BULLSEYES AND BLUNDERS

Lessons from **100** Cases
in Pharmaceutical Marketing

BULLSEYES
AND
BLUNDERS

Lessons from **100** Cases
in Pharmaceutical Marketing

Subba Rao Chaganti

PharmaMed Press

An imprint of Pharma Book Syndicate
A unit of BSP Books Pvt. Ltd.
4-4-309/316, Giriraj Lane,
Sultan Bazar, Hyderabad - 500 095.

Bullseyes and Blunders *Lessons from 100 Cases in Pharmaceutical Marketing*
by *Subba Rao Chaganti*

Published by

PharmaMed Press
An imprint of Pharma Book Syndicate
A unit of BSP Books Pvt. Ltd.
4-4-309/316, Giriraj Lane, Sultan Bazar, Hyderabad - 500 095.
Phone: 040-23445688, 23445600; Fax: 91+40-23445611
E-mail: info@pharmamedpress.com
www.pharmamedpress.com/pharmamedpress.net

Cover Design:
    J. Siva Prasad, Hitha Design Science

ISBN: 978-93-88305-61-7 (Hardbound)

Dedicated,

To Chaganti Mahalakshmi, My partner for life

Who took equanimously all my

Bullseyes and Blunders

For over forty-five years and continuing to take...

PREFACE

The title of the Book – Bullseyes, and Blunders is not my original idea. I borrowed it from a 1987 book by Robert F. Hartley with the same title; Bullseyes and Blunders: Stories of business success & failure. The book was about twenty-four case histories of leading brands in Automobile, Hamburger, Beer, Motorbikes, Sports shoes and Personal computers. The book was interesting and illuminating. However, more than anything else, I was mighty impressed with the title of the Book – Bullseyes and Blunders. Very apt. Fits the subject like a perfect glove. Nay, it hits the bullseye!

Three years ago, when I was compiling the cases for this book, I suddenly recalled the title of the book and thought it would be the most appropriate title of this book. It is only the title that is common. There is nothing else that is even remotely similar – not even the industry on which all these hundred cases originate.

Bullseyes and Blunders: *Lessons from 100 Cases in Pharmaceutical Marketing* is a first-of-its-kind of a book. The book is an invaluable resource for the practitioners as well as the students of pharmaceutical marketing. The case studies presented in the book offer many experiential insights into how some of the world's renowned pharmaceutical marketers built, launched, defended and managed their brands, and steered them clear of competition. The Bullseyes in the book present snapshots of these winning brands.

Studying the Blunders or failures or flops too is significant for the practitioners and students of marketing alike. Because they provide the much-needed insights into the essential, *Don'ts* while building and managing their brands. Above all, learning from others' blunders is highly cost-effective.

Bullseyes and Blunders provides a more practical understanding of various topics that are highly relevant for the Pharma brand managers and marketing managers. These are market opportunity analysis, product positioning, product launches, life cycle management, building and defending a disease-franchise among others.

About half of the hundred cases presented in this book are from the world's leading research-based pharmaceutical industry (the United States), and the remaining half are from the world's leading branded-generic market (India). Thus the book provides a holistic view of how the pharmaceutical industry develops, launches and manages its brands.

The sources for each case discussed in the book have been far too many to attribute. The primary sources have been attributed at the end of each case where applicable, and almost all the references are mentioned in the reference list. While every case offers some valuable lessons, more important and less apparent lessons are presented at the end of some cases. The rest of these cases do not mention lessons in the end as the lessons that those cases offer are so obvious and self-explanatory.

The book has ten chapters that are essential reading for any pharmaceutical marketer. They are — the pharmaceutical market; the pharmaceutical product; therapeutic leadership; product launch strategy; the life cycle management; pharmaceutical marketing practices — good and bad; disease branding; Blue ocean strategy; the pricing strategies; Pharma and social media. Each chapter presents a brief discussion on the topic followed by the relevant cases under that topic. The book ends with a summary of the key insights and practical lessons from the hundred cases.

Writing this book has been an immense learning experience for me. I believe reading it will be an equally rewarding experience for you, and you will gain many valuable insights and practical lessons from these one hundred cases to create, build and nurture your prescription drug brands.

Subba Rao Chaganti

ACKNOWLEDGEMENTS

First and foremost, I must acknowledge my thanks and heartiest congratulations to all those brand teams who were behind the one hundred cases that are presented in this book. They had done some brilliant and outstanding work and taught many valuable insights and practical lessons to all of us, pharmaceutical marketers and to all aspiring pharmaceutical brand managers in the future. Without them, this book would not have been created. They are the *raison d'être* for this book.

A book of this magnitude can seldom be claimed as the work of one individual. Many people have helped me in producing of this book. It is not possible to individually acknowledge all my colleagues and competitors (in the field) and teachers, who have helped me in widening my horizon and broadening my perspective of marketing in general and pharmaceutical marketing in particular.

Here are a few Individuals, whose help and support have been truly significant. Without their physical, intellectual and moral support, this book still would have been in a conceptual stage. I sincerely thank Mr. J. Siva Prasad, Head, Graphics Studio, Hitha Design and Science for giving a fantastic cover design and for suggesting the basic layout for this book. My thanks are also due to Mr. Anil Shah for his faith in this project. He apart from being a publisher with vision has been virtually pushing me to bring about this book. I must also thank Mr. Nikunjesh Shah for making digital versions of this book available. My thanks are also due to Mr. Naresh Daver for designing this book. Also, I owe a special thanks to my son, C. Srinivasa Phanindra who did all the illustrations in this book.

Last but not least, I owe my thanks to Mahalakshmi, my better half both literally and figuratively and my three children and their spouses (Srinivasa Phanindra, Geetha, Lavanya, Aditya, Soumya, Chaitanya) for supporting and even pushing me to write Bullseyes and Blunders. I must be grateful to my grandchildren - Aditi, Eesha, and Surya who watched me with awe while I was writing this and that inspired me a lot and gave me a tremendous amount of satisfaction.

Subba Rao Chaganti

CONTENTS

The Pharmaceutical Market

World Pharmaceutical Market, Key Drivers, Brakes, The Turf, Research-based Pharma Industry, The Generic Drug Industry, Evolution of a Research-based Drug Company, The Turf Wars, Surviving Patent Expiration: Defensive Strategies by the Big Pharma, Exploiting Patent Expiries: Generic Drug Firms' Offensive Strategies, Voluntary Licensing (VL) - An Alternate Strategy? Compulsory Licensing, Paragraph IV Filing, Lessons, Market Opportunity Analysis, Elements of Market Opportunity Analysis, Market Opportunity Analysis: A Step-by-Step Approach, Market Opportunity Analysis: An Example, The Served Market, Difficult Task, Defining Your Served Market: A Checklist, Market Segmentation: Points to Ponder, Strategic Options, A. Concentrated Marketing, B. Differentiated Marketing, C. Un-differentiated Marketing

Cases:

1. Prozac: The World's Leading Antidepressant Could not Survive its Patent Expiry Blues! **16**
2. Dr. Reddy's Exploits a Loophole in the Patent Term Extension Act! **18**
3. Biovail Buys Cardizem Patent, Breathes New Life into it! **19**
4. Natco Pharma Gets the First-Ever Compulsory License for Generic Nexavar in a Landmark Decision! **20**

The Pharmaceutical Product 53

The Product Concept, What is a Brand? The Augmented Product Concept, Product Augmentation in the Indian Pharmaceutical Industry, Language of Branding, A Rose by Any Other Name, Product Life Cycle, Key Questions, Usefulness of Product Life Cycle, Market Life Cycle, Extending Product Life Cycle, Determining the Phase of Your Brand in the PLC, New Product Adoption Process, Three Major Propositions, The Individual Adoption Process, Adopter Categories, Product Life Cycle and Adoption Process, Implications for the Marketer, Product Portfolio Analysis, Boston Matrix, Portfolio Analysis in Pharmaceutical Marketing, Product Positioning, Why is Positioning a Must? Positioning Prescription Drugs, Positioning: A Definition, Positioning and Target Market Selection, Sustainable Differential Advantage, Key Questions, Ground Rules for Positioning, Lessons, Product Policy and Strategy, Governing Factors, New Products, Product-mix Decisions, Optimal Product-mix, Product Strategy, Market Penetration and Market Development Strategies, Product Development, Diversification, New Drug Adoption by Physicians in Branded Generic Markets: A Two-step Approach, Communication Hierarchy and the Adoption Process, Product Management, Management by Persuasion, Product Manager as a Gardener? Some Problem Areas, Product Management in the Indian Pharmaceutical

Industry, Making Product Management More Effective, Managing New Products, Standing Still is Going Backwards, The Costliness of New Product Development Process, Types of Risks, Why Develop New Products? The Importance of New Products on Profits, A Program for New Product Evolution, Basic Principles, New Product Development Process, Evaluating New Products, New Product Performance Review, Organizing for Success

Cases:

Therapeutic Leadership 207

Building A Disease Franchise for Achieving Therapeutic Leadership, Why Therapeutic Leadership? Defensible Strategy, From Niche toFranchise Enduring Success

Cases:

04 Product Launch Strategy 235

New Product Launch, Success Secrets, Making Your Drug Launch A Success, Factors That Shape Launch: A Checklist

Cases:

05 Life Cycle Management 259

Life Cycle Management, Drug Life Optimization, Drug Life Optimization: Key Tactics, Ten Commandments of Life Cycle Management

Cases:

06 Pharmaceutical Marketing Practices: Good and Bad

Declining Reputation Good Practices, Pharma's Bad Practices, Factors Associated With Reputational Damage, The TARES Test

Cases:

07 Disease Branding

Disease Branding, Origins of Disease Branding, Dual Advantages, Three Strategic Approaches, Five Questions, Benefits of Disease Branding

Cases:

08 Blue Ocean Strategy

Blue and Red Oceans, Value Innovation, Henry Ford Creates A Blue Ocean, How to Formulate A Blue Ocean Strategy, The PMS Map, Blue Ocean Strategy: Key Questions, Identifying Non-Customers

Cases:

The Pricing Strategies 483

Price and Pharma Marketing Mix, Pricing Objectives, Pricing Decisions, Bases for Pricing, Cost-based Pricing, Demand-based Pricing, Competition-based Pricing, Price Comparison, Market-based Pricing, Pricing Strategies, Skim the cream Strategy, Penetration Strategy, Marginal Cost Price Changes, Strategy, Pricing Management, Customers' Reactions to Price Changes, Price Communicates, Psychological Effects of Pricing, Desensitizing the Consumer to Price, Predatory Pricing: An Emerging Trend, 'Me-too' Pricing Strategy for 'Me-too' Products, Periodical Review

Cases:

Pharma and Social Media 511

What is Social Media? Social Media Marketing, Physicians on Social Media, Patients Are In Control, Insights From Social Media Conversations, Challenging Regulatory Environment, FDA Guidance on Social Media: Implications for Pharma, How Can Pharma Comply with the FDA Guidance on Social Media? Pharma Must Embrace Social Media, 6 Ways Pharma May Use Social Media, Content is King! Gamification, Five Key Elements, How Gamification is Beneficial, More Apps, Slow Rate of Adoption, Engagification, not Gamification! Pharma and Social Media: the Indian Scenario, Presence Vs Engagement, Patients on Social Media, Physicians on Social Media, Digital Initiatives of MNCs in India, Social Media and Indian Pharma, Social Media, Public Relations and Crisis Management, 13 Golden Rules of PR Crisis Management, Tylenol: A Classic Example of Crisis Management, Social Media in Crisis Management

LIST OF ABBREVIATIONS

4-S Study	The Scandinavian Simvastatin Survival Study
AAN	American Association of Neurology
AAP	Association for Academic Psychiatry
ABC	Association of Black Cardiologists
ACE	Angiotensin Converting Enzyme
ACG	American College of Gastroenterology
ADD	Attention Deficit Disorder
ADHD	Attention Deficit Hyperactivity Disorder
AED	Antiepileptic Drug
A-HEFT	African-American Heart Failure Trial
AHP	American Home Products
APA	American Psychiatric Association
APA	American Psychological Association
API	Active Pharmaceutical Ingredient
ARB	Angiotensin II Receptor Blocker
ASCI	Administrative Staff College of India
BCG	Boston Consulting Group
BMA	Bone Measurement Act
BPH	Benign Prostate Hyperplasia
CAGR	Compound Annual Growth Rate
CBC	Congressional Black Caucus
CCB	Calcium Channel Blocker
CHADD	Children and Adults with Attention Deficit Disorders
CHF	Chronic Heart Failure
CME	Continuing Medical Education

CML	Chronic Myeloid Leukemia
CNS	Central Nervous System
CRAMS	Contract Research and Manufacturing Services
CRM	Customer Relationship Management
CSR	Corporate Social Responsibility
DGTD	Directorate General of Technical Development
DLO	Drug Life Optimization
DOP	Department of Pharmaceuticals
DPCO	Drug Price Control Order
DTC	Direct To Consumer
DTCA	Direct-To-Consumer-Advertising
ED	Erectile Dysfunction
EU	European Union
FDA	Food and Drug Administration
FDC	Fixed Dose Composition
FDF	Finished Dosage Form
FERA	Foreign Exchange Regulation Act
GI	Gastro-Intestinal
GERD	Gastro Esophageal Reflux Disorder
GIDH	Glaxo Wellcome Institute for Digestive Health
GSK	GlaxoSmithKline
HCP	Healthcare Professional
HCV	Hepatitis C Virus
HIPAA	The Health Insurance Portability and Accountability Act
HPV	Human Papilloma Virus
IBD	Inflammatory Bowel Disease
IND	Investigational New Drug Application
IPAB	Intellectual Property Appellate Board
KOL	Key Opinion Leader
LCM	Life Cycle Management
M & A	Mergers and Acquisitions
MAPE	Maximum Allowable Post Manufacturing Expenses

MOA	Market Opportunity Analysis
MSD	Merck Sharp and Dohme
MSL	Medical Sales Liaison
NAACP	The National Association for the Advancement of Colored People
NCE	New Chemical Entity
NDA	New Drug Application
NIH	National Institutes of Health
NIMH	National Institutes of Mental Health
NME	New Molecular Entity
NPPA	National Pharmaceutical Pricing Authority
NSAID	Non-Steriodal-Anti-inflammatory-Drug
OAB	Over Active Bladder
OCD	Obsessive Compulsory Disorder
ORG	Operations Research Group
OTC	Over-The-Counter
PAG	Patient Advocacy Group
PCP	Primary Care Physician
PMDD	Premenstrual Dysphoric Disorder
PMO	Post Menopausal Osteoporosis
PMS	Pre-menstrual Syndrome
POM	Prescription Only Medicine
PTSD	Post Traumatic Stress Disorder
RA	Rheumatoid Arthritis
RLS	Rest Legs Syndrome
SAD	Social Anxiety Disorder
SEO	Search Engine Optimization
SKU	Stock Keeping Unit
SSRI	Selective Serotonin Reuptake Inhibitor
STI	Sexually Transmitted Infection
SWOT	Strength, Weakness, Opportunity, Threat
UCPMP	Uniform Code of Pharmaceutical Marketing Practices

US FDA	United States Food and Drug Administration
US	United States
UTI	Urinary Tract Infection
V-HeFT	The Vasodilator Heart Failure Trial
WHO	World Health Organization
Y & R	Young & Rubicam

The Pharmaceutical Market

World Pharmaceutical Market

The pharmaceutical industry across the world continues to reel under pressure from all sides. Patents of one blockbuster drug after another are expiring. The innovator-drug industry is caught up in a gap of revenues that is widening continuously between an old way of developing drugs that is increasingly tapped out with each blockbuster patent expiry. What is more, it is becoming increasingly difficult to replenish the drying pipelines with blockbusters-to-be drugs.

Managed-care companies in the US, the world's largest generics market are successfully pushing patients away from high-priced new drugs and toward low-priced generics to reduce their already-overstretched drug outlays. Governments even in other developed countries in the European Union and Japan are also driving aggressively cost-containment to check the increasing healthcare expenditures.

All these pressures that the industry has been facing slowed down the rate of growth for prescription drug sales to a snail's pace of 1.8 percent between 2011 and 2017. However, the growth rate is likely to improve to a healthy CAGR of 6.4 percent for 2018 through 2024 according to the forecast of Evaluate Pharma, a leading consultancy firm.

Evaluate Pharma, in their World Preview 2018 Outlook to 2024 for Pharmaceutical Industry present a snapshot of key drivers and brakes.

Key Drivers

1. Increase in the number of new drug approvals doubled from 27 in 2016 to 55 in 2017.
2. Increased focus on orphan drugs. Orphan drugs to generate an additional $124 billion between 2018 and 2024.
3. Oncology drugs to grow almost twice as rapidly as the market at 12 percent during the next six years.

4. Advanced therapies to the fore. Advanced therapies to generate an additional $5billion in the next six years.

Brakes

Factors hindering performance or putting the brakes on the growth are:

1. Continued payer-pressure on budget-growth.
2. Patent cliff. The impending patent expiries during the next six-year period affect a total sales volume of $251billion.
3. Increase in R&D costs. Increase in average spend per new molecular entity (NME) since 2007 to $3.97 billion suggesting that a significant improvement in R&D efficiencies is needed.
4. Reducing R&D spend by industry at the same time from 20.9 percent of drug sales in 2017 to 16.9 by 2024 suggests a reduction in innovation.

The Turf

Turf implies ownership, possessiveness, and protectionism in that order. The point of conflict in the globalization process lies in the ambivalent attitude of gaining market access and denying market access to one's products. Understanding the sensitivities involved in gaining market access assumes paramount importance. The shades and hues of social, political, cultural and technological colors make the management of diversity a challenging task.

The world pharmaceutical industry can broadly be divided into two categories — single-source and multi-source products. Single-source products industry is the research-based pharmaceutical industry popularly known as the Big Pharma. Since its products have patent protection, they enjoy market exclusivity as long as the patent lasts and therefore available only from one source and hence called single-source, which is the innovator or discoverer of the drug. Although the life of a pharmaceutical patent is 20 years from the date of filing, its effective patent life is ten to twelve years on average as the gestation period of a pharmaceutical product — from concept to commercialization is quite long and takes an average of eight to ten years for a drug to reach the market from the lab.

The Federal Drug Administration (FDA) approves marketing of generic versions or copies of the original drug subject to their matching the bio-equivalence with the original drug after the drug's patents expire. After patent expiry, there can be any number of generic versions available in the market. As these are available from multiple companies (sources), these products are also known as multi-source products. When a drug's patent expires and generics enter the prices fall drastically — sometimes by 80 to 90 percent of the original drug's price before patent expiry.

Research-Based Pharma Industry

For many years, it was fairly simple and straightforward to outline the structure of the research-based pharmaceutical industry. One could classify the companies into three easily identifiable and separate segments in the industry such as:

A. Big Pharma comprising large prescription-drug companies, which discover, develop, manufacture and market New Chemical Entities (NCEs).

B. Biotechnology companies such as Amgen, Biogen, and Genzyme, which focus on discovering, manufacturing and marketing biological products.

C. Generic drug firms, which produce the bio-equivalent products of the research-based pharmaceutical companies when their patents expire. Notable examples of generic drug firms are Teva, Mylan, and Sun Pharma.

The following table illustrates the blurring lines between Big Pharma and Biotechnology segments of the pharmaceutical industry. Only one company - Amgen out of the ten companies in the following table has started as a biotechnology company. The rest of the nine pharmaceutical companies, who have been a part of the Big Pharma for a long time, boarded the biotechnology bandwagon in time and had become active participants garnering a sizable share of the rapidly growing biotechnology pie.

Table 1.1 Big Pharma Companies and their Biotechnology Share in 2017

Company	Total Sales (US $ Billion)	Contribution of Biotechnology Products to Total Sales (%)
1. Merck & Co	35.4	31
2. AbbVie	27.7	70
3. Bristol-Myers Squibb	19.3	47
4. Amgen	21.8	88
5. Novo Nordisk	17.0	74
6. Eli Lilly	18.5	49
7. Pfizer	45.4	24
8. Roche	41.7	82
9. Johnson & Johnson	34.4	41
10. Sanofi	34.1	40

(Source: Evaluate Pharma)

Today, it is not quite as simple to divide the industry in this way. The merger and acquisition (M&A) activities and licensing arrangements have blurred the traditional lines dividing these segments. Patricia Danzon, the Celia Moh Professor of Healthcare Management at Wharton School, University of Pennsylvania clearly explained this phenomenon:

> The biotechnology revolution has transformed the nature of drug discovery and the structure of the industry. Increasingly, new drugs originate in small firms, which often out-license their products to more experienced firms for late-stage development, regulatory review, and commercialization.

It is not that only the dividing lines between the Big Pharma and biotechnology are blurred. That is happening between the brand-name drug companies and generic drug companies too. Consider the following facts for example:

- ▶ Pfizer, which has the world's largest generic platform termed Pfizer Established Products alongside its substantial Greenstone (subsidiary generic company) business took a significant step to reinforce the generics business with the $16 billion acquisition of Hospira.

- ▶ Endo Pharmaceuticals acquired PAR pharmaceuticals, a generic drug company for $8 billion.

The Generic Drug Industry

The US generic drug industry, which has the largest share of the world generic drug market in terms of value is experiencing dramatic growth with generic prescriptions approaching almost the 90 percent level and it is poised for even rapid growth with impending patent expiries worth a whopping $251 billion in sales value. The generic drug industry is in for a dramatic change with a consolidation spree sweeping it.

The aggregate value of the generic drug industry on a global basis exceeded $900 billion for the first time in 2016 according to the estimate of Torreya Partners, the leading consultants to the generic drug industry. It was only $150 billion a decade ago. Furthermore, the global generic industry accounted for about $200 billion in total sales in 2015 is expected to reach $380 billion by 2021, growing at a CAGR of around 10.8 percent between 2016 and 2021.

Evolution of a Research-Based Drug Company

What is the ultimate goal of a generic manufacturer, be it in the developed world or developing world? When you ask this question, you are likely to get three types of responses.

A. Some of the leading generic drug companies in the specialty space would like to be research-based pharmaceutical companies.

B. A few others would like to compete in the generic space that is rapidly growing and become international generic drug companies.

C. And then, there are others would like to position themselves as 'partners-of-choice' or preferred partners in the CRAMS (Contract Research and Manufacturing Services) space that is expanding fast.

Whatever be the space in which a company chooses to compete, every company wants to become an integrated company competing across the pharmaceutical value chain. The journey or transition or perhaps the metamorphosis from a generic drug industry to a research-based pharmaceutical company is tough and arduous to say the least. The evolutionary process (Figure 1) would take anywhere between 20 to 25 years provided one works towards this goal with unflinching determination. It can take a minimum period of ten years for a generic drug manufacturer to graduate into a branded generic drug company and to an international generic company with the right investment and the relevant capabilities. From an

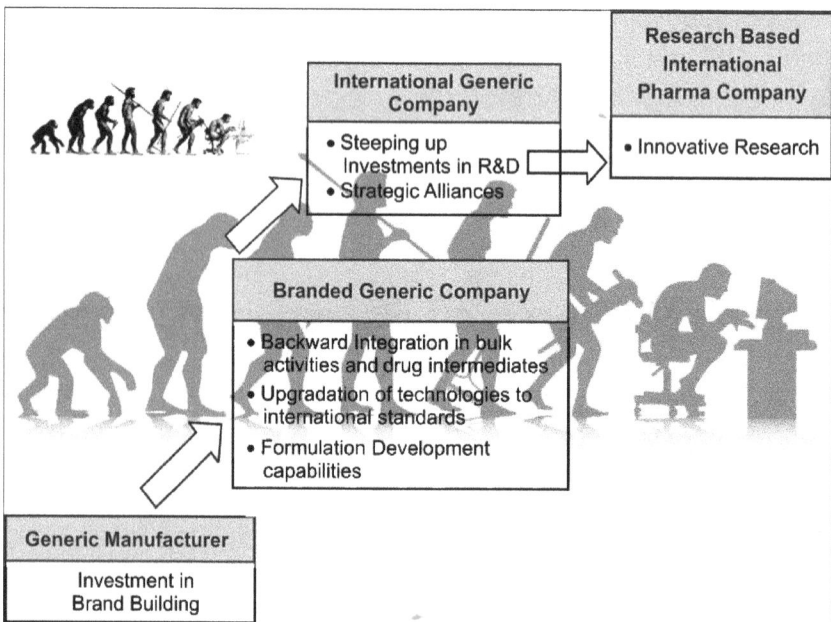

Figure 1. 1 Evolution of A Research-Based Pharma Company

international generic company to a research-based pharmaceutical company it could take ten to fifteen years with the right combination of competencies, capabilities, strategies, and investments.

There seems to be a well-defined hierarchy of goals in the pharmaceutical industries in the pharmaceutical world. All firms virtually start off with as manufacturers and marketers of finished-dosage forms (FDFs) which are generally known as formulations or Active Pharmaceutical Ingredients (APIs) and drug intermediates. Then they integrate backward or forward depending upon the point from where they started, to become fully or vertically integrated pharmaceutical companies.

Vertical integration gives a significant and sustainable advantage to a pharmaceutical firm. It gives the firm the much-needed control on costs, timely availability, and quality of inputs. The underlying assumption here is that the integrated firm has cost-effective processes, superior technology, and therefore holds the key to successful integration.

Fifteen to twenty years ago, Teva, the Israeli drug major was perhaps the only fully integrated international generic drug company in the world. Teva, today, is among the top twenty of the Big Pharma with its own New Chemical Entity (NCE) that had become a billion-dollar molecule. Taking a cue from Teva's journey to become a research-based pharmaceutical company, a few other international generic companies are on their way to compete with the Big Pharma on their turf — with their drug discovery programs.

The Turf Wars

The battle lines are clearly drawn between the Big Pharma and the generic drug firms. The Big Pharma wants to protect their patents and exclusivity as long as it can whereas the generic drug firm wishes to enter the market as soon as a drug's patent expires. Till the mid-1980s, the brand-name drug firms dominated the industry. In fact, when generic drugs first emerged in the 1980s as a potentially formidable source of profits, the major pharmaceutical companies controlled much of the segment through ownership of generic firms.

From the late 1980s, brand-name drug companies have come under increasing pressure from generics since the passage of the Hatch-Waxman Act, which is instrumental in creating the modern generic drug industry as we know today. Not content with their achievements, some of the leading generic drug companies are raising the bar constantly and shifting the battle lines by entering the turf of the innovator drug companies by fielding their new drug candidates and launching their New Chemical Entities (NCEs) after they reach the required critical mass to invest in the drug development process.

Innovator drug companies too are taking the battle to the generics camp with their offensive moves such as launching their own generic versions and authorized generics to hit them where it hurts most — their profits during the market exclusivity period. The battle lines are shifting and blurring. The fighting is all over the field. The world's leading generic drug company – Pfizer Established Products, for example, is the subsidiary of a Big Pharma major, Pfizer. Likewise, the world's largest generic drug company – Teva Pharmaceutical Industries is also a top-twenty company in the world pharmaceutical league table with its innovator drug that has over a billion dollars in worldwide sales.

Innovator-drug companies are launching generics, partnering with generic companies to fight generic companies. The generic drug companies are into discovery research already with a combined pipeline of over one-hundred molecules covering a wide range of therapeutic areas at various stages of development.

Truly when titans clash the turf shrinks!

Surviving Patent Expiration: Defensive Strategies by the Big Pharma

When the generic drugs first emerged in the 1980s, they were considered as a potentially formidable source of profits and growth. Some of the drug majors owned and controlled the segment to beef up their profits and growth. However, the potential did not result in a promising performance, and it did not take much longer for the

Pharma majors, who were disillusioned with their generic-arms to divest and keep a distance from them ever since.

Big Pharma companies, therefore, are continuously exploring ways and means to fix the situations that they are in. They are looking at every strategy in the book and are also evolving new strategies to defend themselves against the generics onslaught.

The 1984 Hatch-Waxman Act put the US Pharma industry on an innovation treadmill. Within a year of the bill's passage, nine of the industry's top-ten best-selling drugs had new generic rivals forcing sales precipitous declines rather than a long, slow tapering off sales as in the past. Faced with the prospect of continuing patent expirations and with not enough products to replenish the declining sales, innovator-drug companies have started applying every strategy they could think of for protecting their patent rights as long as possible (ever-greening patents) and delaying the generic entry as long as possible. Innovator-drug companies have been working more vigorously than ever before to defend their market and profit shares. Here are fifteen of the more important and commonly applied strategies by the Big Pharma to delay the generic drugs from entering on to their turf.

1. Strategic Patenting
2. Strategic Lobbying
3. Strategic Litigation
4. Metabolite Defense
5. Pediatric Exclusivity
6. Citizen Petition
7. New, Improved Successor-Drug Candidates
8. New, Improved Dosage Forms
9. New Uses (Indications)
10. Predatory Pricing
11. Aggressive Marketing
12. De-Marketing - Launching Own Generics
13. Reverse Payments

14. Prescription-to-OTC-Switches
15. Voluntary Licensing

Exploiting Patent Expiries:
Generic Drug Firms' Offensive Strategies

The generics drug industry has come a long way since its humble beginnings in the 1980s. Three factors are mainly responsible for changing the complexion of the generic drug industry to the pink of health that it is in today:

1. Many generics companies have become highly competitive and built up their capabilities across the pharmaceutical value chain.

2. The rise in health care costs, while painful for the big pharmaceutical companies, has considerably benefited the generic drug firms. Substitution laws and managed healthcare system from the Health Maintenance Organizations (HMOs) to hospitals in the US and elsewhere create significant pressure on physicians to prescribe *generics first* to contain healthcare costs.

3. Generic drug companies have been setting their sights high and are aspiring to become fully integrated, research-based pharmaceutical companies. Once they reach the critical mass required, they move up from process to product development. As generics manufacturers have improved and moved rapidly upstream in the pharmaceutical business system developing R&D capabilities, they have sharply increased their technology and in-licensing skills.

Generic drug firms have not only been trying to defend their turf but also are launching their offensives and taking the battle to the Big Pharma's turf. Here are seven commonly followed offensive and defensive strategies by the generics drug industry:

1. Paragraph IV Filings
2. Strategic Litigation
3. Strategic Lobbying

4. Strategic Alliances
5. Branded Generics
6. Transformational Strategies
7. Compulsory Licensing
8. Invading the Innovators' Turf

While it is beyond the scope of this book to discuss all the strategies that the research-based and generic pharmaceutical companies apply to defend their respective turfs, three specific strategies need a special mention. They are – Voluntary licensing, which the research-based Pharma practices, and Compulsory licensing and Paragraph IV filing, which the generic drug firms try to exploit.

Voluntary Licensing (VL) - An Alternate Strategy?

Voluntary licenses, as the name indicates are licenses that patent holders give at their discretion to other parties on an exclusive or non-exclusive basis, the right to manufacture, import and distribute a pharmaceutical product.

Ever since the government of India gave its first compulsory license of Bayer's Nexavar to Natco Pharma, multinational pharmaceutical companies have been rethinking about strategy to launch their new drugs in India. The strategy? Voluntary licenses. Here are the details of some of the voluntary licenses that MNC pharmaceutical companies gave to their local partners in India.

▶ MSD Pharmaceuticals gave Sun Pharma an exclusive marketing license for marketing two patented diabetes drugs - Januvia and Janumet in India.

▶ Novartis, a top-ten Big Pharma company, entered into a marketing tie-up with Lupin, the Indian drug major for its Onbrez inhaler.

▶ Bayer plans to license most of its patented products for India to its local joint venture company, Cadila Healthcare - Bayer.

▶ Gilead Life Sciences gave voluntary licenses to seven Indian generic drug manufacturers – Cadila Healthcare, Cipla, Hetero

Drugs, Mylan Labs, Ranbaxy, Sequent Scientific and Strides Arcolabs for its blockbuster hepatitis-C drug Sovaldi (sofosbuvir).

Voluntary licensing to a local partner under mutually agreed terms will not only help patent holders to expand the market but also avoid compulsory licensing action. While government intervention through a compulsory licensing will lead to a drastic reduction in price as it is typically without the consent of the patent holder, voluntary licensing may get a more remunerative price albeit much lower than its original price.

Innovative drug companies with patented drugs realize that voluntary licensing is a wiser option to avoid a likely invocation of the compulsory licensing Act. Besides, a voluntary license offers two advantages:

A. A voluntary license helps minimize loss and also ensures better access of the patented drug to more domestic patients.

B. It helps counter one of the most common reasons for issuing a compulsory license — inadequate patient access.

Compulsory Licensing

A compulsory license is an authorization given to a third-party by the government to make, use or sell a particular product or a particular process, which has been patented, without the need of the permission of the patent owner. Compulsory licenses, therefore work against patent holders. However, then, they are given only in certain cases of national emergency and health crisis.

There are certain prerequisite conditions, which need to be fulfilled if the government wants to grant a compulsory license in favor of someone. At least three years should pass from the date of grant of a patent before anyone interested in making an application to the controller for grant of compulsory license on any of the following three conditions:

A. That the reasonable requirements of the public concerning the patented invention have not been satisfied or

B. That the patented invention is not available to the public at a reasonably affordable price or

C. That the patented invention is not worked in the territory of India

Thus, the use of a compulsory license effectively withdraws a patent from a drug completely if it is seemed prohibitively expensive to a domestic market and a vital public health need.

Paragraph IV Filing

Certification under the Paragraph (IV) is called Paragraph IV certification. It is the most complicated of the four certifications as the generic drug companies required to notify the innovator drug company about the NDA filing and explain the reasons it believes the generic version will not infringe the listed patent or the listed patent is invalid. Within forty-five days of receiving the notification, the innovator company has to file an infringement suit. The FDA withholds the approval of Abbreviated New Drug Application (ANDA) for 30 months or until the case is decided if the innovator files a lawsuit. The Act Permits such an action by the patentee even if no infringement is taken place in reality. FDA will approve the ANDA depending on the outcome of the case. If the generic product is found to be non-infringing, FDA approves the ANDA.

The following four cases illustrate how the innovator and generic pharmaceutical companies try to fight for their turf.

Prozac: The World's Leading Antidepressant Could not Survive its Patent Expiry Blues!

Prozac, the world's best-selling antidepressant almost since its introduction in 1988 accounted for about 26 percent of Eli Lilly's $10 billion sales in 1999. Its compound patent and a subsequent pediatric exclusivity expired on August 2, 1001. Barr Labs, the US generic company, had set its sights on this opportunity quite early. Barr filed its ANDA with a Para IV certification in 1996 claiming that its version of Fluoxetine did not infringe on Lilly's patents and the patents were unenforceable.

After five years of litigation, on August 9, 2000, the Court of Appeals vacated lower court's decision ruling in favor of Barr invalidating one of the patents of Prozac. The judge ruled that the patent not be valid because of so-called double patenting but upheld another patent, which prevented any generic drug maker from making a generic version of Prozac until February 2001. FDA extended the patent in November for another six months because Lilly planned to test the antidepressant on children.

Barr finally launched its generic version of the 20 mg strength of Fluoxetine on August 3, 2001, as soon as Lilly's patent expired and grabbed 65 percent of Prozac's prescription share within two months after the launch. Prozac lost 46 percent of its total prescriptions to Barr's generic in the very first month. By the end of the six-month exclusivity period, Prozac lost 82 percent of its prescriptions to the generic version. In the eleven months after launch, the sales of Barr's generic Fluoxetine reached $367.5 million, which accounted for 31 percent of the company's total sales in 2002.

Barr doubled its profit margin too during the same period. The stock price of Barr spiked to $86.38 from $66 in July 2001, when the Court of Appeals ruled in favor of Barr's generic version.

Around the same time, Dr. Reddy's Laboratories, the international generics firm from India, filed its ANDA for the 40 mg strength of Fluoxetine with Paragraph IV certification. The District Court of Indiana gave a ruling in favor of Dr. Reddy's invalidating a December 2003 patent protecting Eli Lilly's Prozac in a final judgment delivered on July 27, 2001.

Dr. Reddy's launched 40 mg strength of Fluoxetine with 180-day exclusivity and recorded sales of $ 70-million in the first year of its generic launch.

Lessons

Patent life is finite. Twenty years from the date of filing in the United States. Patent expiry is inevitable. There is only so much you can do with lifecycle management by getting approvals for additional indications and by introducing new dosage forms and new drug delivery systems. You cannot extend it forever.

The only way you can keep revenue streams is by fielding successive drug candidates to defend your disease franchise. Launching successive patentable products is the only way you can save your drop off the patent cliff.

Dr. Reddy's Exploits a Loophole in the Patent Term Extension Act!

Dr. Reddy's Laboratories, a leading International generics player from India, found a loophole in the law that granted patent term extension. The company found that the Congress had not extended the original patents, but just the exclusive rights to sell the drugs themselves.

As with other drugs, Pfizer's Norvasc's (amlodipine) original patent protected both the chemical structure of Norvasc and a host of sister compounds or salts that are nearly identical and work equally well. Dr. Reddy's legal team realized that the patent extension did not protect these sisters, opening the doors for look-alike that had the same effect but a different composition or a slightly different chemical structure.

Dr. Reddy's scientific team took the call enthusiastically and exploited this opportunity. They developed a Norvasc look alike, which Pfizer itself had used in extensive testing, and filed a Paragraph IV ANDA. Pfizer sued but lost the case in New Jersey in late 2002.

Biovail Buys Cardizem Patent, Breathes New Life into it!

Cardizem (Diltiazem), a popular calcium-channel blocker provides an excellent example of how incremental therapeutic improvements by both a big pharmaceutical company and a specialty player can extend a patent's life. Cardizem's original patent expired in 1988. Aventis was able to create a new blockbuster with a sustained release version, Cardizem CD, a twice-daily formulation, but was unable to develop further as once-daily formulation.

Biovail, the well-known drug-delivery company, bought the Cardizem patent in 2002. With its focus and expertise in drug delivery and reformulation, Biovail developed a long-acting version of the drug, Cardizem LA, and breathed new life into the drug, 14 years after its original patent protection ended.

Natco Pharma Gets the First-Ever Compulsory License for Generic Nexavar in a Landmark Decision!

Bayer, the German Pharma major, invented sorafenib (brand name: Nexavar) used in the treatment of primary kidney cancer and advanced primary liver cancer and priced it at Rs. 2.80 lakh for one month's supply of the drug (120 tablets) in India. The price being exorbitant, the drug reached only 2 percent of the patient population.

Natco Pharma, an Indian generic company, requested Bayer for voluntary license to manufacture and market the drug in India, which Bayer denied. Natco then filed an application with the Controller of Patents for grant of a compulsory license of the drug, sorafenib. The Controller granted a compulsory license to Natco to manufacture and sell a generic version of Nexavar under the following conditions.

A. Nato would pay a 6 percent royalty on the net sales every quarter to Bayer.

B. Further, it could only charge Rs. 8,800 for a monthly dose of 120 tablets of the drug and

C. Donate free supplies of the drug to 600 needy patients each year.

The Controller of Patents granted a compulsory license in this case as he found that all the three criteria for the grant of a compulsory license as per the Indian Patents Act were satisfied.

Bayer supplied the drug to only 2 percent of the patient population and thus, did not meet the reasonable requirements of the public for the patented drug.

Bayer priced the drug exorbitantly high at Rs. 2.80 lakh for a month's supply of the drug. It was unreasonably high as it was many times more than the per capita income in India in 2011. The per capita income in India in 2011 was the US $1,575 whereas the cost of the drug per year was the US $69,000. Compare this with the price of Natco's generic version of US $2,120.

Bayer did not sufficiently work the patent in India.

Later, Bayer challenged the order passed by the Intellectual Property Appellate Board (IPAB) in Bombay High Court, which upheld the IPAB Order.

(**Source:** Adapted from S. S. Rana &Co's Blog article on Working of patents statements in India)

Market Opportunity Analysis

Inherent in the law of marketing success is the consistent need for market opportunity analysis (MOA). Unless you continuously practice a systematic opportunity analysis and keep your antennae high and ears close to the ground, you can neither unearth the dormant opportunities nor discover those that are looming considerable over the hemisphere of your potential market. Here are seven cases emphasizing and amplifying the need and importance of market opportunity analysis and how crucial it is for business success in the Indian pharmaceutical industry.

Anti-tubercular Market: A Tale of Two Companies!

The anti-tubercular market was Rs. 104-crore large and growing at an annual rate of 28 percent in 1972. Tuberculosis was affecting approximately 14 million people at that time. The main line of treatment in the 1970s included drugs like PAS, Isoniazid, Thiacetazone - alone or in a combination of two or more drugs.

Two companies, Pfizer, a multinational on a fast track (ranked 8th with a sales volume of Rs. 89-crore in 1992) and Biological E. Limited, a medium sized Indian company with an impressive track record (ranked 44th with a sales volume of Rs. 29-crore in 1992) were acknowledged leaders in the anti-tubercular market in the seventies with their respective brands of PAS, isoniazid, thiacetazone and their combinations.

However, the eighties had seen the emergence of new and more potent drugs such as ethambutol (introduced in 1978 and gained significant market share in the 1980s), pyrazinamide and rifampicin. The earlier anti-tubercular medicines like PAS, INH, and thiacetazone accounted for a mere 3.5 percent of the total anti-tubercular market (INH in combination with rifampicin, however, accounted for 48 percent of the entire anti-T.B. market) in 1992.

However, Pfizer and Biological E. Limited, the two leaders in the anti-tubercular market of the 1970s did not visualize the changes in the market and the shifts in the line treatment, in their very own served markets.

The Result: From a leadership position in the 1970s, the two companies virtually became non-entities within a few years in the anti-tubercular markets. While Pfizer in 1992 had a meager 1.4 percent share of the total anti-tubercular market as a leader in a vanishing sub-segment of the anti-tubercular market, Biological E. Limited had driven itself out of the market.

Lost opportunities? Marketing Myopia? Are there any lessons to be learnt from this? You decide.

Anti-tubercular Market: Exploiting the Opportunities - The Secret of Lupin's Success!

While the two leaders, Pfizer, and Biological E. Limited, of the anti-tubercular market in the 1970s were resting on their laurels, Lupin, a fledgling company began flexing its muscles in the late seventies and was actively looking for opportunities to satiate its ravenous appetite for rapid growth. Lupin ranked 62 with a sales volume of a mere Rs. 3-crore in 1981, took the anti-tubercular market by storm with its introduction of rifampicin. It had introduced all other modern, potent anti-tuberculous drugs like ethambutol, pyrazinamide and a formulation of rifampicin and INH in quick succession. In seven years, Lupin had become an undisputed leader in the anti-tubercular market with a formidable 29.7 percent share in 1988. Lupin during this period had also moved up to the 12th rank in the Indian pharmaceutical industry with Rs. 33.3-crore. Lupin, further went on to consolidate its already stronghold in the anti-tubercular market to a dominant position. By 1992, Lupin had achieved an invincible 50 percent share of the total anti-tubercular market in India.

Lupin's range of anti-tubercular drugs introduced since 1981 alone had accounted for over 61 percent of the increase in sales volume in these eleven years. That is what identifying, uncovering and exploiting an opportunity can do for a company!

Once A Leader, Not Always A Leader!

The Year: 1976.

The segment: the largest and the fastest growing segment of the lot. The Rs. 395-crore sized antibacterial market. This large market had been a testing ground in the Indian pharmaceutical industry for the fluctuating fortunes of many a company.

Sarabhai Chemicals, the No. 1 pharmaceutical company in 1976, was also the leader in the antibacterial market with as many as eight of its eleven brands occupying pride of place among industry's top 120 brands. Narrow-spectrum antibiotics and oral penicillins accounted for over forty percent of the total antibiotic sales of the company in 1976, whereas these sub-groups formed about twenty-eight percent of the systemic antibacterial group. The antibacterial market had been undergoing rapid changes since then. More potent, broad-spectrum, semi-synthetic antibiotics had been gaining prominence. Products like ampicillin, amoxicillin, cephalosporins, doxycycline, cloxacillin combinations, trimethoprim with sulphamethoxazole combinations had been registering unprecedented growth rates. These newer antibiotics had grown at an average annual growth rate of over eighty percent since 1976, thus improving their share of the antibacterial market to a staggering 44 percent in 1988 from 21 percent in 1976.

About the same time, the narrow-spectrum antibiotics and the oral penicillins were losing their share of the market. The industry leader,

Sarabhai Chemicals did not notice the significant fall of 14 percent in the market share points. Even if it was seen, the responses and reactions were too slow. The loss of the market share of narrow-spectrum antibiotics and oral penicillins from 28 percent in 1976 to a mere I per cent in 1988 might have been a case of missing the wood for the trees, since these segments (narrow-spectrum antibiotics and oral penicillins) too had grown at a respectable pace of 20 percent per annum on an average. That may have lulled the leader into complacency in retrospect. What had led to the shrinking of the market share of the narrow-spectrum antibiotics and the oral penicillins during the period between 1976 and 1988? Well, elementary as it may seem, it is the fact that the total antibacterial market during the same period had registered an average annual growth rate of over 40 percent, i.e., twice as fast as the narrow-spectrum antibiotics and the oral penicillins. To top it all, the newer antibiotics had grown even more quickly than the market! At eighty percent growth rate that is twice as fast as that of the antibacterial market. Here's a snapshot of the growth rates of the three sub-segments of the antibacterial market between 1976 and 1988:

▸ Narrow-spectrum antibiotics and Oral Penicillins at **20** percent
▸ The anti-bacterial market as a whole grew at **40** percent
▸ Newer antibiotics grew at a rate of **80** percent

The Net Result? The company that once was a leader and a sort of emperor in the antibacterial market had to contend to remain a king, who had surrendered all new markets to a one-time upstart-turned-emperor! Complacency? Lack of alertness? Whatever may be the reason, one should remember that in the market place, it is axiomatic that once a leader is not always a leader or at least, not necessarily!

One Company's Complacency, Another Company's Vision!

In the same anti-bacterial market around the same time (1976-88), another company, relatively small in size (rank 30, sales volume Rs 5-crore in 1976), but big in dreams was working hard to realize them ever since. Ranbaxy Laboratories (now a part of Sun Pharma) literally ran to the top of the league in Indian pharmaceutical industry in just about twelve years (rank 4, sales volume Rs. 58.6-crore in 1988). What is the secret of its success? It had unearthed, uncovered and exploited the opportunities in the rapidly changing anti-bacterial market, which was the largest and fastest growing segment of the total market. What the industry leader, Sarabhai Chemicals failed to visualize and capitalize, Ranbaxy had grabbed hard and held on to firmly. Ranbaxy in these twelve years had entered every sub-segment of the newer, potent, broad-spectrum antibiotics market and drove itself to success. In 1988, it had achieved the leadership position with a 10.8 percent share in the largest segment of the Indian pharmaceutical industry, which is antibacterial by nudging the leader Sarabhai Chemicals (market share 10.4 percent) to the second position.

Ranbaxy was not content with its achievement. Its objective was to achieve a dominant leadership position in the antibacterial segment that was large and rapidly growing. The company had chosen the fastest growing subsegment (quinolones) of the antibacterials and pursued a very aggressive strategy with the introduction of Cifran (ciprofloxacin) in 1989. In less than four years, Cifran had become the most critical brand for Ranbaxy accounting for about one-fourth of its domestic formulations sales. Cifran had given it the much needed competitive edge. Ranbaxy had become the unquestioned leader with a 12.7 percent share of the total anti-bacterial therapeutic group by 1992. Ranbaxy was way ahead of the competition in its chosen segment with the nearest competitors - Cipla (6.9 percent) and the once-upon-a-time leader Sarabhai Chemicals (Market share 6.7 percent) trailing far behind.

The formula for success is not difficult to understand because there is no such formula. What is crucial to the whole business of winning at the marketplace is the ability to uncover the opportunities and the energy to exploit them!

You cannot be Immune to Change, Even if you are a Leader in Immunologicals!

The market for immunologicals is yet another example of a leader in the 1970s being pushed to the second position. The immunological market in 1976 comprised Sera and Vaccines (Anti-tetanus serum, tetanus toxoid, and DPT vaccines mainly) and gamma globulins. The market had grown from Rs. 1-crore in 1976 to Rs. 9-crore in 1988. In addition to this, the government of India had embarked on a massive nation-wide primary immunization program against diphtheria, pertussis, tetanus and polio and measles. That is an addition of Rs. 5-crore to the Sera and Vaccines market, making it a sizable Rs. 14-crore market. Increasing literacy levels and growing urbanization were also expanding the immunological market. The demand for other vaccines like measles vaccines, anti-rabies vaccine, oral polio drops was continually increasing.

However, Biological E. Limited, the market leader in the Immunological market in the 1970s, remained oblivious to these changes and developments. It had not introduced any new product in this category despite the numerous new product opportunities that had come its way. The company seemed to have taken its leadership position for granted and felt immune to the changes and developments. So the inevitable happened. The company slid down to the third position in 1988 with a market share of only 15.2 percent.

The company did not see the writing on the wall, which was large and bright enough. Consequently, its share of the immunological market had further eroded to a mere 6 percent by 1992 pushing the company to fourth place.

The marketplace has got its own laws. First and foremost among them is that the consequence of complacency is the loss of leadership, however firmly entrenched the leader might have been once upon a time!

Booster Doses are Essential to Boost Sales and Market Share!

As in immunology, booster doses seem to be essential in the immunological market. Because that was what Serum Institute, a young, little-known company in the early 1970s had done to climb the coveted leadership position in the immunological market in India. The company was quick on the draw and capitalized every single opportunity that had come its way. It was the first company to introduce new vaccines in all emerging categories and positioned itself firmly as the Immunologicals company. The name Serum Institute of India reinforced this image. The outcome? The company emerged as a leader in the immunological market in India, with no challenger in sight (market share 40.2 percent in 1988).

Perhaps this had lulled the company into complacency. It had taken its leadership position for granted and did not take cognizance of emerging competition. Hoechst (Sanofi now) and Alidac (a division of Zydus Cadila) had been watching the immunological market with considerable interest.

Hoechst had entered the market with its brand of anti-rabies vaccine, Rabipur in 1986 and within a short span of six years achieved a dominant leadership position by introducing new products and by promoting its sera and vaccine range aggressively.

The market share of Serum Institute had shrunk to 16 percent by 1992, and the company had to be content with a distant No.2 position.

Another important law of the market place is that there is no time for respite. You cannot take anything for granted in marketing. Not even your leadership position however formidable it may seem to be!

One is Enough!

Hoechst India is another company, which confirms to the maxim of the marketplace, that if you uncover just one right opportunity and back it up with all your might, you are sure to be a winner.

Hoechst, though a very late entrant to the immunological market in India (December 1986), uncovered a significant opportunity in the anti-rabies vaccine area and exploited it with the introduction of a truly superior product, Rabipur anti-rabies vaccine. The company had vigorously promoted the product and within a short span of two years achieved the No.2 position in the immunological market (market share 28 percent in 1998). Surely one is enough if it is the right one!

The dramatic success of Rabipur vaccine only whetted the appetite of Hoechst for further increase in market share. The company expanded its winning range of products in the sera and vaccines market with new products like anti-RHO-D, Beriglobin, Human Albumin, and Berirab. Within six years, Hoechst had achieved the leadership position in the immunologicals market with a formidable 58 percent share of the market (1992).

Elements of Market Opportunity Analysis

The common thread that runs through these cases is that constant analysis of market opportunities is imperative to the success of any company. Market opportunity analysis includes:

A. Strengths of your product attributes (unique customer perceptions) in your served market as well as in your competitors' served markets (as opposed to their product offerings).

B. Analysis of any possible gaps between customer needs and your (as well as your competitors') product offerings. The gap is the opportunity area.

C. A detailed analysis of whether the identified gaps or opportunities (currently unmet needs of customers) can be exploited profitably. In other words, is the new segment viable?

D. Look for any possible weaknesses existing in your product offerings as compared to changing customer needs and how your competitors have been responding. It is necessary to prevent the invasion of your competitors into your served markets and to reinforce your product strengths by appropriate product development strategy.

E. Whether exploiting the emerging new segments or markets involves directly or indirectly any internal threats, environmental, social, competitive or otherwise. Quantitative analysis of the segment and your new product regarding:

  ▸ The demand analysis
  ▸ The profitability
  ▸ The competitive edge that it would give the company's product-mix
  ▸ The likely impact it may have on your existing products — Eg. Whether it would lead to cannibalization of the existing products and if so, what is the net impact on the company's bottom-line?
  ▸ A detailed analysis of competitors and their likely responses to the new segment — like what would be the response

time involved? How soon can the competition enter? What plans do you have to counter any possible attack by competitors?

▸ What is your feedback system? How effective is it? What improvements are needed to improve its promptness? Its speed?

Once you are equipped with all this information and a determination to succeed and are quick enough on the draw, you are sure to win in the marketplace as many other companies have done in the past. Sounds simple? Well, it takes much hard work!

Before deciding on any line-extension strategy, further analysis of the available data is essential. Because, if your brand does not enjoy a considerable strength in the market, using the same brand name for all possible line extensions with a hope of building a successful or winning flagship brand will end up only as a fond hope! Like athletes need strong legs and excellent coordination to compete in a race, brands too need a strong foothold to be successful in the marketplace that is merciless.

While all this may sound elementary, look at how many companies have ignored such opportunities even in the antacid, anti-flatulent market. Here is a case in point:

Opportunity Overlooked?

The industry leader Glaxo (GlaxoSmithKline now) introduced in 1977 Almacarb tablets in the antacid, anti-flatulent market, and positioned it for acid reflux cleverly and clearly. The new positioning earned the company a respectable share of the (over two percent) market within a short time. Later the company had started promoting this product through its second division Allenburys, which is considerably smaller than the Glaxo Pharma division both in sales and coverage. Glaxo, which is known for its innovative marketing strategies, somehow decided to ignore the relatively more significant and more prosperous segment of antacid suspension. The antacid suspension market accounted at the time for about two-thirds of the total antacid market with tablets contributing for the rest of the one-third market. Entering the suspension market would have been a logical decision, even an elementary one for Glaxo, particularly in the light of Almacarb's initial success and the company's marketing muscle. Because the company had got an enviable combination of brain and brawn! The company had been hugely successful even with me-too re-launches like Piriton Expectorant in an over-crowded cough and cold preparations market a few years ago!

But somehow, the company chose to ignore the larger sub-segment of antacid, anti-flatulent suspension. Opportunity overlooked?

Market Opportunity Analysis:
A Step-by-Step Approach

Step One: Analyze your existing markets.

What is your directly competing market? List out all the existing markets in which you are competing in terms of market size (in units and value), growth rate, number of competitors, the top three competitors in each market, their sales in units and value, market share, the rate at which they are growing, your sales in units and value, growth rate in each market. You can thus arrive at the size of your directly competing market.

Step Two: Build on your strengths.

Have you realized, capitalized and exploited all the possible opportunities in your existing markets? Do a SWOT (Strength, Weakness, Opportunity, Threat) analysis of your products in all your current markets. The fundamental questions to ask are:

Are there any unmet needs in your existing markets, not fulfilled by you as well as your competitors?

Are there any significant sub-segments where you do not have any product? What about your competitors? How are they faring in the sub-segments? What is the contribution of their products in these sub-segments to their total sales in the market?

▸ What are the strengths and weaknesses of your products as compared to your competitors? Is there any need for product development, to create a perceptible differentiation?

▸ What are the opportunities that the current markets offer? Can you plot the trends and spot any emergence of new markets early enough as Lupin did in the anti-tubercular market and Serum Institute of India in the case of the immunological market?

▸ Are there any shadows or threats lurking in your markets? Do you have any early warning system so that you can pull out of the market with little or no damage? Like Schering A.G.,

Nicholas Piramal, and Allenburys division of Glaxo pulled out of the high dose estrogen-progesterone market, which vanished due to a government ban? These threats could be from the changing opinions of customers, shifts in the treatment pattern, or line of therapy or governmental policies. You should develop a feedback system to monitor the changing trends and the likely changes. Developing an early warning system is as essential as a stitch in time.

Building on strengths is crucial for success. You should reinforce your already strong position in your existing markets with new products, expand and extend your served markets. Because, if you don't, your competitors will!

Step Three: Explore new market opportunities.

Always be on the lookout for new market opportunities. Find out the fast-growing markets. Large markets, and the ones, which are less entrenched. List out the new markets regarding their size, growth, competitive intensity, and vulnerability. Prioritize them in the order of their importance or attractiveness to you.

Also, analyze how the markets identified or short-listed will match with the resources of your firm. What is the level of congruence? So how will these new markets affect your existing ones? Will there be any cannibalization of the products? How many new markets can you enter?

Step Four: Evaluate new opportunities in new segments.

The main points to consider, when you are evaluating new market opportunities in new segments are:

▸ Find out whether the market is large enough and is growing rapidly enough.

▸ Whether the segment is over-crowded; what is the intensity of competition?

▸ Who are the major competitors? What are their strengths? What about their coverage? How does your firm compete with them regarding resources?

▶ What about the attributes of your product (to be introduced) vis-a-vis the competitors? Have you created a differentiation that can be perceived by your prospective customers?

The answers to these questions will be helpful in giving a direction to your marketing strategy.

Market Opportunity Analysis: An Example

Assume that you want to introduce a non-steroidal anti-inflammatory drug. What should you consider as your market? Your actual market (directly competing market) would mean an aggregate of the sales volume of all non-steroidal anti-inflammatory drugs in the market. That is limiting the market and restricting the opportunities.

Looking at the potential market would mean widening the horizon of opportunities. The potential market, in this case, would be the anti-arthritic market as a whole, since physicians use Non-steroidal Anti-inflammatory Drugs (NSAIDs) widely in the treatment of arthritis because of their safety and efficacy. When you analyze the prescriptions of doctors, you will observe that the anti-arthritic market includes in addition to NSAIDS, muscle relaxants, steroids, topical rubifacients, anti-gout preparations, and analgesics, etc. With the help of prescription audit report figures, it is possible to quantify the size of each segment. You can find out exactly how many prescriptions are written for each competing product in each segment.

Consider for example the gout segment of the anti-arthritic market. The prescriptions written for gout include apart from the anti-gout preparations like Zyloric (Burroughs Wellcome then and GSK now) and Benemid (Merind then and MSD now), NSAIDs (Non-steroidal Anti-inflammatory Drugs) and analgesics. By referring to prescription audit, you can find out the exact number of:

A. Prescriptions written for NSAIDs in gout
B. Prescriptions written for analgesics in gout
C. In addition, to the total number of prescriptions written for the more specific anti-gout preparations

Armed with this ammunition of information, you can now aim to be going great guns with your new NSAID against a bigger anti-arthritic market (potential market) rather than confirming yourself to a smaller NSAID market (actual demand).

Similarly, when you analyze each of the major segments like pain, lumbago, sciatica, bursitis, synovitis, spondylitis, sprains, osteoarthritis, rheumatoid arthritis, etc., (based on diagnostic profile), you would observe that the actual market of NSAIDS allows itself to expand into a much more significant potential (anti-arthritic) market!

You can do a similar analysis taking into account all the aspects of exploring and evaluating new opportunities in all the markets you want to enter.

The Served Market

It is Bruce Henderson, Chairman of the famous BCG (the Boston Consulting Group), who has originated the Served Market concept. So far all the definitions of the market have been somewhat implicit and included elements like your customers, products or services and your competitors' products or services. Since all customers, their needs and requirements (physical, physiological or psychological) are not alike, it is useful to think of them as segments of the total market. You can group them based on factors such as homogeneity, or commonality of needs, which helps to sharpen your focus on the customer needs of different customer groups even more effectively. This explains why so many creative and innovative marketers the world over are looking for niches and turning the science of segmentation into a fine art.

The served market concept is the ultimate step and the state of the art way of defining market segments and understanding market structures. This involves an examination of your market segments from a competitor's point of view. In any given market there are different segments of the market, comprising groups of customers with varying needs. These customer groups select the competitive offerings that best suit their needs. This process creates market segments. Each competitor, thus, has some group of customers where he holds an absolute advantage over all other competitors. This is his forte. Because he offers a benefit-package of products and services that is best suited for his specific target customers. That is his served market. Here is a graphic presentation of the served market (figure 1.2).

The Served Market

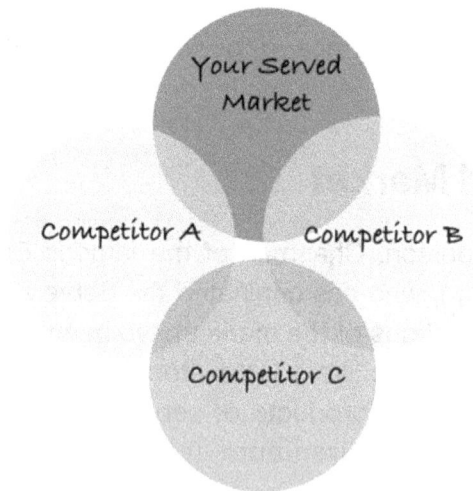

Figure 1.2 The Served Market Concept

What is more important to note in the served market concept is that each competitor has his boundary lines. Moreover, by definition, those areas offer zero-competitive advantages. At those boundaries, neither you nor your competitor has an edge to provide those particular customers. What are the implications of this to the marketer?

Firstly, all competition in a market must take place along the boundary lines of the served markets as all differentiation, competitive advantages that are stronger at the core, become increasingly thinner and as you move to the periphery and they become entirely imperceptible and indistinguishable at the boundaries or borders.

To expand your market and increase your market share you will have to create a discernible competitive advantage and communicate it with all your might to your customers and prospective customers around the zero-advantage boundary line and, indeed to those in your competitor's served market. That is not only necessary for growth but also essential even for survival.

Always, remember that the boundary lines of the served markets of yourself as well as your competitors' change over time since the marketing environment is such a dynamic one where change is the only constant factor. Also, this change occurs as one competitor acquires a competitive advantage over another and occupies part of his territory. So an appropriate definition of your served market is that particular one in which, you have a combination of customers and products and services, where you have an absolute advantage over all other competitors in your market (the total market).

To expand your served market, you have to:

A. Develop a clear understanding of your served market and the served markets of your competitors.
B. Defend your served markets by communicating the advantages of your products and services persuasively to your existing customers as positive reinforcement.
C. Create a distinct competitive advantage and communicate them to persuade the customers of your competitors (and those around the zero-advantage zone).

The name of the game of business growth and market expansion, therefore, is differentiation that can be perceived by the customers. In mature markets, this assumes even greater importance. Here is an example (case 13) of what differentiation can do to your product. It can catapult an obscure brand into the leadership position.

Antacid Market: Emergence of a New Leader!

Gelusil of Warner Hindusthan (now Pfizer) had been enjoying brand leadership in the Rs. 78-crore large (1992) antacid, antiflatulent market. It was a brand leader since its launch in 1973.

Its served market had been considerably large with other prominent brands like Aludrox, Divol and Digene , etc. Although introduced in 1968, it was only during the 1970s that Digene created a perceptible product differentiation by adding an anti-flatulent (Methylpolysiloxane) and pushed the product aggressively into the competitors' territory. Its volume had grown, market share had moved up significantly making Digene the undisputed brand leader in 1992 with a 20 percent share of the antacid-antiflatulent market.

Difficult Task

Developing a clear, thorough understanding of your market is a challenging task. You may find this a demanding or perhaps even an impossible exercise.

What you should do is define exactly how much you understand about your business and by extension, what new information you have to acquire to develop intelligent, meaningful, appropriate competitive marketing strategies. To help you get started on this task, here is a checklist:

Defining Your Served Market: A Checklist

1. Define the total market by size (volume and value), growth rate, customer-types, and competitors.
2. Define your served market concerning your customers' needs and how your product attributes satisfy those needs. Mention the specific competitive advantage of your product.
3. Define your competitors' served markets regarding their respective customer needs, and the competitive advantages their products offer in satisfying those needs.
4. Identify the areas of zero-competitive advantage.
5. Find out ways of creating a perceptible differentiation and turning it into a distinct competitive advantage.
6. Prepare a persuasive communication strategy to drive home the distinct competitive advantage you have created.
7. Invade your competitor's territory with all your might.

Market Segmentation: Points to Ponder

While market segmentation is essential for success by creating a niche for a product, one should not splinter the market and lose sight of the opportunities that may have been lying dormant at his doorstep. This sort of tunnel vision has cost many companies very dearly. Business history, the world over is replete with the success stories of companies, which have been alert to spot the opportunities in time that others could not, and at the same time, innumerable are the failures of those companies, who could not recognize the opportunities waiting in front of them. Theodore Levitt, the well-known professor emeritus of marketing at the Harvard Business School in his classic and landmark article, *The Marketing Myopia* published in 1960 had most vividly described this. It is relevant even today.

The points, therefore, you have to remember while segmenting the market are:

A. Define your served market and the potential market as clearly as possible. Definition of your potential market includes and involves a thorough understanding of your competitors' served markets.

B. List the critical characteristics and attributes that are unique to your products. Also, list the essential features and unique aspects of your competitors' products.

C. Find out whether there are any unmet, unsatisfied needs in your competitors' served markets.

D. Monitor the changing needs and be alert to notice, recognize, and record any developments taking place in the total market. Unless you are the first to observe and understand the changing trends and events, you cannot be the first to meet the changing needs of your customers (yours as well as your competitors) with an appropriate and satisfying mix of product offering. Remember the cardinal principle of marketing — you have got to be the firstest with the mostest if you want to reap an abundant harvest in the market.

Strategic Options

Now that you have defined, redefined and refined your market definitions and analyzed it, how should you go about deciding on your market finally? What are the strategic options?

A. **Concentrated Marketing:** Should you segment the market by the customer specialty, I.e., pediatric market, orthopedic market, psychotropic market, the gynecology market, the dermatological market, etc.?

The implications of such segmentation would mean practicing the strategy of concentrated marketing. In other words, you have to design a marketing-mix explicitly targeted at the chosen segment and go the whole hog. The apparent advantages of concentrated marketing are:

You can carve out, a niche for your company and its products.

A concentrated approach will give you a distinct and definite competitive advantage as you will be in a better position to monitor and predict the trends and the likely shifts in the line of treatment and customer needs in the market than your competitors. It is truly invaluable. Consequently, your customer service will be better than your competitors' because of the specialized knowledge of your sales force, your product management, and product development teams.

Of course, concentrated marketing is not without its disadvantages. The primary problem is that a failure could be devastating. It could cost the company very dearly since you are putting all your eggs in one basket. You have got to be thorough in your analysis and should have products, which are perceptibly different and distinct from the existing products. Equipped with this, when you go all out in promoting your product with an appropriate promotional-mix, you are bound to succeed. However, you must do much homework, monitor your tactics, strategy and competitors' responses closely. As a Jewish proverb says, *'there is nothing wrong with keeping all your eggs in one basket, so long as you watch the basket closely.'*

The other disadvantage of concentrated marketing is that the segment may not be viable and the company, in its enthusiasm to create a target-specific marketing-mix may be losing sight of some of the opportunities. After all, even the insignificant many may also count in the long run. However, in the final analysis, concentrated marketing wins hands down when the segmentation criteria are right.

Schering A.G. Concentrates on Gynaec Market and Beats the Retreat in Time!

Schering A.G. was concentrating only on the gynecology market in India in the late 1960s. The company was specializing in the female sex hormones and had many winning brands like Primolut N, Duogynon and a wide range of oral contraceptives under the brand names - Gynovlar, Primovlar, Anovlar, etc. The company's image in the gynecology segment was arguably the best in the industry. Subsequently, the company had become a part of German Remedies and started practicing differentiated marketing, promoting even German Remedies' products. The company today does not have the exclusive image of the company in the Gynaec market any longer.

Schering A.G.'s retreat was just in time and appropriate. The Gynaec market had been undergoing a substantial change with some of the earlier hormones like progesterone and estrogen (certain esters of these hormones) coming under attack due to side effects, including the fear of breast cancer. The oral contraceptive market had not been growing fast enough. The company was, therefore, left with two options:

A. Either introduce newer and safer hormones, or
B. Pull out of the market

While the company had not withdrawn itself from the Gynaec market, it pulled out of the controversial segment of high-dose combinations of estrogen and progesterone, which were supposed to be used mainly for pregnancy diagnosis (but misused for termination of pregnancy more often than not, much before the medical termination of pregnancy was acceptable socially and legally). The company (German Remedies), which acquired Schering A.G. had been practicing differentiated marketing by product-market diversification (promoting other products of German Remedies) thus freeing itself from the threat of vulnerability.

Later, German Schering as the company was known then started promoting only the hormonal and other original products and not the different range of German Remedies for reasons best known to them.

Today, German Schering is part of the Zydus Bayer joint venture as Bayer acquired German Schering. Later Bayer has formed a joint venture with Zydus Cadila in 2011.

The case of German Schering brings home one major disadvantage of practicing concentrated marketing. The vulnerability. When you are concentrating only in one segment of the market, you may become vulnerable, if market conditions change and you do not have anything to fall back upon. What has been a major strength once, i.e., excessive specialization , may turn out to be a weakness when the market conditions change and when you are less flexible (due to excessive specialization).

B. Differentiated Marketing: The second strategic option is Differentiated Marketing.

When an organization markets in many segments, each with a differentiated marketing-mix, it is practicing differentiated marketing.

One significant advantage of practicing differentiated marketing is that it minimizes or eliminates the vulnerability factor. It allows a firm to be more flexible that way. The second advantage of practicing differentiated marketing is that the significant marketing costs, like selling and distribution, are spread over many products. As a result, you can compete in relatively smaller-yet-profitable segments, more effectively.

There seems to be an increasing trend among some companies to practice concentrated marketing strategies mainly targeted at the institutional market in the pharmaceutical industry. Some companies in the late 1980s and 1990s created an institutional sales division or a hospital products division. It has later evolved into a process called Key Account Management (KAM), which is a more integrated and scientific approach to focus on the institutional market that comprises large accounts, which are crucial to sales success.

Before deciding on any strategy or a combination of these strategies you should ask the following questions:

A. What are the resources of your company? (financial, technological, manufacturing and marketing)

B. What are the competitors doing?

C. Is the market new to the company?

C. Undifferentiated Marketing: Undifferentiated marketing, as the name suggests, is precisely the opposite of differentiated marketing or segmented approach to marketing. There are a few products in the consumer market and several more in the industrial market that are sold to many buyers and not to any particular sub-group. In so far as the pharmaceutical industry is concerned, you can only view the institutional market as a mass market. While some marketers feel that in the emerging generic market too can be considered for undifferentiated marketing, without some degree of differentiation regarding the quality or better value for money, it is not possible to market even the generics successfully. That is why the corporate-branded generics are making their presence felt, albeit at a slower pace in the so-called undifferentiated market. It is the company name and the corporate image that gives a brand status to the generic product. Undifferentiated marketing seems to be more of a myth than reality in the present day world, where branding even commodities is becoming a necessity to market them successfully.

The Pharmaceutical Product

The Product Concept

What is the product may sound like a superfluous question. However, there is more to a product than meets the eye. A product is not what it is, but what it does to the consumer. People do not buy products. They buy the benefits that the product offers. A person does not buy a TV because it is a TV. He buys it because it fulfills his need for entertainment. The needs could be real, felt or imaginary. Charles Revlon, the entrepreneurial genius behind the Revlon company, said it beautifully: *in the factories we make cosmetics. In the marketplace we sell hope. The hope of romance*. Thus, a woman who dabs on some Intimate or a man who sprays some musk onto himself is fulfilling probably the perceived need. A person who buys some Aspirin is not buying Aspirin as such, but he is buying relief from a headache (a benefit).

Similarly, when a doctor prescribes a different antibiotic like ciprofloxacin, he is not prescribing because it is the latest antibiotic. He is prescribing it because of its superior antibacterial power and its ability to control the infection better and faster. He too is buying the benefits it offers. Thus a product can be said to be a bundle of benefits and a need-satisfying entity.

What is a Brand?

What constitutes a brand? While a generic product is an undifferentiated (similar) product, a brand is a differentiated product. For example ranitidine, the anti-ulcer drug is a generic product, but when you call it Zantac, a different image is conjured up before us. The image of the world's largest selling prescription drug.A potent anti-ulcer drug. Zantac is the brand. The next question is, what is the difference? Is the difference between the brand and the product — is it only in the name? No, there is more. Much more.

The brand name gives a distinct identity to the product. However, this mere christening of the product does not provide or create the brand image. Designing and building up a brand image is a more complex, painstaking process, which is known as branding a product. Moreover, like Rome, brands too are not built in a day!

It is the communication that makes the brand and gives it a distinct personality. Communication here includes all the internal elements of the marketing-mix, popularly known as the Four Ps - Product, Price, Promotion, and Place (distribution). Each of these 4 Ps communicates and in the process creates a personality for the brand.

Moreover, until the communication about a product is transmitted and received, accepted and found rewarding, it will not become a brand. No, not for long. A product, therefore, must provide specific benefits (leading to rewarding experiences) to a large enough number of users. Only then can it become a brand.

A branded product, therefore, has the extra plus — the promise of customer satisfaction and customer-satisfying benefits. A Brand is not a mere name that you give a generic product and put on the label to differentiate it physically from other similar products. The American Marketing Association has defined a brand as *a name, symbol or design or a combination of them, which is intended to identify the goods and services of one seller or groups of sellers and differentiate them from those of competitors.* However, there is indeed more to a brand than this differentiation by name. Sidney J. Levy and Burleigh B. Gardner emphasize this in their 1955 Harvard Business Review article on P*roduct and the Brand* when they say:

> *A brand name is more than the label employed to differentiate among the manufacturers of a product. It is a complex symbol that represents varieties of ideas and attributes. It tells the consumers many things, not only the way it sounds (and its literal meaning, if it has one) but, more important, via the body of associations it has built up and acquired as a public object over a period.*

A brand name will convey meaning, which its advertising, merchandising, promotion, publicity and even sheer length of existence have created! The net result is a public image, a character or personality that may be more important for the overall status (and sales) of the brand than many technical facts about the product.

Professor Levitt of Harvard Business School has been saying this for a long time that *a branded product is not what the engineers say, but also what is implied by its design; its packaging; its channels of distribution; its price and quality and activities of salespeople. It is a transaction between the seller and the buyer; a synthesis of what the seller intends and buyer perceives.*

The Augmented Product Concept

What we are discussing here about the brand and branding is similar to what professor Levitt calls the augmented product concept. Without indulging in the game of semantics, let us decide and agree that a brand is and should be an augmented product, which is the result of voluntary improvements brought about in the product by the manufacturers. These improvements are neither suggested by the customers nor even expected by them. The marketer, on his own, augments by adding an extra facility or an additional feature to his products. It is essential to create a significant, meaningful and perceivable differentiation in the product.

Augmentation of the product is essential in branding, particularly in the pharmaceutical industry in India. The severe competition demands and dictates that. This augmentation can be created in the primary product itself, or the packaging, communication, and additional services or a combination of these areas.

Product Augmentation in the Indian Pharmaceutical Industry

In the Indian pharmaceutical industry, product augmentation is a must for the survival and growth of brands. It is necessary because many newer drugs are being developed making the existing products obsolete at a faster rate. The main reason is the licensing policy of the government, which encourages the small-scale sector even in sophisticated, high technology industry like pharmaceuticals. The result is the mushrooming of pharmaceutical companies churning out many brands (brands here are only namesakes reduced to mere identification marks of generics; otherwise there are virtually no product differentiations). Companies, which consider that branding means augmenting the product by creating and communicating that extra plus are bound to succeed. In fact, only those companies succeed.

For example, there is umpteen number of brands of paracetamol in India (products with different names only and not brands in the real sense), but only Crocin, Calpol, and Metacin are very successful in India.

Let us take different brands of B-complex in the country. They are Innumerable. However, the successful brands are only a handful such as Becosules, Cobadex, and Becozyme. The situation is the same for any product group in the country.

Branding by product augmentation, in the pharmaceutical industry, is achieved by creating differentiation in the manufacturing process, changes in the formulation, packaging, communication, and by giving an appropriate, suggestive, memorable brand name. Consider these Cases:

The Silent Salesman Adds Value!

An example of product augmentation by packaging is Lederle's (Pfizer now) Prenatal capsules. Prenatal capsules are hematinic capsules specially meant for pregnant women as the name suggests. In fact, the name tells it all. They have brought about an innovative and voluntary improvement in the packaging. They introduced a beautiful and innovative pack of 120 capsules for their Prenatal in the shape of a feeding bottle, which is reusable. It would also ensure that the consumer buys at a time 120 capsules. The product was doing very well even before this packaging innovation. The new packaging would have probably taken the brand further up even to a brand leader position. However, the company took the pressure off this product, and as a result, the brand slipped from its rank and market share. Prenatal was a brand to reckon with in its heydays. The silent salesman did add value!

Innovation Makes All the Difference!

Another example of product augmentation is Fefol, the pregnancy hematinic from SmithKline French known as Eskay Labs in India in the late 1960s (GlaxoSmithKline now). Fefol was no more than a hematinic formulation containing 150 mg of ferrous sulfate and 0.5 mg of folic acid. Nothing was exciting about the formulation. Many hematinic formulations were containing these two ingredients in even higher quantities. However, the product augmentation was achieved in Fefol by its superior formulation, which can be said to the forerunner of new drug delivery systems, that are sweeping the pharmaceutical market today. Even the presentation of the product is distinctly different. It was a different kind of a capsule called Spansule, which contains the active ingredients in the form of tiny pellets - hundreds of them inside each transparent capsule. These pellets are coated especially to ensure timed-disintegration. Apart from the technical benefits it offers, the product too is a beautiful see-through capsule with hundreds of multi-colored time-release pellets. The benefit: freedom from side effects associated with oral iron therapy. They have very dramatically and persuasively communicated this benefit package to doctors in the country. They introduced a new brand, Fesovit (iron with multivitamins) in the same Spansule form of capsules. They had promoted these brands vigorously and achieved a leadership position with a market share (combined for both Fefol and Fesovit) of 15 percent in 1999.

Language of Branding

A Brand, the American Marketing Association, has defined as *a name, term symbol, design, or a combination of them which is intended to identify the goods and services of one or groups of sellers and to differentiate them from those of competitors*. Becosules, Cobadex, and Basiton Forte are some of the leading brands of the therapeutic group called B-Complex Oral Solids, in India.

A Trademark is a brand that has been given legal protection, thus ensuring its use exclusively by one seller. A brand has to be registered with the Registrar of Trademarks to get the legal protection, i.e., the trademark. Nowadays, it takes anywhere from 2 to 3 years to get a trademark registered in the pharmaceutical industry in India.

Individual Brand Strategy as the name indicates, is having a separate brand name for each product. The company can search a winning name for each of its products and can introduce a variety of brands in a single product class. If any one brand fails or proves to be inferior, the other brands of the company are not affected and victimized by the name. For instance, in the multivitamins and minerals group, Lederle in India had many brands like Prenatal, Vi-Magna, Gevral, Folviron, Stress Caps, Autrin and Incremin.

Family Brand Strategy as the name suggests is having a familiar brand name (family) for all related products. The main advantage here is that the company can cash in or capitalize on the image of a highly successful brand name. In the pharmaceutical industry, family brands are quite familiar because many drugs are present in different dosage forms for various indications and different age groups, as in the case of pediatrics and geriatrics. Some of the highly successful family brands are - Terramycin of Pfizer, which tends to extend its image to the other products marketed in the same product class by the company. Glaxo in India has an excellent image with consumers in India, and the company was a household name as they manufactured baby foods and protein food supplements in the past. By the heavy direct advertising, it was the best known name among the pharmaceutical companies in India at the time. The company's packaging cashed in on this by displaying Glaxo in big bold letters and very prominently. Glaxo's company brands like Complex B-Glaxo, Ostocalcium-B12 Glaxo were big sellers in India.

While a corporate or company brand strategy attempts to cash in on the favorable image of the company, a brand that is hugely successful, reinforces the already well-established and desirable image of the company itself. Thus the company image and the brand image can be mutually reinforcing. Here is case in point.

The Brand that Catapulted a Company into the Top Position!

Septran, an anti-bacterial drug, which is a combination of sulphamethoxazole and trimethoprim, commonly known as cotrimoxazole (generic name), was introduced in India in 1974 by Burroughs Wellcome. Cotrimoxazole was the product of a joint research program of two well-known multinational pharmaceutical companies - Burroughs Wellcome (GSK now), and Hoffman La Roche. The drug, as usual, was introduced in the UK and some other European countries first and following its successful launch, it was launched in India a few years later. While the drug was reasonably successful in other countries wherever the company introduced it, in India, it was an unprecedented and spectacular success. Septran had made history. Septran remained the most significant selling prescription drug in India even after fifteen years of its introduction in India. Nowhere in the world has Cotrimoxazole made to the top.

Consequently, Septran catapulted Boroughs Wellcome into the top six companies in the Indian pharmaceutical industry from a below-twenty position. Septran accounted for about 55 percent of the company's sales volume in 1988.

Boroughs Wellcome in India had pursued a very aggressive marketing strategy for Septran right from the word Go! It was somewhat uncharacteristic of the company, which was very conservative in the past. The image of the company in India was always excellent, and the company was considered to be a reliable, dependable pharmaceutical company with a high-quality research profile, having little or no profit orientation, as it was a subsidiary of Wellcome Foundation, which was considered to be a nonprofit organization. Their sales force in India were also communicating the same message to the doctors in the late 1960s and even in the early 1970s.

Septran hugely changed all this. There was excitement. The company backed up the Septran promotion with many marketing initiatives. It provided specially designed visiting cards to the medical representatives, special visual-aids, booklets, and product literature giving detailed prescribing information of the product. Besides, persuasive detailing by its field force, documentation of clinical trials conducted, special Septran allowances and incentives to motivate the field force to call on as many doctors and chemists as possible within the shortest time and incentive on Septran sales accentuated Septran's progress in the market. The company had achieved the highest call average of customers during the Septran launch. The individual visiting cards differentiated the representatives' Septran interviews from the regular, routine doctors' calls.

The rest was history. Although Roche, the original research partner of cotrimoxazole too had introduced their brand - Bactrim around the same time, it did not make it as significant. The launch of Bactrim also was a success in India, but it had to contend with a distant second position with a sales volume that was less than half of Septran's. Many cotrimoxazole introductions immediately followed the success of Septran under various brand names. There were more than two hundred cotrimoxazole brands, which were struggling to carve a place for themselves in the 1990s.

Septran had achieved about one-third of the cotrimoxazole market in India and was growing strong even after fifteen years after its introduction in India. In the process, it had made cotrimoxazole one of the biggest subgroups in the Indian pharmaceutical market. To further consolidate its position the company has introduced a double-strength formulation of cotrimoxazole under a different brand name - Sepmax. This move had reinforced its already strong position in the cotrimoxazole market with a formidable and unprecedented market share of over 46 percent.

Multiple Brand Strategy is marketing virtually the same product with two or more different brand names. The idea here is to get a more significant share of the market. It is a problematic strategy in a sense, if not planned and communicated very carefully it could lead to cannibalization of brands. Cannibalization of brands means that one brand is losing prescriptions, sales and market share as a result of a new introduction by the same producer or manufacturer. In other words, one brand eating into the share of the other brand of the same company rather than taking the share of the competing brands. Multiple brand strategy, as opposed to cannibalization, is to ensure that both brands gain a significant share of the market and achieving a dominant position in the market.

Glaxo had used the multiple brand strategy very successfully. It, of course, had promoted these brands through its different marketing teams (Glaxo and Allenburys divisions). Becadexamin (Glaxo) and Multivite FM (Allenburys) are the multivitamins, and mineral capsules have identical formulations. Only the brand names were different. Both the brands were late entrants to the market. Both had achieved at one time a combined market share of 45 percent in the multivitamin minerals market (1988).

Private Brand or a middleman's brand strategy implies that the owner of the brand does not manufacture the product. The middleman or the distributor of marketer owns it. The equivalent of this private brand strategy is rapidly growing in the Indian pharmaceutical market. You see an ever-increasing number labels and cartons of new products, which read - *manufactured by so and so and marketed by so and so*. The main reason for such a proliferation of trading activity of new brands is the government's licensing policy. A small-scale manufacturer need not go through the rigmarole of registering his product with the Directorate General of Trade and Development (DGTD) nor is it controlled by the Drug Price Control Order (DPCO). All he needs is a drug license. To save valuable time and to avoid the fear of rejection of the license for the proposed new product, even the leading pharmaceutical companies resort to this backdoor method of getting the drug manufactured by a small-scale manufacturer but market it themselves.

Product Item is a distinct unit within a product line that is distinguished by size, dosage form, price, appearance or some other attributes.

Product Line describes a group of related products with a similar function. Factors such as the assortment of sizes, dosage forms, strengths, the concentration of active ingredients, flavors, price range offered within each product line determine the depth of a product line.

Product-Mix is a complete list of all the products offered by a company for sale. The number of product lines it offers measures the breadth of the product mix.

A Rose by Any Other Name!

What's there in a name? Maybe Shakespeare had his reasons to say that there is nothing more to a name. However, in marketing, that too in the age of brands, a rose by any other name is not a rose and it does not smell as sweet! Not only do we see what we want to see, but we also smell what we want to smell.

In today's me-too world, a name is a vital tool that can cut through the chaos and confusion in the marketplace, where the number of brands multiplying like that of rabbits.

A name is a hook that hangs the brand on the product ladder in the prospect's mind. A name should tell the prospect what the product is and what its major benefit is.

Let us look at what Al Ries and Jack Trout, the strong advocates of the positioning strategy and in fact, who introduced to the concept of positioning into the marketing lexicon. Here's what they said in their landmark article, *The Positioning Era Cometh* in the Advertising Age more than forty-five years ago:

> *Choosing a name is like driving a racing car. To win you have got to take chances. You have to select names that are almost, but not entirely generic. A strong, generic like, descriptive name will block your me-too competitors from muscling their way into your territory. A good name is the best insurance for long-term success.*

What one should look for in a name is not the goodness but appropriateness. Would Septran by any other name, have been successful?

Would Becosules, ABDEC, Fefol have been successful? Of Course, it is difficult to say in retrospect, but the chances are that they may not have been as successful.

It is not enough if the name is short, rhyming and descriptive as illustrated in the case of the impossible name.

CASE

18

The Impossible Name!

Tips & Toes understandably is a perfect name for nail polish. The brand, backed by excellent promotion has become a big success. Inspired by this, another company wanted to introduce a lipstick. The company was planning to launch some cosmetics simultaneously. The company wanted to have a catchy, memorable brand name for their lipstick. It should be suggestive, short and sweet. They came up with the name - Kiss & Tell. Suggestive, crisp, and rhyming. They promoted it vigorously. The brand was a miserable failure. Not because the name was bad. The brand name had all the characteristics of an ideal brand name. However, it was simply an impossible name, because it prevented customers from asking for the product. Can any woman walk into a store and ask for Kiss and Tell?

Realizing the importance of the name in branding a product, the US Department of Commerce listed out some characteristics of a good name, in a guide issued to developing and selling new products. An ideal brand name should meet the following criteria:

▸ Short
▸ Simple
▸ Easy to spell
▸ Easy to pronounce
▸ Easy to read
▸ Easy to recognize
▸ Easy to remember
▸ Pleasing when reading
▸ No disagreeable sound
▸ Cannot be pronounced in several ways
▸ Does not go out of date
▸ Adaptable to package or label
▸ Can be easily connected with the trademark
▸ Not offensive, obscene or negative
▸ Descriptive, or suggestive of product and use
▸ Connoting a good image of the product and the company

Product Life Cycle

Products are like people. They gestate, are born, grow, mature, become old and ultimately die. The product life cycle concept describes the product's life history starting from its birth to old age or death. In fact, it is not a cycle, but a span. The span popularly called life cycle can be divided into four phases for better understanding and study. These phases as shown in Figure 2.1 are:

A. Introductory phase
B. Growth phase

C. Maturity phase

D. Decline phase

Every product, as they say, has a unique life cycle very much like a human being. Just as it is difficult to predict the future of a human being, it is tough to predict the future life cycle of a product.

PRODUCT LIFE CYCLE

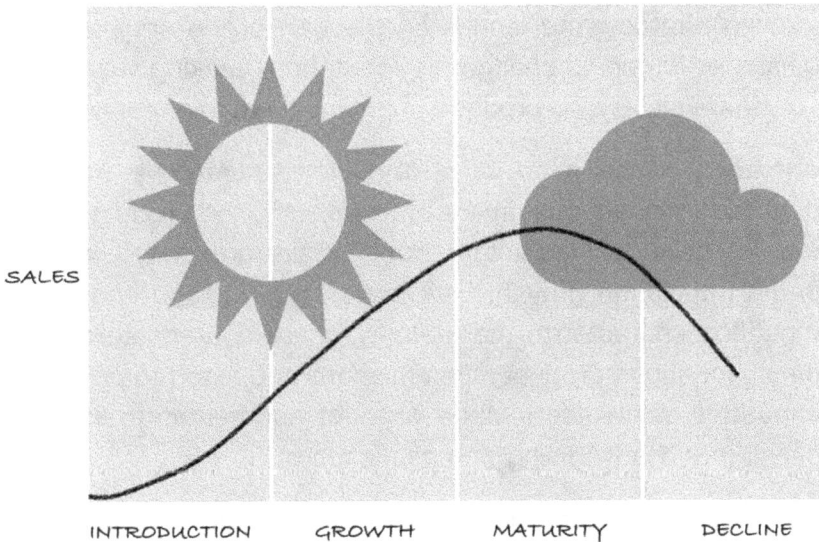

SALES

INTRODUCTION   GROWTH   MATURITY   DECLINE

Figure 2.1 Product Life Cycle

The value of the division of the product life cycle (PLC) into the four phases mentioned above lies in determining the marketing inputs that the product needs at various stages. It is just like the human organism where the requirement of calories, proteins, carbohydrates, vitamins and minerals, and fiber are different at different stages of human life to maintain optimum growth. Likewise, marketing inputs also vary at each stage of the product lifecycle.

The introductory phase is also the phase of market development because neither the demand for the product nor has the product proven its capabilities to fulfill the customers' needs yet. The marketing has to direct its effort here towards getting the customers to try the product.

Indeed a great deal of marketing effort is needed at this stage. The sales are usually low and creep along slowly. The duration of the introductory phase depends on the complexity of the product, the degree of newness and its fit into customer needs.

The growth phase of the new product is also allowing the growth phase of the market. The demand for the product accelerates. The market too expands, as potential competitors, who have been waiting and watching till now, jump into the fray. It calls for a different marketing strategy and tactics on the part of the originator. The originator is forced to change his focus from seeking ways to get the customers to try the product, to getting them to prefer his brand.

The maturity phase is indicative of market saturation in the sense that all the potential customers have taken to the product, except those who have decided not to adopt it. Sales growth will be on par with the population growth. Leveling-off the demand and intense competition characterize the maturity phase. Competitors at this stage try for subtle product differentiations and resort to price wars. Competitive strategies include product augmentation efforts in packaging and advertising communication.

The decline phase is the terminal point of the product life cycle. The marketers' insight and foresight that has gone into their product planning determine whether the product life cycle is to be extended by injecting new blood, thus prolonging the maturity phase and avoiding the decline phase or whether to let the dying product die.

Key Questions

The fundamental questions to which a marketer should address himself are:

1. To what extent can the shape (or the curve) and the duration of each stage be predicted?
2. How can one determine at what stage an existing product is?
3. How can this knowledge be used?

Usefulness of Product Life Cycle

The product life cycle is a theory, and it seems unlikely that it can ever be proven experimentally. However, this does not diminish its usefulness or importance. As the famous economist Kenneth Boulding once observed, *'there is nothing quite so useful as a theory that works.'*

The product life cycle concept is useful because it helps you to anticipate future events and prepare the best response to coming changes.

The life cycle concept is of immense value for managers who are about to launch a new product. No doubt, it is tough to foresee or predict the slope (or the curve) and the duration of each phase of the PLC very accurately. However, this does not mean that one cannot make useful efforts to foresee and visualize the scope and duration of a new product's life.

Product planning can become more rational with an understanding and appreciation of the PLC concept. It helps to create valuable lead-time for significant strategic and tactical moves after introducing the product. It can be of great help in developing a series of orderly competitive moves — be it stretching or extending the life of a product or accelerating an introductory phase, or phasing out and deleting an old product.

Market Life Cycle

So far our discussion on product lifecycle has revolved around a product lifecycle than a brand of a particular company and its strategic implications and the likely impact on that specific company. However, when you consider a product in generic terms, you have to think regarding a product class or therapeutic category, or indeed even as a market (segment). It is because, when a market is, say, nearing maturity it does not necessarily mean that all the companies competing in that market will have the same sales history curves.

Consequently, the strategic options available to each of the competing companies are not the same. Their responses too will be predictably different.

It is reasonable to expect that in any maturing market, for that matter even in a growing or declining market, there will be large, medium and small-stake players. It is quite apparent that there will be differences in their margins, economies of scale and break-even levels.

MARKET LIFE CYCLE

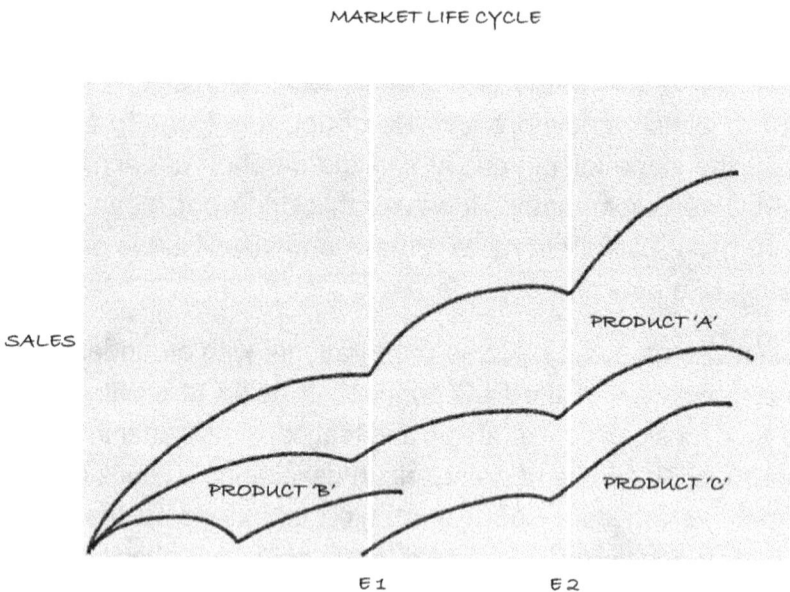

Figure 2.2 Market Life Cycle

The market life cycle (MLC) concept which, simply stated, is the aggregate life cycle consisting of several competing brands and companies in a given market, therapeutic category or product class. The micro-level characteristics or reality described as higher investment needed, little or no profits, rapid growth, peak profit levels refer to a product or, more specific to a brand of a particular company and not the market as a whole. Figure 2.2 presents this schematically.

As can be seen from Figure 2.2 the market life cycle has been extended twice (E1 and E2). Product 'A,' which was introduced around the same time as the market was emerging had also extended its life cycle once, running almost parallel to the market life cycle, but unable to exploit the opportunities when the market started its second extension with a dramatic growth phase (E2). That was the time when product 'C' entered the growth phase and even reinforced the growth phase of the market life cycle itself. Product 'B' never really took off in the real sense of the word, plateaued very early, and declined somewhat prematurely even while the market had been in its growth phase.

In the pharmaceutical industry, a market life cycle curve may consist of various brands and even different molecules, product classes or sub-segments in a particular therapeutic category.

Consider the case of the anti-tubercular market in India, which offers a close parallel to the schematic sequence of the market life cycle as shown in Figure 2.2.

Anti-tubercular Market Extends its Market Life Cycle While Eradicating Tuberculosis!

The anti-tubercular market in India was Rs. 341-crore (1988) with an annual growth rate of 0.5 percent. The main line of treatment consisted of drugs like streptomycin, INH, PAS and thiacetazone till the late 1970s. Subsequently, in the 1980s, newer and more potent drugs like ethambutol, pyrazinamide, and rifampicin were introduced. The medical profession accepted these newer drugs readily. These new drugs had even made it possible to treat tuberculosis at home instead of at a sanitarium. Tuberculosis, which was once labeled as a killer disease is not dreaded as before thanks to these newer drugs. It is curable.

Each of these newer drugs had extended the anti-tubercular market life cycle on their introduction. The conventional drugs like thiacetazone and PAS had reached their maturity phase and even started declining. At the same time, INH had extended its life cycle (as a sub-segment and not as a brand) when the combination of INH with rifampicin had gained acceptance and even preference to single ingredient formulations of the newer, more potent anti-tubercular drugs. The newer anti-tubercular drugs accounted for over 90 percent of the anti-tubercular market in 1988, whereas the conventional anti-tubercular drugs accounted for a meager share of less than 10 percent as they were declining.

One can see that while the anti-tubercular market's life cycle was in its mature phase (1988), some of the products such as thiacetazone, and PAS (sub-segments as these are molecules comprising a handful of brands) are in the decline phase. At the same time newer anti-tubercular drugs like ethambutol, rifampicin, pyrazinamide are in the growth phase of their life cycles (as these molecules are subsegments each containing a number of branded generic formulations). INH by virtue of the increasing demand of its combination with rifampicin and other newer drugs was also enjoying the extended maturity phase.

The advantages and the strategic implications of the juxtaposition of the product life cycle curve and the market life cycle must now become obvious the discerning marketer. The MLC and PLC of a brand for any particular company may be close or far apart for many reasons. The marketing actions dictated by this juxtaposition may also correspondingly vary. The marketing actions, which would best exploit that product life cycle, are not dependent on the market alone but on the phase, where the individual brand is present.

The original producer or the innovator bears most of the costs and risks of the product and market development. Competitors are only waiting on the sidelines watching the product and how it is likely to behave in the marketplace at this stage. Therefore, the introductory stages of the product and market life cycle are virtually the same.

Once the market accepts the product, others join the fray. The competition intensifies. It is at this point that the difference between curves and life cycles of the market and the product begins, with many competitors trying to create product differentiation, to capture as big a slice of the market as possible. As a result, the competitive pressure on the originator increases. If the originator has plotted the PLC for his new product even before its introduction, anticipating the possible entry of competition and their likely moves, he will be better off in countering the competition. He does this by critically examining the vulnerability of the product before introduction and by planning the product development and diversification strategies accordingly. If the originator is not forearmed or well-equipped, his unit sales and contribution will be adversely affected. Consequently, there will be a premature decline for the originator's product while the market may well be on its growth or maturity phase.

Figure 2.3 shows a hypothetical market life cycle graphically. As you can observe from this, While the market life cycle phase like introduction, growth, maturity, and decline unquestionably depend on the aggregate of various products, may differ significantly for many individual brands. The difference in the resources, competencies, and strategies for the different brands competing in the same market causes this.

The life cycle for a given market or therapeutic group extends, when some of the competing producers innovate, extend their product usage, and modify their existing products. The total of this expansion of the served markets of individual products results in the extension of the market life cycle. At the same time, products that are less competitive and unable to exploit the opportunities due to a slow or sluggish response may bite the dust even when the market life cycle is in its growth phase. Consider the following case (Case 20) for example.

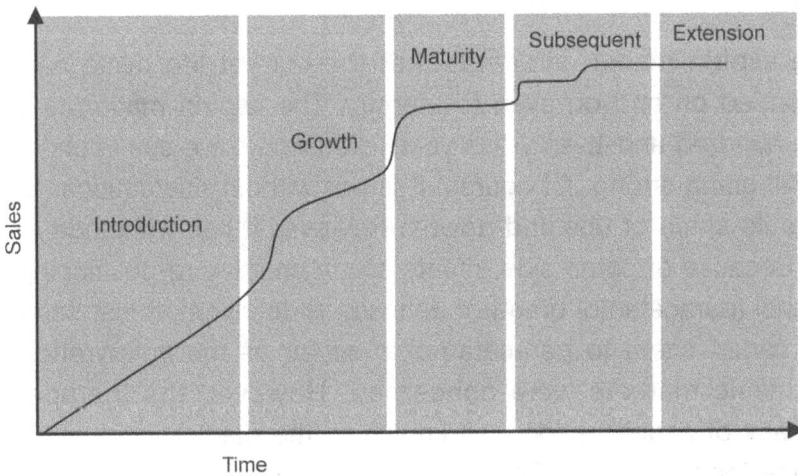

Figure 2.3 Hypothetical Market Life Cycle

The Centurion Gets Younger and Stronger by the Year!

The aspirin market indicates that the market life cycle can be extended on and on even to eternity. The aspirin market is over one-hundred-and-twenty-five years old (should we say young) and is still going strong. Of course, it is not without fluctuations. It did have its share of ups and downs. However, it has withstood them all. Because of some side effects and a creative re-positioning by Tylenol (paracetamol brand of Johnson & Johnson), it lost some of its market share to paracetamol in so far as the antipyretic and analgesic markets were concerned. However, the therapeutic efficacy of aspirin is too well known to the medical and scientific profession to ignore it. Some innovative marketers introduced safer dosage forms of aspirin such as enteric-coated, buffered tablets and dispersible tablets. These brands like Dispirin (Reckitt Coleman), Microfined Aspirin (Nicholas) in India and Bufferin (in the US) did well at the marketplace, while the numerous lesser-known brands vanished from the market. However, the market life cycle and the PLCs of successful brands had got a new lease on life.

Research findings in the mid-1980s have given a further boost to the centurion. It is believed and proven that regular intake of aspirin will minimize and even prevent heart attacks in high-risk patients. The aspirin market was on a growth phase once again. New bulk drug manufacturers have entered the market while the existing ones were busy expanding their capacities!

Extending the Product Life Cycle

Likewise, one can extend the life cycle of a product or avert its decline. What one needs are a broader perspective and holistic thinking. You should think regarding your product or products in the context of the relevant therapeutic category or product class. You should also think about expanding your served markets. You should not lose sight of these and think about your products in isolation. That would only limit and restrict even the existing opportunities. Here are a few ideas as a starter to extend your product lifecycle in the pharmaceutical market.

▸ Find out new usages for your products. What are the new indications in which you can promote your product?

▸ Enter new markets by covering new geographical markets or expand the existing market coverage. Expand your served markets.

▸ Modify existing products. Introduce different pack sizes. Introducing larger pack sizes of tonics and enzyme preparations has improved the product sales considerably and extended the growth phases of many a product.

▸ Introduce new flavors. New dosage forms. Introduce flanker products.

Keep track of competition and develop your products continually. Be alert to spot new opportunities and introduce new products early enough in your existing markets (therapeutic categories). Update, and keep abreast are the two most essential watchwords.

The pharmaceutical industry has countless examples of products well past their life and which in theory should be either in maturity or decline stage, but are still selling at high volume and producing acceptable profits.

You should use the PLC concept as a framework for thinking through and develop winning marketing strategies based on the phase of the product in its life cycle, and for that, planning activity must take place now to preempt decline in future years, so that you can to prevent it. In fact, that should be the sole purpose of planning. Remember what Peter Drucker, the great management thinker said about planning? It is the futurity of the present decisions.

Today in the pharmaceutical industry, more than ever before, successful maintenance of mature products becomes an increasingly vital part of product planning and management. The declining rate of new drug launches dictates this.

A crucial point to remember regarding the concept and application PLC in pharmaceutical product planning is that as a product, which is competing in different market segments, is at a different stage or phase in each segment. Product management should consider their decisions based on this.

Here are a few cases of companies that have extended the PLCs of their brands by extending their usage (promoting in new indications) successfully.

Anti-allergic Stimulates Appetite for Growth!

Periactin (cyproheptadine hydrochloride) of Merck Sharp and Dhome (later Practin of Merind) was being promoted initially as an antiallergic and antipruritic. In the late 1960s, the company produced new evidence that Periactin stimulated appetite. They had gone all out in detailing Periactin as an appetite stimulant ever since. Many new brands entered this new segment. The product sales grew faster because, not only did the doctors who were using it as antiallergic and antipruritic continued to use it, but even many new doctors (new to the product) started prescribing it in the new-found indication of stimulating appetite.

New Indication Widens the Growth Spectrum!

Flagyl (metronidazole) of May & Baker (later Rhone Poulenc and now Sanofi) was being used mainly to treat giardiasis. The company had found out in the 1960s that their product was very effective in treating amoebiasis, which was very prevalent in India. The company launched an aggressive promotion of Flagyl in the treatment of amoebiasis and replaced the conventional therapy of amoebiasis with emetine hydrochloride injections. Many other brands of metronidazole joined the bandwagon. Flagyl even today remains one of the favorite prescription drug brands in the treatment of amoebiasis.

New Indication Attacks Competing Brands while Preventing Heart Attacks!

Betnesol (betamethasone) injections had always been one of the most important brands of Glaxo (GlaxoSmithKline now), the industry leader in the mid-1970s. Betnesol injections were lagging behind Decadron injections (dexamethasone) of MSD in the late 1960s. Glaxo, by promoting in one new indication, i.e., a ten-ampoule course in myocardial infarction, changed their position dramatically. The product image as a life saving drug got a big boost indeed, and the product became a brand leader and more importantly remained a brand leader for many years!

Determining the Phase of Your Brand in the PLC

Understanding the characteristics of the different phases in the life cycle concept will help the discerning marketer to determine the stage of the life cycle for his existing products. This coupled with an understanding of the market life cycle will enable you to plan, preempt and execute winning strategies. Consider this case:

The Antacid that Neutralized even the Competition!

A medium-sized, rapidly growing pharmaceutical company had introduced an antacid brand 'x' in the Rs. 44-crore large antacid, antiflatulent (actual) market. When you add the anti-peptic-ulcerants, to this the (potential) market becomes larger by another Rs.31-crore (1988).

The company was well aware that the potential market (antacids, antiflatulents, and anti-peptic ulcerants) was in its growth phase and there were more than one hundred and one brands already fighting for their survival and growth. Introducing yet another antacid at this stage was no easy task. However, the company was determined to enter this large market as part of its product diversification strategy and to make the most of it.

The company had meticulously planned a new product with a perceptible differentiation — a new ingredient, different flavor, new additional benefits and impactful communication package coupled with attractive sampling to induce trial, specialized training to the field force — in short, the whole works.

Besides, the company's marketing team had a stormy brainstorming session to plot the PLC for their product and to preempt the likely moves of competitors (top five competitors accounted for over 90 percent of the actual market) and new entrants. The launch had been a success by all standards. In less than one year the product picked up a 2.4 percent market share, which no other antacid introduced during the preceding five years had achieved. However, the product had not made any dent in the top five brands. Being alert, ever-vigilant competitors, they had responded quickly and stepped up their promotional inputs and mounted an offensive on this fledgling brand.

Since the company had preempted and anticipated the signature moves of competitors, it did not catch itself off-guard. The company was well prepared to meet the competitive challenge. The company had plotted the PLC and the strategic action for their brand 'x.' The company's analysis was somewhat like the one presented in Table 2.1.

While these may sound or look like over-simplified statements that is what exactly happened. The competitors' responses were indeed predictable in retrospect, for they had acted as anticipated by the company even before the introduction of its brand 'x.'

Though brand 'x' was yet to achieve the preeminent position that it has set out to (the brand, as well as the market, were still in the growth phase in the early 1990s). In the final analysis, brand 'x' seemed to be successful not only in neutralizing the acid but even the competitors' offensive!

Table 2.1 PLC and Planning for a New Antacid Brand

1. **Introduction:** Brand 'x' should be different from all other antacids available in the market and should be perceived as such by our prospective customers. The differentiation should be created in: (a) Composition (b) Shape (c) Color (d) Flavor (e) Pack (f) Promotion at doctor level as well as at chemist level (g) Price - Skimming strategy: Although the pharmaceutical industry is subjected to rigorous price controls and markups by the government, since the active ingredient in brand 'X' was not listed at the time in any controlled categories, some flexibility in pricing exists. (h) Launch itself

Table 2.1 Contd...

2. **Likely Responses of Competition:** The pharmaceutical market in India is virtually a me-too market. The possibility of new competitors joining the fray once the product is accepted is certain. The primary competitors, who are currently taking their respective shares of the market for granted but for a few skirmishes around the borders of their served markets, face no threats. The shares of the market leaders were more or less frozen. The success of brand 'x' might shake them out of their complacency. That would mean waking up the sleeping giants. With their resources, they can launch a major offensive. Brand 'x' therefore, must initiate product development and product diversification strategies before the introduction so that it need not be caught napping during the crucial growth phase.

3. **Product Development:** The company and the brand 'x' better be right the first time. Since the company is fighting the international giants in the market and the target customers are educated and enlightened, qualitative differentiation (in addition to aesthetics) is, of course, a must. Not only that, to counter the competitors' moves effectively during the growth phase, but also product development effort should be concentrated in significant areas such as:

   - Acid neutralizing capacity
   - Taste. Since antacids are chewable, the flavor becomes a considerable factor.

   It is critical to initiate the necessary changes to improve the product before introduction.

4. **Product Diversification:** To develop new flavors since the competitors might try to introduce different flavors. The company should be prepared to launch more flavors of brand 'x' during the maturity phase (essential to maintain novelty and sustain the interest of the early majority), or earlier if the competitors' moves warrant it.

   To look for new segments and enter with necessary product modifications (like a combination of local anesthetic, the small but attractive segment) to prolong, extend and indeed avert the decline phase.

New Product Adoption Process

New Product adoption is a process, and it takes time and effort. Regardless of the intrinsic value of a product, many potential customers will tend to resist change. Some may accept change, but most do not.

For many products, the process of the adoption follows a somewhat uniform pattern, from the time the new product is developed until the ultimate consumer widely accepts it. In the case of pharmaceutical products, it is the intermediate customer, the doctor, who decides whether to accept or not to accept a product.

Researchers have charted a course of the new product by determining when people adopt it. Graphically presented, the adoption process looks like a simple probability curve, in cumulative as shown in Figure 2.4.

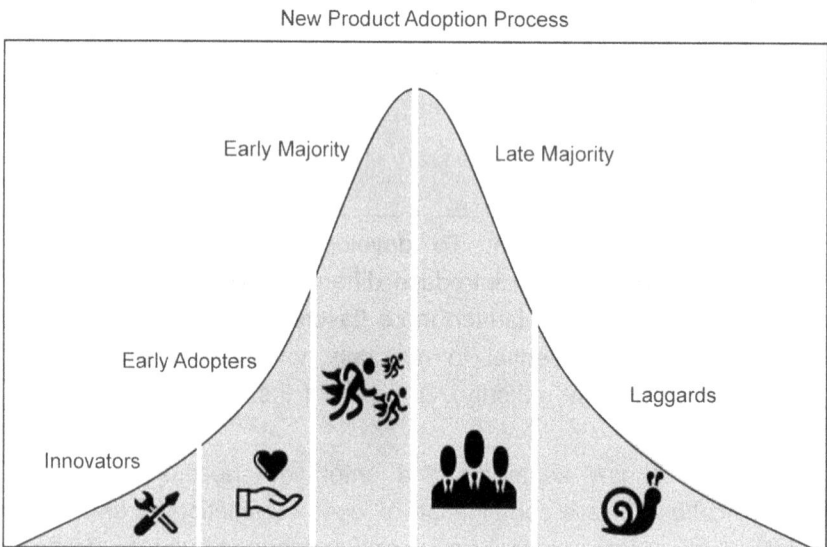

Figure 2.4 New Product Adoption Process

A few people adopt a product first, then a few more, followed by a slightly sharp increase and finally leveling off, when most of the potential consumers have taken the product.

The adoption of a new product can be viewed as a special kind of attitude change. Almost by definition, such a change encounters resistance. The product or idea usually alters or replaces something, which is already a part of the individual's pattern of thought. If the change under consideration is a major one, it is quite likely that it will encounter significant resistance and consequently will take longer to adopt. The customer may even reject the idea of the product of change. On the other hand, if the change is trivial, the resistance may not be much and may take less time to adopt.

Three Major Propositions

1. The greater the complexity of change, the more resistance is aroused and the longer the period that is required for adoption.
2. The more costly the item, the longer it takes before it is widely adopted.
3. A change, which has more rapid and visible results, is adopted more quickly than a change with slower, less visible effects.

The Individual Adoption Process

To adopt or not to adopt is not a simple question with a simple yes or no answer. It is not a simple *go* or *no-go* decision either. It does not happen at once. When an individual faced with the possibility of a change, he goes through several mental stages before he makes up his mind to adopt or not to adopt. They are:

1. **Unawareness:** At this point, the customer has no idea about the product.
2. **Awareness:** At this point, the customer has a general idea about the product.

3. **Interest or Information Stage:** At this stage, he collects more information about the product. If his interest continues to grow, he wants to know what the product can do for him.

4. **Evaluation Stage:** Would I be better off with this product? Would I be worse of without it? The customer evaluates.

5. **Trial Stage:** This is the final stage before adoption. The trial stage appears to play a crucial role in the decision process. Because a customer, who is satisfied with the trial is very likely to take up the product in full scale. Marketers in general and pharmaceutical marketers, in particular, have been aware of the value of free trials for many years. This explains why they spend a significant part of the promotional expenditure on Physicians' Samples.

6. **The Adoption Stage:** The customer adopts the product after a successful and satisfactory trial, at least until some other product comes along to replace it. Then the adoption process starts all over again.

Adopter Categories

Some people adopt very quickly. Others wait a long time before they take up the new product and there are some others, who never adopt. Depending upon how quickly or how slowly the new product adoption takes place, customers are categorized as:

A. Innovators

B. Early Adopters

C. Early majority

D. The late majority, and

E. Laggards

Innovators are defined as the first 2.5 percent to adopt the new product. They are highly educated with established practice, successful and venturesome. They are respected but not held to a very high degree of esteem, watched but not followed readily by neighbors.

Early adopters are defined as the next 13.5 percent of the people, who adopt the new product. They are relatively young but not younger than innovators, well educated, socially active. They are the sources of information to the community.

Early majority comprises the next 34 percent of the people who adopt the new product taking the total adoption to 50 percent. The number of adoptions increases rapidly after this group begins to adopt. They are slightly above average in age, education, less active in formal activities than innovators and early adopters as leaders, but active members of their organizations. They must be sure that the new product or idea will work before they take it.

The late majority is the fourth category, which comprises the next 34 percent of the consumers, who take to a new product after the early majority have adopted.

Laggards are the final 16 percent of the customers, who adopt a new product (or idea). They may even include non-adopters if everyone does not use the product. They do not participate in community activities and are usually suspicious of salespersons.

Product Life Cycle and Adoption Process

Product life cycle and the adoption process are rather intimately linked. Product life cycle describes the rate of acceptance or rejection of a product. The adoption process explains about the individuals who adopt a product, how quickly and how slowly and categorizes individual adopters accordingly.

A fit of these customer categories based on the adoption process and the four phases of the product lifecycle reveals these (Figure 2.5).

   A. The introductory phase reflects product acceptance by the innovators.

B. In the growth phase, the sales are due to the early adopters and the early majority.

C. In the maturity phase, the late majority would have jumped in.

D. The laggards who almost never come in probably hasten the decline phase and those few, even if they join, are too insignificant to avert the decline.

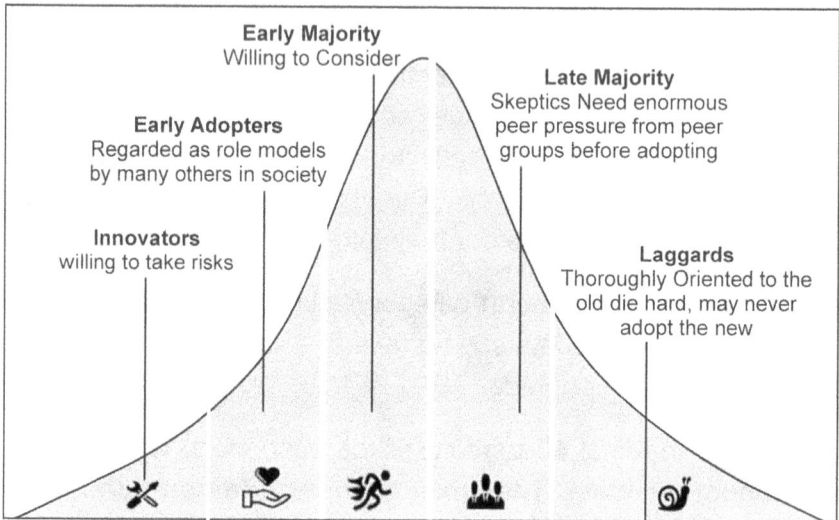

Figure 2.5 Product Life Cycle and Adoption Process

Recognition of the fact that the phases of the life cycle of a product are closely related to its adoption process can be of great strategic importance. It enables the marketers to arrive at important, responsive strategies required at different stages.

For instance, the identification of prospective innovators is crucial for a new product launch. The introductory phase or the market development phase can be accelerated by proper, accurate identification of the innovators and by convincing them. You can see the relationship between the product life cycle and the new product adoption process can in Figure 2.6.

Product Life Cycle and Adoption Process

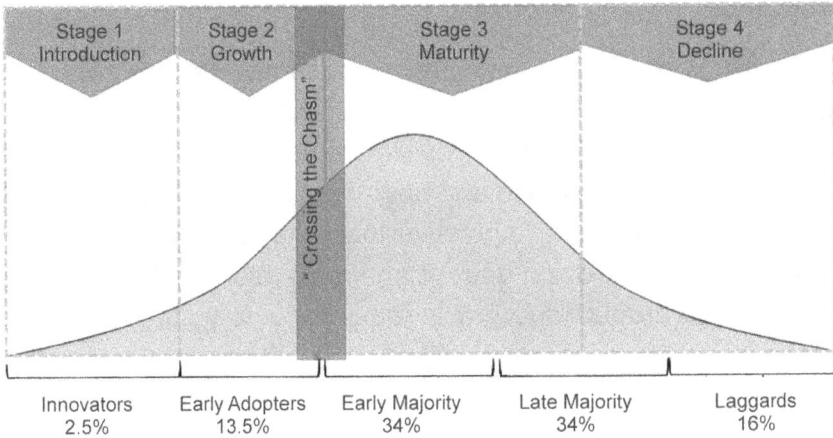

Figure 2.6 Product Life Cycle and New Product Adoption

Implications for the Marketer

When you understand the product life cycle concept and the new product adoption process, your ability to plan for new products improves significantly. Here are some of the more apparent advantages:

When you are introducing a new product, you have to identify the innovator and the early adopters carefully and target your communication and promotional inputs oriented explicitly towards them. In the pharmaceutical market, how does one identify the innovators and early adopters? Apart from the psychographics profile like their educational qualifications, lifestyles, social affiliations, media habits, a more reliable way is to observe their prescription habits. Since the innovators and the early adopters take to new products quickly (almost instantaneously), they are also likely to give up these products rapidly. Remember that these are the trendsetters and take to anything new immediately. Change, constant change in their prescribing behavior is there for the discerning observer to see. Their brand loyalty is by definition is less. It is not to say that they stop prescribing your product once the newness is gone. The regularity and intensity of prescriptions are bound to decline unless your positive reinforcement is strong enough.

Therefore, you will have to identify these trendsetters by monitoring their prescription habits from the retail chemists. You will observe that it is this small group of doctors who have started the prescriptions of virtually every new product that has entered the market. It is, therefore, imperative that your identification of these doctors be accurate and your promotional package target specific for your new product success in the introductory stage.

The next logical sequence is to increase your prescriber-base and penetrate the market. You have to preserve with your early and late majority categories of prescribers. The early and late majority prescribers determine your rate of growth at this stage. Another significant advantage with these prescribers is, while they may take a relatively long time to take up your product, they are equally conservative in dropping off your brand from their prescriptions. Their brand loyalty is undoubtedly better, and it is imperative and essential during the growth and maturity phases of your brands' product lifecycle. Like everything else, even in marketing perseverance certainly pays!

Product Portfolio Analysis

It is rather apparent that a review of a company's different products at any point would reveal different stages of growth, maturity, and decline. The objective of any company is not to make a fast buck, but to achieve consistent growth in profitability. A regular review and analysis of the company's products and markets are essential to pursuing an active and aggressive policy towards planning effective strategies for products in the growth and mature phases and an innovative new product development strategy to ensure tomorrow's profitability and to prepare for divestment or harvesting of declining products in shrinking markets.

Thanks to the pioneering work done by the Boston Consulting Group (BCG), you now have a systematic procedure for classifying every product your company makes, regarding its present position and concerning future profit earning potential. It is known as product portfolio analysis, and it provides a basis for allocating today's resources to optimize returns by exploiting tomorrow's business potential. The idea of portfolio analysis for a company is to meet its objectives by balancing sales growth, cash flow and risk. There are two essential aspects of the conceptual framework of the portfolio analysis. One is the market share, relative market share to be specific, and the other is market growth.

Managing your product portfolio is very much akin to the management of a portfolio of stocks. You need to acquire some for current dividends, some for growth, and some should be divested to free capital for more profitable investment.

It is useful and simple to visualize all this on a grid with one dimension representing the relative market share and the other representing the market growth rate. That market share is a crucial element in strategic planning is universally accepted. Consider the case of Cheminor Drugs, the young Turk of the bulk drug market in India.

Dr. Reddy's Laboratories and the Cost Leadership!

Cheminor Drugs and Dr. Reddy's Laboratories, the bulk drug units belonging to Dr. Reddy's Laboratories group of companies, had done remarkably well in the manufacture and marketing of bulk drugs. Within four years, the company had achieved cost leadership in manufacturing at least three bulk drugs, namely ibuprofen, methyldopa, and norfloxacin. How did the company accomplish all this in such a short time? There are two reasons. Firstly, the economies of scale. The company was the third largest producer of ibuprofen and methyldopa in the world at that time. The higher volumes had given the company the cost leadership. The second reason is that the company had also achieved technological superiority.

The case of Dr. Reddy's Laboratories indicates that market share is closely related to profitability. Higher market share means higher sales volume. It is a well-known fact that we become better at doing things the more we do them. That is why this phenomenon is known as the experience or learning curve. It manifests itself with items such as labor efficiency, work specialization, and methods improvement thus resulting in improved productivity and increased profitability. There is an overwhelming body of evidence supporting this experience effect. Simply stated, this means that the greater your volume, the lower your unit cost should be. In other words, if you have the largest market share (hence bigger volume), your profitability should be relatively higher. That is how and why Dr. Reddy's Laboratories were able to bring down the price of a novel antibacterial drug, norfloxacin, whereas their competitors could not. Cost leadership is crucial to competitive advantage. No, cost leadership is the competitive advantage!

The relative market share is an essential dimension in portfolio analysis since it gives you an idea about the degree of competitive advantage or disadvantage that your product (or company) has in a given market. Relative market share also indicates the product's ability to generate cash as compared to the competitor's product. The relative market share is expressed as a ratio and can be arrived at by dividing your market share with the market share of your most significant competitors.

The rate of market growth is the other important determinant since it indicates the direction in which the market is moving and its potential.

Boston Matrix

The Boston grid or matrix combines these concepts in a straightforward manner, which has profound implications for the company. It is worth noting that the Boston Matrix does not consider profits or profitability as a determinant of this matrix. It is because profits are not always an appropriate indicator of portfolio analysis and performance. Market share is chosen instead as a determinant because market share indicates that the higher your volume, the lower your unit cost should be. In other words, if you have the largest market share (hence the most significant volume), your profitability should be relatively higher than all your competitors. Profits do not always indicate the scope of future development as they often reflect changes in the liquid assets of the company as inventories, capital equipment, and receivables. Cashflow has been taken as a crucial determinant factor since it reflects the cash generating ability of the company, which is essential to develop its product portfolio.

The basis of classifying your products on the Boston matrix is according to their cash generating ability and cash utilization for promotion. Figure 2.7 presents a model of the Boston matrix for your portfolio analysis.

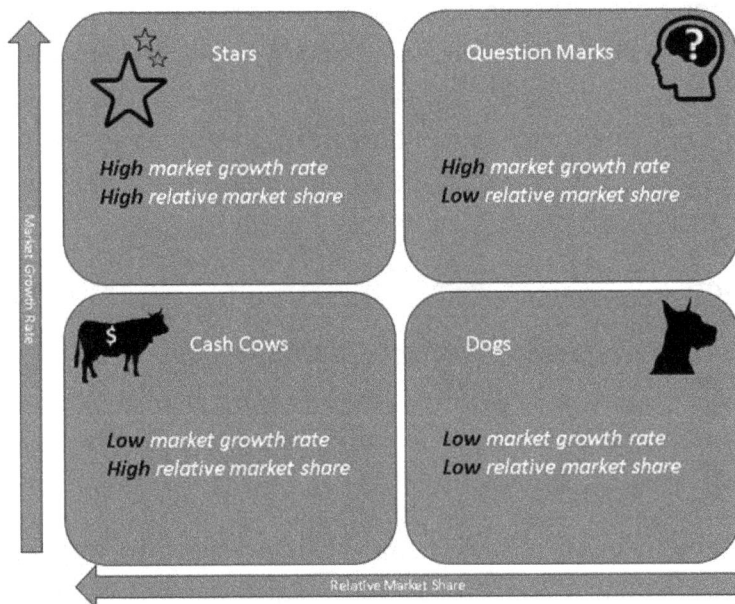

Figure 2.7 Boston Matrix and Portfolio Analysis

Though the axes on this grid are labeled arbitrarily, they are widely usable. Market growth is classified as low when it is less than ten percent and high when it is more than twenty percent.

Relative market share is shown as a ratio. For example, if your market share is twenty percent, and your major competitor's share is also twenty percent, then the ratio is 1:1, and if your competitor's market share is only ten percent as against your twenty percent then the ratio is more favorable (to your company) 2:1. This ratio is, in fact, the measure of market dominance.

The graphic labels attached to each of the four categories of products give some indication of the prospects of the products in each quadrant. Each quadrant of the grid shown in Figure 2.7 has different strategic implications.

Quadrant - I

Products in this quadrant have a very appropriate name, Stars, as they are products with a high market share in high growth markets. They represent the basis of tomorrow's business. They may or may not generate sufficient cash flow today to finance their rapid growth. One needs to do a careful analysis regarding their present position, and potential. They require careful nurturing. You should not starve them of funds that need to fuel their growth even if their cash flow today is not so positive. That would only result in preventing them from becoming major sources of cash flow in the future.

Quadrant - II

Products in this quadrant are the most difficult to deal with and often lead to the classic question that Shakespeare's Hamlet was faced - To be (promoted vigorously) or Not to be (promoted because of the low market share).

That is why they are called Question Marks. These products often lead to a marketing man's dilemma because their cash flows are usually not adequate to fuel their growth. They require massive transfusions of cash to build market share and increase volume, so that they may someday become significant cash generators. While the market growth rate is very attractive, the investment is considerable. Hence the Question mark.

Quadrant - III

Products in this quadrant are excellent sources of cash. While their market share is high, they are in slow growth markets. So building up the further market share is too expensive, even prohibitive. Therefore, the cash generated by these products should be invested preferably in Stars (high growth products and prospects), or even in Question marks after careful analysis. Since these products generate adequate cash to finance the future profit earners of the company, they are known as Cash Cows. There is one caution, however. You should never milk these cash cows to death because there may be many productive and profitable years ahead of them. The discerning marketer can exploit these through creative extensions of the life cycle of these products.

Quadrant - IV

The products in this quadrant are low share products in slow or no growth markets. These products may not be earning an acceptable return on investment (ROI). They require a disproportionate amount of marketing effort. Their prospects too are very bleak. They are often a cash drain on a company. The name given to these products is Dogs. They are underdogs at that. While it is human nature to support the underdog, in marketing one should avoid any emotional attachment to these products (Peter Drucker very aptly called these products as *investments in managerial ego*) and dispassionately adopt a strategy of either harvesting or divesting so that funds can be freed for investing in the top dog products i.e., Stars.

The art and science of product portfolio management become a lot clearer now than ever before. The ideal product development sequence involves developing Question marks into Stars and Stars into Cash cows. Inherent in this perfect product development sequence is the judicious use of the surplus cash generated by the cash cows in stars, which in turn will be tomorrow's primary profit earners (cash cows) and in some selected question marks, which are likely to become tomorrow's stars and perhaps, day-after-tomorrow's cash cows. It is more or less a cyclical process, and the marketer should be alert while playing at this wheel of fortune. One thing about this cyclical process is that its movement is anti-clockwise, as can be seen in Figure 2.8.

The cyclical movement shown in Figure 2.8 is no doubt hypothetical. However, it is useful in the sense that it indicates the likely direction and the ideal sequence in which a company can develop its products. As physicists are obsessed with the idea of perpetual motion so are marketers with the idea of the perpetual product development cycle.

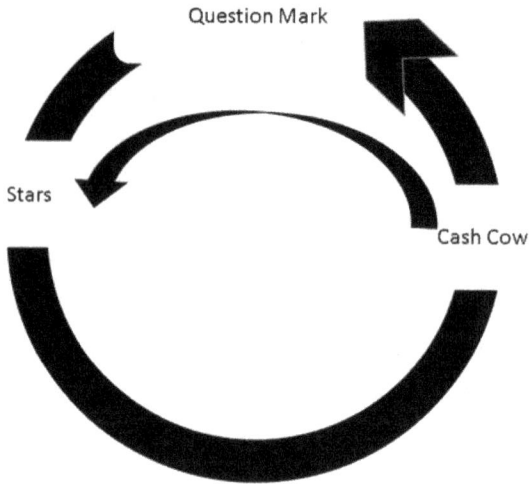

Figure 2.8 Perpetual Product Development Cycle

Portfolio Analysis in Pharmaceutical Marketing

It is useful to do the product portfolio analysis in pharmaceutical marketing at two levels. Firstly, at the level of the individual product or brand for each of your major brands. Secondly, for each of the therapeutic categories in which you are competing. Such an approach would help in identifying and formulating effective strategies to exploit even the relatively small but could be tremendous opportunities of tomorrow, that is, the star opportunities in each therapeutic category that may not be as obvious today. You have to be alert and look for the emerging sub-segments.

The concepts of PLC and product portfolio analysis are rather closely related. Product review must, therefore, include both PLC and portfolio analysis. Here are some important reasons:

The basic premise of PLC is that it is a valuable planning tool and provides essential strategic directions during the different phases of both product and market life cycles.

Secondly, PLC analysis also suggests the levels of promotional efforts required during the different phases of the life cycle of a product and its market.

Thirdly, a careful study of PLC will enable a marketer to exploit the hidden or dormant opportunities by extending the life cycle of a product and indeed even of the market. PLC is thus futuristic.

Product portfolio analysis takes the cash generating ability of a product and cash usage into cognizance for classification of products into today's profit earners and tomorrow's potential profit earners. Thus, the product portfolio analysis essentially provides the strategic directions to the company. The primary purpose of portfolio analysis is to optimize the process of resource allocation.

The relative market share and the rate of market growth act as key determinants to identify the present position of the company's products and to decide on the desirable course of action for the future of the company's products.

Thus, on closer examination, you will observe that while the significant purpose of portfolio analysis is to optimize the resource allocation for the company's products based on their current position and desired future direction and determine the promotional effort needed. The basis for analysis of PLC and product portfolio and critical determinant factors may be different, but the purpose remains the same.

Product review and analysis from different angles, dimensions, and directions would give a better idea, better insight and a broader perspective of necessary strategic actions, and you need to take them at different phases of product and market life cycles. Such an analysis would enable you to bring stability to the company through present profit earners and ensure future growth opportunities by nurturing and developing the stars and by extending the product life cycle through innovative marketing strategies.

Product Positioning

Product positioning is a concept borrowed from military strategy. The earliest known writings about positioning in military strategy can be found in the writings of a Chinese general Sun Tzu, who was a contemporary of Confucius, the famous Chinese philosopher. In his classic work, *The Art of War*, Sun Tzu, being the master strategist that he was, discussed the importance of positioning in the military strategy context — troop disposition, ground, terrain, the relative strength of opposing forces and the mental attitudes of the opposition. His primary target was the mind of the opposing commander. These concepts are very much relevant in the present-day marketing context.

Jack Trout, a strong advocate of positioning, wrote in a 1969 article entitled - *Positioning is the game people play in today's me-too marketplace*. What can be more me-too than the pharmaceutical market in India, choking with over 100,000 products?

David Ogilvy in 1971, pointed out that *the result of our campaigns depend less on how we write our advertising than on how a product is positioned*. The 1970s have ushered in a new era in marketing — the era of Positioning. Accurate positioning has become the most crucial step in effective marketing.

Why is Positioning a Must?

It is the information explosion that has led to this realization. It is the ever-increasing noise level in the marketplace, with the number of brands multiplying like rabbits that have made positioning a must for survival and growth. Let us consider the pharmaceutical industry in India. Over 10,000 companies are churning out over 100,000 products. An urban doctor on a typical working day meets about 20 to 25 medical representatives who in turn detail about 5 to 8 products. That means exposure to anything between 100 to 200 products. Add to this the information through newspapers, magazines, professional journals, radio and television messages. The Total number of messages that he is exposed to is genuinely mind-blogging. A marketer must virtually fight for the attention of the doctor for his product. While the human mind has a remarkable ability to cope with such an information overload, how it deals and processes this excessive volume of information is indeed not helpful to the marketer. One is the screening and selective process of perception. The other is that the human mind rejects any information that is not related to its prior knowledge. The human brain has no room for something that is new unless it is in some way connected to or matches with previous information and knowledge. The simplest example is that learning the alphabets of any language is essential for learning words in that language. Without the prior knowledge of alphabets, new words sound like gibberish.

Furthermore, research indicates that people rank objects, events and even other people in their minds. It is necessary to organize the ever-increasing information to cope with it. Therefore, consumers rank products in their minds. If the product is distinctly different in that product category and if it fits with a similar, equivalent perception of the consumer, then, only then the product is likely to be ranked higher in the consumer's mind. The closer and the more perfect the unique product-attribute and the consumer perception-fit, the higher the ranking of that product. It is here that the positioning of a product is going to play a vital, crucial role. Much depends on how the product is positioned.

Positioning Prescription Drugs

Today, in the Indian pharmaceutical industry where the rate of brand proliferation is behind only that of rabbits, the success of new or even modified versions of existing products depends more on proper positioning. Failure to recognize or understand positioning can lead to major marketing mistakes frequently associated with significant changes in the product line:

A. The introduction of a new or modified product fails to generate adequate sales and profits or

B. The new product launches succeed, but at the expense of other products (illusion of success)

If undetected, this could result in misdirected marketing efforts by the company. On the other hand, an appreciation and understanding of positioning can produce increased profits through marketing innovations. The importance and crucial nature of positioning are very aptly summed up by David Aaker:

> *Product positioning is so central and critical that it should be considered at the level of a mission statement...It comes to represent the essence of a business.*

Positioning: A Definition

Webster's dictionary describes positioning as:

A. A relative place, situation or standing

B. Perceived images consumers have of one product concerning their needs

C. Perceived images of similar products marketed by competing companies

Positioning is the process of establishing a product, person, even, company or even an object in the minds of the members of a target market in such a way that it is perceived to answer the needs of that market. Positioning thus refers to identification and communication of differential advantage.

Profitable positioning is a strategy for creating a unique product image, which increases total profits. Firms that are planning modifications of existing products or the introduction of new products will naturally, in keeping with their marketing objectives strive to position their products' entry so that it will produce maximum sales and profits.

The three primary tasks of product-positioning in the drug industry are:

A. The type of conditions for which the product will be prescribed

B. The kind of patient for whom the product will be considered suitable

C. The products with which the product will compete closely

Positioning and Target Market Selection

It is imperative to emphasize the interaction of positioning and selection of the target market. Target market and positioning strategies are like two sides of the same coin. They are inseparable.

A brand must be positioned to appeal to a target customer segment (target market), and likewise, a consumer segment too will respond to a brand that occupies the position preferred by it.

Sustainable Differential Advantage

Uniqueness or rather perceived uniqueness is a product's only protection against commodity status. The primary task of marketers, therefore, is to create a perceivable uniqueness, I.e., differential advantage. A differential advantage should satisfy three fundamental criteria.

A. It should differentiate the product from all others in the product class by creating a perception of uniqueness.

B. It is essential or can be made to seem relevant to the target audience.

C. It should be sustainable over time against the competition. The primary task of marketers is to create a differential advantage. The secondary task is to defend it with all their might. There are two basic approaches to achieve this. One is to increase the importance of unique product features or attributes and their benefits. Alternatively, one can reduce the significance of the individual product features or characteristics and the benefits of competitors' products. Here are two cases highlighting these two approaches.

The Fabulous Success Story of American Remedies in the Systemic Anti-Fungal Market!

American Remedies, one of the fastest growing companies in the Indian pharmaceutical industry had spotted an opportunity in the early 1990s (Dr. Reddy's Laboratories later acquired the company) in the systemic anti-fungal market. Griseofulvin was the most widely prescribed anti-fungal for systemic use at the time (77 percent of the market in 1992). Only two companies - IDPL and Glaxo with its two brands (Grisovin FP and Dermonorm) — had accounted for over two-thirds of the total anti-fungal market. American Remedies, being a small company could not have thought of succeeding with another brand of griseofulvin in the systemic anti-fungal market. It had to do something different — an obvious differential advantage not only over the other brands of griseofulvin but also over other brands of emerging new anti-fungal molecules like ketoconazole.

After a thorough inquiry into the perceptions and the needs of the target consumers and users, the company identified a vacant, unoccupied slot in the perceptual space of the target consumers — the convenience of dosage. The recommended dosage for all griseofulvin brands was one tablet four times a day. When you consider the low levels of gastric tolerance associated with griseofulvin, suddenly a specific vacant slot becomes obvious. What other companies were oblivious to, became apparent to American Remedies. The company found out that it is possible to offer a once-a-day griseofulvin brand by reducing the particle size further, down to about 400 microns. The company introduced Gris OD (griseofulvin once-daily) and communicated this differential advantage very forcefully and persuasively. The convenient dosage regime became far more critical to the prescribing physicians. This differential advantage of the once-a-day brand of the well-established griseofulvin molecule paved the way for the dramatic success of Gris OD. The brand was on its way to achieving the leadership position in the systemic anti-fungal market.

A seemingly simple, even obvious positioning slot, when exploited well can result in fabulous success!

Undermining Others' Differential Advantage?

Zantac's pre-emptive strike against Losec (now Prilosec) offers an excellent example of undermining the differential advantage created by potential competitors. Zantac (ranitidine) of Glaxo (GSK now) had achieved the distinction of being the world's largest prescription drug brand (sales US $2.7 billion in 1991-92). Losec (omeprazole), an original research product of Astra, belongs to a different class of drugs (proton pump inhibitor) even though it is in the same therapeutic category of anti-ulcerants. Losec offered a distinct advantage regarding faster ulcer healing and very low (if not absent) relapse rates. Glaxo, sensing this, decided to undermine the differential advantage, and launched a pre-emptive strike against Losec, internationally creating a dissonance among the prescribers. It succeeded in making Losec a reserve drug to be used as a second line treatment for some time.

Meanwhile, Glaxo had pursued a market development strategy by expanding the usage of Zantac in non-ulcer dyspepsia, gastritis, etc. Glaxo could do this primarily from its preeminent position. It had built up much credibility. Astra (AstraZeneca now) had also built up a substantial clinical evidence and got Prilosec cleared as a first line drug in gastric ulcers.

Glaxo surely had bought time by undermining the differential advantage created by Astra and defended its leadership position for Zantac in the anti-ulcer wars!

Key Questions

Positioning is perception. Positioning is deciding on what your product is going to do and for whom. After deciding on this, the next step is how to make the customer perceive it the way you want him to. The key questions that one should ask and answer before positioning a product are:

1. What position do we already own in the prospect's mind? (for existing products)
2. What position do we want to own?
3. What is the Gap?
4. What companies should we out-gun, if we are to establish that position?
5. Do we have enough marketing resources, both regarding money and creative talent to occupy the position we want to?
6. Do we have the conviction and guts to stick with the one consistent position?
7. Does our creative approach match our positioning strategy?

Ground Rules for Positioning

Let us now look at some of the ground rules for positioning a product. These are not rigid rules but are some of the basic principles that are derived and formulated from a detailed and exhaustive study of many product successes and failures. Some of the important ground rules are:

1. **You cannot appeal to everyone:**There is no room for panaceas in the marketplace. A product that tries to appeal to everyone winds up appealing to no one. This attempt to appeal to everyone is in fact, the antithesis of positioning. If anyone claims that his product has a lot to offer from pediatrics to geriatrics, in many conditions, a sort of cure-all, who is going to believe it? The credibility will be near zero if not a real zero. Many pharmaceutical brands in India have achieved uncommon success through precise, non-ambiguous, no-nonsense positioning. Here are two cases in point:

2. **You Cannot Beat Them - The Brand Leaders head On!** There are some positions, which cannot and should not be contested. You cannot make a direct, frontal attack on the brand leader who is firmly entrenched. Over 2,400 years ago Sun Tzu recognized the folly of attacking a superior and firmly entrenched competitor head-on. He said: *There are some roads not to be followed, some armies not to be attacked, some cities not to be seized, some positions not to be contested.*

If you want to introduce an antacid brand now, you cannot afford to attack either Gelusil or Digene. That would be setting you on a collision course. You can take a different position, but you should create the necessary differentiation and make your brand stand out distinctly. You should, of course, relate your product to competition, but only to say that it is different and better than others. The differentiation must be perceived.

Unless you base communication on a unique idea, and position, the message often goes into the mental slot reserved for the leader in that product category. That is why with every addition of a new product that is not differentiated in a particular product group, and you find that the brand leader is gaining share continually further strengthening its position. Consider the case of a new antacid that had made the waves in the antacid, anti-flatulent market.

3. **You Can Re-position Your Brand:** Even if you do not find any gaps in the market as it is currently defined and perceived, it may be possible to alter the market map and thus create new opportunities. You can do this by introducing a new attribute and making it salient for the target market. It is repositioning by changing the frames of reference. You can reposition your brand against the competitor. Repositioning is undercutting an existing concept or a product. One should not be afraid of conflict or controversy while repositioning a product. Consider these cases.

Precise Positioning Improves the Blood Picture of Two Brands in the Hematinic Market!

Let us take the multi-hematinic market in India. It is a highly fragmented market with over a hundred plus brands. The market size in value was around Rs. 20-crore with an annual growth rate of 1.2 percent in 1992. Majority of these brands did not have a clearly defined positioning strategy. A typical list of indications for a no-position hematinic looks like this: *in anemias due to diverse causes such as increased requirements of hematinic during pregnancy, lactation, convalescence, due to malnutrition, due to a restricted diet, in obesity, chronic infectious diseases, tuberculosis, anorexia nervosa, chronic diarrhea, achlorhydria, post-gastrostomy, or gastro-jejunostomy, chronic hemorrhoids, hookworm infestations etc.*

Only two brands, Fefol of Eskaylabs (GSK now) and Livogen Capsules of Allenburys (GSK now), had a clear positioning strategy. Both were positioned as pregnancy haematinics, which is the most significant indication for hematinics accounting for about 70 percent of the hematinic usage according to prescription research. Fefol stayed with the theme *part of the routine of pregnancy and lactation* consistently.

They had put their might behind this position (the mother and baby contest was one unique promotional strategy they had adopted to reinforce their positioning strategy) and reaped an abundant harvest of prescriptions.

Close on their heels was Livogen Capsules, which stayed on with its powerful, persuasive and distinct theme, *11(blood-building factors) for the mother and 5 (mg of folic acid) for the fetus.* Although the other hematinics were not promoted in pregnancy, pregnancy was one of the several indications in which other hematinic brands were prescribed. Pregnancy was not an exclusive indication for other hematinic brands. Whereas both Fefol and Livogen Capsules were positioned only in pregnancy and stayed on with that position unwaveringly. Unflinchingly!

It has always been a neck-to-neck race for Fefol and Livogen Capsules with a negligible difference of less than one percent in terms of market share points, Fefol having a market share of 11.6 percent and Livogen Capsules having 10.9 percent in 1992.

Clear Positioning Steers Glaxo Clear in Anti-Asthmatic Market!

Another case in point is Betnelan tablets of Glaxo (GSK now). Each tablet of Betnelan contains 0.5 mg of betamethasone valerate, a potent corticosteroid, which can be used in a number of conditions like: *asthma, severe allergic disturbances, leukemia, rheumatoid arthritis, collagen diseases, various inflammatory skin diseases, nephrotic syndrome, ulcerative colitis, pemphigus, sarcoidosis (especially with hypercalcaemia), rheumatic endocarditis, ankylosing spondylitis, blood dyscrasias, agranulocytosis, and thromobo-cytopenicpurpura, etc.*

Betnelan introduced sometime in the 1950s was being promoted in all these conditions till 1973. The company had a relook at its marketing strategies in 1973 and positioned Betnelan in bronchial asthma and promoted it vigorously. Betnelan, not only achieved the leadership position but also remained a strong leader even fifteen years after this clear, decisive positioning in bronchial asthma. That is what a clear, precise positioning can do to a brand.

The reason for this specific positioning and its success with a such a versatile drug like betamethasone valerate was that Glaxo at the time was also marketing it in the same strength of 0.5 mg of the drug per tablet in a soluble tablet form under a different brand name, Betnesol effervescent tablets. Betnesol tablets were positioned differently.

Glaxo, by virtue of its clear positioning strategy and the conviction with which it stayed on, achieved a formidable position in the systemic corticosteroid market, with a market share of 48 percent. Its positioning strategy paid off handsomely in marketing the twin brands of betamethasone very successfully. Both Betnelan and Betnesol continued to grow from strength to strength. There was no cannibalization of brands either. Positioning, clear positioning had ensured harmony and growth instead.

The New Antacid's Guerrilla Warfare!

Biological E. Limited, in 1987 introduced a new antacid that jostled for space among a crowd of 151 antacid brands in an Rs. 45-crore large antacid, anti-flatulent market. The company knew beforehand that it could not fight the brand leaders - Digene of Boots (market share 19.9%) and Gelusil of Warner Hindusthan (market share 13.1%) head on. Therefore, the company chose to create perceptible product differentiation. It formulated the product differently and promoted it as a sodium-free antacid. This concept caused enough dissonance since it has been common knowledge that sodium intake is restricted in hypertensive patients.

Furthermore, it is highly likely that middle-aged patients who are susceptible to hypertension are also likely patients of hyperacidity. The company chose a different name for its brand that is suggestive and powerful enough to cut through the clutter. *pH4* is a highly suggestive name since that is the normal gastric pH level. The product became synonymous with the normal gastric pH. The company reinforced its product differentiation in many ways and communicated its differentiation persuasively. The net result is that the product found a niche for itself and gained a foothold in the minds of physicians, which no other antacid introduced during the previous six years was able to. While the new brand — *pH4* did not take any share from the brand leaders, it certainly awakened the sleeping giants, who stepped up their promotional efforts to defend their market share.

(Boots later became a part of Abbott Healthcare, and Warner Hindusthan later became a part of Pfizer due to a series of acquisitions.)

Alert makes it Good!

There are over a hundred brands of antihistamines in the anti-allergic market in India. Although many of them contain different ingredients, customers (doctors) continued to perceive these various brands as antihistamines with little or no difference. A few differences like price, which is of concern to the dispensing or purchasing of doctors and hospitals, and action of duration, of course, existed in the served markets of different competitors. There were no significant perceptible differences among the brands in the total market as such. The brand leaders - Avil (Hoechst, which is Sanofi now) and Foristal (Ciba Geigy, which is Novartis now) had been guarding their respective served markets zealously. All other brands had insignificant shares of the total market with very small served markets.

Enter Incidal of Bayer. Incidal contained a different ingredient. Furthermore, with clear product differentiation and a smart re-positioning strategy, Bayer invaded the served markets of various competitors and grabbed the business (prescriptions) right from under their noses. They promoted Incidal as an Alert and Daytime Histamine vigorously. The Alert theme created a strong product differentiation in the minds of customers as all other antihistamines cause drowsiness or sedation and cannot, therefore, be prescribed to patients while driving vehicles and who are busy at workplaces during the day. With its clear and clever repositioning as an Alert, Daytime antihistamine, Incidal overcame the current limitations of all antihistamines in one stroke and stormed the antihistamine market and achieved the second position in the market in a short span of few years.

Repositioning Strategy Replaces an Entrenched Brand!

Here is an example of how Tylenol (brand of paracetamol) in the US was repositioned against the mighty Aspirin and won the battle. The Tylenol ads said:

> *For millions who cannot take aspirin...if your stomach is easily upset, if you have an ulcer... or you suffer from asthma, allergies, iron deficiency anemia; it would make a good sense to check with your doctor before you take aspirin. Aspirin can irritate the stomach lining, can cause hidden gastro-intestinal bleeding... Fortunately, there is Tylenol...*

Tylenol is a leading brand of analgesic-antipyretic in the US and many other countries. The repositioning strategy paid rich dividends indeed!

A few years later, an over-the-counter (OTC) brand of ibuprofen was trying to invade the served market of the mighty Tylenol brand with its own repositioning strategy.

Positioning or repositioning strategies discussed here may look obvious and over-simplistic. The simplicity is deceptive. One can apply the principles of positioning strategy after thoroughly analyzing the various aspects like the current position of his brand, the desired position and the existing gap between the two. One should not mimic or imitate another product's theme just because it happens to be a similar product or falls into the same product category. Such practice of imitative strategy could be disastrous. Consider this case.

Me-too Strategy Meets with a Disaster!

Imitation may be the best form of flattery. However, it could falter when overdone or without proper analysis in marketing.

Inspired by the success of Tylenol's classic repositioning strategy, Burroughs Wellcome (GSK now) in India marketed their brand of acetaminophen, Ridake (manufactured by Litaka Laboratories). The company had chosen the OTC route. Large ads of Ridake appeared in leading newspapers. The copy was almost similar to the copy of the Tylenol ads when it was introduced in the US many years ago. There was a strong objection to these ads as they were hypercritical about the popular Aspirin. Comparative (or combative) advertisements were almost non-existent at that time in India. The resistance to their advertising strategy was so high that the company had to withdraw these ads. The company finally got rid of the product that was supposed to rid the pain (hence the name Ridake)!

Synergistic Power of a Successful Repositioning Strategy!

Septran, the anti-bacterial that catapulted the company, Burroughs Wellcome (GSK now) into the limelight (from a mere Rs. 4-crore company in 1973 to an Rs. 75-Crore giant in 1992). The company repositioned its Septran against the mighty tetracyclines in 1973.

Septran was the Indian pharmaceutical industry's leading brand (sales Rs. 31.3-crore, growth 3.1% in 1992). Septran, a combination of sulphamethoxazole and trimethoprim positioned itself as an ideal alternative to the widely prescribed tetracyclines (rather indiscriminately used) that were reigning supreme up to the late 1970s. What is particularly noteworthy is that the synergistic power of Septran backed by an unprecedented promotional effort of the company pushed the brand to the dizzy heights of the industry's number one position even when other sulfa drugs were on the decline.

Rocephin Stands Out in a Crowded Market!

Hoffman La Roche, the Swiss drug major, launched its broad spectrum injectable antibiotic in the United States in 1993. The injectable antibiotic market was indeed crowded at the time. Injectable antibiotics are used mainly in hospitals to treat very serious and even life-threatening conditions. The ability to kill the invading germs or the killing power was the main criteria for selecting the drug for the hospitals and physicians. Almost all the competing brands of injectable antibiotics were claiming that their brands were the most potent killer antibiotics. Not only the market was crowded, but also the messaging.

Rocephin had a tough challenge as any new entrant would. How to stand out in the crowded segment of antibiotic injectables? The brand, Rocephin, however, had a distinct advantage. It had a very convenient once-daily dosage. All the other brands had to be given two to three times a day. Once-daily dosage is a tremendous advantage. However, the physicians at the time did not think so. They felt that once-day dosage was a significant disadvantage. Surprising as it may seem, they were apprehensive that despite the substantial evidence confirming the efficacy of Rocephin, its effects might taper off reducing the antibacterial power over twenty-four hours before the next dose leaving patients vulnerable to toxic pathogens. The hospitals too might become susceptible as a result and become a target of costly lawsuits.

The brand team of Rocephin after thorough research of the advertising and messaging practices of competing brands observed that all the competitors were harping on their respective 'kill powers' and often showing images of scary, open, infected wounds and blown up microscopic pathogens. The Rocephin team decided to follow a different route that would give them a distinct identity in the crowded market space. That would make Rocephin stand out.

Instead of engaging in a head-to-head competition highlighting Rocephin's power to kill bacteria, the team focused on what the hospitals and physicians were looking for. Better outcomes. Quickly and safely discharging the patients who recovered completely from the severe conditions. In other words, Wellness. On getting better. Rapid recovery from infections. The communication too was simple, direct, straightforward. The advertisement showed an image of an apple, denoting the simple, yet powerful folksy adage that an apple a day keeps the doctor away.

It's simplicity at its best. There was no need for any rational argument. It resonated with patients, physicians, the hospital staff and the payers.

Rocephin became a blockbuster and passed the $2.8 billion mark in sales in 2005, the year of its patent expiry. Understandably, generics eroded 55 percent of its market by 2007.

Lessons

The case of Rocephin is a classic example of how to create a distinct brand identity in a crowded marketplace.

Rocephin's communication strategy focused on what customers want and not on what the brand has, and brand does. It focused on the outcomes such as healthy recovery, safe discharge from the hospital and wellness.

As Vince Parry, the thought leader of healthcare advertising strategies says in his insightful book, *Identity crisis*. Brand identity is a distinguishing set of essential values or ideas of a product, company or services perceived by the customer.

Rocephin's brand communication was the essence of simplicity. It resonated with all the stakeholders that matter. Rocephin, as a result, owned 'wellness' and not severe problems like competition.

(Source: Adapted from Vince Parry's book, Identity Crisis, Parry Branding Group, 2017)

Late Entrant Emerges as A Leader in A Crowded Market Place!

In the late 1990s, antihypertensives was a crowded market space in the United States pharmaceutical market. Novartis had launched its Diovan (Valsartan) as the second brand in the angiotensin II antagonists category. Merck's Cozaar (Losartan) pioneered the class two years before in 1995. Close on heels of Diovan's entry were two more significant competitors, Bristol Myers Squibb's Avapro (Irbesartan) and AstraZeneca's Atacand (Candesartan) in 1997 and 1998, making the market even more crowded. Diovan, as a result, in its first year could only bank a disappointing $80 million in sales. The brand team of Diovan persuaded the top management to endorse a long-term strategy to establish the brand's presence.

The antihypertensive market in the US at the time was large and growing. There were about 50 million hypertensive patients including approximately 36 million untreated patients. The angiotensin II antagonists class was small accounting for a mere eight percent of the market as compared to the twenty-four percent for beta blockers and angiotensin-converting enzyme (ACE) inhibitors, and twenty-one percent for calcium channel blockers (CCBs). The following table (2.2) presents the details of their patent expiration:

Table 2.2 Patent Expiry Schedule of Diovan and Its Competing Brands

Brand	Year of Patent Expiry
Norvasc (Amlodipine), the world's best selling antihypertensive	2007
Cozaar (Losartan) of Merck	2009
Avapro (Irbesartan) of Bristol Myers Squibb	2011
Atacand (Candesartan) of AstraZeneca	2011
Diovan (Valsartan) of Novartis	2012

The Diovan brand team started investing in a five-step relaunch strategy of Diovan following its disappointing launch performance:

1. Compete out-of-class with angiotensin-converting enzyme (ACE) inhibitors and calcium channel blockers (CCBs) for first-line use

2. Differentiate from other angiotensin II antagonists in efficacy and selectivity

3. Pursue new indications, dosages and combination products

4. Support all of the above with the most extensive clinical trial program in its class

5. Pursue an aggressive publication strategy in medical journals and increase the share of voice

The medical profession and the scientific community perceived the angiotensin II antagonists (AIIA) class as a second-line therapy at the time. Novartis' repositioning strategy of Diovan had helped the repositioning of the entire class of angiotensin receptor blockers (ARBs). Diovan had only a modest clinical advantage, the same efficacy as the leading ACE inhibitors and CCBs and better tolerability. However, Novartis exploited Diovan's marginal advantage in its new global position - *Protective, Effective and Selective.*

Repositioning alone would not push Diovan's ranking in the marketplace. Cardiologists need clinical evidence, and Novartis did generate enough of it. The company launched an aggressive Phase IV clinical program to support new indications and formulations. New indications included congestive heart failure, post-myocardial infarction, and high-risk hypertension and obtained approvals from the FDA through 2002 to 2005.

The Diovan's relaunch strategy did work effectively, and the brand team did deliver. Diovan became a blockbuster by 2001. By 2007, it was generating a whopping $5 billion in annual sales. In 2010, Diovan passed $6.1 billion in sales, making it the best-selling drug in Novartis' history!

(Source: Adapted from Francoise Simon and Philip Kotler's book, *Building GlobalBiobrands*, The Free Press 2003)

4. **There is Not Much Room Over There!** The human mind can no doubt store and process an incredible lot of information (about 12 billion bits of information is the estimated capacity of the human brain, but scientists say that hardly 10 percent of it is used by an average individual. The brightest seem to be using about 15 percent). According to the Harvard psychologist, Dr. George A Miller, the ordinary human mind cannot deal with more than seven items at a time in its working memory. Ask anyone to name all the brands he can remember in a given product category. For a high-interest category, the chances are that they will hardly get past seven. Usually, it is much less.

Your product has got to occupy one of the seven positions, to be remembered and recalled and to be successful. If your product fails to occupy one of the seven rungs on the product ladder in the prospect's mind, it has no chance of survival. In any product category, the few top brands (usually 5 to 7) account for about 90 percent of the market. The Indian pharmaceutical industry is no exception to this.

Moving up the ladder is very difficult, particularly when the above brands are firmly entrenched and the gap is wider. A detailed analysis of the competing brands and their positions is a must before one plans to climb up the ladder.

If you have a genuinely new product, it is often better to tell the prospect what the product is not, rather than what it is. That is because the mind has no room for what is new and different unless it is related to the old and matches with prior knowledge.

The classic example of this is that the first-ever automobile was positioned as a horseless carriage. Among cough syrups for children in India, a non-narcotic brand was the leader in the 1990s. Patients certainly prefer (and therefore, doctors too) a pain-free injection. In the anti-inflammatory market, non-steroidal drugs are preferred. Non-staining ointments are highly acceptable among topical preparations as they have a cosmetic appeal. Sodium-free and Sugar-free preparations are sought after by many a health conscious person.

5. **Credibility is the Foundation for Success!** The foundation of a successful positioning strategy is its credibility. Whether it is possible, to tell the truth, the whole truth and nothing but the truth is beside the point. Unless the consuming public believes the message conveyed by the product promotion, the positioning game is lost.

In a highly competitive, over-crowded market like the Indian pharmaceutical market, in a me-too, rather *me-me-too* market many companies claim that they are different. However, merely claiming that one is different is not going to create a unique, distinct position. At best it will change the me-too market into a me-different or *me-me-different* market.

Only when the consumers perceive the difference, will the product be successful. Genuine product differentiation alone can create the desired position for the product in the minds of consumers. It means differentiation in both words and deeds.

Finally, what is axiomatic about the whole business of positioning is this: the best policy for an effective, successful positioning strategy is honesty itself.

Product Policy and Strategy

Product policy and strategy is the keystone of a marketing-mix since a product is the most tangible and often the essential expression of any business endeavor. Customers satisfy their needs only through the use of products. Customers' image of a product and decisions to buy your products or not in future is influenced only by their experiences with your product. The satisfied customers with rewarding experiences of your products are likely to indulge in repeat purchases. Others with not-so-positive experiences may switchover to competitors' products. Decisions relating to products, therefore, are crucial to marketing strategy.

There are two main reasons why a company adds a product or two to its existing product mix. Firstly, when it realizes that its current products do not have the potential to attain the growth and profit objectives the company has set itself.

The second reason is that the company spots new product opportunities that it can exploit since they are matching its resources or that the company is confident of mobilizing.

It is vital that a company's product-mix must represent a dynamic equilibrium between current profitability and future growth and stability in the ever-changing marketplace. Adoption of the product portfolio analysis suggested by BCG is beneficial for this purpose. You classify the products by their current market share, market or sales growth, and profitability. When you look at products this way you will observe that:

A. Products with high market share and low growth are today's profit earners (Cash Cows)

B. Products with high market share and high growth represent tomorrow's (potential) big profit earners (Stars)

C. Products with low market share but high growth are high-risk investment (Question Marks)

A company should have a properly balanced mix of products that includes today's as well as tomorrow's profit earners.

Governing Factors

Product strategy, therefore, is concerned with decisions on the range of products a company must offer to achieve its objective of profit, growth and market share. The policies will specify the action plans and programs that will be implemented to meet the strategic goals. The factors governing the product policy and strategy decisions are:

1. **Resource Utilization:** Optimum use of resources holds the key to improved profitability. Productivity must be improved.

Will the product policy and strategy decisions lead to better utilization of resources in all areas such as raw materials, installed capacities, market position, corporate image, reputation, and quality? Will the product decisions lead to better utilization of the existing resources?

2. **Stability:** Stability in sales, profit, return on investment, earnings per share are essential for continued success. A company, which is robust (financially speaking) and can venture to expand further must avoid excessive fluctuations and should not stretch beyond limits. One must avoid the temptation to buy market share at any (promotional or otherwise) cost. Aggression tempered with prudence pays dividends in the long run.

3. **Flexibility:** A company's product policy and strategy should be feasible enough to adapt to ever-changing customer needs and marketing environment and exploit them.

4. **Profit:** Profits are the lifeblood of a company. A company must continuously strive to improve profitability by improving performance in all areas and activities of the company. It is the profits that fuel the growth opportunities and maintain the existing business.

Product planning, therefore, is crucial for attaining marketing objectives. The key result areas are:

A. A regular review of product range and product-mix becomes mandatory to ensure optimization of sales and profits of all items in each product line.

B. A constant improvement in marketing and manufacturing efficiencies to improve product image, promotional effort and ensure better capacity utilization.

C. To maintain a balance between price and value based on customer expectations and perceptions. Maintaining acceptable quality is essential. Excessive quality (beyond the acceptable limits and levels) may be very costly and need not necessarily reap any additional benefits either to the customer or the company.

D. It is necessary to anticipate the competitors' moves, reactions and responses to your product strategies to stay ahead and defend your products' market share.

The decision regarding the product policy and strategy, therefore, affect a company's future significantly. The choice of products of a firm influences all the other elements in its marketing program, and may have significant implications for such functional areas as finance, production, and personnel. That is why product policy and strategy have been called the micro-marketing functions that center on a firm's marketing programs, and its organization and management of marketing. The basic interacting triad suggested by David J. Luck that forms the foundation of the entire product program is:

A. *Objectives*: Provide the ends towards which the management must steer.

B. *Policies*: Provide the guidelines along which and the channel within which the firm should proceed towards meeting its objectives.

C. *Strategies*: Conceptualize and direct the means whereby the firm moves towards its objectives.

Stated simply, product policy and strategy decisions center around what goods and services a firm should offer for sale and what characteristics and attributes they should have. These decisions involve matching the company's resources and needs with market opportunities.

Formulation of product policy, therefore, requires careful analysis of existing and potential (new) products relative to the characteristics of both the market and the firm. Here is a checklist of all essential properties and other aspects for reviewing a pharmaceutical product (Table 2.3)

Table 2.3 Pharmaceutical Product Review - A Checklist

1. Physical Properties of a Product

(a) Dosage form – Capsule
  - What should be the color, shape, size, and texture (hard gelatin or soft gelatin) of the capsule?
  - What are the ingredients and their strengths?
  - Should the brand name be printed on the capsule? Linear printing or circular printing? Are the colors selected for printing approved?

(b) Dosage form – Tablets
  - What should be the color, shape (round, oblong, flat, square) and the size of the tablets?
  - Should the tablets be sugar-coated, film coated, enteric coated or uncoated? Should they be scored?
  - Should the brand name be embossed on the tablet?
  - What are the ingredients and their strengths?
  - Should they be chewable or swallow tablets? If chewable, what should be the taste and flavor?

(c) Packing for Oral Solids
  - Should the capsules or tablets be packed in glassine poly or aluminum foil, blister or all alu blister packing? In glass bottles or plastic containers?

(d) Dosage form - Oral Liquids
  - Should the product be in suspension or syrup form?
  - Should it be free from sugar?
  - What should be its color, smell, taste, and flavor?
  - Should it be packed in glass bottles or PET containers?
  - Should there be a measuring cup or a dropper (in case of pediatric syrups)
  - What is the composition?

(e) Dosage form – Parenteral
  - Should it be in ampoules or vials?
  - What is the composition? What kind of preservatives should we use?
  - Should it be packed in disposable syringes? Auto-injectors?
  - What are the storage conditions? Should it be transported through a cold chain like some vaccines?

Table 2.3 Contd...

(f) Dosage form - Topical Ointments
  - What should be the smell and color of the ointment?
  - What are the ingredients?
  - What should be the base? Cream or oily?
  - Should there be an applicator (as In the case of hemorrhoidal ointments)?

(g) Dosage form - Topical Solution
  - What are the ingredients?
  - What should be the color, smell of the topical solution?
  - Should it be in a glass bottle or a roll-on bottle?

(h) Dosage form - Topical Powder
  - What are the ingredients?
  - What should be the texture of the powder?
  - Should it be packed in glass vials, plastic containers or tins? What should be the pack size?

2. Medical Rationale
  - Medical rationale for each product and each dosage form
  - Details regarding why and how the product works
  - What is the recommended dosage?

3. Indications and Claims
  - What are the indications?
  - What are the product claims? How can they be substantiated?

4. Trade Mark Position
  - Is the trademark registered? It is always necessary to apply for trademark registration for proposed new products, at least three years in advance in India.

5. Patent Position (Basic drugs)
  - It is necessary if you are exporting to those countries, which are signatories to GATT on intellectual property rights.

6. Registration and Licensing Status (If the product is not decontrolled)
  - Have you obtained the DGTD registration?
  - Have you received the drug license for manufacturing?

7. Pricing
  - What category does the proposed product fall into as per the Drug Price Control Order (DPCO)?
  - Have you got a price approval from the National Pharmaceutical Pricing Authority (NPPA)?
  - If the product does not come under the purview of price control, what pricing strategy should you adopt? Skimming the cream or penetration strategy?

Table 2.3 Contd...

8. Sizing up the Competition
  - ➤ What is the intensity of the competition?
  - ➤ How many competitors are there? Their market shares?
  - ➤ What is the combined market share of the top three competitors? What are their product attributes and benefits? How do they compare with yours?
  - ➤ What are their resources? Their promotional effort? Their distribution? Their sales force and their competence? How do they compare with yours?
  - ➤ How do they compare with you regarding all resources?

9. Sales Potential
  - ➤ What are your sales forecasts? What is the projected profitability in the next five years?

10. Launch Plans
  - ➤ Detailed launch plans

New Products

Speaking of new products, Professor William J.Stanton of Colorado University in the US states that, "*It is not important to seek a very limited definition of a new product. Instead, we may recognize several possible categories of new products.*" The three recognizable products categories are:

A. **Innovative:**These are products, which are really innovative and genuinely unique like hair-restorer, or Cancer cure. For these products, there is the real need, and there are no real satisfactory substitutes. Products, which are entirely different replacements for existing goods serving existing markets, can also be included in this category. H2 Antagonists like cimetidine, ranitidine, famotidine among anti-ulcerants, anti-hypertensives such as atenolol, nifedipine, captopril and the quinolone derivatives like ciprofloxacin, norfloxacin, ofloxacin among antibacterial drugs are some notable examples of the genuinely innovative products in the pharmaceutical industry.

B. **Replacements:** Products, which are primarily of the same type, but with a significant differentiation from the existing product, can be classified under this category. Ibuprofen sustained-release capsules - Fenbid, Fenlong,   Ibubid TR, and ferrous sulfate and folic acid Spansules (Fefol) are some examples in this category. The basic idea here is to create a product differentiation even if the drugs are the same, by combining them with another drug (to achieve synergy); or a drug delivery system (to obtain a higher degree of safety and minimize the dose), and to gain a larger share of the market.

C. **Imitative:** Products in this category are new to the company but not to the market. The purpose of introducing products in this category is that a company merely wants to capture part of an existing market with yet another brand of a current type of product. The pharmaceutical industry in India is virtually flooded with imitative products, and it is this category of products that have made the pharmaceutical market in India the fiercely competitive market that it is today.

Product-Mix Decisions

Product-mix decision is an important and indeed a crucial product policy decision for a company since it tends to reflect not only the nature of the market, and the resources of the firm but also the underlying philosophy of the company's management.

There are many options available for a firm in this area. One firm may pursue a policy of diversification. Some other firm may prefer to concentrate and specialize in a specific area and offer a narrow product-mix. For example, Serum Institute of India specializes only in the area of immunologicals. It is important to note that market opportunities for the firm's product-mix serve to determine the upper limits of potential corporate profitability while the quality of the marketing program tends to determine the extent of the achievement of such potential.

Optimal Product-Mix

As Philip Kotler says, it is challenging to define an ideal or optimal product-mix. One can say that the current product-mix is optimal if no adjustment will enhance the company's chances of achieving its objectives and improving its performance.

Diagnosis of a sub-optimal product-mix, therefore, is essential. Unless you regularly conduct a SWOT (Strengths, Weaknesses, Opportunities, Threats) analysis of each product in your product mix, you would not be able to diagnose whether your product-mix is sub-optimal.

The usual symptoms are:

▸ Chronic or seasonally recurring excess capacity in a firm's production and inventories of finished products. Tapering or sluggish demand often leads to this.

▸ A very high proportion of profits coming from a small percentage of products.

▸ Inefficient use of sales force skills.

▸ A steady decline in profits and sales.

▸ A steady increase in complaints from dealers about slow or non-movement of products from their shelves.

▸ A steady increase in claims for refund on date-expired products

This situation, if not corrected immediately will only lead to disaster. The strategic options available to a firm for remedying this situation are:

A. **Deletion:** Deletion strategy involves decisions regarding product discontinuance or abandonment of individual items or even of an entire product line.

B. **Product Modification:** You can achieve product modification by changing either tangible or intangible product attributes. Reformulation, redesigning, changing the pack size or shape, changing the taste or flavor and removing specific features are some of the methods commonly adopted in product modification strategies. By successfully planning and implementing product modification strategies many companies have extended the life cycles of their products, resulting in a more extended, healthier, more profitable lease of life for both products and the company.

C. **Introduction of New Products**: The introduction of new products is crucial for the survival and growth of any business endeavor.

Here is a case that illustrates the importance of diagnosing the sub-optimal product-mix in time to avoid any catastrophe.

Poor Diagnosis Proves Dearer!

Unichem (now acquired by Torrent Pharma) is a large pharmaceutical company in the Indian sector with a considerable reputation. The company manufactured bulk drugs and many formulations (about 75 stock keeping units in 1988).

Two products - Uni-enzyme tablets and EP Forte (high dose combination of estrogen and progesterone) accounted at one time for over one-third of the company's total sales volume. Though the company was among the first to get a license to manufacture newer anti-tubercular drugs lIke ethambutol and rifampicin, the company had not persevered with ethambutol and had marketed rifampicin and INH combination under Anticox. Consequently, despite a head start, the company had only a token share of 2.5 percent of the anti-tubercular market.

Coming back to the company's stronghold - Uni-enzyme tablets, a brand leader in the digestive preparation category for years and EP forte, also a brand leader in the high-dose estrogen, progesterone combinations-the company seemed to have taken its position for granted and not monitored and reviewed the changing trends or even tap the opportunities available.

Take for example the market for digestive preparations. It was as large as Rs. 34.7-crore with an annual growth rate of 8 percent in 1988. This market comprised oral solids and liquids, with oral solids accounting for about 33 percent and the liquids for the balance 67 percent. Uni-enzyme tablets had been enjoying the brand leadership for many years. The company seemed to have ignored the large oral liquids market for it did not introduce digestive enzyme syrup all these years. A line extension of Uni-enzyme brand as syrup or tonic, backed by massive promotional effort would have made the brand far more formidable. However, by 1988, many companies entered the market with their brands of digestive enzyme syrups and took a significant share of the digestive preparations oral liquids market. Aristozyme of Aristo and Bestozyme of Biological E. Limited had taken a sizable share from the veteran brands like Vitazyme of East India Pharmaceutical Works and Digeplex of TCF.

As a result, Unichem from its dominant position of brand leadership has gone to a slightly vulnerable position, where even the brand leadership position was at stake in the total digestive preparations market. Had the company been alert and instituted a diagnostic screen of detecting the symptoms of the sub-optimal product mix early enough, Unichem would have reinforced its already formidable position in the digestive enzyme market invincible rather than vulnerable?

Consider now the market for a high-dose combination of estrogen and progesterone. The combination had been enjoying brand leadership for years with EP Forte. However, the Government of India banned the formulations containing high doses of estrogen and progesterone around 1986. While other companies such as German Remedies, Nicholas and Allenburys had withdrawn their products in time and planned for some new products in different therapeutic categories, Unichem did not. Sudden withdrawal of EP Forte left a void in its product mix. The company was unprepared to meet this sudden loss of sales.

Other companies, while their stakes in the high-dose estrogen-progesterone market were not as high as they were for Unichem, their brands Duogynon Forte, Orasecron Forte, Disecron Forte, and Secrodyl contributed significantly enough to their total sales respectively. However, those companies noticed the storm signals early enough and sustained their growth by concentrating on other products and by introducing new products in different product categories. However, Unichem seemed to have been caught napping without a proper diagnostic screen. It failed to detect the symptoms or perhaps was too complacent to act quickly.

The net result was that this lack of systematic review of product mix had been showing a decline of about ten percent per annum for the next two years and the company's rank fell from 16th in 1986 to 22 in 1988 and slid down further to 30th position on the Indian pharmaceutical league table in 1992.

The importance of regular and systematic evaluation of a company's product-mix and development of diagnostic screen to detect or spot the symptoms of a sub-optimal product-mix can never be over-emphasized. Companies that take cognizance of the early storm signals and act fast are bound to succeed. Companies that take their position for granted and close their eyes and ears to the early warning signals are sure to join the dinosaurs club.

Product Strategy

How do you go about formulating the product strategy? From the very beginning. From a clear, precise, statement of objectives for each product. Because any decision on strategy depends upon your goal (where you want to go). Once you decide on a strategy, the means (tactics) by which you want to achieve your objective become much clearer. A detailed understanding of objective, strategy, and tactics will be of help.

Objective

An objective is like your destination. Where you want to go. An objective should be clear, precise, non-ambiguous, quantifiable, measurable, realistic and achievable. At the same time, it should not be too easy to accomplish with little or no effort.

The stretch factor should be built into it to make it challenging. There are three levels of setting objectives. They are:

A. Corporate objectives

B. Marketing objectives

C. Product objectives

Strategy

A strategy is like a route or a road you want to take to reach your objective (destination). A decision on strategy, therefore, involves all aspects like your target audience, your product's key attributes, allocation of your resource-mix and the segments you will attack.

Tactics

Tactics are the means or vehicle that will take you all the way (strategy) to the destination (objectives). Tactics are the specific action plans. Deciding on tactics would mean deciding on your entire promotional mix.

Market Penetration and Market Development Strategies

Market penetration and development suggests that you increase the market share and profits of your existing products in your current markets. Five main ways in which you can achieve this are:

1. Widen the customer base. Increase the coverage of doctors like promoting to different groups of specialists, who are not presently covered by your sales force.

2. Increase the call frequency of your sales force to top prescribing doctors.

3. Find new uses for your products. Find out new indications in which you can promote your products. Like May & Baker did with their Flagyl when they had started promoting it in amoebiasis in addition to the earlier indication of giardiasis. Another example is when Merind (Merck now) began promoting their Practin (Periactin earlier), formerly an anti-allergic and anti-pruritic as an appetite stimulant, and anti-inflammatory drug aspirin, which is currently being promoted to reduce the incidence of heart attacks in high-risk patients.

4. Add flanking products or line extensions in the same therapeutic category either under the same brand name (it would mutually reinforce the brand image if it is already well established) and facilitate the entry of the new product. You can also introduce it in another dosage form or combine it with another drug if it leads to synergy.

5. More aggressive promotion than ever before is another way of increasing sales, profits, and market share. For products with OTC profile (over-the-counter products where a prescription is not needed), attractive dealer incentives will help boost the sales.

Product Development

Product development strategy should be a constant exercise. Product development aims to improve the quality and efficacy of the product or to minimize the undesirable attributes. Inherent in the product development strategy are:

A. Constant monitoring and analysis of competitor's products. It is the equivalent of reverse engineering of the Japanese electronics industry, which is one of the major secrets of their success. It will enhance and sharpen your competitive edge.

B. Offering better value for money by modifying pack-sizes. Family packs for protein-food supplements, tonics, and multivitamins for consumers and dispensing packs for doctors are some examples of this.

Diversification

Diversification is both costly and risky. You can practice related diversification. A pharmaceutical company diversifying into OTC healthcare products, hospital products, and animal healthcare products are a few examples of related diversification. The more unrelated the diversification to the existing business of the company, the more costly and risky it is. Here is a case in point.

CASE

38

Unrelated Diversification Eludes Success for an Otherwise Highly Successful Company!

Cadila Laboratories is probably one of the most successful companies in the Indian pharmaceutical industry. From a position of 37th in 1976, the company moved to the prestigious second position in the Indian pharmaceutical industry by 1988. The company successfully planned and implemented market penetration, market development and product development strategies in copybook style. The company also pursued an aggressive and imaginative new product planning and development strategy during these twelve years and reaped rich dividends.

Inspired by this success, the company went into a diversification program totally unrelated to its existing business. It began manufacturing color televisions and mopeds. It could not make any mark in these two unrelated areas, whereas everything the company had touched in the areas related to its core business of pharmaceuticals turned into gold. The Midas touch was not to be seen in the unrelated diversification and success eluded the otherwise highly successful company.

New Drug Adoption by Physicians in Branded-Generic Markets: A Two-Step Approach

The study of new drug adoption by physicians, particularly in a branded-generic market such as India involves two steps. It is particularly important for pharmaceutical marketers in India since the basic research effort is very minimal and consequently new-to-the-world drugs are scarce. The moment a new drug is discovered elsewhere in the world, it is launched by more than one company in India in quick succession. The new drug launch thus is virtually a me-too-new-drug launch. It is this simultaneous introduction of the same new drug (the same new molecule or the generic drug) by various companies that makes pharmaceutical marketing in India a different ball game as compared to the highly regulated markets in North America, Western Europe, and Japan. It is, however, changing gradually, after India recognized the product patents in 2005.

The marketing tasks involved here are two-fold. Firstly, the marketer has to facilitate the new drug adoption process by physicians at the molecule level. Secondly, he should ensure the adoption of his brand of the newly adopted drug in preference to competing brands within that molecule or generic drug category. The strategy, tactics and the relative emphasis on the promotional elements at each of the different stages would be different for the new drug adoption and new brand adoption.

The pharmaceutical marketer may have to adopt a rational approach — a strong reason why communication to persuade the physician to accomplish the new drug adoption. It is the vital first step. The second logical step is to gain the preference of the physician towards his brand of the newly adopted or accepted drug. The motivating factors behind these steps could be different.

We have already discussed that the primary motivations behind a physician's choice of drug therapy must be considered rational. The physician chooses a molecule based on the rational elements such as efficacy, safety, and total cost of treatment. However, when it comes to selecting a brand of a molecule, which he had already decided, the selection may not necessarily be rational alone, and emotional elements too can play an important role.

Communication Hierarchy and the Adoption Process

The communication objectives for the new drug adoption and new brand adoption are different. To get to the root of the difference, a brief discussion on communication hierarchy would be helpful. The widely accepted communication hierarchy in any buying process tells us that the consumer moves from many stages — be it an idea or a tangible product. These stages are:

- ▶ Unawareness
- ▶ Awareness
- ▶ Understanding
- ▶ Comprehension
- ▶ Liking
- ▶ Preference
- ▶ Conviction
- ▶ Action

The consumer passes through these stages every time he makes a purchasing decision. These stages are not isolated. They are on a continuum. All these stages may not be elaborate, apparent, and visible. It depends on the purchasing decision and the extent of the stakes involved for the consumer. The marketer through his skillful and creative communication strategy attempts to make the movement of the consumer as swift and as sure as possible. These stages may appear condensed or sandwiched at times. They may not be visible, but indeed they are all there in every buying decision we make. The discerning marketer would also realize that these stages include both rational and emotional components. You can group all the elements concerned with knowledge and information broadly under different logical elements. The emotional elements include all other aspects related to liking, preference, and action.

Compare this with the physician's new drug adoption process we discussed earlier. Physician's decision process on the selection of a new drug includes the following stages:

- Awareness
- Interest
- Evaluation
- Trial
- Adoption

These stages are similar to those in the communication hierarchy model we discussed earlier. On closer examination, one would observe that the physician's new drug adoption model is a more rational model of decision-making. The marketing implications of these should be clear by now. When the physician's choice of drug therapy is more rational, the task of marketing communication should be to convince the doctor regarding the new drug, its superiority and advantages over the current line of therapy. The orientation, therefore, is relatively more technical and product-oriented. You should substantiate the product claims with the results of clinical trials, success rate and so on to reinforce confidence in the new drug. The importance of this becomes clear when we understand that every time a physician chooses a new drug, he is taking a risk. That is why he should have all the reassurance and confidence that one can. It is possible only when you have all the relevant details backed by evidence. That is the first vital step.

Once you gain his acceptance and conviction regarding the choice of the new drug, the second crucial step is to make the physician prefer your brand of the new drug selected and more importantly to get him to act — to prescribe. This step is second only regarding the sequence and not in terms of importance. This step may often be simultaneous. There need not be any time-lag between the first step and second step.

The preference or the new brand adoption have certain emotional components in the decision-making process of the physician, unlike the new drug adoption process. Favorable predisposition towards the company in general, his experience with the company's earlier products, his response to advertising communications, his opinions and attitudes towards the company's medical representatives and their persuasive power — all those factors are likely to influence his choice of a brand considerably.

There are many new drugs like naproxen, Piroxicam, cimetidine, Ketoprofen, which were very successful abroad, where they originated from, but failed to take-off in India. It is not that these drugs were not used in India. In fact, these drugs were substantially superior alternatives for many of the drugs in use in the respective therapeutic groups at that time. What could be the reasons? Here is a possible explanation or reason.

These new drugs, which were very successful abroad, were discovered elsewhere and marketed by the companies that created them. These companies had gone the whole hog with their irrefutable evidence and convinced the physicians in those countries regarding the superiority of these new drugs over the current line of therapy. They had also gained; as a result, acceptance, and preference of their brands of the new drugs. The drug choice and brand preferences were almost simultaneous in the western world, where the international patent law is recognized. There are very few brands available with the same generic drug. The competition is more at the choice of the generic drug level itself and not so much between different brands of the same new molecule or drug. It is because, in the first-world markets, a patented new molecule is marketed as a brand exclusively by its innovator until the patent expires. The molecule and the brand are one. Only the names differ in the sense that the molecule has the chemical name, and a brand name has a more straightforward catchy name. Only when the originator's patent expires, do other branded generics enter the market. Whereas in India, the competition is almost always between different brands of the same drug.

Moreover, none of the companies that discovered these drugs were the first to introduce them in India. Some of the companies that discovered these drugs did not introduce them in India at all. As a result, the companies that introduced these drugs earliest in the country may not have had the same degree of commitment, pride, conviction, detailed documentation of research results, as those companies that discovered these drugs would have. That is why and how the companies that introduced drugs in India had probably not exploited the opportunities thoroughly. Instead, they could only tap the peripheral segments of the physician populations, like innovators and early adopters, whose awareness and acceptance of anything new and worthwhile are naturally high. These companies probably had not persisted adequately to gain a firm conviction in the minds of prescribing physicians. Instead, these companies probably had got a tiny, insignificant share of the prescriptions more out of the novelty element than on conviction. That explains why these new drugs never took-off in the Indian market despite a definite need for those products (those therapeutic groups are rapidly growing) and despite their overwhelming success abroad. The following cases would further amplify this point.

Fasigyn gives A Shot-in-the-arm to Tinidazole

Tinidazole, an anti-amoebic drug, was introduced some years ago by many companies in India. Some of the companies that introduced Tinidazole in India were considerably large in size and known for their marketing skills. However, tinidazole, after an initial spurt in prescriptions and sales, began to plateau somewhat prematurely. It could not stand against the mighty metronidazole and its combinations, which accounted for over two-thirds of the anti-amoebic market in the late 1980s. Pfizer, the company that discovered the drug - Tinidazole, could not introduce it earlier in India due to specific government regulations applicable to multinationals. Later Pfizer, after diluting its equity to attain non-FERA status under the then Foreign Exchange Regulation Act (FERA), introduced tinidazole, its research product in India under the brand name Fasigyn.

The introduction of Fasigyn, if the initial response was any indicator, gave tinidazole a much-needed shot-in-the-arm. The tinidazole market, which was hitherto not progressing, had all of a sudden become buoyant.

Pfizer quickly gained the conviction of the prescribing physicians regarding the superiority of Tinidazole over other amoebicides in the first place and increased preference to its Fasigyn brand of tinidazole. The two-step approach of new drug adoption and new brand adoption is evident at work.

Tinidazole had found at long-lost and ardent spokesman, an advocate in Pfizer, its discoverer, to gain a firm foothold in the physicians' minds. Other companies who had been marketing tinidazole so far, were quick to realize that the drug was gaining conviction among the prescribing doctors and joined the tinidazole bandwagon with renewed promotional effort and communications strategies aimed at gaining brand preference. The result? A resilient tinidazole market with a number of tinidazole brands showing rapid growth apart from Fasigyn, which moved to the brand leadership position within a very short period showing a very progressive trend!

Pioneer Fails to Take Off!

Cimetidine, the popular anti-ulcer drug is an original research product of Smith Kline Corporation, Philadelphia. The drug was indeed a pioneer among the H2 receptor antagonists. Tagamet, Smith Kline's brand of cimetidine had reached a preeminent position the world's largest selling prescription drug before it was dislodged from that position by another H2 receptor antagonist, ranitidine, a research product of Glaxo, UK Zantac was the brand name.

When Eskayef introduced Cimetidine in India, the government did not allow brand names for new single-ingredient drug formulations. Eskayef, the subsidiary of Smith Kline Corporation in India (GSK now) could not introduce the drug due to government regulations covering multinationals. Many Indian drug companies introduced cimetidine under the generic name in India. The doctors, who were aware of cimetidine quickly took to the product. The product had been picking up in prescriptions and sales, but its progress was no way comparable to the success that it had achieved in the first world markets, where product patents were recognized, and brand names were allowed.

Subsequently, due to a stay order of the Supreme Court of India, even the new single-ingredient formulations were allowed to be marketed with brand names. All companies marketing cimetidine christened their products appropriately.

In the meantime, the Zantac brand of ranitidine by Glaxo (GSK now) was remaking history in the anti-ulcer market worldwide. As soon as the government cleared ranitidine for marketing in India, many companies including Glaxo had introduced their respective brands of the drug. Glaxo had gone all out to make their Zantac brand of ranitidine (Glaxo used a phonetically similar but a different brand name Zinetec in India) the leader in the fast-growing anti-ulcer market in India. Ranitidine did not face any competition from its arch-rival cimetidine in India, against, which it had to fight with all its might in the rest of the world.

Instead, the focus of the competition in India was among different brands of ranitidine. It is because cimetidine did not gain the conviction of the prescribing physicians. Had Eskayef introduced their Tagamet brand in India before the introduction of ranitidine, probably cimetidine would have found a spokesperson and strong advocate for itself. However, then, Eskayef had introduced their brand of cimetidine very late and after the introduction of Glaxo's Zantac brand of Ranitidine.

It was rather too late for Tagamet to make any impact! The reason why cimetidine, the pioneer among the H2 receptor antagonists, did not even take off in India was that — even before the drug was adopted by prescribing physicians, its marketers in India shifted the competitive focus to brand preference. The brand preference in the case of cimetidine was literally the company preference, as brand names were not allowed at the time of its introduction. Cimetidine never really gained a firm conviction and a strong foot-hold in the prescribing doctor's mind.

Zinetec's Cakewalk!

The success of Glaxo's ranitidine brand of Zantac is all too familiar to the pharmaceutical marketers the world over. Zantac quickly marched forward to become the first-ever prescription drug to cross the coveted US $ 1-billion mark in the world.

In India, Glaxo was one of the earliest companies to introduce ranitidine, the world famous anti-ulcer drug. Glaxo had put a never-before-kind of promotional effort towards gaining the conviction of the doctors regarding the superiority of ranitidine over cimetidine and then their preference for Zinetec brand of ranitidine.

The result of this well-orchestrated two-step approach towards gaining the conviction of the prescribing physicians in the new drug adoption and the subsequent preference of the brand Zinetec over others is brand leadership with almost one-quarter of the Indian anti-ulcer market under its belt!

Conquering the Indian anti-ulcer market was a relatively tame affair for Glaxo, for neither cimetidine nor Tagamet was a force to reckon with in India. The real growth of the anti-ulcer market started only with the advent of ranitidine and Zinetec in India. From that point, winning the anti-ulcer market in India had been literally a cakewalk for Zinetec!

Product Management

The concept of product management or brand management originated in 1927 by Proctor &Gamble, has undergone several refinements over the years. Today, product management has carved out a niche for itself in the organizational structure of many forward-looking, dynamic and fast-growing companies the world over.

Camay soap was the first-ever product in the marketing history of the world to have been assigned exclusively to a product manager in 1927. Since then, neither Camay soap nor the product management system has looked back.

Today, an ever-increasing number of consumer, pharmaceutical and industrial products are being assigned to product managers specifically with a hope to develop and nurture these products into winning brands.

What is product management? Is it a panacea, a sort of cure-all for all kinds of ills and problems that marketers face? No, certainly not.

Product management is a system of decentralized business management. Product management is an application of perhaps the most essential marketing principle. The principle of concentration.

A product manager, when assigned with specific responsibility for a product or product line, can do some real solid, concentrated thinking on problems and opportunities that exist for his product. This focused thinking, in turn, is bound to result in more appropriate and better strategies for his product.

The product management system creates a focal point of planning and responsibility for individual products, says Philip Kotler. The product manager's role is to generate product strategies, plans, see their implementation, monitor the results and take corrective action.

David Luck termed product managers as the vital organizational loci for the focus of marketing interfaces. The essential interfaces with which product managers interact frequently are:

- The buying public
- Distributors
- Salesforce
- Advertising agencies
- R & D
- Production
- Suppliers
- Finance
- Governmental agencies

The Tasks of a Product Manager are:

- Developing a long range and competitive strategy for the product.
- Preparing an annual marketing plan and forecasting sales.
- Working with advertising and merchandising agencies to develop copy, programs, and campaigns
- Stimulating Interest in, and support of the product among the sales force and distributors.
- Gathering continuous intelligence on product performance, customer and dealer attitudes, on competitors' moves, new problems, and opportunities.
- Initiating product improvements to meet changing needs.

Advantages

The product management system offers many benefits. Here are some of the important ones:

- A product manager, with his focused approach the system facilitates, can balance and harmonize the various functional marketing inputs a product needs.
- A product manager is in a position to react quickly to problems in the marketplace without involving in several different people and lengthy meetings.

▸ A product manager can also be alert to spot, identify and capitalize on the opportunities that exist for his product.

▸ Smaller brands, which do not have the necessary attention in a functional marketing organization, find a champion in a product manager who will pursue their cause.

▸ Product management is an excellent training ground because it involves the manager in virtually every area of company operations. The product manager is the hub of the entire marketing activity.

Management by Persuasion

Product management is management by persuasion. If a product manager needs particular output from the sales force and production from the plant to gear up for a big advertising campaign, he has to sell the idea to people, who report, not to him, but managers in charge of sales and manufacturing. If his data and instinct tell him that his product needs different packaging, a more focused commercial or a reformulation of ingredients, he must impress upon the appropriate support groups with the importance of paying particular attention to his brand. If a product manager is worried that swings in one of his basic ingredient costs will erode into his profit margin, he might go to the purchasing department.

A product manager is responsible for his product's sales and profits. At the same time, he has very little authority and virtually no margin for financial risk. Still, product managers feel just about as entrepreneurial as a young executive could in an established hierarchical organization.

Competitive Edge

The product management system is necessary when:

A. A company's product lines need specialized marketing programs, or

B. A company markets many products, heterogeneous in nature, which are thus beyond the capacity of a functional marketing organization. Product management does not replace the functional organization but serves as another layer of control. Product management provides the much-needed cutting edge in the ever-increasing competition that exists in today's business world.

Product Manager as a Gardener?

A product manager is like a gardener. He owns his garden (is possessive about the garden), and at the same time, he does not own it (the garden does not belong to him as he has no right to the produce). However, he sows and plants the seeds (product ideas), cares, nurtures and nourishes them (prepares plans, gets the support of other departments and campaigns for his products) and ensures their proper growth. He is happy when the plants bloom (products become winning brands). He guards them zealously from intruders and trespassers (competitors trying to take a share of his products), takes out the weeds (deletes the products that are on the road to decline and obsolescence) and ensures that his plants are healthy (profitable, that is in sound financial health).

Some Problem Areas

Product management has come to stay. It offers many advantages and a distinct competitive edge. However, product management has its share of problems. The problems in a product management system are not insurmountable. There are some areas of conflicts. These are:

1. **Responsibility for Profits:** The product manager is accountable for profits. Dominguez in his book on Product Management, calls a product manager a profit manager. One of the most critical functions of the product manager is to ensure an increasing profit volume. The two problems of a product manager are:

A. Reduced gross profit volume because of rising ex-factory costs

B. Increasing media and promotion costs

The product manager has no control over both these costs, and yet he is held responsible for the profits of the products he manages! He, therefore, has to arrive at a balance between the promotion budget he can spend and the sales he can achieve with that input.

2. **Conflicts of Costs:** As far as media and promotion costs are concerned, the product manager has to accept these and find ways of spending the promotion budget most effectively. However, when there are rising ex-factory costs, there is a conflict between product management and production/ purchase management, who should be able to control costs by rationalizing production and purchasing at the most economical price.

3. **Implementation of Promotional Plans Through Field Force:** An excellent promotional plan can become ineffective if the implementation is improper. The product manager is responsible for the plan but, he has to get it implemented through the field force, which is not directly under his control. He, therefore, has to sell the plan to the field force and motivate and persuade them to implement the program correctly and effectively.

4. **Conflicts with Distribution:** This conflict arises when the distribution is centralized in a company handling different product lines like cosmetics and pharmaceuticals. In this case, the cosmetic range would require a wider distribution than pharmaceuticals. If for some reason, the field force does not get along with the product manager, all his promotional plans, they tend to ignore. Thus the desired results are not achieved.

Let us take a specific example. A product manager planned to launch a new anti-acne cream in the top 30 towns in the first year and worked out promotional plans and sales estimates accordingly. If the field force in their anxiety to achieve the sales targets, stock up markets outside the 30 specified towns, there would be problems of shortages initially and later on complaints that stocks have not moved from dealers' shelves in those markets where they did not plan the promotion.

Product management may have an objective of increasing new outlets. It may so happen that distribution, to save costs, may set a high minimum order value. It could lead to conflicting objectives. Problems arise where the distribution function is not under the control of the marketing or product management department. Conflict arises because the product management team is eager to sell, whereas distribution is concerned with having the lowest inventory carrying costs and waiting for the most economical transport, not realizing that the market will take stocks at the time when it wants, where it wants and on what terms it wants.

5. **Conflict Between Product Managers:** Product managers have to compete with one another for financial and staff support for their products, even for shelf space at a dealer level. Therefore, in a product management system, there could be conflicts. For example, there could be a clash of a promotional plan between a product manager, who is handling throat lozenges and another looking after a pain-relieving balm. Both would like to promote their products actively during the winter. There would be a problem of which product would receive more emphasis and which they should promote first. It is the area where the head of the marketing division or the group product manager will have to handle the situation without affecting the effectiveness of either of the product managers.

Yes, conflicts exist in product management. We, therefore, could say that a product manager is not merely a manager of products but a manager of problems and conflicts too. Perhaps, that is why product management is more challenging than most marketing tasks.

Product Management in the Indian Pharmaceutical Industry

We have discussed the product management system and its growing importance and their role, tasks, and responsibilities of a product manager.

Now let us take a look at the product management system with specific reference to the Indian pharmaceutical industry; how the product management system and pharmaceutical companies in India practice it and how product managers function, their attitudes towards their job and their aspirations.

There seems to be a wide gap between the product management system practiced in the western world and India, particularly in the pharmaceutical industry. Product managers in companies engaged in marketing consumer products and industrial products in India seem to be better off regarding responsibility and support from the top management.

A study conducted among 50 product managers and product executives in the pharmaceutical industry in India (there is virtually no difference between product managers and product executives and these designations are given differently in different companies) makes the following observations:

A. The product management system in the FMCG (fast moving consumer goods) companies was significantly different as they have been practicing product management as it was intended to. The same was not true in the case of pharmaceutical companies in India untill the 1990s.

B. Some large pharmaceutical companies in India used to home-grow their brand of product managers in the 1970s. They used to select the product managers from area sales managers and give a two or three-day orientation program internally. Some companies also followed the policy of job rotation between product managers and area sales manages every two or three years. However, of late, the trend in pharmaceutical companies, particularly the young ones, is to recruit graduates or postgraduates in pharmacy with diploma business management with one or two years' experience. This practice of hiring qualified pharmacists or biochemistry postgrads with management diplomas is increasing as the industry is introducing more and more complex products requiring thorough scientific knowledge. The changing complexity of product mix is making this change in recruitment practice a necessity.

C. In many Indian pharmaceutical companies, product managers do not have the specific responsibility for their products' sales and profits. Many companies were not used to share the cost data even with their product managers as it is considered sensitive. This practice is, however, changing slowly.

D. Product managers did not have much say in the annual marketing plans for their products in the real sense. Their participation in this area was moderate and restricted to do the basic tasks such as working out the preliminary details.

E. There was no systematic appraisal or evaluation of product managers in many companies in India. Many product managers due to lack of exposure did not seem to have the big picture.

The following case gives a broad view of the product management practices was in the late 1980s.

The Plight of a Profit Manager!

Some time ago in 1988, a special training program on product management in pharmaceutical product management was conducted in the prestigious Administrative Staff College of India (ASCI) at Hyderabad. Some of the giants of the Indian pharmaceutical industry had sponsored their product managers for the program. When it came to discussing the product policy, strategy alternatives, there was a sudden silence. Fictitious cost-data (for doing simulation exercises) was provided to the participants for analysis and presentation during a case study. Many a product manager drew a blank. It was for the first time that they were exposed to any cost data, fictitious or otherwise. This explains the plight of the profit managers in Indian pharmaceutical industry!

The study also points out to what product managers in the Indian pharmaceutical industry were doing mostly. Here are some of the more critical tasks that pharmaceutical product managers mostly do:

A. Preparing detailing stories (communication) creating the product visual aids for their products

B. Preparing sampling strategy — broad guidelines to field force on what products they need to sample, and in what quantities and to which doctors

C. Fieldwork with representatives and independently to find out the movement of their products as well as competitors' products in the marketplace and to monitor the levels of implementation of their strategies and their impact

D. Analyzing the ORG (Operations Research Group) retail store audit (PharmaTrac AWACS or IMS data now) for their products and competitors' products and presenting to the management and field force every month

E. Analyzing the internal sales of the company, product-wise, region-wise and submitting it to the head of the marketing department and respective sales managers

F. Briefing the sales force on promotional strategies at briefing sessions or cycle meetings

G. Follow-up with suppliers of gifts, and other sales promotional materials

This trend, however, seems to be changing with increasing competitive intensity and the role of pharmaceutical product management expanding gradually. Product managers are also involved in designing stalls or booths and in-the-stall activities at medical conferences and CME (Continuing Medical Education Programs). They are also involved in preparing speaker notes for key opinion leaders (KOLs) who conduct product symposia on behalf of the company the programs sponsored by the company.

Making Product Management More Effective

Effective product management is crucial to a company's success in the marketplace. How to make the product managers more effective? By giving them responsibility. By building accountability into their jobs.By giving it due importance both in words and deeds. These answers may be simple, but the implementation often is not.

Often there is a conflict between the line and staff functions. Which is more important? It is as mindless a question as which vital organ of the body is more vital? The heart? The brain? The kidneys?

When you build a well-knit team of sales managers and product managers who understand and appreciate their mutually supportive and reinforcing roles, you are in fact, and in effect building up a winning team that is formidable. You are enhancing the distinctive competence of your company. Here is a case of one company that found a somewhat unique way of nurturing and building a highly competent product management team.

Unique Brand of Brand Managers!

A medium-sized pharmaceutical company a few years ago faced with a conflicting situation wherein divisional sales managers, and product managers were up-in-arms against each other. While apparently, the relationships with each other were smooth, they were limited to common courtesies. The divisional managers felt that the product managers were having a jolly good time, having a ball for themselves without any responsibility (for sales) while they (the divisional managers) were sweating out on the field.

The product managers on the hand felt that they had been brought from the field to head office (they were field managers, that is front-line managers earlier before they became product managers) and were given a raw deal. They were not clear about their position in the organizational hierarchy and had not advanced or progressed in their careers as they envisaged. There was a growing dissatisfaction since they were also suspicious that the divisional managers were getting a better remuneration package and incentives on achieving sales targets. No divisional or field manager was willing to join the product management team.

The company realizing this, albeit belatedly, reacted positively. The company had clarified that the divisional managers and product managers were and would continue to be at the same level on the organization ladder, though their functional responsibilities were different. It had also standardized their remuneration and clearly defined the job descriptions. The attributes or qualities that the company had been looking for in product managers ever since were:

- ▸ Technical knowledge
- ▸ Communication skills — written as well as verbal
- ▸ Creativity
- ▸ Inter-personal communication skills
- ▸ Perseverance
- ▸ Enthusiasm
- ▸ Analytical ability

The company launched an ambitious program of building up a top team of product managers that would be a model to and envy of the industry. The company introduced a job rotation program between product managers and the divisional managers to communicate that the divisional managers and product managers are at the same level and are equally important. Such a job rotation program would lead to personal as well as organizational development. It would also develop a core team of product managers and divisional managers. They would have a better understanding, a better insight and a broader perspective of formulating and implementing marketing strategies. The quality of strategy formulation and implementation would significantly improve.

The result would be an elite regiment of *esprit de corps*, which is built on the bedrock of mutual respect based on each others'competence. That was the logic behind the structural changes. The company, while sticking to its promotion from within policy in all functional areas, had recruited a few product managers, who were technically qualified with excellent scholastic records to strengthen and fill the void of training its field force in product knowledge and also to remain ahead of the competition in strategy formulation. The company was planning to enter into new therapeutic categories and wanted to improve its knowledge base. Superior technical knowledge and information were essential in these new segments.

Furthermore, the company had given field sales assignments to its newly recruited product managers to gain perspective and insight into the dynamics of pharmaceutical selling and to get the much-needed hands-on experience. The company had thus planned meticulously a blend of product managers with selling skills (promoted from within) and product managers with superior technical knowledge (recruited from the universities).

In addition, the company had planned out to the minutest detail — a one-year curriculum, which included reading assignments, marketing research assignments, fieldwork assignments, weekly classroom discussions and case study presentations. After successful completion of one year's learning while earning (on the job), the product managers would be presented a Post Graduate Diploma in Pharmaceutical Product Management ceremoniously. While this is not a university or any institute-recognized certificate or degree, the perceived value of this diploma would certainly not be inferior to those in any manner. The company had really planned an effective way of developing its own successful brand of brand managers and above all to retain them, which is even more difficult!

Managing New Products

Standing Still Is Going Backwards!

In today's business world, where competition is at its fiercest, standing still is tantamount to going backward. A company that only wants to defend its existing markets with its current products and not venture into new markets or update its product mix with more modern and better products is not planning for the future. It will undoubtedly cost the company very dearly in the long run. Business history is replete with such examples. There are many reasons for this. One is product obsolescence.

A company must plan for new products even to defend the market share of its existing products in its current markets. Otherwise, it will be caught in the whirlpool of product obsolescence. It must offer replacements for products that are on their way to obsolescence. If not, the products, which ones ruled the market may become extinct like dinosaurs.

No corporate function, probably has a more significant impact on the successful long-term growth of a company than new product development. David J. Luck in his book *Product Policy and Strategy* said a *product mix could remain competitively viable only when you can replenish it with modern new products and strengthen with improvements in current products.*

Developing and managing new products, of course, is a costly and risky business. Costly because of the enormous investments required in R & D for the development of new products. Risky because of the high degree of uncertainty and high rate of failure of new products. The high rate of failure further makes new product development even more expensive. General statistics for over fifty years in the US have shown that four out of five new products fail. While such statistics are not available in India, it is reasonable to presume that the failure rate is even higher, since research and development are still in a stage of infancy in India. All this puts a higher premium on planning, developing and managing new products. Whether it is a breakthrough product, an improvement of the existing product, or even a cosmetic change of an old product, it requires innovative thinking and application.

Innovation naturally implies risk. If you are unwilling to experiment and take risks, then you cannot innovate. If you decide not to take risks, you are in fact taking the biggest risk of all — the risk of doing nothing. It is not enough to do what our predecessors did even if what they did was excellent. Managers need to generate new ideas and better ways of doing things for future growth.

Success with new products requires a very disciplined approach. Innovation is neither a mystical nor mysterious process. It is a functional skill that can be taught, learned, assimilated and practiced.

Managing new products effectively and successfully involves a disciplined approach. It requires skillful, creative planning, innovation, and hard work. You cannot achieve Innovation by mere inspiration. Thomas Alva Edison, the greatest inventor, known to mankind, once said *innovation is one percent inspiration and ninety-nine percent perspiration.*

Whether you agree with this composition of the formula or not, you will have to agree with this axiom. Companies that pursue success in the ever-changing marketplace must promote and encourage an innovative culture, and institute a systematic new product planning and development process. Otherwise, success will elude them. The writing on the wall is loud and clear. Innovate or Perish!

The Costliness of New Product Development Process

The internationally known management consulting firm, Booz Allen & Hamilton Inc. conducted a study of 51 companies with excellent track records in new product development. It found that an average of 58 new product ideas was required to produce one successful new product.

Further analysis of their study revealed that out of every fifty-eight ideas, about twelve passed the initial screening test, which showed them to be compatible with company objectives and resources. Only about seven of these twelve remained after a thorough evaluation of their profit potential. Out of these seven too, only about three survived the product development stage, two the test marketing stage and only one was commercially viable. Thus about fifty-eight new ideas must be generated to find a good one that is commercially viable. What is more, you have to price this one successful idea at a level profitable enough to cover all the money lost by the company in researching the fifty-seven other ideas that failed.

Types of Risks

The product planner needs to judge the degree and likelihood of possible losses that would result from many risks that a new product faces. David J. Luck categorized them broadly into four types:

1. Technical failure is the risk that no viable product may emerge even after lengthy and expensive development risk.
2. Product failure may be due to the various faults and snags that may develop in a product after it presumably has been perfected and placed in use.
3. Demand failure occurs when the expected demand for a product proves to be non-existent or when the actual demand fades.
4. Competition is an omnipresent product risk unless firmly protected with patents. The pharmaceutical industry in India has become so fiercely competitive because it did not recognize international patents and intellectual property rights (IPR) for products until 2005.

That is why some of the large trans-national companies were hesitant and apprehensive to introduce their research products in India. Now that India recognizes the product patents they are gradually introducing their major research products in India too.

Why Develop New Products?

If new product development is such a costly process and a risky undertaking why develop new products?

Products need to be resurrected, rejuvenated, and replaced. It is vital to ensure a steady flow and growth of profits into company both in the short-term and the long-term. By studying the life cycle of new products, one can conclude that sooner or later every product is preempted by another, or else it may degenerate into a profitless price war.

When a company does not update or modernize its product-mix, sales growth is not only difficult to achieve but also becomes an expensive affair. The competition intensifies its attack with new products. The company's selling and distribution costs keep on increasing. The profits stop growing along with sales, reach a plateau, and start declining. It is because the company to maintain the sales volume in the face of stiff competition with newer and better products is forced to offer profit-less price cuts, discounts, trade offers. Discounts and price cuts can never be a substitute for newer improved products with better profitability. Furthermore, there will be little or no impact of such price cuts on sales after a particular point.

Another important reason is that since business success tends to be governed not only by what you do but also by what others do, you have to stay ahead of the competition in your planning and execution of business strategy. You can do this by differentiating your products and introducing new products with better margins. Profits generally can be sustained in the long run only by a continuing flow of successful new products.

The Impact of New Products on Profits

New products can have a profound impact on the entire firm. They can change the fortunes of the companies. Here are two cases illustrating and amplifying the kind of impact new products can have on a firm, its sales, and profit volumes.

CASE

44

Tagamet Pushes SmithKline into the Forefront!

The SmithKline Corporation is a pharmaceutical company headquartered in Philadelphia, Pennsylvania. In 1976, SmithKline introduced a new product in the United Kingdom followed by its introduction in the US a year later. The new product was Tagamet, an anti-ulcer drug. Tagamet was being sold in over one-hundred countries around the world at that time. It was one the most remarkable successes of the 1970s.

By 1979, SmithKline's revenues reached the US $1.35 billion, a gain of 125 percent over 1975, the year before it introduced Tagamet. Profits during the same period shot up by a staggering 266 percent. Tagamet accounted for more than a third of the entire company's sales about half of its profits in 1979. By 1980, Tagamet's worldwide sales were over US$ 649 million. It was more than the entire company's total sales before Tagamet.

Tagamet surely pushed SmithKline (GSK now) into the forefront of the international pharmaceutical industry.

Zantac Wins the Anti-ulcer Race!

Glaxo (GSK now), the British pharmaceutical giant subsequently introduced Zantac, also an anti-ulcer drug in the United Kingdom. Following its success there, Glaxo introduced Zantac in the US and many other countries. Zantac had become the first-ever prescription drug in the world to cross the coveted US$ 1-billion mark, a landmark that eluded its predecessor, Tagamet. Not only that, by 1989, Zantac pushed Glaxo into the prestigious fourth position on the world pharmaceutical league table. Zantac continued to defend its prestigious position as the number one prescribed drug brand in the world with a sales turnover of US$ 1.7 billion. Glaxo's fortunes have indeed changed with the introduction of Zantac.

Closer home, the success of Burroughs Wellcome's Septran is all too familiar to us. Septran had catapulted Burroughs Wellcome from under the twenty-fifth position into the top ten of the pharmaceutical league table in India. Septran continued to be the most extensively prescribed drug in India even in 1990. Such is the success that winning new products can bring to a company.

Companies that have been growing faster than their competitors in the Indian pharmaceutical industry are the ones that have been pursuing new product development and launch strategies very aggressively. There seems to be no exception to this rule. Another validating factor for this no-exception rule is the fact that all those companies that have been sliding down in terms of rank and market share in the industry are the ones that have insignificant new product development and planning activity. New product planning and development seems to be the common denominator between winners and the also ran. Consider these cases.

Cadila's Climb!

Started sixty-seven years ago in 1951 at Ahmedabad, Cadila Laboratories had made very rapid strides and reached the coveted fourth position in the Indian pharmaceutical industry in 1986. Cadila's progress was indeed spectacular.

Cadila, in 1976 was ranked 37th in the industry with a sales volume of Rs 3.87 crore. Ten years later in 1986, Cadila had catapulted itself into the fourth position. How did Cadila achieve this? By careful, systematic new product planning, market expansion plans and timely execution and implementation of those plans.

Cadila had expanded into newer markets by increasing its market coverage substantially during this period. From around 140 representatives in 1976, Cadila had increased the customer coverage markedly by adding more than two-hundred and fifty medical representatives thus bringing the field force strength close to 400 by 1986.

At the same time, Cadila had pursued a very aggressive new product planning and development strategy. Cadila had diversified into fast-growing product groups. In 1976, the size of Cadila's directly competing market was around Rs. 164-crore, a mere 39 percent of the industry's total sales. By 1986, Cadila had improved its therapeutic coverage up to 90 percent of the entire pharmaceutical market in India by launching new products in all the critical therapeutic segments. As a result, the company had registered a staggering growth of 705 percent in increasing the size of its competing market.

Cadila's market share too had grown from a meager 0.9 percent in 1976 to a very respectable 3.1 percent by 1986.

Cadila had introduced as many as 19 new products in the fastest growing therapeutic groups like systemic antibiotics, psychotropic drugs, non-steroidal anti-inflammatory drugs, and anti-peptic ulcer drugs between 1978 and 1986. These 19 new products had contributed to about 60 percent of the increased sales volume of Rs. 42.15-crore.

Not content with the dramatic progress achieved so far, Cadila embarked on a new game plan. It was relatively easy for Cadila to diversify into new product groups and new market all these years because:

Earlier (1976) the size of its directly competing market was only 39 percent of the total industry's sales. By 1986 Cadila had expanded its directly competing market to 90 percent of the overall industry's sales.

The company's base was also very meager with 0.9 percent share of the total market in 1976, which had grown to a sizable 3.1 percent by 1986.

Cadila, realizing that it could be tough to maintain the same pace of progress from its current position (rank 4, Market share 3.1 percent in 1986), had appropriately changed its game plan to move further up in the Indian pharmaceutical market faster than the competition.

Cadila continued its aggressive stance in introducing new products. To facilitate a stronger and faster new product introduction program, Cadila started a second trading face - Alidac. The dramatic success achieved by Glaxo in managing multiple trading faces effectively to promote a wide range of products probably had inspired Cadila to start Alidac.

After 1987, Cadila had introduced many new products through its two trading faces, i.e., Cadila and Alidac. Cadila had added many new products in the rapidly growing therapeutic segments such as cardiovascular (Envas, Linvas, Diltime), quinolones (Negafloz, Ciprobid, Ciprodac), anti-pepticulcerants (Famonit, Aciloc), antihistamines (Stemiz, Zoter) and protein supplements (GRD) among others. All these new products introduced after 1987 by Cadila had accounted for about 50 percent of the company's overall growth between 1987 and 1991.

One can thus conclude that it was the new product planning, development and their effective implementation of the plans were responsible for the phenomenal growth (from a 37th position to a prestigious 3rd place) that Cadila achieved between 1976 and 1991.

Later in 1995, Cadila had divided itself into two different companies - Cadila Pharmaceuticals and Cadila Healthcare (later re-christened as Zydus Cadila Healthcare).

Ranbaxy's Runaway Progress!

Ranbaxy, established in 1961, has been showing a very impressive and enviable growth rate. Ranked only 30th in 1976, Ranbaxy leaped into the big league by reaching the sixth position in the Indian pharmaceutical industry by 1986.

Ranbaxy, during this period of accelerated growth, meticulously followed a three-pronged strategy. Firstly, it expanded into newer markets and increased its customer coverage substantially in the domestic market. Secondly, it diversified into new product groups and launched as many as 23 new products between 1976 and 1986. Thirdly, Ranbaxy went international by setting up joint venture projects in countries like Nigeria, Thailand, Malaysia, and marketing operations in many other countries. Ranbaxy increased its group turnover from around Rs. 6-crore in 1976 to Rs. 96-crore by 1986. The pharmaceutical division of Ranbaxy alone increased its turnover from Rs. 4.9-crore to Rs. 38.9-crore during this period.

A closer look at the product-mix of Ranbaxy would reveal that it expanded in the fastest growing therapeutic groups like systemic anti-bacterials (Roscillin, Sporidex, Gramoneg) anti-tubercular (Tibrim, Tibrim-INH), non-narcotic analgesics (Fortwin), tranquilizers (Calmpose) during the first phase of its acceleration. Ranbaxy introduced about 23 new products between 1978 and 1986, which contributed to over 60 percent of the increase in the sales volume of Ranbaxy's pharmaceutical division.

In the five years that followed, Ranbaxy changed its focus from the therapeutic groups like tuberculostatic drugs that were price-controlled to rapidly growing decontrolled product groups like anti-pepticulcerants (Histac), quinolones (Norbactin, Cifran), rejuvenators (Revital), antihistamines (Trexyl). It had further consolidated its leadership position in the most significant therapeutic segment of the Indian pharmaceutical market, I.e., antibacterials with another new-generation cephalosporin drug (Keflor).

All these winning moves earned the coveted second place for Ranbaxy in the industry. Ranbaxy also started a second marketing division - Stancare in the late 1980s. Stancare, in the late 1980s, introduced many successful brands like Gramogyl in the intestinal anti-infective segment, Zanocin in quinolone segment. It further reinforced Ranbaxy's position at the top, bridging the gap between Ranbaxy and Glaxo, the industry leader.

One of the key factors of Ranbaxy's rapid growth from a 30th position in the industry to the top two (group turnover Rs. 333-crore in 1991-92) in just fifteen years, was a systematic approach towards new product planning and implementation exploiting opportunities all the way!

Lupin's Leap-frogging!

Started in 1968, Lupin was able to reach only an obscure 98th position in the Indian pharmaceutical industry by 1976, with a mere Rs. 2-million in sales. In the ten years that followed, Lupin chose the rapidly growing anti-tubercular segment as a vehicle for its rapid growth. The company introduced many new anti-TB drugs between 1976 and 1986. Lupin introduced its brands of all the new molecules that dramatically changed the approach towards anti-tubercular therapy like ethambutol (Combutal), pyrazinamide (Pyzina), rifampicin (R-cin) and rifampicin combinations (R-cinex). Lupin also started manufacturing these bulk drugs.

Lupin very aggressively promoted all its anti-TB brands with the sole objective of achieving the leadership position in that segment. The company achieved a formidable leadership position with a dominant 35 percent share of the total anti-tubercular market in India by 1986. The anti-tubercular range of Lupin accounted for almost one-half (49 percent) of the company's total sales in 1986-87.

Lupin thus moved from a token presence (98th rank) in 1976 to a very prominent 20th position in the Indian pharmaceutical league table by 1986-87.

Lupin continued to accelerate its growth with the objective of reaching the top of the league. In five years, I.e., by 1991-92, the company had moved to the coveted ninth position. During this process of acceleration, Lupin further consolidated its already formidable position (1986-87) with 8.4 percent of the total anti-tubercular market to an Un-impregnable position with virtually one-half of the market tucked under its belt (50.5 percent in 1991-92).

Having leapfrogged during the past fifteen years to secure a place among the top ten of the Indian pharmaceutical industry, what is Lupin up to now? Lupin seems to move further up at a faster pace. Its objective of crossing Rs. 1,000-crore mark is now common knowledge. Lupin had set up a joint venture at Thailand, stepped up its effort on the export front and integrated backward to manufacture its major product — rifampicin, right from the basic fermentation stage.

All these plans notwithstanding, Lupin's heavy concentration in the anti-tubercular segment is also indicative of its vulnerability. Its anti-TB range accounted for 60 percent of the company's formulation sales in India, and these drugs are price controlled. Even during the last five years, it is the anti-TB range that had contributed significantly to the overall growth of the company (over 40 percent). Other new products introduced by the company contributed to around 20 percent. Having realized this, Lupin had become active in the rapidly growing cephalosporin segment (Ceff, Odxyl, Cezolin) and also planned an ambitious new product development program in the anti-viral segment as well. Lupin, though belatedly made an entry into the fastest growing segment — quinolones with its Ciprova. This move propelled Lupin once again from its 9th position into the top 5 in Indian pharmaceutical industry by 1995.

Torrent - True to its Name!

Torrent Pharma seems to be living up to its name. There had been an abundant stream of new products ever since Torrent Pharma appeared on the Indian pharmaceutical industry in 1959.

In 1976, Torrent was not having national operations and was not listed in the ORG retails store audit's 165 companies. However, by 1986, Torrent stormed its way into the top fifty companies in the Indian pharmaceutical industry. Torrent was ranked 50th with a sales volume of Rs. 10.8-crore in 1986.

Torrent seems to be following the firstest with the mostest policy regarding new product planning. Torrent was the first company to introduce new products in many therapeutic categories.

Between 1980 and 1986, Torrent chose the psychotropic drugs segment as the principal avenue for growth, subsequently achieving and maintaining the leadership position in the segment till 1992.

New products introduced after 1980 accounted for 84 percent of the sales volume of Torrent in 1986. Torrent introduced new products in three of the fastest growing therapeutic segments, namely, psychotropic, cardiovascular and anti-pepticulcerants.

Torrent identified the rapidly growing anti-pepticulcerants and cardiovascular segments to accelerate growth and consolidate its position in the late 1980s and the early 1990s. True to its tradition of being the first to introduce new drugs in the segments of its choice, Torrent introduced the first brands of different molecules like ranitidine

(Ranitin), famotidine (Topcid), and omeprazole (Omizac) among anti-pepticulcerants. This move of entering all conceivable sub-segments secured a third place for Torrent with an 11.3 percent share in this crowded and fast-growing anti-pepticulcerants segment that was Rs.80-crore large (1992).

In the cardiovascular segment, Torrent introduced Dilzem, the first brand of diltiazem in India. With this, Torrent was firmly in the saddle riding the cardiovascular market that is Rs 137.6-crore large, with an unassailable share of 13 percent in 1992.

Even in the relatively smaller antihistamine segment, Torrent was among the first two companies to introduce two new molecules namely astemizole (Astelong), and terfenadine (Tefril). Torrent's steady stream of new products was responsible for its extraordinary success. New products introduced between 1980 and 1986 contributed about 80 percent to the growth of the company during that period.

The secret of Torrent's success can be attributed to its very aggressive new product planning and management. In just about twelve years, the company really galloped into the 13th position in the Indian pharmaceutical industry virtually out of nowhere.

A Program for New Product Evolution

Before birth, a new product goes through a gestation or prenatal process that may be short or long depending upon the complexity and the degree of newness, that virtually shapes the nature and survival of a product. These evolutionary phases, christened initially by the well-known consultancy firm, Booz Allen and Hamilton have become a standard. These are:

A. **Exploration:** The search for a new product idea to meet the company objectives and goals.

B. **Screening:** A quick analysis essentially to determine which ideas are relevant and practical, requiring a detailed investigation.

C. **Business Analysis:** The expression of current ideas through a detailed analysis of concrete business recommendations including product features, action programs, and financial implications.

D. **Development:** Turning the idea-on-paper into a product-in-hand that can be demonstrated.

E. **Testing:** Designing and conducting the commercial experiment to verify the first business judgments.

F. **Commercialization:** Launching the product in the market.

No rigid rules are governing this six-stage new product development process. Different practitioners may call these stages by different names. These stages may either be coupled or sub-divided depending upon the company's needs, goals and policies.

Basic Principles

Admittedly, there is no magic formula for new product success. If you study the success stories and failures of companies with their new products and analyze them carefully, you will find that there is a common thread running through them all. Some basic principles emerge. These basic principles are:

A. You need effective market research to understand and track changing customer needs. Market research helps you in identifying the new product opportunities on which you can capitalize. You minimize the chances of success if you fail to do adequate market research. Market research does not necessarily mean all the sophisticated and latest techniques and multivariate analyses. What you need from market research at this stage is to know what new growth opportunities it has uncovered here and now.

B. The second logical step, of course, involves innovation. How can you innovatively develop a new product to meet the needs of customers that your market research has helped uncover? New products must have a clear, significant, perceptible difference — a valid reason for being — that is related to a need in the marketplace. Yes. Differentiation, noticeable differentiation is the name of the game.

C. The formulation and implementation of the most aggressive marketing strategy is the crucial third step, without which, even the most effective market research and product development efforts will be severely undercut.

D. To execute this effectively, you need the total support and commitment of the top management.

New Product Development Process

While there is no formula for success in developing new products, a systematic approach towards new product planning and execution will certainly help minimize the failure rate. Here is the step-by-step approach towards planning and implementing new product development in the Indian pharmaceutical market. The suggested steps are:

1. Develop a new product blueprint and strategy.
2. Analyze and rank potentially attractive therapeutic categories.
3. Generate ideas and develop concepts within the selected therapeutic categories.

4. Screen concepts and set priorities.

5. Conduct business analysis of selected concepts.

6. Work with R & D closely and help them develop the product as per the selected concepts and identified market needs.

7. Develop a launch plan and commercialize the new product.

8. Prepare a detailed marketing and communication strategy and tactical plans for the launch year.

9. Monitor the performance regularly as per the plan.

1. **Developing a New Product Blueprint:** Your blueprint for new product development should clearly define the direction and role of new products as related to the company's overall objectives of growth and strategy. For example, you should spell out the role that new products have to play in the achievement of the growth objectives of the company. Do they have a modest growth role, high growth role or only a survival role? What type of new products should the company develop in the future?

It depends in no small extent on the role you envisage for the new products. If you envision a survival role, you will only be preparing a me-too new product plan. Your approach to new product development is merely reactive. On the other hand, if you assign a high growth role, your posture towards new product development is proactive and an aggressive one at that. You will be directing your energies towards developing genuinely innovative, even new-to-the-world type of products. In the Indian pharmaceutical industry, it is tough to think of the new-to-the-world kind of new products, as the development costs are genuinely prohibitive. You can, however, plan to be the first in introducing a genuinely unique product developed abroad. No matter what roles you assign to the new products and what objectives you set for them, your blueprint for new products should include:

A. A description of the role that new products will play in the overall growth plan of the company.

B. Budget estimates that indicate all developmental expenditure and capital investment for the new product effort.

C. Product-wise sales and profit volume objectives for the five-year period, for all new products.

D. Guidelines and benchmarks for successful new product performance.

2. **Analyzing and Ranking Potentially Attractive Categories:** What product categories should you defend (in your existing markets) and what new categories should you enter by introducing new products? The answer to this question depends to some extent on the growth roles you assign to your new products. Your new product blueprint would have prescribed some guidelines. Also, you have to determine the therapeutic or product categories you want to enter based on their attractiveness regarding:

A. Size of the potential market

B. The growth rate of the potential market

C. Extent of competition

D. Compatibility with your existing product lines regarding manufacturing facilities and marketing capabilities like customer coverage, distribution channels.

E. Degree of newness

F. Profitability

It is vital that you defend your share of your existing markets with existing products as well as update your product mix by preempting competition and planning in advance for product obsolescence that is inevitable in any case. If you want to stay ahead of the game, the introduction of new, improved products in your existing markets (therapeutic categories) is a must.

For determining the attractiveness of the therapeutic categories identified, and ranking them in order of their importance or attractiveness, you can give specific weights to each of the six attributes discussed earlier and develop evaluative criteria. The items or attributes to use, the scoring system, the weights and other details of this screening process are unique to each company. There are just no rules for how to do it and that is how it should be.

There is, however, one point to remember. Use items where you can decide on low-cost, quickly available information. If you try to focus your attention on the details, on the point of precision at this stage, that will only diffuse your resources instead of concentrating them. Moreover, accuracy in new development is more often an illusion.

The purpose of doing an attractive category analysis is to determine the priorities regarding category selection in an objective manner. In pharmaceutical marketing, defending your market share and leadership position in a given therapeutic category involves some degree of cannibalization. Product obsolescence is a matter of fact and way of life in the pharmaceutical market. When some other company introduces a new, more effective and superior therapeutic agent, it is bound to affect your product position. It is, therefore, better to plan for product obsolescence yourself, at least in therapeutic categories where you enjoy a dominant position. Like Ranbaxy did it in the urological market and indeed even in the antibiotics market as such. That is what the industry leader Glaxo had done in the corticosteroid market even in the 1990s. Glaxo introduced the latest topical steroid combinations with an anti-bacterial and anti-fungal under their new *Eumosone* brand, thus making their position even more formidable in the topical corticosteroid market with over half of the market under their belt. The moral, therefore, is that if cannibalization despite imaginative positioning is inevitable, it is better if your new product does it rather than your competitors'.

3. **Generate Ideas and Develop Concepts within Categories Selected:** Idea generation is a significant first step. How many ideas should you generate? One way to answer this difficult question is to ask another question. How many new products do you want to market each year? If you're going to introduce one major new product each year, then on an average you

should plan to generate about 50 to 60 ideas each year. Remember the general statistics indicating the new product success rate in the US show that only one in 58 new product ideas is commercially successful.

What is even more important is that you should track and monitor the changing customer needs in the marketplace. What new needs you can fulfill in the market? What new sub-therapeutic groups or categories are emerging? What changes are taking place in the line of treatment of certain major ailments? What novel and more potent drugs are currently under development abroad? You should be alert in monitoring these changes in the therapeutic categories where you are actively involved. Your priority in idea generation too should take this into cognizance.

4. **Concept Development:** Once you generate some ideas and initially screen them, the next step is to develop a concept statement for each of the selected ideas. A concept statement is a statement of the problem that the product is supposed to solve, and a brief description of the need that you think exists. It also should define briefly the characteristics or attributes of the new product that makes the solution possible.

    You must keep the language simple and direct while writing down a product concept. Do not be vague. Don't make statements that are judgmental such as, that it will be better, superior. Be precise and clear.

    A clear, precise concept statement can ensure the success of your new product. It makes the task of product development and the preparation of communication strategy more meaningful.

5. **Screen Concepts and set Priorities:** Once you define the product concepts, screen them carefully and set the priorities after evaluating them. Here are a few questions you should answer when you are evaluating the new product concepts.

    A. Are they likely to enhance the company's present position in the marketplace?

B. Can your sales force handle these new products successfully? Is there a need to train them mainly for the new products?

C. What about distribution? Are the existing channels adequate?

6. **Business Analysis:** The next step is to conduct the business analysis of selected product concepts. The primary factors to be considered during a business analysis are:

A. *Sales Volume Potential*: Before making any estimates of expected sales, it is important to size up the opportunity. What is the size of the total market? What is the extent of competition, both direct and indirect? The indirect competition includes all the products you can use as substitutes for the same condition or indication. Adding up the sales volumes of all competitive products, you can arrive at the size of the total market. You should also find out the growth trends of the market. What share of the market could your product-entry reasonably expect to capture during the first year and second year? Answers to these questions will be helpful in shaping up your product strategy and plans.

B. *Profit Potential*: The fundamental questions to answer in evaluating or assessing the profit potential of your product are:

▸ What will be the product's gross margins? How are they comparable to your existing products? To competitive products in the same category?

▸ What levels of marketing expenditures do you need to achieve the projected sales volumes in the first year and second year?

▸ What is the breakeven point? By what time are you likely to achieve the breakeven point as per the projected sales volumes?

▸ Are the raw materials and packaging materials freely available and their costs stable? Are there any shortage forecasts for these that might lead to cost escalation?

▶ Do the returns on investment projections for the product under consideration offer the best alternative use of capital?

▶ Considering that the price of the product is at par with the competition and since the trade margins are virtually the same for all competitors in a given product category (the retail margins are fixed by the DPCO 1987), will the product generate a gross margin equal to or more than for current products?

▶ What is the projected pay-back period or breakeven point in capital investment?

▶ Introductory marketing investment in terms of months after the product introduction date?

C. *Product Line Compatibility*: If the proposed new products are compatible with the existing product lines of your company, then the risk and costliness of developing them are minimal. You can measure the degree of compatibility can in two broad functional areas, namely marketing and production. The important aspects to consider from the marketing point of view are:

A. The degree of competitiveness of the proposed new products with the existing products is essential as it indicates the likely extent of cannibalization among your products. You can plan to minimize or avoid this if you are aware of it. If cannibalization of your brands is inevitable then you can still decide to introduce the new products, provided your company can achieve a better position in the category than before or balance the likely loss of sales and the possible gain of new product sales.

B. Whether your existing distribution channels are adequate for marketing your product profitably? Are additional distribution channels needed? Are they cost-effective?

C. Whether the proposed new products can be handled by your existing sales force effectively? Do they require new skills and knowledge? What are their new product training needs?

D. Whether the target customers for the proposed new products are currently on your company's visiting list? If not, should you include them after proper prospecting? Can they be reached effectively without affecting the coverage of existing customers? Alternatively, is there any possibility of rationalizing the existing customer list? For example, if you are planning to launch some cardiovascular drugs for the first time and if your company is not covering cardiologists currently, you will have to include them in your visiting list of customers naturally. Whether you can cover these new doctors effectively with your existing sales force or you have to add more medical representatives to your sales force is what you have to decide.

E. *From the production point of view you have to consider:*

▸ Whether you can manufacture the proposed new product in your existing manufacturing facilities.

▸ If not, what is the level of capital investment needed to create the facilities and to acquire the new equipment required?

F. *Competitive strength evaluation:* The extent of competitive intensity in the category or market you are planning to enter with your proposed new products is also a significant factor to be considered. The fundamental questions to be answered while evaluating the competitive strength are:

▸ The intensity of competition in the market, whether it is highly fragmented or dominated by a few competitors.

▸ The production facilities and capabilities of your major competitors.

▸ The marketing strength of the major competitors, their coverage, distribution network, sales force capabilities.

▸ The relative strengths and weaknesses of the products of your major competitors.

▸ The levels and expenditure of the promotional efforts of your major competitors.

▶ You can give a rating to the financial evaluation, product line compatibility, competitive intensity, and other aspects of business analysis to determine the relative attractiveness on a ten-point scale, as you have done earlier to rank the categories in order of their importance.

7. **Product Performance, Customer Acceptance, and Market Tests:** Working closely with R & D and production in translating the selected concept into a usable product and testing its performance in the marketplace is the next step. Test marketing is not a common practice in the Indian pharmaceutical industry. As regards to product acceptance tests by customers, the company launching a product for the first time in the country conducts only the mandatory clinical trials for registering the drug. Some companies as a part of their promotional strategy, organize focal clinical trials with many doctors. However, if you have a genuinely new concept, it is worthwhile to conduct multi-center clinical trials as well as the focal clinical trials with all the key opinion leaders.

8. **Product Development and Preliminary Marketing Plans:** Now that you have decided that your product idea is viable, it is time to look into all other aspects of products' development and preliminary marketing plans. Here is a checklist:

▶ Write down the raw material specifications

▶ Develop the production specifications

▶ Determine the shipper sizes

▶ Select the brand name. Since getting the brand name registered takes a minimum of two to three years in India, it is better to have many brand names registered beforehand in the categories you would like to enter. Whenever you are ready with a new product, you can select a brand name from your already registered list.

▶ Develop the packaging including specifications of packaging materials. Check whether you labeling is following the drug laws.

▶ Decide on the price.

▶ Fulfill all the licensing and other legal requirements. For example, you need a test license for development purpose.

Drug license for manufacturing and DGTD registration for commercializing the product are required. Price approval is necessary before you market the product.

9. **Marketing Strategy and Tactics:** Prepare a detailed tactical plan for marketing the new product. The plan should cover all the details for the launch year and include the core concept. You should also write the broad guidelines for follow-up promotion in the second and third years. It is necessary to maintain continuity and consistency for building the brand image. Here is a checklist:

1. Develop the advertising strategy
2. Develop the sales training program
3. Develop the sales and promotional material including product monographs, literature, leave-behind leaflets, brochures, detail-aids and so on.
4. Fix the sales targets territory-wise
5. Develop the feedback systems
6. Select the key customers depending upon your segmentation strategy
7. Anticipate competitive reaction
8. Chalk out a detailed tactical plan for launching the product

This list is by no means exhaustive. You may add some more details, which you consider appropriate and vital. Many of the items on this list are very close to your everyday business activities. Commercializing a product concept means translating the idea into everyday business reality and activity. These items are significant, if not crucial. If you do not give due importance and attention, they can become critical. If you allow them to be critical, you will put your new product project in jeopardy.

Speed by All Means but not Rush

There will be much pressure to get your new products to market as quickly as possible. Top management wants to recover investment as fast as possible. The project team intends to complete the project at least on schedule, if not ahead because time is indeed money. Speed, therefore, is vital. A new product project should move at a brisk pace. At the same time, one should not rush things. All these pressures should not lead you to introduce a product to the market before it is ready. Until it is one hundred percent marketable. Do not even be tempted to say or listen to the danger words — we will take care of that later.

10. **Monitor Your Performance Regularly:** Elementary and fundamental as it may seem, monitoring the performance of new products on a regular basis is an almost forgotten step in many companies. Once the product is commercialized, probably the newness and the consequent or in-built excitement are gone. The common temptation is to revise the forecasts for new products for six months or even longer instead of analyzing and finding out reasons. Monitoring the performance of new products regularly against the original plan forecasts can provide significant insights and help you leverage the development of successful new products.

Evaluating New Products

What makes some companies more successful in new product planning, development, and management than others? What is that quality that separates the professionals from the amateurs? Well, the answer is the experience. By experience, we mean here the learning experience. The experience of learning from past mistakes and the ability to build upon previous successes is beneficial. Learning from past performance requires capitalizing on the things that were done right and correcting the things that were wrong. Tracking, monitoring and evaluating the new product performance of both past and present new products (past new products being the ones that you introduced less than five years ago). You can set a shorter time limit for reviewing the new product performance, provided your rate of new product introduction is higher. There are no rigid rules. However, it is advisable to determine the phase of the life cycle of the product group before you set any time limit.

A new product diagnostic audit is a very beneficial tool that can be used to pick up the blueprint to guide the future. Here is what it can do for your new product development program:

▸ Quantifies the past new product performance regarding revenue generated and profit earned.

▸ Identifies the reasons and underlying causes for each new product success and failure.

▸ Compares actual performance to original product forecasts.

▸ Helps identify the company's strengths and weaknesses.

▸ Helps in estimating the developmental costs and launch costs with a reasonable degree of accuracy.

▸ Helps in improving the success rate of new products.

There are five significant steps in evaluating new product performance. These are:

1. Review the new product performance regarding sales volumes and profits for the preceding five years.

2. Assess the new product performance against the original objective.

3. Check new product survival rate.

4. Identify the causes behind the new product's success or failure.

5. Identify the strengths of top new products' competitors.

New Product Performance Review

1. **The fundamental questions to ask during a new product performance sales and profit volume review are:** How much money was generated by each of your new products during the past five years? List all new products introduced by you year-wise during the past five years and the revenues generated by them each year and cumulatively.

   ▸ How much profit volume was generated by each of these new products each year and cumulatively?

   ▸ What were the developmental costs and the marketing expenditure for these new products each year and cumulatively?

- What were the net profits (before tax) earned by these new products each year and cumulatively?
- What were the payback periods for each of these new products?

2. **New Product Performance Vs. Original Objectives:** Is there a performance gap? The next step of the new product diagnostic audit is to assess the new product performance against the original plan objectives.

3. **What is Your New Product Survival Rate?**

How many new products did you introduce during the past five years? How many of them are moving out the chemists' shelves today actively? How many of them are gathering dust on the retail counters currently? How many of them are non-existent, whether in the marketplace or the doctor's mind? How many of them do you actively promote even today? What is the survival rate of your new products?

4. **Secrets and Reasons:** While the hard data arranged in the formats suggested for the purpose of conducting the new product diagnostic audit, an in-depth analysis based on these facts is likely to unfold precious information. The secrets of your new product success and the reasons behind the failure of other new products are hiding behind these facts. An open mind, a questioning attitude and analytical ability are what you need to uncover these facts. The many lessons that one can learn from such an analysis will be of immense help in planning and implementing a winning new product program. To identify the reasons behind the successes and failures, you have to examine:

- The assumptions made in the business analysis; how did your information and interpretation differ from your observations in the market?
- Data and analysis behind the original forecasts and the variance between planned objectives and actual performance.

▸ Whether any external factors influenced your performance — like competitive responses, distribution, and consumer-demand shifts.

▸ Whether any internal factors affected your performance such as insufficient research, inadequate funds, top management commitment, inadequate facilities and so on.

▸ The quality of the implementation of the launch plans.

5. **Analyze Your Major Competitors:** How are your major competitors faring in their new products? What is their success rate? What is the survival rate of their new products? As the first step to this analysis, you have to identify the top two or three competitors, for each of your new products. You may find that one or two competitors, who pursue a very aggressive and dynamic new product program, turn up more than once as familiar competitors for several new products. Prepare a list of competitors for each new product launched and the type of new products developed by each competitor during the same period. Collect as much data as you can on their sales volume, growth rate, market share, advertising to sales ratio, cost of manufacturing, from published sources and the feedback reports of your own sales force.

Compare the performance of your major competitors with your performance in each new product category. Ensure that you evaluate the reasons behind the varying degrees of success. The significant advantage of identifying and analyzing a competitor's new products activity is that you are sure to gain insight on how they might respond to new products that you launch in their served markets.

Organizing for Success

The most critical part of a successful new product development strategy is people. There is no doubt about that. All the models, analyses, and methods are of no value if the wrong people or worse by the right people in the wrong organization use them. Assigning the right people and ensuring the right organizational structure for them to function effectively is, therefore crucial for the success of any new product development program. That is the critical responsibility of the top management. What is the right organization structure for new product development? Where should the responsibility lie? Should it be with the R & D department since it is the scientists, technicians, and engineers, who finally assess the feasibility and develop the physical product? While this seems and sounds logical, there are a few drawbacks.

One is that a majority of new product failures are not technical failures, they are market failures. Since R & D personnel are not likely to be close to the market, they may end up a developing a product that has no market. The second drawback is that since R & D people are likely to think far ahead into the distant future, there is a possibility that they will focus on products that are just far ahead of their time and not on those, which can earn profits immediately.

Is the marketing department a logical choice for shouldering the new product development responsibility? Since marketing personnel is closest to the market, are they the logical and automatic option? Convincing as it may seem, there are certain drawbacks even with this type of organizational structure.

Experience has shown that new products developed by marketing departments tend to have minor product differentiation of the existing product lines, and that too, very often no more than cosmetic changes. The second major drawback is that since marketing personnel have full-time jobs managing current products and are somewhat bogged down with their day to day problems, they are not likely to focus the kind of attention that new product development demands.

That leaves two more options — starting a new product development department or forming a new product development committee. What should be the composition of these? Ideally, they should comprise of talented people from marketing, R & D, and production. Many companies seem to be paying lip service towards the formation of such committees. Instead of seconding the most talented and innovative personnel from their respective departments, they seem to be sending the people whom they can spare to such committees. Furthermore, in a committee, accountability is not clearly defined.

As regards the new product development department, the department usually is not given adequate importance in the organizational hierarchy and does not create the much-needed atmosphere of involvement and commitment of the other functional departments. They are (the new product people) usually labeled as dreamers.

The critical question is how to create a climate that nurtures and develops the spirit of innovation? Some companies seem to have found an answer. Companies that are more aggressive on the new product front have created venture teams. The talented personnel from all major functional areas such as marketing, finance, R & D, and production are brought together to form a venture team for a specific new product project. They are empowered to cut through the red tape. They are made accountable for the particular task they are chosen to accomplish. They have a team leader who coordinates the activities of the venture team and provides feedback to the top management. Venture teams pick only the best performers from all the functional areas. The importance, the recognition and the rewards given to these venture teams are the primary motivating factors. These factors also act as excellent pressure points and ensure that the venture teams accomplish their tasks. Some of the companies that have achieved an enviable strike-rate with their new products followed the *product champion* concept. A product champion is an empowered, committed, and die-hard new product development manager. The idea is to promote entrepreneurship within an organization.

Whatever organization structure a company may choose, the most critical factor to remember and act upon is that the new product program must have the unqualified support of top management.

Therapeutic Leadership

Building A Disease Franchise for Achieving Therapeutic Leadership

The pharmaceutical market is not one specific market. It is composed of many highly diverse segments called therapeutic segments. What singles out a pharmaceutical company from being a winner and an also-ran is its ability to build and defend its franchise in a given therapeutic area or segment. It is not enough if you have a successful brand or two as the effective patent life of these is usually ten to twelve years after which generics invade your market and erode all your margins. You need to be ready with successive product candidates to maintain your position in your therapeutic segments. Only then you will be able to build a franchise and even own a therapeutic segment or part of it.

It generally takes years, if not decades to build a therapeutic franchise and once a company establishes in any specific therapeutic area, it will do all it can to stay to defend its position in that therapeutic field. When you build a therapeutic franchise, you are not achieving just high sales. You are, in fact developing relationships with your customers - whether hospital specialists, general practitioners, primary care organizations (PCO) or even patient focus groups. It is these relationships that help you build a robust marketing platform to achieve the dominant leadership position in a particular therapeutic area of your choice.

Besides, these relationships have a snowballing effect resulting in a virtuous cycle. These relationships lead to a group of influential local, regional and international opinion leaders, who are preeminent in their fields. These key opinion leaders are usually physicians or surgeons, who will work on early development trails and will act as experts at the time of regulatory approvals. These experts are the ones who publish papers on the product and discuss its uses and its place in the management of the diseases in question at global conferences and important technical meetings.

Why Therapeutic Leadership?

When you build a robust position in a therapeutic segment, your relationships with the thought leaders will also be mutually beneficial. These expert physicians tend to work with a select group of companies that have the know-how and whom they know and trust. Such relationships also create a barrier to entry in the given therapeutic market for a new competitor.

Pharmaceutical companies, large and small therefore are exploring many ways to build a franchise.The two most common strategic routes that they take are:

A. Large pharmaceutical companies facing the patent cliff and with no successive product candidates to carry on the legacy are actively looking for licensing-in opportunities of late-stage new chemical entities (NCEs) in their therapeutic areas from small and medium-sized biotechnology companies.

B. Small biotech companies with scarce resources to take their new drug candidates to market are seeking strategic partnerships with large established companies.

These strategies may not always work successfully. Once the patent on the branded drug expires and the generics swarm the market like vultures, it will lead to the disappearance of a franchise if there is no successor candidate or a defensible strategy. What can be a defensible strategy?

Defensible Strategy

Some pharmaceutical companies with foresight such as GlaxoSmithKline were following an innovative defensible strategy and at least buying some time until they come up with a follow-on drug candidate. GlaxoSmithKline (GSK) achieved a dominant position in the Asthma market by introducing successive new compounds at regular intervals. What is more, the company developed many of its drugs for asthma using a proprietary delivery technology that delivered the drugs directly to the lungs via inhaler devices. GSK's investment in delivery technology helped in maintaining the company's market dominance in the asthma market long after the patents on certain drugs expired. The company had bought time to field successor candidates. Another case in point is Novo Nordisk's dominance in the diabetic segment with its insulins. It is the delivery technology of the company with its Novopen devices that helped the company stay as a leader.

Device innovation is not easy although its developmental pathways are shorter than the drug development. However, a mix of product and delivery device has created significant boundaries and even barriers to entry of new competitors in inhaler markets, and insulin markets. Similar strategies are also emerging in new drugs as well as diagnostics in other areas of pharmaceutical medicine.

The following cases show how some pharmaceutical companies are building and defending their franchises in their chosen therapeutic areas.

Eli Lilly's 90-Year Old Diabetes Franchise!

Every pharmaceutical and biotechnology company dreams of optimizing their franchise in the therapeutic areas of their choice. How do you maximize your therapeutic franchise? While there is no simple answer to this question, Eli Lilly's success story in building and managing its diabetic franchise provides us with valuable insights into building and maintaining a disease or therapeutic franchise.

It all started in 1923 when Eli Lilly sourced Iletin, the world's first insulin product from Frederick Banting and Charles Best of the University of Toronto. Lilly had to wait for almost six decades for its second breakthrough in its diabetic franchise. In 1982, the company launched Humulin, human insulin sourced from Genentech. Humulin was the first therapeutic that Genentech developed using recombinant DNA technology. Humulin was a huge success, and it passed the coveted $1 billion mark in annual global sales before its US patent expired in 2001. Lilly had already introduced in 1996 an analog of Humulin, Insulin Lispro under the brand name Humalog in the US and switched the user base of Humulin to Humalog. Humalog is a fast-acting insulin analog with greater dosing convenience and improved glucose control. Therefore, switching was not difficult. It was a case of switching for something better!

While the sales of Humalog were going steadily over the next few years, Lilly had also introduced a new formulation, Humalog Pen (cartridge for injection containing Humalog mix 75/25). Humalog patents were valid until 2013 in the US. Besides, to reinforce its position in the diabetes therapeutic area, Lilly licensed oral diabetic drug, Actos (pioglitazone) from the Japanese pharmaceutical firm, Takeda in 1999. Actos patent was valid till 2006 in the US.

Lilly launched three drugs in the diabetes therapeutic area in quick succession between 2014 and 2015. In August 2014, Lilly introduced Jardinace (empagliflozin) a once-daily medication for treating type 2 diabetes. Although Jardinace is the third brand in a new class, it is the first drug to show cardio-protective effects in high-risk patients. Also, Lilly launched Trulicity (dulaglutide), a once-a-week injection that comes with a smart pen in 2014. In 2015, Lilly quickly followed up its Jardinace and Trulicity launches with the introduction of a combination drug - Glyxambi, a combination of empagliflozin and linagliptin as an adjunct to diet and exercise in patients with type 2 diabetes. The company focused its promotion of Trulicity initially on the specialists and later rolled it out to primary care physicians.

Every which way you look at it Eli Lilly had built an enduring diabetes franchise.

Lessons

The case of Eli Lilly's diabetes franchise illustrates and illuminates as to how to build and manage a therapeutic franchise. The critical success factors for developing an enduring therapeutic franchise are:

1. Early development of multiple indications.
2. Early development of new dosage forms and formulations.
3. The launch of new molecules before the patents on the initial brands expire, as it allows for switching patients to the company's successive (new) brands.

This is undoubtedly, a high cost and high-risk approach with significant expenditures of new trials. However, then, the benefits of such an effort include:

A. Added exclusivity

B. Penetration of new segments, and

C. Potential strengthening of physician loyalty through a one-stop-shop for all possible therapeutic solutions in the therapeutic area.

(Source: Adapted from Francoise Simon and Philip Kotler's Book, *Building Global Biobrands*, The Free Press, 2003)

The Everlasting Life of Xylocaine (Lidocaine)!

Astra launched Xylocaine (Lidocaine) in 1948 in a dental formulation. Today, Xylocaine has become the most widely prescribed anesthetic in the world. Astra made it happen through a multitude of developmental efforts in bringing out various formulations. Also, the company pursued a vigorous clinical trial activity in getting the regulatory approvals for multiple indications over the years. The company had developed several formulations for treating multiple indications as diverse as:

▸ Surface anesthesia to anti-arrhythmla
▸ Ointment to epidural injections
▸ Suppositories to dental cartridges, and
▸ Pump spray to patches

The following table presents the different formulations and indication approvals timeline.

Xylocaine Formulations and Indications Development Timeline

Year of FDA Approval	Formulation Developed
1948	Xylocaine (Lidocaine) in a Dental Formulation
1949	Ointment
1968	Xylocaine Epidural Injection
1969	Xylocard (anti-arrhythmia)

Table Contd...

Year of FDA Approval	Formulation Developed
1969	Xylocord Suppositories
1974	Xylocaine Dental Catridges
1990	Xylocaine Pump Spray
1993	Xylocaine Patch

The Xylocaine family, even after fifty-two years of its introduction recorded $200 million in global sales in 2001. The forecast for 2018 to 2022 for the Xylocaine range looks robust. It is as though Xylocaine would have life everlasting!

(Source: Adapted from the book, Building Global Biobrands by Franchise Simon and Philip Kotler, The Free Press, 2003)

The Brand that Helped the Company in Building a Franchise in Neurology!

UCB Pharma got approval for its second-generation antiepileptic drug (AED) Keppra (levetiracetam) in 1999 from the US FDA. Despite the stiff competition from the industry's majors brands such as Lamictal (lamotrigine) from GlaxoSmithKline, Neurontin (gabapentin) from Pfizer and Topamax (topiramate) from Johnson & Johnson, UCB's Keppra carved a specific niche for itself in Epilepsy segment. Keppra achieved this although all of its major competitors had a higher promotional spending and larger field forces than itself. Within three years of its launch, Keppra had become the number one prescribed second-generation AED in the US. How did UCB achieve this?

Firstly, Keppra had new and rather compelling clinical data showing a higher rate of seizure freedom in very refractory patients treated during the registration process. Secondly, the company leveraged its small size, sharpened customer focus and quickly communicated its robust clinical data forcefully among the physician base with its high-quality sales force. Thirdly, the company implemented a carefully planned expansion of its indications as well as other geographical markets to cover a larger patient base. Keppra repeated its success story in all the markets that it entered.

A more significant factor that contributed to Keppra's success is that the company moved the market expectations. In the past, success was measured as the number of patients, who achieved a 50 percent reduction in seizures. With its continuing educational efforts, the company had moved this to the concept of seizure freedom, something that dramatically improved the prospects for the patients concerned.

From Niche to Franchise

Having created a niche for itself in epilepsy, UCB committed itself to improve the lives of people with epilepsy around the world and stepped up its research first in the area of epilepsy. The company, which has over twenty years of experience in the research and development of antiepileptic drugs, is determined to become a preferred partner for the global epilepsy community. The company strives to create super-networks with world-leading scientists and clinicians in academic institutions, pharmaceutical companies, and other organizations that are committed to the cause of improving the quality of life of people with epilepsy.

To supplement its strong position in a niche area of the broader neurology segment, UCB decided to bring other therapeutic solutions to the neurology physician. As the next logical step, the company has been researching to find treatments for diseases such as Parkinsonism, Restless Legs Syndrome, which are of central interest to its key customers, neurologists. The company thus would be able to build a franchise in the area of neurology by leveraging the trust, and confidence that it had created among neurologists.

The company has been taking many around-the-pill and beyond-the-pill initiatives to reinforce its position first in epilepsy therapy area and then in the neurology segment as a whole. Here are some of the more critical actions:

A. *Epilepsy Advocate Website*, where epilepsy advocates, who are people living with epilepsy and caregivers strive to inspire others by sharing their personal success stories online and with local communities.

B. *Canine Assistants Program*, which is a non-profit organization that is dedicated to providing service dogs that are seizure responsive to children and adults with epilepsy, physical disability, and other special needs. This organization works together with The Epilepsy Company – UCB Inc. in the training of every dog. This partnership ensures that each dog gets the extensive training that it needs to meet more needs of the epilepsy community.

C. *UCB Family Scholarship Program* offers educational scholarships to people living with epilepsy to help them fulfill their dreams. The company has so far (2018) awarded over $ 2-million in scholarships to more than 400 deserving people for pursuing their undergraduate and graduate studies.

UCB has been leveraging its capabilities in neurology segments in general and epilepsy therapy area in particular meticulously ever since it launched Keppra. The brand indeed has helped the company in building a franchise in Neurology. The company today has a multi-billion dollar presence in Neurology, even ten years after the Keppra's patent expiration.

The company followed a carefully crafted strategy of lifecycle management to minimize the impact of generic erosion after patent expiry and fielded successor candidates for treating epilepsy to sustain and reinforce its strong position. The following table presents a glimpse of how successfully UCB has built a franchise in epilepsy and neurology.

Keppra's Life Cycle Strategy Timeline

Year	What the Company did
1999	Keppra first approved in the US
2000	Keppra approved in the EU (European Union)
2000 to 2007	Keppra received several supplementary indications as an adjunctive therapy across both partial and generalized seizures in the US; also approved as monotherapy in the EU for the treatment of partial onset seizures in adults with epilepsy

Table Contd...

Year	What the Company did
2008	Keppra gets the US FDA approval for its extended release dosage form, Keppra XR in September 2008 US FDA grants Keppra Pediatric Exclusivity on June 06, 2008, Exclusivity expires on January 2009 Mylan launches its generic version of Keppra on November 1, 2008 before the expiry of its pediatric exclusivity
2008	Gets the US FDA approval for Vimpat (Lacosamide), the successor NME (new molecular entity) for Keppra and launches it as an add-on therapy for adult patients with or without secondary seizures
2010	Keppra gets regulatory approval in Japan and subsequently follows on indication expansions resulting in larger treatable patient base. This minimizes the impact of generic erosions of US and EU revenues
2014	Vimpat (lacosamide) gets US FDA approval as a monotherapy for treating epilepsy in adult patients and markets Vimpat in different dosage forms — tablets, oral solution and IV injections
2016	Gets approval for Briviact (brivaracetam) another NME for treating partial onset seizures in patients 16 years of age and above in the US and EU Further reinforces the presence of UCB in the epilepsy therapeutic area

What made Keppra so successful? It is Keppra's positioning strategy focusing on three key messages – Efficacy, tolerability, and ease of use that made Keppra a huge success. Because, no other anti-convulsant was comparable to Keppra in offering all the three without a tradeoff.

(Source: Adapted from articles: Anthony Vacchione, *MM & M All-stars small marketing team: Keppra*, MM&M, December 15, 2008).

Johnson & Johnson Extends its Antipsychotic Franchise Strategically!

How do you extend the life of your blockbuster antipsychotic's life by another five years? By mimicking the drug's metabolism in the liver and making that metabolite in the laboratory and formulating it as a new drug. The patentable research can get your old drug a five-year extension under the Hatch-Waxman Act.

That's what Johnson & Johnson had done with their antipsychotic blockbuster - Risperdal (Risperidone). Risperdal has been one of the best-selling drugs for Johnson & Johnson with 2005 sales of US $3.5 billion. It was due to expire in 2007 and generics could be available by 2008.

The company thought out a clever strategy. When a patient swallows a dose of Risperdal, usually a tablet a day, the liver metabolizes the drug into paliperidone, the active substance in the body. Johnson & Johnson performed this act of metabolism inside the lab and made pills of it, which would release the chemical over 24 hours. The company obtained the FDA approval for paliperidone New Drug Application (NDA) with a five-year exclusivity extending its anti-psychotic franchise. Johnson & Johnson launched paliperidone under the brand name Invega. This was the first leg of the strategy. The table below details the steps of the multi-leg strategy that Johnson & Johnson crafted, with timelines.

Strategy to Extend the Antipsychotic Franchise by Johnson & Johnson with Timelines

Timelines	Strategic Initiatives
1993	Risperdal first approved. Initially available in color-coded tablets ranging in strengths from 0.5 mg to 4 mg and 1mg/ml oral solution.
2003	• FDA granted approval for oral disintegrating tablets, Risperdal -M tablets of 0.5 mg, 1 and 2 mg. • US FDA also approved *Risperdal Consta*, a long-acting intramuscular injection with strengths of 25 mg and 50 mg supplied in pre-filled syringe to be injected every 2 weeks. The injection offers a significant advantage of overcoming compliance issues inherent in daily oral dosing of patients with antipsychotic disorders.
2003	In December 2003, Mylan and Dr. Reddy's, two of the leading international generic companies submitted Abbreviated New Drug Applications (ANDAs) with Paragraph IV certificate against the Risperdal patents triggering a 30-month stay until May 2006, 18-months before the patent expiry.
2006	• Johnson & Johnson gained another FDA approval for the indication of irritability in children with Autism, which gave them six-months of Pediatric Exclusivity against generics of Risperdal until May 2008. Risperdal's key patent was due to expire in November 2007. • The FDA granted approval to Johnson & Johnson's Invega (Paliperidone) extended release (once-daily).
2006	In October 2006, the District Court of New Jersey ruled that the Risperdal patent was enforceable, and infringed by the Mylan and Dr. Reddy's.
2008	Generic oral Risperidone entered the market duly as the patent expired by mid-2008
2009	FDA approved Invega Sustenna, a long-acting intramuscular injection of Paliperidone

Soon after the generics of oral Risperidone entered the market, the total sales of Risperdal franchise dropped from the US $4.2 billion in 2006 to the US $3.4 billion in 2008. A year later the sales further eroded by 60 percent to the US $2.3 billion. Only Risperdal Consta (the long-acting intramuscular) injection had grown by 9 percent as there was no generic competition against it. While it had been extending and defending its Risperdal franchise, Johnson & Johnson had also been developing a successor - Invega (paliperidone) both as a once-daily oral tablet form and a long-acting, once-a-month intramuscular injectable dosage form.

Invega once-daily oral formulation did not offer significant advantages over Risperdal other than dosage convenience from twice-daily to once-daily and a slightly more favorable side-effect profile. There was no difference in efficacy. In fact, Risperdal's onset of action was faster than Invega. The product differentiation created in Invega was not adequate to command the price premium it had. Realizing the modest advantage of their new drug over the old, Johnson & Johnson priced Invega slightly lower than Risperdal to encourage psychiatrists to switch patients to the new drug.

Invega Sustenna, the once-a-month intramuscular injection containing Paliperidone has a significant advantage over Risperdal Consta. Johnson & Johnson, therefore, could effectively switch patients from Risperdal Consta to Invega. Although Risperdal Consta had market exclusivity in the US until the mid-2012, the company transferred its loyalties to Invega Sustenna earlier.

While Johnson & Johnson had lost much of its oral antipsychotic market to generic Risperidone, the company successfully defended its antipsychotic franchise by switching injections from a dependency on Risperidone to Invega Sustenna.

Lessons

Did Johnson & Johnson manage its antipsychotic franchise successfully? There were good and bad elements in the overall execution of the company's strategy.

The company managed its move from oral Risperdal to intramuscular Risperdal (Risperdal Consta) well and around half of the franchise of sales survived the expiry of the basic Risperidone patent. The company was successful in switching patients from patent-expired oral Risperdal to the patented Risperdal Consta (intramuscular dosage form).

On the negative side, Oral Invega was just not differentiated enough from the oral Risperdal to stand a realistic chance of success once the generic Risperidone became available. The advantage of once-daily instead of twice-daily was not strong enough in persuading the patients and psychiatrists to pay the huge price differential between the Invega brand and the generic Risperidone.

On the plus side, Invega Sustenna's superior dosing schedule and the absence of generic competition in the injectable dosage form segment enabled to move Risperdal Consta sales to Invega Sustenna.

(Source: Adapted from the book, *Pharmaceutical Lifecycle Management* by Tony Ellery, Neal Hansen, John Wiley & Sons, 2012)

Ranbaxy Defends its Leadership Position by Updating its Products in the Urological Market!

Ranbaxy occupied the No.1 position in the Rs. The 6.6-crore urological market in India in 1986 with its Gramoneg brand of nalidixic acid. Gramoneg continued to be the largest selling brand of nalidixic acid in the urological market even after the introduction of norfloxacin, the broad spectrum antibiotic with a high cure rate in urinary tract infections. However, norfloxacin as a sub-category has carved out a 51 percent share of the total urological market.

Cipla, another company on the fast track in the Indian pharmaceutical industry, introduced Norflox, which had become the largest selling brand of norfloxacin in the country. Ranbaxy too had introduced Norbactin, their brand of norfloxacin almost simultaneously in 1987, and aggressively promoted it to retain its leadership position in the urological market. Ranbaxy had to contend with a No. 2 position for their Norbactin in the norfloxacin sub-segment after Cipla (Cipla's Norflox had a market share of 19.4 percent, and Ranbaxy's Norbactin had a market share of 16.3 percent). However, Ranbaxy did defend its leadership position in the urological therapeutic category with a formidable share of 44.2 percent (Gramoneg, Norbactin combined).

The introduction of ciprofloxacin, a new quinolone molecule in 1989 changed the complexion of the quinolone market by making it the largest and fastest growing subsegment among anti-bacterials in India.

The ever-alert Ranbaxy grabbed this opportunity and made Cifran, their brand of ciprofloxacin the fifth largest brand in the Indian pharmaceutical industry in less than three years (sales Rs. 18.9-crore in 1991-92). Consequently, Ranbaxy could further consolidate their leadership position in the quinolines sub-segment with a formidable share of about one-fourth of the total market under its belt. Updating the product mix certainly helped Ranbaxy not only to defend its market share but also to remain far ahead of the competition by achieving therapeutic leadership!

Sovaldi's Unprecedented Launch Success Leads to a Therapeutic Leadership with its HCV Franchise!

Gilead Sciences' Sovaldi has had the most successful Pharma launch in history. It made $8.5 billion in sales in the first nine months during 2014 and passed a whopping $10 billion in global sales for the first full year. How did Gilead achieve this unprecedented success with Sovaldi? Here is how it did what it did.

Gilead did not develop Sovaldi (sofosbuvir). Pharmasset, a small Pharma and Biotech company based in Princeton, New Jersey did. Gilead saw great potential in Pharmasset's developmental drug candidate - sofosbuvir to treat Hepatitis C infection and acquired the company for $11 billion in November 2011. Gilead submitted a New Drug Application for sofosbuvir (Sovaldi), which the FDA approved in 2013 with a breakthrough therapy designation in the treatment of Hepatitis C.

Everything seems to be unprecedented in the case of Sovaldi including its price which is unimaginable. The price of a single tablet is $1,000. The complete course of therapy is one tablet a day for twelve weeks and costs the patient $84,000.

Stiff Opposition

While Sovaldi's success was nothing less than amazing, it was not without opposition. Sovaldi had to face formidable opposition that lined up against its introduction because of its exorbitant pricing. Here are some of the major opposing forces against Sovaldi's pricing:

- ▶ The US Congress repeatedly tried to intervene with Gilead's sales of the product demanding public explanations for Sovaldi's $84,000 price tag for complete therapy.

- ▶ There were many attacks by major insurance and Pharmacy Benefit Management (PBM) companies such as Express Scripts claiming that Gilead's pricing of the product was unsustainable and greedy.

- ▶ Medicaid agencies in many states have refused to pay for Sovaldi, and others have placed severe restrictions on access to the drug. Because Sovaldi's cost will wipe off their annual prescription drug budgets.

- ▶ The adverse impact that Sovaldi's reimbursement costs on the overall prescription drug budget too is unprecedented. Consider for example that if the total number of 3.2 million Hepatitis C patients in the US are to be treated with Sovaldi, it would cost about $300 billion for the US healthcare system. Some critics have even suggested that the US government would be better off by buying Gilead Sciences for $150 billion, which can reduce the treatment costs by half.

Despite mounting pressures against its price, Gilead did not waver throughout 2014. To communicate its strategic intent in pricing the product, Gilead introduced another new, once-a-day formulation for treating Hepatitis C–Harvoni with a 96 percent cure rate in 12 weeks and priced it even higher than Sovaldi - at $95,000 per therapy.

Sovaldi's Success Secrets

How did Gilead achieve the highest ever launch sales in the history of the pharmaceutical industry in the face of all the stiff opposition to its pricing? What are the keys to its success? What is its secret sauce? Tom Norton gives Gilead's keys to success in his article, *How Gilead Blew out the lights* in Pharmaceutical Executive (November 2016). Here's the gist:

1. *The cure story*. Sovaldi has very high cure rates. Thousands of patients who could access the drug despite access

restrictions have got cured and the word about its amazing cure rates spread. Moreover, the patients suffering from Hepatitis C in America were doing whatever they must to access the drug. In the first year about 117,000 hepatitis C patients were prescribed Sovaldi. The value of these prescriptions was around a whopping $10 billion.

2. *The Cost-effectiveness story*. Gilead has put forth a highly persuasive argument against all the allegations and accusations of its pricing that it was greedy and socially irresponsible among others. And it is not about pricing; it is about cost-effectiveness. Hepatitis is a chronic disease, and its patients are high-cost consumers of medical care. The prognosis is usually a downward slope; even with proper 'pre-Sovaldi prescription care,' there is little or no improvement. As Hepatitis C virus eventually destroys the liver, the patients may reach a point where a liver transplant is necessary. A liver transplant costs about $650,000 in the first year. This does not include the costs of possible rejection and other complications that may arise. Therefore, a complete course of 12 weeks with Sovaldi at $84,000 per patient is a very cost-effective solution. Once the therapy is concluded, chances of spending for further treatment of Hepatitis C are essentially over. Sovaldi is, therefore, a logical medico-economic solution for patients suffering from Hepatitis C.

3. *Smart pricing decisions for foreign markets*. Gilead addressed the pricing concerns in the international markets very rapidly. The company entered into a series of agreements that range from $300 for a full course of Sovaldi to $840 under authorized generic agreements in low-income countries and developing countries. Even in the 'G 20' countries such as the UK, Germany and Canada Gilead is offering about 45 percent discounts on its US prices. Gilead made these smart pricing decisions as the US accounted for less than 2 percent of the Hepatitis C patients, and providing the drug access to the vast majority

of the patients around the globe is essential for its success. The company entered into pricing agreements with as many as 91 countries.

The Competition

Even as Sovaldi started basking in its spectacular success, competition quickly entered the hepatitis C market. AbbVie got its hepatitis C drug, Viekira Pak, a fixed-dose combination of three drugs – ombitasvir, paritaprevir, and ritonavir approved for treating Hepatitis C. The competition got heated up more with Merck also entering the market with its Zepatier, a fixed dose combination of elbasvir and grazoprevir. Bristol-Myers Squibb introduced its Daklinza (daclatasvir) in July 2015. AbbVie, Bristol-Myers Squibb and Merck priced their hepatitis C drugs much lower at approximately half the price of Gilead.

AbbVie later in 2017, entered the market with its Mavyret, a fixed-dose combination of glecaprevir and pibrentasvir and quickly grabbed a 7 percent share of the new prescriptions of Hepatitis C. Mavyret has a distinct advantage of shorter treatment of eight weeks over Sovaldi's twelve weeks. The following table gives the FDA approval dates of hepatitis C drugs in the US.

Approval Dates of Hepatitis C Drugs by the US FDA

Company	Drug	Approved in
Gilead	Sovaldi	December 6, 2013
Gilead	Harvoni	October 10, 2014
AbbVie	Viekira Pak	December 19, 2014
Bristol-Myers Squibb	Daklinza	July 2015
Merck	Zepatier	2016
Gilead	Epclusa	June 28, 2016
Gilead	Vosevi	July 18, 2017
AbbVie	Mavyret	August 3, 2017

Mounting pressures on Gilead's pricing of Sovaldi and Harvoni, availability of effective and more economical therapy alternatives started having an impact on Gilead's hepatitis C franchise sales. The declining sales trend can be seen in the following table. Increased competition from other Hepatitis C drugs leading to market share erosion and lower net prices and a fall-off in new starts due to the drugs' efficacy contributed to the considerable decline in Gilead's HCV franchise sales.

Declining Sales of Gilead's HCV Franchise

Year	Sales from HCV Franchise ($ Billion)
2015	19.14
2016	14.83
2017	9.14
2018 (estimate)	3.75

(Source: BiopharmaDive)

Gilead Defends its HCV Franchise

Having built a strong hepatitis C franchise, Gilead is determined to defend it with all its might. Gilead quickly followed its spectacular Sovaldi launch with another highly effective fixed combination drug, Harvoni in less than a year. When competition came in the company introduced two more new drugs to strengthen its HCV (Hepatitis C Virus) franchise - Epclusa and Vosevi. With its four-drug HCV franchise, Gilead is equipped to provide treatment options for all the six genotypes of hepatitis C virus.

The company has made its Sovaldi accessible to the hepatitis C patient populations in 91 countries with its authorized generics agreement. However, Gilead continues to face strong criticism in the US for its pricing. How can the company give 99 percent discount in countries such as India and Egypt and charge a prohibitive $1,000 per pill in the US? Does the company expect its US patients to subsidize the costs of Sovaldi therapy for the whole world?

Gilead Life Sciences finally decided to launch authorized generic versions of its controversially priced hepatitis C drugs – Harvoni and Epclusa via the newly created subsidiary, Asegua Therapeutics in January 2019. The generic versions of these drugs will be available at a list price of $24,000 per a course of therapy. Gilead took a step in the right direction.

Lessons

The case of Sovaldi reinforces once again the importance of scientific expertise and knowledge in developing and marketing a pharmaceutical product. Gilead's scientific acumen is evident in identifying the potential of the developmental candidate – Sofosbuvir of Pharmasset and buying the company for $11 billion.

There are essential takeaways in the manner Gilead managed its HCV franchise with a continuous focus on developing cures for all genotypes of Hepatitis C and in its quick reflexes in responding to increasing competition.

It is axiomatic that the quality of the cure can command a premium. However, it is essential that it should be a premium based on the principle of an adequate and reasonable return and not the one that reflects one's greed. A price of $1,000 per tablet does not sound reasonable no matter how persuasive your cost-effective argument may sound. When you consider that it costs about $130 to manufacture Sovaldi, you realize how outrageous its pricing is. Gilead claims that the pricing reflects the value of Sovaldi and deserves a premium because of downstream health savings. Every which way you look at it, the pricing of Sovaldi does not reflect the company's social responsibility.

David Evans reported in The Fair Pricing Coalition (FPC) applauds the Wyden-Grassley US Senate bipartisan Sovaldi investigation spotlighting a greed-driven pricing strategy behind Gilead's $1,000 per pill Hepatitis C drug launch on December 3, 2015. He wrote that the Fair Pricing Coalition condemns Gilead Sciences on the high price of new Hepatitis C drug Sovaldi and urges rapid and wide dissemination of support program details for the uninsured, and underinsured people living with Hepatitis C.

It is important to listen to the public sentiment and take cognizance of public criticism against the organization and respond suitably. The recent pricing strategies and price gouging approaches by select pharmaceutical companies are exposing the greedy nature of the organizations. If this continues unabated, the government may intervene and may even bring in legislation regulating prices in the pharmaceutical industry as a whole. Many governments in developing nations and developed nations have already started doing that.

(Source: Adapted from: 1. Tom Norton's article, *How Gilead 'Blew out the lights with Sovaldi'* in Pharmaceutical Executive, November 18, 2014; 2. Ned Pagliarulo, *Gilead forecasts steep slide in 2018 hepatitis C revenues*, BiopharmaDive, February 6, 2018)

Enduring Success

In today's fierce pharmaceutical marketplace, whether you are a marketer in the Brand-name drug markets or branded-generic markets, it is not enough if you have a few successful brands. You need to build and maintain a successful franchise in the therapeutic areas of your choice. In fact, you should aim for therapeutic leadership in the segment of your choice. It is the vital difference between enduring success and eluding success!

Product Launch Strategy

New Product Launch

Pharmaceutical companies depend on product launches to fill the gaps in their product portfolios and to drive growth in the face of rapidly approaching patent cliffs and mounting pressure on margins. Moreover, product launches in the pharmaceutical industry are getting smaller and more complex. New product launch is crucial to the survival and growth of every pharmaceutical company. About two-thirds of all drug launches fail to meet the pre-launch sales objectives during the first year of the product on the market. According to McKinsey, research indicates that:

▶ Only 30 percent of new chemical compounds (NCE) that enter the market recover research and development costs.

▶ Less than half of products achieve less than fifty percent of sales forecasts for the launch year.

Pharmaceutical companies, therefore, need a successful commercialization strategy that drives their growth expectations. How can they overcome the current underperformance? How can they achieve launch excellence? Eric Dalton, executive vice president at HealthCast, suggests, in his article, *4 Secrets of successful drug launches marketers must know* (PM360, October 18, 2017). The four success secrets are:

Success Secrets

1. *Be specific and precise in your launch efforts*. Physicians and patients, though have become a lot savvier with their research of therapies and medications with the influx of new product information at their fingertips, they do not have time to sift through what is essential and what is not. Pharmaceutical companies can do more than creating awareness about the indications or disease conditions. They can help physicians identify appropriate patients who are candidates for their new

drug even before product launch. They should then focus on the physicians who are likely to treat more often those patients to educate them on the value of the product. Just as research and development focus is shifting to targeted treatments, marketing should also target their focus on the appropriate patients and the physicians that treat those types of patients. Reaching everyone is like throwing a dart in the dark. If you want to hit the bullseye, you need to make your marketing more meaningful by focusing on the segments that matter.

2. *Look at behavior, not just access*. Everyone talks about access these days. It is a comprehensive term that encompasses anything from formulary status to pricing structures of a drug. Reimbursement, of course, is a significant component that improves patients' access to the drug. Formulary status alone does not guarantee success for the drug. One needs to prioritize the needs of the physicians and patients appropriately to drive the usage of their drug. Marketers need to find ways and means to understand the process of change and what makes physicians change their routine. Today, many digital tools provide more information than ever before to help us understand how patients are complying with the product and to see if they are getting better. Go beyond the formulary. Go beyond access. Focus on what you need to do to change the behavior of your physicians and patients regarding switching to your new drug.

3. *Involve other product influencers*. The importance of stakeholders other than physicians is increasing in the new product success. There was a time when new drug success formula was relatively straightforward. You discover a drug, position it appropriately and focus on the high-prescribing physicians and generate more prescriptions. Your success depended on the sheer ability to generate more prescriptions than your competitors. You need to get the drug on the formulary of as many payers as possible to gain maximum

access. However, that also depended mostly on your key opinion leader (KOL) and physician advocacy development skills. That is Changing. You need to look to other stakeholders too. Of course, physicians are still critical. Pharma marketers also need to identify the patient advocates, caregivers and others such as media and analysts, who have a stake in the product. You need to find out how these groups are perceiving the product and what they can do to ensure that they have the right knowledge and complete understanding of the product. They also need to figure out what they need to do to improve the engagement and support continuously among all the stakeholders. What is crucial is to address the community and not just the prescribers.

4. *Focus on the long-term*. While launching a new drug, it is important to think the entire lifecycle of the brand and how to achieve long-term, sustainable growth. Undeniably, it is the launch sets the momentum.

While these four secrets provide broad guidelines on how to launch, what you have to do to make your drug launch a success? Here are twelve points to ponder, plan and implement a successful new drug launch.

Making Your Drug Launch A Success

New drug launches face more intense competition today than they faced a decade ago. Bain & Company research shows that the average window of time in which a drug remains on the market before competing products arrive has fallen to four years, down from eight years between 2000 and 2004. Today, data from phase III trials is not enough to differentiate your product in the eyes of doctors, regulators and health insurers. You need to do the following things right for launching your new products successfully, as suggested by Rafael Natanek, in his insightful article, *How to Make Your Drug Launch A Success*, in the Bain & Company Report:

1. Differentiate the new drug through messaging, post-launch data and services. While many pharmaceutical marketers understand the importance of these factors, they often do not pay the necessary attention. Communicating the critical clinical and non-clinical benefits to physicians and other decision makers is crucial for success.

2. Pharmaceutical companies with an excellent new product launch track record often use post-launch data and services to differentiate their product from the competition further. They transform market data into actionable insights to make their product stand out.

3. You must build and substantiate your marketing messages with clinical data and convert them into benefits your physicians and patients are seeking. Your messages should satisfy the unmet needs of your physicians and patients.

4. Conduct post-launch studies early enough, at least eighteen months before launch to close any gaps in data and ensure superior data quality over competing products and new entrants in differentiating your product. Doing so will enable you to generate a steady stream of data substantiating your product immediately after the launch. When you continuously give new evidence (messaging) supporting your product's competitive advantage, you keep your product at the forefront of your physicians' minds.

5. You can increase the effectiveness of your message by including a competitive, companion service offer to address patient and physician pain points. Physician services such as diagnostics, patient identification, and onboarding to improve medication adherence, reimbursement support to name a few play a significant role in successful launches.

6. Provide superior customer experience and reinforce customer advocacy and broaden it. Physicians today consider a much broader set of factors beyond clinical data when deciding which drug to prescribe. They consider factors such as clinical

protocols, drug price, the type of patient to whom they can prescribe a drug, and overall treatment regimen. What is more, they are rapidly shifting to a broader array of information sources such as online sites, and peers.

7. Bain research shows that at least 40 percent of physicians' brand preference is attributable to customer experience factors beyond the product. These factors include for example, how Pharma companies support physicians by providing consumers with appropriate patient education, identifying patients, and connecting physicians with peers.

8. Many Pharma companies, however, focus their advocacy on the most influential physicians in a given field - the key opinion leaders - and miss the opportunity to create advocates among the day-to-day prescribers. Leading companies look beyond the key opinion leaders and turn day-to-day prescribers into advocates by providing them with superior customer service. They understand that a physician's overall customer experience is a sum of individual interactions with a Pharma company.

9. Understand that every interaction or episode is an opportunity to engage with a customer in a positive dialogue. How can you provide superior customer experience in every interaction? Consider for example that providing easy and accurate medical sales liaison contacts within 24 hours of the physician's request. Bain study showed that some of these interactions have a more significant impact on prescribing behavior than others.

10. Bain research shows that physicians give pharmaceutical companies an average Net Promotion Score® of negative 11 percent across all their interactions with them. That negative score is a significant opportunity to increase launch success by designing and delivering a superior customer experience to physicians. (medallia.com defines the Net Promoter Score is an index from-100 to 100 that measures the willingness of

customers to recommend a company's products or services to others. Marketers use It as a proxy for gauging the customer's overall satisfaction with a company's product or service and customer loyalty to the brand).

11. Organize your launches as micro-battles, which means you create a company within a company to launch the new drug. The new launch teams have the authority and agility to make decisions that are best for the patient and the brand. The micro-battle approach allows the launch teams to focus on strategic issues, adapt more rapidly to competitors, regulatory changes, and new insights.

12. How does a micro-battle strategy work? Firstly, you assemble a cross-functional team of 10 to 20 high performing individuals who report to a launch Head. The launch Head reports directly to the company CEO. The team members collect customer feedback before, during and after the launch and make rapid adjustments as needed to the launch strategy. They would continue monitoring the progress of the new drug against the milestones and launch objectives and make the necessary course correction to keep the new drug launch performance on the track.

When you think of it, a new drug launch is much like launching a rocket. Hundreds of activities need to happen at pre-defined moments to a certain standard. You need to ensure that nothing falls between cracks. Here is a checklist of the essential factors that shape a new product launch in the pharmaceutical industry.

Factors That Shape Launch: A Checklist

1. Size of launch indication and indication sequencing. How big is the opportunity for each of the indications in which the drug is useful? Is there substantial clinical evidence that is superior to the competition in these indications? Who is our target audience regarding patients, physicians, and other influencers?

2. Robustness of data for approval and access. How convincing is our clinical evidence regarding efficacy, safety, and dosage convenience?

3. The shift in the treatment paradigm needed. Is our new drug a novel therapy?

4. Marketing effort intensity. Is our sales force combat fit and battle ready? Is there a necessity to reallocate resources from other therapeutic areas? If we are entering a new therapeutic area, are we building critical skills adequately? Are we hiring from competition for the new therapeutic area?

5. Launch order. A detailed schedule of launch activities along with a monitoring mechanism.

6. Unmet needs and therapeutic value. What unmet needs does our new drug meet? What is the strength of our scientific evidence? Are we emphasizing enough on the vital difference that our drug can make?

7. What are our public relations efforts? Is there a need for direct-to-consumer advertising (DTCA) campaign to increase disease awareness among patients?

8. What is our strategy for outreach and services? What is our key opinion leader (KOL) development program?

9. Do we have a robust patient advocacy engagement program in place? What is our approach? Funding support? New compliance approaches?

10. Payer environment and reimbursement at launch. How extensive is our coverage? What do we need to achieve greater coverage? What is our action plan to meet it?

11. Behavior and mindset of physicians and key opinion leaders (KOLs). How robust are our KOL relationships? How many advocates do we have among physicians? What is our Net Promoter Score® among KOLs? Physicians?

12. Switching potential (or new patients only)?. What is our strategy for switching patients from our earlier brand in the same

therapeutic area? And for switching patients from competitors' brands?

13. Competitive pressure (number and quality of alternatives). What is the intensity of the competition?

14. Company experience in indication. What is the strength of our franchise in this disease condition? What is our equity in this disease area? How does the new drug reinforce it?

There is a significant difference between a product launch that is new to the world (new chemical entity) and a product launch that is new to the company (branded generic). The primary difference is in scale, and that is huge. The research and development effort, clinical trials, in particular, are significant both regarding costs and the time it takes in the case of new chemical entities.

Although, Branded generic marketing is a different ball game, most of the marketing approaches and strategies are similar. Companies marketing branded generic prescription drugs follow or even mimic most of the strategies practiced by the brand-name Pharma companies. This is probably because they are mostly similar save one vital difference. Brand-name pharmaceuticals are innovators, and branded generics are imitators. They operate in the same marketing environment and ecosystem. The success factors for launching a new product, therefore, will be useful and applicable to a large extent for all pharmaceutical marketers whether they are operating in a brand-name or branded generic environment.

The following cases show how some companies have hit the bullseyes with their brilliant launch strategies and execution by achieving remarkable success, while others with their blunders have pushed their new drug brands into the oblivion. These cases provide useful insights as to what it takes to launch pharmaceutical brands successfully and what blunders one must avoid to prevent launch failures.

Exubera's Irrational Exuberance!

The idea of Exubera was brilliant: Deliver insulin via an inhaler instead of a shot. A Pfizer CEO once even called it a major medical breakthrough. However, then, the idea was not new. Within three years after Banting and Best introduced insulin from the University of Toronto in 1921, German researchers first introduced the concept of inhalable insulin in 1924. After decades of failure, everyone almost forgot about it. The reason for the failure was evident. The required dose of insulin was too high and the resultant blood levels too low. It was not until the 1990s that the problem seemed solvable. Scientists have realized that the new technologies make it possible to turn insulin into a concentrated powder with particles sized for inhalation.

The idea of taking a century-old active substance, and that too a biologic at that and create a new patient-friendly route that has been eluding scientists all these years is exciting by itself. That is why Exubera, Pfizer's inhalable insulin was being welcomed even before its launch. Touted as the most significant medical breakthrough in recent years, Exubera brings a world of convenience to millions of patients around the globe. Never again people with diabetes have to insert a needle into the skin of their belly or buttocks from one to four times a day.

Predictably enough, patient satisfaction tests had shown that a clear majority of people with diabetes would prefer to be prescribed inhalable insulin rather than the traditional subcutaneous injections.

Pfizer collaborated with two other companies to market Exubera. Firstly, Pfizer had an arrangement with Hoechst Marion Roussel (Sanofi now) for the supply of recombinant insulin. Secondly, it had entered into an agreement with Nektar Therapeutics for providing a delivery system that would deliver the dry insulin powder deep into the lungs where it is quickly absorbed into the bloodstream, using a handheld inhalation device. The delivery device converted the insulin powder into an aerosol and did not require the use of a propellant. The agreement stipulated that Pfizer would lead the clinical development and Nektar Therapeutics would develop the technology necessary for packaging the product.

FDA requested Pfizer for additional clinical data because of the novelty of the therapy and also raised questions about the drug's long-term effectiveness. New clinical data revealed that patients on Exubera were four times more likely to develop antibodies against their insulin than those taking injectable insulin. There was a further delay in May 2002, as treatment with Exubera was shown to be associated with a small reduction in lung function as well as a mild-to-moderate cough. Subsequently, Pfizer and Aventis were able to announce the acceptance of their regulatory submissions in Europe first in 2004 and later in the United States in 2005.

A bullish Pfizer agreed to pay the US $1.3-billion to Aventis to buy out their interest in Exubera. The deal included full ownership of insulin production facility that they jointly owned in Frankfurt, Germany. The company made Exubera's forecasts with irrational exuberance. One estimate was as high as the US $ 4.8-billion in annual sales. Perhaps, the bold move of Pfizer to own the full rights to Exubera prompted analysts to go wild with their predictions and forecasts.

Finally, the US FDA approved Exubera on January 27, 2006. Hank McKinnell, the CEO of Pfizer at the time proudly announced, *"Exubera is a major, first-of-its-kind medical breakthrough that marks another critical step forward in the treatment of diabetes, a disease that has taken enormous human and economic toll worldwide."*

Criticism started mounting against Exubera within weeks of its launch. Michael J. Russo and David Balekdjian wrote in the Business Week that under rigorous outcomes-based access (OBA) analyses, Exubera did not offer an acceptable value proposition. No data has been generated to support Exubera's price, which was expected to be up to four times more than injected insulin.

Even after getting the approval, Pfizer kept delaying the launch and finally launched it on September 1, 2006, seven months after it obtained the FDA's approval in the United States. It is reported that Karen Katen, the Vice-chairman of Pfizer announced in this context that," *education programs and manufacturing preparations are time-consuming and that the company was taking the time necessary to do the job right.*" However, just weeks later of its launch, Pfizer announced that it was delaying a full-scale rollout to general practitioners until early 2007.

The New York Times reported by April 2007 that Exubera looked like becoming an expensive flop. After marketing for six-months to doctors, Exubera was receiving only one out of every 500 prescriptions for insulin written in the United States.

What went wrong? There seem to be many reasons, which were probably taken for granted or overlooked in the irrational exuberance of the concept of inhaled insulin. Consider these for example:

The best business case scenario was the idea of inhaled insulin itself. That inhaled insulin was more convenient than injections and avoided the needle pricks. In the real world, however, this argument was not working.

1. The Exubera inhaler was cumbersome and unwieldy about the size of a can of tennis balls. Doctors and patients alike were unhappy with it.
2. It now seemed that most diabetics were not that dissatisfied with injections. The needles used today are smaller and less painful than they used to be.

3. Exubera's dosages were not the same as injected dosages. They were more complex and converting them could be tricky.

4. Safety warnings were increasing. Long-term insulin inhalation could reduce pulmonary function and damage the lungs. As a result, potential Exubera patients had to be screened using lung function tests before they could be prescribed the product and this was discouraging both to physicians and patients.

High costs, lack of convenience, increasing safety concerns were weighing heavily on Exubera's chances of success. On October 19, 2007, just a year after launch, Pfizer announced that it was withdrawing Exubera from the market and taking a US $2.8-billion pre-tax charge in the third quarter. The product sold only $12 million in the first nine months of the year.

The impact of Pfizer's dismal failure with Exubera was so high on the industry that Novo Nordisk and Eli Lilly discontinued their inhaled insulin projects - Aerx and AIR respectively. Only Mannkind persisted with their Afrezza which received approval in June 2014.

(Source: Adapted from the article: Avery Johnson, *Insulin Flop Costs Pfizer $2.8 billion*. The Wall Street Journal, October 19, 2007).

Zelnorm: A Case of Misplaced Hopes

Novartis had high hopes at their drug - Zelnorm (Tegaserod) for indigestion, constipation, stomach pains, and other symptoms, which are known as irritable bowel syndrome (IBS) and that it would be their next blockbuster. Because there were fewer treatments for this condition at the time and about 15 percent of the population, mostly women suffered from such problems. Marketing people loved the drug, but clinicians suggested easing off of large-scale clinical trials doubting whether the syndrome even existed. Even if it did, they argued that it would be hard to prove that the drug worked because the symptoms were so subjective. As a result, most people had lost interest in the drug.

That's when Dan Vasella, the CEO and Chairman of the company came along and saw the way the teams were trying to bury the drug. He recalled that he had treated numerous patients who had suffered from IBS when he was a physician. Vasella pushed the clinical trials, which meant an investment of $ 100-million at the time. He promoted the new trial's chief Dr. Jorg Reinhardt, to head the drug development. Reinhardt has been a fast mover. In fact, one magazine described him as a risk-taking sports car enthusiast, who likes to zip down the Autobahn at 150 mph. The marketing team, enthused by these developments planned a massive TV campaign for Zelnorm when it was approved on July 24, 2002.

Zelnorm grossed $ 561-million in annual sales in 2006, but its commercial success had a very short life. On March 30, 2007, the US FDA asked Novartis to suspend Zelnorm's US marketing and sales activity because of a safety analysis that found a higher chance of heart attack, stroke and unstable angina in patients treated with Zelnorm compared with those, who were treated with a placebo. The FDA said in their announcement that they are treating Zelnorm like an investigative new drug (IND) and restricting Zelnorm's use to the treatment of irritable bowel syndrome with constipation (IBD-C) and chronic idiopathic constipation (CIC) in women younger than 55 and who have no known or pre-existing heart conditions.

On April 2, 2008, Novartis voluntarily discontinued Zelnorm putting an end to its blockbuster hopes.

Xigris Ends its Ten-Year Odyssey

In the early 2000s, Eli Lilly was facing the loss of patent protection for one of its most significant blockbuster drugs, Prozac. The company was in dire need of a blockbuster and launched its new drug – activated drotrecogin alfa (Xigris) for treating severe sepsis in high-risk patients. Lilly saw Xigris as a potential blockbuster, and some even predicted an annual sales of US $ 2-billion in three years. Because, Lilly considered sepsis as a phenomenal opportunity with doctors in intensive care units, practically an untapped market at the time.

The FDA approved Xigris in November 2001. However, sales were not as brisk as expected. What went wrong? Sidney Taurel, then CEO of Eli Lilly said, " Sales were down by a narrow label and prescriber caution and unique therapeutic options. It would take considerably more time, effort and investment to fulfill the promise of Xigris."

A year later, in 2002, the authors of a New England Journal of Medicine article stated that that the data on Xigris are encouraging but insufficient to make the standard of care.

Five years after its launch, Xigris in the first-half of 2006 sold just the US $ 98-million worldwide, which was 16 percent less than what it sold during the corresponding period of the previous year. On top of that, a New York Times article reported that three research investigators at National Institutes of Health (NIH) – Peter Eichacker, Charles Natanson, and Robert Dinner criticized Lilly for its questionable efforts in promoting Xigris. These three authors in a New England Journal of Medicine (NEJM) accused Lilly of financing a task force called–Values, Ethics, and Rationing in Critical Care – to spread the word that doctors were rationing the expensive Xigris. Lilly funded the task force with the US $ 2-million according to NPR (National Public Radio). They also wrote that Lilly used marketing strategies masquerading as evidence-based medicine.

What is even more damaging is that a group of physicians – many with financial ties with Lilly - funded the Surviving Sepsis Campaign. Lilly provided the vast majority of funding, the NPR reported. A Lilly spokeswoman, however, denied that the company masterminded the ethics task force or scientists that devised the guidelines.

On October 25, 2011, Eli Lilly announced that it was withdrawing Xigris, its drug for treating severe sepsis from all markets in the world including the United States, in the wake of a new study called, PROWESS-SHOCK. The study showed that the drug did no better than a placebo in reducing mortality.

(Source: Adapted from Fierce Pharma article, *Xigris: Pharma's biggest flops*)

Highly Effective Launch of Januvia and Janumet by MSD in India!

Merck (known as Merck Sharp and Dohme in all markets other than the US and Canada) launched its first-in-class prescription drug brands - Januvia (sitagliptin), and Janumet (fixed dose combination of sitagliptin with metformin) in the US first and later in the European Union with phenomenal success.

As a part of its geographical expansion strategy, MSD got its patent for Sitagliptin in India in 2007 launched its brand of sitagliptin (Januvia) in 2008. India accounts for over 30-million diabetic patients, which made it the diabetic capital of the world.

Januvia is a unique product that is much superior to the existing diabetic drugs. It has fewer side effects. One of the main concerns of physicians treating diabetes is that many anti-diabetic drugs may cause hypoglycemia and Januvia does not cause hypoglycemia.

To improve drug access and reach, MSD has worked out a differential pricing making it affordable to Indian patients. In addition to competitive pricing, MSD has also planned many initiatives to add value to diabetic treatment using Januvia in India.

The Strategy

The company has built its strategy on seeking out patients who are on metformin and convince, encourage physicians and patients to make Januvia the next step. This is because Januvia is the perfect add-on to metformin. Metformin is widely used and growing rapidly in most parts of the world. The strategy, therefore, is to hit that sweet spot.

Pre-launch Activities

A. The company conducted rigorous market research - both quantitative and qualitative involving 350 physicians and 200 patients and arrived at differential pricing.

B. Devised an integrated disease management program involving physicians and patients.

C. Created awareness of the DPP IV, the new class of drugs to which Januvia belongs through extensive scientific communication in medical journals.

D. Positioned the product with targeted diabetologists and physicians in specified geographical areas.

The Launch

A. Launched Januvia at a differential pricing (India-specific pricing that is different from its international price) at Rs. 42 a day.

B. Launched at CME events at both national and regional levels. KOLs from other countries conducted many of the National level CMEs. Regional KOLs conducted regional CMEs. The company has undertaken over 100 CMEs and workshops in 60 cities in two months.

C. Also, MSD representatives organized group meetings of 7 to 8 physicians and diabetologists to discuss and exchange information on DPP-IV class and its role in the management of diabetes.

D. The focus of marketing has been on the product's clinical profile and not on selling the drug. The company followed scientific marketing.

E. MSD made corporate social responsibility (CSR) an integral part of the strategy, which helped in creating goodwill among physicians and patients.

Post-Launch Activities

A. MSD has conducted many post-launch activities to sustain the interest and increase prescriptions from physicians and usage rate among patients. Some of the more important initiatives are:

B. Committed to Putting Patients First, MSD started SPARSH Health Line, a patient support service in January 2009. SPARSH is an integrated diabetes management program involving physicians and patients. This service is available to patients, who are being treated for type II diabetes and they can enroll to avail the services of SPARSH with their physician's recommendation. MSD has launched this program to complement their prescription-focused efforts and to support the patients with educational and other resources that help them manage their condition better. Here are the services offered by SPARSH:

(a) Counseling. Counseling over the telephone by trained personnel based on needs assessed by physicians, patients, and counselors. Counseling with customized diet-charts and personalized follow-ups. Exercise counseling with suggested lifestyle changes. Dos and Don'ts.

(b) Home-delivery of medicines

(c) Reminder alerts to keep the appointment

(d) HB A1C and lipid profile monitoring. MSD tied up with Thyrocare, a diagnostic company that provides specialized tests for a comprehensive health checkup.

(e) Disease awareness campaigns. Awareness about the disease and its management.

Over 85,000 patients have experienced SPARSH (www.sparsh msd.com) so far (May 2018).

Joint Venture with Sun Pharma to expand the market reach and share. Sun Pharma will sell Sitagliptin and under a different brand name, Istavel (launched in June 2011) and the Sitagliptin with Metformin

FDC (Fixed-dose combination) under the brand name, Istamet (Launched in August 2011) as a part of the company's India-specific strategy. The joint venture with Sun Pharma has helped Sitagliptin franchise achieve a dominant position in the oral hypoglycemic market in India.

MSD repeated its success story of Januvia and Janumet in India too with a brilliant strategy and impeccable execution and established a strong franchise in the diabetes market.

(Source: Adapted from: 1. Charmi Popat, *Product Management Assignment: Profile of a Pharma Blockbuster, Januvia*, SCRIBD; and 2. www.sparshmsd.com)

Acomplia Beats a Hasty Retreat without Accomplishing!

Obesity is a virtually untapped, multi-billion dollar market that draws drug developers like a moth to a flame. Sanofi Aventis thought that it had a winner with its Acomplia (rimonabant), a first-in-class selective cannabinoid receptor CB1 antagonist that blocked hunger signals to the brain. Touted as the first major weight-loss drug since Fen-Phen (fenfluramine / Phentermine), Acomplia was considered to be a blockbuster. Sanofi at one time even predicted an annual sales of US $ 3-billion. The European Union (EU) approved Acomplia in 2006, and it was selling at the time in 56 countries around the world. US FDA never accepted it.

Post-launch, Acomplia's problems began to mount. Reports were coming in about the drug's side effects that were worse than clinical studies indicated. Of primary concern were the increased instances of depression and suicidal thoughts. The European Medicines Agency (EMA) decided in 2008 to pull the drug out from the market, as Acomplia's risks no longer outweighed its benefits. The company withdrew Acomplia from the market in 2009.

Merck, which was also developing a CB1 antagonist also found that subjects who were taking the drug became irritable and depressed and abandoned the project.

(Source: Adapted from Fierce Pharma article, *Acomplia - Pharma's biggest flops*)

Life Cycle Management

Life Cycle Management

Pharmaceutical products are different. While the life of every product in today's fiercely competitive marketplace limited, the life of a pharmaceutical product is even more limited. A new pharmaceutical product typically has a life of twenty years from the date of the patent. However, about nearly half of it or more (10 to 12 years) is spent in the developmental phase. After the approval of the new product by the Federal Drug Administration (FDA), a drug has only about eight to ten years of patent life (exclusivity) left. Generics enter the market immediately after patent expiry and reduce the value of the innovator drug by eighty to ninety percent of the patented drug by price erosion. Every new pharmaceutical product, therefore, seeks to maximize its value during its limited lifetime and implements life cycle management (LCM) strategy.

Drug Life Optimization

Most pharmaceutical companies use the conventional product life cycle management approach that goes through the stages of introduction, growth, maturity, and decline on patent expiry. Every company seeks to maximize the return on investment during each of these stages. Stan Bernard of Bernard Associates LLC, in his article, *Rethinking Product Life Cycle Management* in the Pharmaceutical Executive of February 01, 2013, cogently argues that, unfortunately, the limited methodology of the conventional product life cycle management approach often results in flawed business decisions. Instead, he suggests a Drug Life Optimization approach to manage the life cycles of pharmaceutical products.

A standard product life cycle management entails making critical investments corresponding to four commercial stages of a product's life cycle - introduction, growth maturity, and decline. However, drug life optimization (DLO) enables pharmaceutical marketers to view the entire life of the product - not just the life cycle of a product, to make appropriate, timely and strategic decisions to maximize its lifetime sales. Unlike most other products, pharmaceuticals are unique products which do not have one life cycle, but rather three different periods:

A. An extensive early development period
B. A highly competitive mid-life period
C. A significant late post-patent period

These three periods together constitute the real life of a pharmaceutical product, running from bench to bedside. Pharmaceutical products have a lengthy, strictly regulated and complex developmental, pre-marketing phase usually lasting a decade or longer. An extremely diversified group of customers and stakeholders have a significant influence during this period of scale-up toward commercialization and impact the conditions of access, utilization, pricing, and sales dramatically.

Drug life optimization (DLO) presupposes that there is more life to your product beyond its expiration date. DLO focuses on maximizing product sales throughout the entire life of the product, even after patent expiry and loss of market exclusivity. It takes a transformational change in the mindset of every pharmaceutical marketer to practice DLO. Here are the significant areas in which the drug life optimization strategy differs with life cycle management strategy:

A. Incorporates early stage development planning.
B. Believes that there is life after patent expiry.
C. Recognizes cumulative product sales.

The DLO too, like life cycle management primarily aims to enhance a brand at its most basic level – its clinical profile. Four fundamental principles drive the likely success of any developmental activities. These are:

1. The ability to provide a meaningful improvement in clinical profile by increasing efficacy and reducing side effects, and drug-drug interactions.

2. The ability to expand the potential real-world patient base for the brand. Getting a new indication approval gets a new segment of patients and help widen the patient-base.

3. The ability to generate a return on investment as the costs of developmental activities can be very high. The size of the opportunity, therefore, should be more significant than the cost of development.

4. The ability to enhance the market exclusivity of the brand franchise through additional patent protection or regulatory exclusivities.

Drug Life Optimization: Key Tactics

Drug life optimization (DLO) takes a holistic approach and goes beyond the traditional marketing and sales promotion practices. It recognizes the importance of cumulative product sales. DLO focuses on maximizing product sales throughout the entire life of the product, including post-marketing exclusivity.

According to a 2011 Leerink-Swann investor analysis, innovative companies can capture as much as 20 t0 30 percent of total value of an innovative product after patent expiration and the onset of generic competition by considering a wide array of cost-effective actions. That is why the DLO approach assumes there is a real business opportunity even for products facing the loss of exclusivity (LOE). Many pharmaceutical companies have been implementing a combination of some of the following activities to maximize the value of their innovative products throughout their lifetime:

1. New formulations
2. New indications
3. Pediatric exclusivity
4. Disease management programs

5. Strategic price change

6. Authorized Generics

7. Combination products

8. Next-generation products

9. New dosing regimen

10. Companion devices or diagnostics

11. Patent litigation

12. Prescription to Over-the-counter (OTC) switches

13. Strategic lobbying

14. Public relations

15. Supporting the patient advocacy groups

Ten Commandments of Life Cycle Management

Dr. Neal Hansen, the expert trainer of the Late Stage Pharma Lifecycle Management course at C.E.L. for Pharma, suggests ten critical success factors to optimize the life of the drug throughout its life. These are not just success factors, they are in fact, ten commandments of successful life cycle management to achieve drug life optimization:

1. Consider lifecycle management as integral not optional to your strategy.

2. Ensure management recognizes the value of life cycle management planning and investment. Top management support and involvement are crucial for success in lifecycle management.

3. Allow time to think of the future.

4. Drive cross-functional alignment through common, shared goals.

5. Establish an active process for lifecycle management. A process mindset ensures successful implementation and timely course correction.

6. Know where your market is going. Understanding the unmet needs and opportunities and threats you may need to address is the foundation on which you build your life cycle management strategy. It is not enough if you understand these opportunities in today's context, you also need to anticipate the future environmental drivers and resistors.

7. Integrate. However, do not ignore uncertainty. Uncertainty remains a crucial challenge even when you are preparing for the next life cycle management strategy with analog research for fielding a successor candidate after the patent expires on the current drug. Fundamental questions to ask are: what else might happen to shape the market? How do we deal with those? We need to look to longer time frames and prepare for dealing with uncertainty as effectively as we can.

8. Put strategy at the heart of life cycle management planning.

9. Get creative with both internal and external solutions. The entire life cycle management team should think and consider different approaches to dealing with common issues reflecting potentially different timescales, how you can apply them to different regions, costs and probability of success.

10. Last but not least, build and maintain a corporate memory. The average life cycle of the team members in a life cycle management team is often shorter than that of the brand life cycle. So identifying the best way to pass on the learnings of previous life cycle exercises to new generations of team members is critical. If the company has a good life cycle management strategy already in place, why reinvent the wheel?

Here are a few cases that show how pharmaceutical companies optimize the value of their innovative prescription drug brands throughout their life.

Bayer Manages the Life Cycle of 'Cipro' in Copybook Style!

Bayer's Cipro (Ciprofloxacin), the second approved drug in the Fluoroquinolone class illustrates how a company can extend the product life cycle even in a crowded segment like antibacterials. Cipro's case was a blend of marketing plusses and minuses. Its main advantage was its antibacterial strength. It was comparable to intravenous (IV) antibiotics that ruled the field at that time.

Team Cipro

In the 1980s, Bayer created a cross-functional team - The Cipro Team drawing people from the vital functions such as clinical, pre-clinical and marketing. The Cipro team had gone the whole hog in building a mass of credible data proving the superior antibacterial power of Cipro. At one point, every hospital in the United Kingdom was testing Cipro for one thing or another. In the US, the team blanketed the country, clinical, and pre-clinical, in vitro, animal models, pharmacokinetics, pharmacodynamics and indeed the whole works. Cipro team was even making a pharmacoeconomic argument much before the heyday of managed care and formularies!

The Cipro team involved virtually every thought leader in the Cipro studies. More importantly, they believed in the study. The German team had presented a model, which forecasted revenues by indication. The model predicted a $ 100-million in the first year. Cipro did achieve $ 100-million in the first year's sales surprising even the insiders. Within six months of launch, Cipro was on 99 percent of hospital formularies.

COLT out of the Bolt!

Cipro dominated the field of UTIs, but in 1996, the team wanted a more significant share of the respiratory market as it had another quinolone - Avelox (Moxifloxacin), which was showing promising results in respiratory infections. By building a franchise in the respiratory area for Cipro would pave the way for Avelox. The company accordingly launched COLT, an acronym for Cipro Oral Launch Team. COLT built pulmonary advisory boards and collected plenty of evidence. The reps promoting Cipro had multiple case studies asserting the drug's efficacy and other support material like slide kits. They garnered massive support from leading pulmonologists and infection-disease specialists.

Operation Surge

Bayer did some solid rethinking and revisited its strategy for the primary indication - UTI. The late 1990s were the period when resistance to the TMP-SMX (Trimethoprim and Sulphamethoxazole) class of antibacterials was emerging as a real and growing global public threat. Bayer spotted that opportunity. The treatment protocol around that time was that the physicians try Bactrim (TMP-SMX) or penicillin first, then move on to a quinolone like Cipro. The Cipro team wanted the physicians to think Cipro First! They wanted to move Cipro to the first-line. If you are in an area of high resistance, it makes more economic sense for the physician and patient to start with Cipro first. The Cipro team set an objective for itself of growing its UTI use from 48 percent to 56 percent of the drug's prescriptions in 1999. They treated it like a re-launch, developing an internal icon and logo. They conducted a large Phase IV study of resistance rates. They appropriately christened the campaign as SURGE, an acronym Strategic Urologic Re-Launch, and Growth Effort. The campaign gave birth to a catchy slogan for Bayer's two quinolones: *Avelox above the belt, Cipro below the belt!*

SURGE succeeded because the team had put into practice the lessons they learned from their past mistakes. For example, their initiative of a Cystitis Pack, a three-day regimen offered in packaging specially designed for women, to gain market share in UTI, where they were already strong did not fly. A post-marketing analysis revealed some of the critical aspects the team had overlooked, and they were:

A. The team did not stay true to their branding. All of a sudden, it (the color scheme) was not the standard Cipro blue.

B. Physicians were accustomed to prescribing a four-to-seven-day therapy of Cipro, and a three-day dosage regimen was against the grain.

C. Pharmacies were already carrying 250, 500 and 750 mg tablets of Cipro and resisted another stock keeping unit (SKU).

Anthrax Attack and Cipro

The Anthrax attack of October 2001 made Cipro the talk of the nation. Cipro's effectiveness against Anthrax was familiar since the early 1990s after the Department of Defense did animal studies to determine its utility. The troops in Kuwait and Iraq in the first Gulf War used it. Bayer continuously worked alongside the government to provide Cipro as needed. It paved the way for Bayer's regulatory submission for approval of a new indication. Cipro obtained approval for its Anthrax indication in 2000. There was considerable pressure on the government to break Bayer's patent so that other manufacturers can produce the drug to meet the unprecedented demand for Cipro post 9/11. Bayer reassured the government and the public that it would be able to supply the quantities needed and also became one of the first companies to authorize a generic version of Cipro.

LCM (Life Cycle Management), Copybook Style

Bayer managed Cipro in a classic copybook style through its life cycle. The company benchmarked Augmentin, the antibiotic that GSK had handled exceptionally well. Augmentin grew at 6 percent per annum even after the launches of generics and its extended release formulation. Bayer too had done pretty well with Cipro. Cipro XR also had contributed by extending its franchise after genericization of Cipro. Here are the key activities Bayer undertook during its life cycle management of Cipro:

Period	Activity
1981-86	Development of the molecule
1987	Cipro Tablet launches - LRTI, UTI, Skin and Soft Tissue Infections, Diarrhea, Bone and Joint infections
1991	Cipro IV
1994	Typhoid Fever
1996	Prostatitis, Intra-Abdominal Infections, Severe Nosocomial Pneumonia
1997	Sinusitis, AECB 750mg; Febrile Neutropenia (IV), sNDA for Cystic Fibrosis
1998	Oral Suspension, Ear Drops
1999	Cipro 250 mg / 3-days; Safety Studies in Children; Reaches Billion Dollars in Annual Sales
2000	Anthrax sNDA; Anthrax Indication
2001	Anthrax Crisis; Sales Peak at $ 1.23-billion
2002	NDA Cipro - Once Daily - Cipro XR Approval
2003	Cipro XR 1000mg Launch; UTI Multi-source Generics Enter Market; 180-day Pediatric Exclusivity Granted; Patent Expires; Sales Drop to $ 750-million
2004	Cipro BID Pediatric Exclusivity Expires, Generics Enter Market

Cipro's Life Cycle Management

Brand-name companies have very high stakes in extending patent protection as long as they can. Bayer had managed its Cipro with all its might in copybook style.

(Source: Adapted from an article, *The lifecycle of Cipro*, by Sibyl Shalo, Senior Editor, in the Pharmaceutical Executive, August 1, 2004)

Merck Wins the Diabetes Race with a First Class Strategy for its First-in-class Diabetes Drug!

First-in-class drugs, when communicated effectively with their stakeholders are naturally accepted and achieve reasonable success at the marketplace. That is what first-in-class should be. When you launch the first-in-class drug with a well-crafted, first-class launch what can you expect? A better performance? More than that. That's what a synergistic approach or action does to a product. However, when you add serendipity to a first-in-class drug launched with a first-class strategy? Uncommon success. That's what Merck had achieved with its first-in-class diabetes drug, sitagliptin (Januvia), a dipeptidyl peptidase - IV (DPP - IV) inhibitor along with its fixed-dose combination (FDC) Metformin /sitagliptin sibling, Janumet. An extraordinary success by every which way you look at it. Here are some of the achievements of Merck's Januvia diabetes franchise:

A. Crossed the coveted $1-billion mark and achieved blockbuster status in its second year of launch.

B. Garnered 14 percent share of all new prescriptions written for oral hypoglycemics by primary care physicians and 20 percent of all new prescriptions written by endocrinologists. These were in the same league as the categories' market leaders.

C. Became the second brand among oral hypoglycemics regarding prescriptions written in the US.

D. Within one year of the launch, Januvia received three million prescriptions and became the most prescribed oral glycemic drug in the US.

E. Reached $5.7-billion in total sales in its sixth-year (2012) and became the best franchise brand in the company's history.

How did Merck achieve all this? What is the company's secret sauce? Two things. One is the company's first-class launch strategy, meticulous planning, and impeccable execution. Serendipity is the second. Before we discuss in detail about the first-class launch strategy, let us look at the part serendipity played in Januvia's success.

Serendipity

Serendipity is the occurrence and development of events by chance in a happy or beneficial way. Januvia's success is due to both an excellent commercialization plan, a first-class strategy well executed and an active element of serendipity. A confluence of external factors seems to have coalesced to create an opportunity for Januvia's success. First, the growing global obesity epidemic, which is directly correlated with the ever-increasing global diabetes type 2 epidemic has contributed to the exponential growth of the overall market for type 2 diabetes products.

Secondly, Januvia could have launched in direct competition to Novartis' Galvus (Vildagliptin) in the US But, shortly before launch, FDA delayed its approval of Galvus due to some side-effect concerns and asked Novartis to submit additional data. It left the field open for Januvia, allowing it to enjoy three years US exclusivity in its class before AstraZeneca and BMS introduced Onglyza (Saxagliptin). Similar market dynamics occurred even in Europe, after Januvia's launch in 2007. Novartis introduced Galvus in Europe a year later in 2008 but has managed sales of just 9 percent compared to Januvia. Chance did favor the prepared mind. Merck's planning was genuinely meticulous.

More importantly, physicians had been using many products to manage their patients' type 2 diabetes, but most of those drugs carried the risk of hypoglycemia and other side effects. Many physicians, therefore were looking for newer, safer approaches to treating type 2 diabetes without these side effects. Januvia's favorable safety profile combined with its efficacy story led many physicians to turn to it making it a huge success.

First-class Strategy

Merck's strategy has been genuinely first-class, with meticulous planning and impeccable execution. Firstly Januvia's dramatic launch was all about speed. It provides an excellent example of the speed with which companies can now get new products to the market. Consider these facts:

1. The US FDA approved Sitagliptin 3.8 years after the drug discovery. Compare this with five years for Rofecoxib and an industry average of 14.2 years for all the drugs launched between 1990 and 1999.

2. Once the drug was approved, Merck began a multifaceted marketing campaign that capitalized on sitagliptin being a new class of drug and its unique mechanism of action.

3. Within 24-hours of approval, thought leaders and key opinion leaders began delivering talks to educate the medical community about the drug. Within 48-hours, education forums delivered, sales representatives had their first contacts, and webcasts and satellite-made broadcasts to thousands of health care providers and investigators.

4. The product websites were functional within 90-minutes of approval. Within eight days, Merck had reached 70 percent of target doctors and made first deliveries of sitagliptin to pharmacies.

5. Merck made sure that they had rapid reimbursement and rapid approval of managed care plans to provide access to patients. Merck clearly understood that the payer community realizes that diabetes accounts for roughly about 15 percent of their total costs and if you add the value of treating the complications, it would cost even more. The diabetes category is thus well covered. That is why, within 14-days, Merck had completed discussions with managed care organizations

(MCOs) covering 188-million patients or 73 percent of insured US population.

6. The launch of a drug often foretells a drug's performance in the market, and Merck put a significant effort in making sure that they had rapid access, and that meant both the earliest possible launch in as many markets as possible. The company launched Januvia in as many as eighty-one countries across the world within four-years of its approval in the US

First-class Strategy: Key Elements

Apart from speed, which is the most crucial element of Merck's winning strategy many vital factors helped Merck win the diabetes race. These are – Key decision points, Education of the new science, Lifecycle management, Unbranded campaigns to earn the trust of all stakeholders, Multichannel marketing, Digital focus and Roping in of celebrities to speed up awareness on the importance of managing diabetes.

Key Decision Points

Ever since the era of blockbuster-decline started, the Big Pharma began to devote a majority of its resources towards in-licensing products to fill its pipelines, as opposed to its earlier practice of internal development. Perhaps the most important decision point in Merck's sitagliptin strategy is bucking this emerging trend. Interestingly though, Merck's DPP-IV project began with an in-licensed candidate from privately held German biotech called Probiodrug AG, all the development has been internal.

The second most important decision point in the whole strategy is that the development team recognized from the start that it is vitally important to demonstrate the efficacy of sitagliptin in combination with metformin, an essential first-line therapy along with sulphonyl-urea drug class for type 2 diabetes around the globe. That is how and why Merck developed sitagliptin as a monotherapy and as a fixed-dose combination with metformin right from the beginning.

The decision to push a metformin combination early in development, before anyone knew if Januvia would even be a success on its own was a significant factor for the brand's success. Later, once the FDA approved it, placing substantial marketing muscle behind the new combination, Janumet, even with blockbuster Januvia on hand. The company jumped on Janumet very early, put the development program in place early on and put a massive promotional effort behind it in all the markets when they launched.

The strategy of seeking out patients on Metformin to encourage the physicians and patients to make Januvia the next step has been another winning move.

Differential pricing in pharmerging markets for Januvia and Janumet is another crucial decision point. A small sacrifice in pricing has gone a long way in building market share and in strengthening the company's diabetes franchise in these markets. Going for rapid and broad access, without holding out for high prices is another critical decision point that made the company's diabetes franchise a spectacular success.

Life Cycle Management

The brand team of Januvia very carefully planned to manage the brand lifecycle in copybook style. Within a year of Januvia's initial approval, the company's Januvia - metformin combination product, Janumet had earned approval as well. Both the brands received approval in the European Union, the second largest Pharma market in the world. Within five years of launching Janumet, the FDC combination of sitagliptin with metformin, the company got its approval for an extended release dosage form of its FDC - Janumet XR. Janumet XR adds once-daily dosage convenience to its power of glycemic control. Both the brands are marketed today in as many as 81 countries across the globe. The following table presents a snapshot of its lifecycle management in action.

Januvia and Janumet : Life Cycle Management

Product / Dosage Form	Approval Date
Januvia (sitagliptin)	October 16, 2006, by US FDA
Januvia (sitagliptin)	March 21, 2007, by European Commission
Janumet (FDC of sitagliptin and metformin)	March 30, 2007, by US FDA
Janumet (FDC of sitagliptin and metformin)	July 16, 2008, by European Commission
Janumet XR (Extended release dosage form of Janumet)	February 02, 2012, by US FDA

Indication Expansion

Starting narrow and going wide – earning a single approval as early as possible and then following it up with a stack of additional indications to broaden the access has been the essence of Januvia's strategy. There was a lot of pre-approval and pre-launch work behind the success of Januvia. The brand team made it a priority to tailor Januvia's clinical programs for different regions to make sure that they had all the data that is required to get reimbursement in different areas. They also had the right indications for various regions and the right studies.

When Januvia was in development, metformin had established itself as the first-line, so Merck knew very well that Januvia would be competing head to head with TZDs for second-line therapy in combination with metformin. With the launch of Janumet, an FDC of Januvia with metformin within six-months of Januvia's launch, Merck changed its approach. The new complimentary marketing approach focused on — Start with the power of Janumet with the goal of targeting patients who are unlikely to respond to metformin alone, bringing Janumet FDC for the first-line patients rather than third-line for many FDCs. By contrast, the marketing for Januvia focused on – Add the power of Januvia aiming for a second-line position.

Getting more indications approved means expanding the market and usage rate. The Januvia brand team added indications for third-line use, added an indication for use with insulin, added an indication for use with TZDs and Metformin. The company followed up rapidly with clinical studies in various indications, filing, and approvals. The following table presents a quick glance at Januvia's indication expansion plan.

Januvia and Janumet : Indication Expansion

Phase	Indications
1st Phase	Add-on to Metformin versus sulphonyl urea - Janumet
2nd Phase	Add-on to sulphonyl urea with or without metformin
3rd Phase	1. Insulin add-on 2. Triple combination with PPar (Peroxisome proliferator-activated receptor) and metformin 3. High baseline HbA1c metformin add-on study 4. Initial comparison with PPAR-y 5. Initial combination with metformin 6. Study in the elderly 7. Mechanism of action studies

Emphasis on Education

Education has been the primary focus of Merck's Januvia strategy. It has been the top priority. Why? Consider these facts. With only about two-thirds of diabetic patients in developed countries aware that they have the disorder, and of those on medication, about two-thirds failing to reach the goal - both diagnosis and treatment have a long way to go. In other markets these numbers are likely to be even higher, the patient needs even more significant. What drove Merck to move faster than ever before in educating their key stakeholders? That unmet patient need. That low awareness.That lower level of attainment of the diabetic patients' therapeutic goals.

Given Januvia's new method of action, Merck understood the need to educate - in a cascading manner all the targeted groups with targeted messages that related Januvia to each stakeholder's needs. Merck focused on primary care physicians (PCPs) and targeted patients who have been on prescriptions of metformin. As Januvia is a perfect add-on to metformin, this made eminent sense. Merck reached all the PCPs with a carefully thought out strategy and followed it up with brilliant execution with the help of thought leaders, key opinion leaders at national, regional and local levels in the shortest time possible. The use of technology such as video detailing and tablet PCs enabled Merck to reach its target audience with specific messages very rapidly across the country.

Merck thus got an early start with physicians not only on type 2 diabetes in general but on incretins and the incretin pathway, which is the mechanism through which sitagliptin worked. The company started with scientific leaders, and then expanded to the specialist community and from there to the office-based physicians before approval and launch.

Post-approval Promotion

If Merck funneled substantial resources into the market before drug approval was secured, what it did was even more focused. Post-approval, branded materials and a rich promotional platform followed online and offline, including training programs for healthcare professionals (HCPs). Merck effectively engaged KOLs, celebrity appearances, direct-to-consumer (DTC) advertising and a sales force stretching across the globe.

Post-approval, Merck started branded campaigns in addition to constant non-branded educational push and pull campaigns around the importance of healthy living, and the potential for long-term complications resulting from uncontrolled diabetes.

Creative Awareness Campaigns

Merck had created many campaigns to build, and improve awareness about diabetes type 2, and how to manage it in an exciting and patient-friendly way. These campaigns not only provided information on diabetes and related topics but also offered many tools to measure, monitor and manage their diabetes. The following table presents a quick glimpse of the most effective and appreciated disease awareness campaigns sponsored by Merck.

Merck's Disease Awareness Campaigns At A Glance

Campaigns and Programs	What they are about
1. discusshypo.com	discusshypo.com was an unbranded disease awareness campaign conceived by the Januvia brand team at Merck to create awareness about hypoglycemia among patients. It was deployed across multiple channels including journal advertising, eDetails, direct mail, and waiting room posters. discusshypo.com campaign was nominated for the best disease awareness campaign at Manny Awards in 2011.
	In this disease awareness campaign, the company put the physician in the patients' shoes, letting them feel the discomforts associated with hypoglycemia. The creative elements were meticulously crafted, and really take HCPs (healthcare practitioners) out of their comfort zone.
2. Restaurant of the Month	An interesting campaign that offers tips for diabetics ordering food in a restaurant, where ingredients and portions are not as controlled as home made fare. The company has roped in the BasketBall legend, Earl, *The Pearl*, Monroe, who is a type 2 diabetic himself, to share his story with patients regarding tips about healthy eating and advice on ordering food at restaurant. All this to accelerate awareness.
	Here is what one can do to celebrate a restaurant of the month.

Table Contd...

Campaigns and Programs	What they are about
	A. Go to MerckDiabetes.com to find the restaurants in your city participating in Diabetes Restaurant Month. B. Visit the restaurants and order the featured diabetes-friendly dishes on the menu. C. Use tips from MerckDiabetes.com to make your next meal diabetes-friendly.
3. BloodSugarBasics.com	Merck partnered with the American College of Endocrinology for an educational campaign called BloodSugarBasics, which provides information to patients about managing diabetes. The company had also roped in a number of celebrities, who themselves were type 2 diabetes sufferers. They share their stories and suggest steps to tackle the disease. The campaign helped in a significant manner to accelerate awareness.
4. JourneyforControl.com	journeyforcontrol.com has become Merck's centralized hub for consumer information on diabetes. The site includes downloadable tools for patients, quizzes, educational resources, doctor discussion guides and more. It also has interactive Conversation Map, created through a partnership with ADA (American Diabetes Association) and Healthy Interactions, a company that facilitates face-to-face dialogue driven sessions guided by a trained facilitator around the disease. Merck has provided under their journeyforcontrol.com program various resources to certified diabetes educators to have a series of small group interactions with patients.

Table Contd...

Campaigns and Programs	What they are about
	Started ten years ago, by three organizations — the American Diabetes Association, Healthy Interactions and Merck, this ongoing program is set out test a simple proposition around diabetes care: could a set of tools focused on lifestyle and behavioral changes help healthcare providers to improve diabetes management for patients? In the first four months,10,000 diabetes educators were trained. Another 10,000 were trained in the first three years. Now, more than 30,000 educators across the country have been trained in the innovative *US Diabetes Conversation Map Program.*
5. Conversation Map Program	The unbranded Conversation Map Program features a candy landesque map that patients can navigate for a more immersive educational experience.
6. America's Diabetic Challenge: Get to your goals	The purpose of this program from Merck and the American Diabetic Association (ADA) is to raise awareness among people with type 2 diabetes about the importance of working with their doctors to set and reach their HbA1c goals. HbA1c is a test that shows what your average blood glucose has been over the past two or three months.

Celebrities to Accelerate Awareness

To accelerate awareness of diabetes and its management among patients, Merck followed a strategy of getting celebrities on board. It is important to note that the celebrities Merck chose for these campaigns have one thing in common: they have type 2 diabetes. The all share their stories with the patients and encourage them to know more about diabetes and how to manage it. The following table presents a snapshot of the celebrities that Merck used to accelerate the awareness of the condition through their unbranded campaigns.

Awareness Campaigns by Celebrities

Celebrity	Purpose
1. Earl, *The Pearl* Monroe, the Basketball legend, who has type 2 diabetes	To celebrate and promote the Diabetes Restaurant of the Month campaign.
2. Randy Jackson, music industry veteran and American Idol judge, who has type 2 diabetes	To participate in Taking Diabetes to Heart campaign to drum up awareness of serious complications, and to urge patients to get in tune with the disease.
3. Mike Golic, NFL (national football) tackle, Emmy winner, ESPN broadcaster	To share his story, give tips to tackle type 2 diabetes in the Blood Sugar Basics Campaign.

Merck Partners with Siemens

Clinical studies show that in-office HbA1c test results improve decision making, patient compliance, and outcomes. In 2008, Merck partnered with Siemens for a diagnostic program to quickly identify potential Januvia patients outside of the United States. The Siemens' point-of-care program with their in-office HbA1c technology helps physicians manage their type 2 diabetes patients more efficiently. Because, it allows the clinicians, who were working in clinics or private practices to measure a patient's HbA1c levels, the key benchmark in determining whether the disease is under adequate control in real time. Merck's initiative helped greatly at the time, as this test was not available at that time, and patients and physicians had to wait for the blood work to be processed at a lab to assess HbA1c levels.

Merck had rolled the Siemens partnership since 2008 in 35 countries worldwide by 2015. Since the program allows physicians to identify with poorly controlled diabetes during the first visit, Januvia can be prescribed on the spot, canceling the need for a followup appointment with lab results.

Multi-Channel Marketing

Merck followed a multichannel marketing strategy for launching Januvia. The company invested in both traditional and digital DTC, e-Detailing, Tablet PC detailing, waiting room posters, multiple websites, YouTube videos, medical education and a significant conventional presence that included webcasts. In communicating directly with physicians and patients, Januvia's brand team had leaned on the good, old-fashioned sales force, still probably the most critical channel.

The company focused on digital and decided to have a robust digital presence for two reasons. One is that digital is efficient and futuristic. That is where the future seems to be moving. Digital enables a company to meet customers where they are at the right time and with the right information. The second is, it is highly cost-effective.

Although much digital space is still a nascent area for the industry, Merck pursued it enthusiastically. The company tried to avoid pushing information out to its key stakeholders at what they would perceive an inopportune time or in a way that is not easily digestible. Instead, the company created an environment where they want to pull information in.

The company's digital bet paid off. In 2011, the L 2 Digital IQ index placed Januvia first in diabetes and fourth among all Pharma brands. This index is a ranking created by L 2 Think Tank in partnership with Healthcare marketing network Vue Group that evaluate pharmaceutical brands' digital presence across four primary criteria, namely e-commerce website, Brand translation, Social media, and Mobile compatibility and optimization.

Earning Physicians' Trust

For a pharmaceutical brand, establishing physicians' trust is of paramount importance. The Januvia brand team put much emphasis on building trust at a company level as it gives a strong foundation for the brand. Also, the company provided much support to physicians in helping their patients. The unbranded campaigns and programs that the company had done gave the company additional credibility with its stakeholders such as physicians and patients. In 2011, The Inaugural Harris Physician Pulse Study of the Physician Trust placed Januvia second among all non-insulin diabetes brands behind only Glucophage. The Harris Physician Pulse Study is particularly gratifying for Januvia brand team as physician trust is closely correlated to prescribing behavior.

Peter Loescher, CEO of Siemens put it succinctly when he commented on Merck's Januvia strategy. He said: *Merck's Januvia strategy is a strategy of investing to win with each product launch - using fewer salespeople, relying more on alternate channels like the internet and putting new emphasis on getting health plans to cover the drug.*

Every which way you look at it, Merck's Januvia strategy is the First-class strategy for a First-in-class drug!

(Adapted from Joshua Slatko's article *Lucky and Good,* 22nd Annual Report, Medicine of the Year: Januvia, MedAdNews, July 2012)

Prilosec, The Famous Heartburn Drug causes Heartburn to its Competitors!

Prilosec, the first proton-pump-inhibiting heartburn drug is also one of the best selling drugs in prescription medicines history. Even after fifteen-months after its patent expiration date of April 2001, there were no generics in sight nibbling at its huge $-6.2-billion pie of the antacid, antiulcerants market!

The reason? Call it marketing paranoia or industry foresight - it is the seven years of planning by a cross-functional team of marketers, lawyers and scientists at Astra Merck, who called themselves the Shark Fin Team. Why Shark Fin Team? Because it symbolized the sales chart shape of what would happen after generics enter the market if they did nothing to defend - an inverted 'V.' The Shark Fin Team was hell-bent on changing that by a proactive, fail-safe defensive strategy and ensure that the shape of the sales curve does not slope even after generics enter.

The deft handling of the task of keeping generics at bay is evident from the fact that there were no generic versions of Prilosec even after fifteen-months after its patent expiry. The team knew that it possibly could not fend off generics forever and decided to transfer its franchise to its successor drug candidate - Nexium.

The Shark Fin Team, which began its work in 1995, came up with 50 possible solutions to defend Prilosec revenues from the inevitable generic onslaught for as long as possible. Some of their more essential approaches were:

A. Launch a new heartburn drug that worked significantly better

B. Construct an elaborate legal defense with an estate of Prilosec patents

C. Lock-in current users with Prilosec's successor through a massive promotional blitz

D. Buy six more months of time through pediatric exclusivity provision

E. DTC (Direct-to-consumers) campaign to make it the most recognizable drug

F. Execute prescription-to-OTC switch of Prilosec

Successful Successor-drug Candidate

The planners evaluated many developmental options and subjected each one of them to a four-way test:

1. Would it be better than Prilosec?
2. Would it be patentable?
3. Would it be technically feasible?
4. Would it be possible to launch before generics hit the market?

Launching a follow-on product is more comfortable when the first drug leaves many patients unsatisfied. To their utter surprise, the Astra-Merck team found during their market research that only about fifty percent of Prilosec users were satisfied and were entirely pain-free. This otherwise bad news became music to the ears of the team, as it would make their task of persuading the unsatisfied users to try the new drug.

The Shark Fin Team despite its lofty goals of coming with a new drug that is significantly better than Prilosec had to contend with a mere me-too drug, which was virtually no better, but patentable thus ensuring several more years of patent exclusivity. Astra-Merck partnership of Merck & Co and Astra AB of Sweden initially sold Prilosec in the US. Astra later bought out Merck's share and merged with another company to form AstraZeneca. Merck continued to collect about a third of Prilosec's US sales and 27 percent of the successor drug.

The company finally decided on Nexium, a new drug that is not only better for common heartburn than the one it would succeed but also could look better with aggressive marketing. The team planned a marketing blitz to lock-in current users of Prilosec to Nexium and priced it as steeply as they did with Prilosec – $4 a pill.

Reinforcing the Legal Defense

Pharma companies patent everything they can think of about their drugs, setting up patent estates that serve as legal minefields for competitors. Astra had started applying for these related patents in 1985, four years before it launched Prilosec in the US.

The company's lawyers were always alert to file patents for Prilosec at every opportunity. Take for instance; when scientists elsewhere found out that ulcers are often the result of bacterial infection, Astra obtained patents on the idea of combining Prilosec with antibiotics and later argued that generic competitors could not launch copycat versions of Prilosec because doctors might prescribe them with antibiotics, infringing its patent on the combination idea.

Astra also patented the metabolite that forms in the body when a patient swallows Prilosec and then claimed that patients who took generic versions of Prilosec would violate their metabolite patent as swallowing the drug (even if it is generic) forms the metabolite resulting in an infringement. Also, the company patented the way it manufactured the drug and claimed that generic competitors were illegally using the same techniques. The company patented the idea of putting two coatings out of necessity to ensure its absorption in the intestine on the active ingredient - Omeprazole. Although this type of coating is common, Astra's lawyers could persuade the patent clerks int he US and Europe that their scientists developed this novel method of triple-layering (usual enteric coating coupled with a thin middle layer that prevents the enteric coating damaging the drug as the standard enteric coating itself is slightly acidic). It was as George Harris in his Wall Street Journal story on Prilosec describes, like patenting the discovery that - *hamburgers are best served with tomato slice sandwiched between the lettuce and the meat, so the bread does not get soggy!*

Switching Prilosec Users to Nexium

The company launched a very aggressive multi-pronged marketing program for switching Prilosec users to Nexium. They had tried every strategy in the book to come up with a persuading strategy to switch prescribers and users of Prilosec to Nexium covering all elements of the marketing mix - right from differentiating the new product, pricing, expand the reach of their communication, sampling, DTC advertising, and a prescription-to-OTC switch.

A. *Differentiation:* Nexium is one-half of the Prilosec molecule - an isomer of it, which gets in the bloodstream more efficiently than the whole Prilosec molecule. The researchers thought that it might be better in healing erosive esophagitis, a condition arising out of the burped-up stomach acid injuring the esophagus. Only one of the four studies conducted by the company comparing 40 mg dose of the molecule - what was to become Nexium with a 20 mg dose of Prilosec showed a marginal improvement in healing rates in erosive esophagitis (90 percent versus 87 percent). That was enough for the strategists to get the approval and to blow their trumpet saying that when the heartburn was so severe that it eroded the esophagus try Nexium, the one with better healing rates!

B. *Extending Exclusivity:* AstraZeneca launched Nexium in March 2001, one month before its Prilosec patent expired. The company bought time for switching Prilosec users to Nexium, by getting pediatric exclusivity, which gave the company time till October 2001.

C. *Distinct Identity:* Prilosec became one of the most recognizable drugs owing to a distinctive purple color, and the company spent hundreds of millions of dollars on direct-to-consumer advertising. Most of the ads signed off saying ask your doctor about Prilosec, the purple pill. After much debate, the Shark Fin Team decided to stick with the purple color even for Nexium to leverage the brand franchise and extend it to the next drug candidate (Nexium) and at the same time differentiating it with racing stripes and changed the pitch to today's purple pill is Nexium. The company spent about half-a-billion dollars in the launch year on the switching campaign.

D. *Promotion to Physicians:* AstraZeneca had 6,000 medical detailers for promoting nine products to primary care physicians in the US. They devote a third of their time to pitch for Nexium, which is three times more than what they do for other products. According to impact Rx, a market research firm, doctors got more pitches for Nexium than for any other heartburn drug. The switch meant cannibalization of Prilosec, and the salespeople, who established Prilosec talked about it only for comparing it unfavorably to Nexium. The marketing strategy paid off. IMS Health reported that Prilosec's share of new heartburn prescriptions dropped to 25 percent just in one year after the launch of Nexium in April 2001, from about 49 percent in 2000. Nexium garnered a 19 percent share of new prescriptions for heartburn during this period. Most of Nexium's prescriptions came at the expense of Prilosec as planned. Impact Rx data confirmed that over 60 percent of Prilosec patients switched over to Nexium when they made a switch from Prilosec. The company was flooding the physicians' offices with free samples of Nexium, a proven success strategy across the industry for doctors give these free samples to their patients as starter doses, and most of the patients would continue using the drug once they find it works.

E. *Pricing Strategy:* AstraZeneca priced Nexium marginally lower – lower by 17 cents at $4.30 as compared to Prilosec's $4.47. The strategy was based on a well-established convention to price the first generic 15 percent lower than the branded version and eventually would fall much lower as more and more generic players enter the market. The company, also cut deals with managed care organizations to sell Nexus for less than Prilosec to hasten the switching process.

F. *OTC Switch:* AstraZeneca chose Proctor & Gamble, the FMCG giant known for its consumer marketing and advertising expertise for launching the over-the-counter version of Prilosec. P&G also has been looking for the significant opportunity in the OTC healthcare segment to beef up its presence. P&G spent five years preparing to launch Prilosec OTC version before prescription generics moved in. By the time the company launched the OTC version in June 2003, Schwarz Pharma's generic version of Prilosec had captured about 70 percent of generic Omeprazole market.

P&G brought its compulsive consumer research and a $ 100-million marketing campaign including a soap-opera star to meet the challenge of winning back defectors of Prilosec to other brands. P&G had a three-year exclusive window from the FDA for OTC versions of Omeprazole from June 2003. P&G priced the Prilosec OTC version attractively - at less than a dollar per pill, which is less than one-fourth of the brand-name version. Backed by its research and marketing insight, the company believed the convenience of picking up Prilosec OTC with the rest of the groceries would be a meaningful point for consumers.

P&G, known for their advertising and branding excellence created a distinct personality for Prilosec OTC. The brand ambassador was a composite array of consumers P&G interviewed. He was not like the stereotypical heartburn sufferer, a late-night beer guzzling guy. The company identified the ideal consumer of Prilosec OTC and christened her - *Joanne, a 35-year-old mother. She shops for her entire household. Also, she has heartburn. Something as seemingly innocuous as a cup of coffee can trigger Joanne's heartburn. You don't have to stuff yourself with chili dogs or guzzle beer to have heartburn.*

The advertising blitz too comprised TV commercials featuring a former male star of Guiding Light and As the World Turns. The slogan: *One pill, 24 hours, Zero heartburn. It's possible with Prilosec OTC.*

P&G created a 24-hour command center. A fleet of 1,200 trucks delivered Prilosec OTC to retailers so that the products hit the maximum number of shelves one minute past midnight that is as soon as it got its OTC approval. P&G drove a purple van through 24 cities in a Burn town Challenge to help promote Prilosec OTC directly to consumers. Also, the company made an unprecedented effort with retailers like Walmart Stores Inc to teach pharmacists how to push Prilosec OTC on shoppers.

Prilosec OTC indirectly got support from big health insurers like Aetna, who are eager to reduce a significant source of their drug outlays. Aetna stopped covering Prilosec OTC and all other prescription generic Omeprazole 20 mg dose formulations steering them to Prilosec OTC. Patients filling prescriptions for competing PPIs had to pay a copayment of $20 to 35, making Prilosec OTC a good deal.

WellPoint Health Networks, another big insurer had gone further by sending many of its PPI users a free 14-pillbox of Prilosec OTC and two coupons for $10 discounts with an objective of swaying more than half of PPI users to Prilosec OTC. PPIs accounted for roughly 8 percent of WellPoint's annual prescription costs of $ 1-billion.

(Adapted from: Gardiner Harris, *Pharma Prilosec Switch to Nexium, Thwarting Generics,* The Wall Street Journal, June 6, 2002)

Humira, The Swiss-Army Knife among Prescription Drugs!

Which is the world's most prized bio-pharmaceutical asset? Undoubtedly Humira, the biologic prescription drug from AbbVie. Humira's lifetime sales of a whopping $136 billion from its launch in 2002, to 2017, make it the most valuable biopharmaceutical product ever with the highest sales.

You might call Humira the Swiss-army knife of prescription drugs. Since its launch in 2002 to treat rheumatoid arthritis, Humira got one FDA approval after another to treat a wide range of diseases. The following table presents the timeline of Humira's indications approved by the US FDA.

Humira's Approved Indications: A Time Line

Year	Approved Indication
2002	Rheumatoid Arthritis in Adults
2005	Psoriatic Arthritis
2006	Ankylosing Spondylitis in Adults
2007	Crohn's Disease
2008	Chronic Plaque Psoriasis in Adults Polyarticular Juvenile Idiopathic Arthritis in Children
2012	Ulcerative Colitis
2014	Crohn's Disease in Children
2015	Hidradenitis Suppurativa

The Science Behind the Product

Abbott saw the prodigious power of Humira much before it became Humira. Abbott did not develop Humira. Knoll Pharma, the pharmaceutical business of BASF in collaboration with Cambridge Antibody Technology developed a compound D2E7 that showed promising results in early clinical trials. It had not been named as Humira yet, and was referred to by its R&D code D2E7. BASF sold its Knoll Pharma to Abbott for $6.9 billion in 2002, and that is how Abbott got to acquire the R&D compound D2E7. D2E7 is later called adalimumab. The suffix *mab* stands for monoclonal antibody, a class of biologic drugs engineered to bind to a single substance. Abbott then named adalimumab as Humira. Before we get into the details of how Humira became the best selling drug in the world, it is essential to understand how it acts and how it treats what it treats.

Tumor Necrosis Factor (TNF) is a protein that triggers inflammation in the body. It is a common root of all inflammatory disorders such as Rheumatoid Arthritis (RA), Ulcerative Colitis and many other inflammatory conditions. Uncontrolled inflammation damages healthy tissues. Adalimumab binds to TNF-alpha and lends it inert, reducing the inflammatory response and symptoms of the disease. The science behind monoclonal antibodies is so important for Abbott that the company stated that it had been the primary reason for its acquisition of Knoll Pharma. To gain access to monoclonal antibody technology.

Abbott understood that Humira was not just a biologic drug. The company saw it as a *pipeline* in a drug. Abbott saw from the very beginning the significant potential of Humira to treat multiple conditions, where inflammation is a problem.

How Humira Became the Best Selling Drug in the World

How did Humira become the best-selling drug in the world? Here are some of the more critical initiatives that Abbott took in making Humira launch an unprecedented success.

1. Product superiority is the number one reason behind Humira's unprecedented success. Although Humira was the third TNF-

alpha antibody at the time of launch, its superior dosing schedule, and improved toleration enabled it to become the best-in-class.

2. Having realized the potential of Humira to treat a number of inflammatory conditions, Abbott quickly invested in clinical trials of five other autoimmune diseases such as psoriasis, psoriatic arthritis, ankylosing spondylitis, Juvenile R A, and Crohn's disease. As planned, sales climbed with the approval of each new indication. The year 2005, for example, brought the approval for psoriasis and sales reached $1.4 billion. Approval of Ankylosing spondylitis in 2006 increased sales to over $2 billion. Furthermore, the company conducted long-term clinical trials for over eight-years for Humira to establish safety and efficacy in R A.

3. In 2004, Abbott received the FDA approval for a self-injectable syringe of Humira, and this helped the product capture about 30 percent of the self-injectable prescriptions for R A that year.

4. As part of its market protection strategy, Abbott created a cluster of over 100 patents, and this should help the company to remain a best seller at least till 2022. Humira won an orphan drug designation for hidradenitis suppurativa in 2015 and a seven-year market exclusivity with it.

5. Abbott started educating the prescribers, payers, and patients as to the severity of the disease and the methods of treatment in preparation for the Humira launch. The FDA does not allow any drug marketing before approval but does not restrict unbranded disease awareness campaigns and education programs. Abbott made good of this opportunity. AbbVie spent $363 million on Direct-to-Consumers-Advertising-Campaign in 2014.

6. Another major initiative that Abbott took at the time of launching Humira was in the area of patient access. Patient access is crucial to any new drug launch and its success in the marketplace. Abbott launched a Medicare Assistance Program, an unprecedented drug-access initiative that provides Humira at no cost to Medicare-eligible seniors.

7. In 2013, Abbott separated into two entities - AbbVie and Abbott Healthcare and placed Humira under the portfolio of AbbVie. AbbVie is the research-based spinoff of Abbot Laboratories. This move enabled the company to sharpen its focus on research and at the same time effectively compete in the pharmaceutical industry with its brand-name products as well as branded generics.

8. AbbVie continued its expansion plans into emerging markets such as Brazil and China.

Milestones and Awards

Humira, in addition to being the world's top-selling drug, has won many awards. It has crossed many important milestones in its successful journey to the top.

▸ Approved by the US FDA on December 31, 2002, Humira is the most successful product launch in Abbott's 115-year long history.

▸ Humira was prescribed to more than 40,000 patients suffering from the potentially crippling joint disease in its first year in the market.

▸ Humira was the most-studied biologic therapy for Rheumatoid Arthritis at the time of its regulatory submission to the FDA with 23 clinical trials involving more than 2,400 patients. Humira was approved earlier than anticipated, just nine months after the company's regulatory submission in the US and Europe.

▸ Humira was named the best new medicine of 2003 by MedAd News.

▸ Humira was one of the ten winners of the Chicago Innovation Award, which honors the local companies for their novel products and services in 2003.

Lessons

The first lesson is that good science always wins. Great science leads. Humira's safety and efficacy are established beyond doubt by extensive clinical data.

The second lesson is that preparation is the key to success in any area of human endeavor including prescription drug marketing. Prepping up the market with insightful, educational campaigns and programs before launch enabled Humira to establish its credentials firmly right from day one.

The third lesson is that access makes all the difference. Improved patient access through Medicare Assistance Program helped Humira significantly not only regarding coverage but also in surmounting the criticism for its high price and subsequent price increases.

The fourth lesson is that indication expansion improves sales by opening the doors to new patient populations and segments and by extending market exclusivity.

Finally, creating a patent cluster of over one hundred patents ensures long life.

All these factors have significantly contributed to making Humira the best selling drug in the prescription drug history!

(Source: Adapted from articles: 1. *One drug. Nine uses. More on the way?*John Russel in Chicago Tribune, September 18, 2015; 2. *The best selling drug since 1996 - Why AbbVie's Humira is set to eclipse Pfizer's Lipitor?* By Simon King In Forbes.com, July 16, 2016;2015, 3. *The Story of Humira: The Swiss-Army Knife of Pharmaceutical Drugs,* LinkedIn, February 17, 2017)

How a Fifth-in-Class Drug became The Best-Selling Drug in The World!

The story of Lipitor (atorvastatin) is also the story of a fifth-in-class drug that became a top-in-class drug in sales. It has many interesting twists and turns to it. The plot thickens with each twist and turn and involves a merger of two companies, a co-marketing arrangement, and a hostile acquisition.

On November 3, 1999, Warner-Lambert and American Home Products (AHP) announced an ambitious merger that would create the world's largest pharmaceutical company with combined revenues of $26 billion and a market capitalization of $145 billion. The following day, on November 4, 1999, Pfizer made the largest hostile takeover bid in the history of pharmaceuticals. Pfizer offered a stock transfer offer of $80 billion for Warner-Lambert and finally acquired it for $90.2 billion February 7, 2000.

Warner-Lambert, founded in the early 1850s had evolved considerably throughout its history to become one of the largest pharmaceutical companies. The company expanded through many acquisitions and mergers over the years to become an international competitor in many businesses. Prescription drug business had always been important to Warner-Lambert with over 57 percent of sales coming from it. The acquisition of Parke-Davis in 1970 further sharpened Warner-Lambert's focus on the prescription drug business.

Warner-Lambert faced many setbacks in its pharmaceutical business in the early 1990s. The following bad press and poor ratings from industry analysts worsened the situation. The company as a part of its recovery process had cut back its resources on R&D. Ronald Cresswell, chairman of pharmaceutical research at the time chose to focus his limited resources on few promising molecules, leaving aside the products in early stages of development. Fortunately (in retrospect) for the company, one of the chemical compounds retained for development was atorvastatin (Lipitor).

The Statin Scenario

The discovery of statins, a new therapeutic class revolutionized the treatment of high cholesterol in the late 1980s. Merck, after forty-five years of research, launched the first-ever statin drug Mevacor (lovastatin) in 1987. Close on the heels of Mevacor's launch, entered three more statins, Pravachol (pravastatin) of Bristol-Myers Squibb, Zocor (simvastatin) of Merck, and Lescol (fluvastatin) of Novartis. Lipitor would be the fifth statin. The fifth-in-class drug as the tradition goes has little chance to succeed in the market. The following table presents the relative market shares of the four cholesterol-reducing drugs before Lipitor's entry into the market.

Cholesterol-Reducing Drugs and Market Shares of Four Statins

Drug Name	Company	Launch Year	Market Share (%)
Mevacor (lovastatin)	Merck	1987	14
Pravachol (pravastatin)	Bristol-Myers Squibb	1991	21
Zocor (simvastatin)	Merck	1992	32
Lescol (fluvastatin)	Novartis	1994	14

The retention of the statin, Lipitor faced severe criticism as it was a fifth statin drug, therefore, a me-too product that would enter an already crowded market dominated by products from some of the most powerful pharmaceutical companies in the world. However, a Phase-I study conducted in 1992 provided a ray of hope for Warner-Lambert that Lipitor could be a powerful cholesterol-reducing agent.

A 1994 Phase II study converted that ray of hope into a belief as it showed 60 percent more cholesterol-reducing power of Lipitor over its competitors in the market. With renewed confidence about the differentiability of their product, Warner-Lambert went into Lipitor's Phase III trials. Lipitor is significantly superior to competitors in its ability to reduce cholesterol levels.

Fifth-in-Class to Top-in-Class: Lipitor's Journey

How did Lipitor move from a fifth-in-class to market to Top-in-class in sales? Having realized that Lipitor is significantly superior to the competition in its cholesterol-reducing ability, Warner-Lambert was determined to realize the potential of its super statin drug, Lipitor. The company took some very important strategic decisions to make it happen. Here are some of its more significant strategic decisions:

1. Decided to run Phase-III trials with people suffering from familial hypercholesterolemia, a fatal hereditary condition resulting in exceptionally high cholesterol to get a fast track clearance from the FDA. A small minority of people suffer from this condition, and any of the competitive statins did not clinically address it. The FDA will consider the drug for fast track clearance (six months as compared to the average 12 months) if it treats a serious or life-threatening condition or addresses an unmet need. The results of the trial justified a fast track clearance, and the FDA approved Lipitor within six months of the New Drug Application (NDA).

2. Another significant decision was to conduct head-to-head clinical trials against the leading competing statins. Marketing group at Warner-Lambert requested this. This tactic is rarely followed in the drug industry because if the new product fails to show significant superiority to competitors, it would be challenging to persuade physicians to switch their patients to the new drug. Of course, it would be an extremely desirable asset if the drug is found superior to the competition. Fortunately for the company, Lipitor was superior to all other

statins in the market. In the head-to-head trials, Lipitor reduced elevated cholesterol 40 to 60 percent across the full dose range (10 mg to 80 mg) and reduced triglycerides by 19 to 40 percent. The best selling competitive cholesterol reducer, Zocor of Merck decreased LDL cholesterol by only about 40 percent.

3. Ronald Cresswell's initiative of integrating regulatory affairs and clinical research into the R&D organization to improve the documentation process was another beneficial strategic decision. He also involved marketing very early in the new product development process. This initiative too helped the company as it brought both R&D and marketing on the same page regarding Lipitor's potential long before its approval.

4. Also, Warner-Lambert developed a compensation plan uncapping performance incentives, which enabled successful performers to earn huge amounts and raise the salesforce morale significantly.

Marketing Lipitor

Warner-Lambert faced many serious challenges in bringing Lipitor to the market. The first challenge is the fact that it is the fifth-statin to enter the market. Although proven to be superior in clinical trials as compared to all other statins in the market, Patients, physicians, and payers saw Lipitor as a 'me-too' drug. To top it, the incumbents such as Merck, Bristol-Myers Squibb had proven products in the market. The competitors, in addition, enjoyed strong relationships with key opinion leaders such as cardiologists. Moreover, they all had experienced sales forces – larger than Warner-Lambert. How could Warner-Lambert, a smaller company fight the dominant competitors and grab a respectable market share?

A successful launch of Lipitor is a marketing imperative. The first six months after a drug launch are very crucial for its success. The initial adoption rate of the drug by physicians can often make or break a new product. The most critical challenge of all is to launch Lipitor effectively. The company brainstormed and arrived at a launch strategy. The key elements of Lipitor's launch strategy were:

1. **Marketing Alliance with Pfizer:** Warner-Lambert decided on a saturation approach to market Lipitor. The market for cholesterol-reducing drugs had many untreated patients and physicians who were mostly content with the therapeutic solutions already available. They were not looking for new therapies. By pursuing a saturation strategy, the company wanted to contact as many physicians as possible which includes the universe of cardiologists in the US at the time. To achieve this broad coverage of physicians, the company needed many sales representatives. Its existing salesforce was not adequate. Recruiting such a large sales force for marketing one product did not make economic sense. The alternative? Co-marketing. Creating a marketing alliance with a reputed pharmaceutical company that does not have conflicting interests in the product promotion. Anthony Wild, Warner-Lambert pharmaceutical sector vice president at the time explained the need for the salesforce augmentation best when he said:

The more soldiers you have out there, the more guns, the more likely you are to achieve your ends.

The company, therefore, decided that a partnership was necessary to address its constrained sales and marketing resources and narrowed down its search for marketing partners to two – Hoffman-la Roche and Pfizer. Its choice of Pfizer as a marketing partner was more a matter of a chance. At one point of the negotiation, a Warner-Lambert fax intended for Hoffman-la Roche accidentally ended up in a Pfizer fax machine. The unintended fax helped convince Pfizer that it needed to make a great offer to get the Lipitor deal. Finally, Warner-Lambert chose Pfizer as its marketing partner, because of its marketing experience, relationships with cardiologists, and its track record of successful product launches. The highlights of the Lipitor Marketing alliance with Pfizer were:

▸ Pfizer paid $205 million in upfront money and milestone payments for the rights to sell Lipitor. Pfizer also agreed to split all future product expenses including advertising, promotion, sampling, and sales force.

- ▸ Furthermore, Pfizer agreed to pay for half of any ongoing and planned clinical trials, which were more than a hundred involving 100,000 patients.

- ▸ In return, Pfizer would receive variable payments based on sales targets established in the agreement. Pfizer had been gaining about 48 percent of net sales.

2. **Product Positioning of Lipitor:** Lipitor was positioned as a superior cholesterol-reducing drug first and foremost. The head-to-head clinical trials proved its efficacy as the most potent statin in the market in reducing the elevated total cholesterol, LDL cholesterol, and triglycerides over a range of comparable doses.

   Lipitor was the first drug approved for reducing triglycerides as well as the more common LDL cholesterol making it an ideal drug for a broad range of points. Although Pravachol (Bristol-Myers Squibb) and Zocor (Merck) are also effective in lowering high triglycerides, neither Bristol-Myers Squibb nor Merck possessed the triglyceride indication at the time of Lipitor launch.

   Ease of use was another important positioning message that Lipitor established in the minds of the physicians. Physicians found it challenging to determine a patient's optimal dose with other statins available in the market. They had to select a starting dose, re-testing the patient's cholesterol after having used the drug for a period, adjusting the dose and repeating the cycle until the proper dose is identified. Fortunately for Lipitor, 72 percent of patients reach the target LDL cholesterol goal at the starting dose of 10-milligrams, thereby eliminating the need for the cumbersome procedure of testing, adjusting, and retesting.

3. **Lipitor's Value Positioning (Pricing):** Lipitor achieved a position of the most-value-for money with its moderate pricing. Warner-Lambert made the already convincing Lipitor value proposition even better with its pricing strategy. Lipitor was positioned as the product with therapeutic superiority, ease of use and yet priced lower than the leading competitors in

the market. The following table presents the comparative prices of leading statin brands in the US in 1997.

Average Prescription Prices of Statin Drugs in the US in 1997.

Statin Brand / Company	Average Price US $ (per 15 tablets)
1. Mevacor / Merck	125
2. Zocor / Merck	95
3. Pravachol / Bristol-Myers Squibb	93
4. Lipitor / Warner-Lambert	84

4. **Lipitor: Promotional Tactics**: Lipitor had put in a massive pre-launch effort. Its pre-launch tactics included:

A. Even before launching Lipitor, Warner-Lambert launched a national cholesterol education program in conjunction with American Heart Association (AHA) to educate patients and physicians that cholesterol needed to be treated more aggressively than it was; they needed to go for the goal established in the guidelines set by the national cholesterol education program. The campaign positioned Lipitor as the drug best suited for achieving these targets.

B. Besides, Lipitor made good use of its pre-market comparative efficacy data by publicizing it in medical journals and at major medical conventions.

C. The company recruited key opinion leaders (KOLs) to use free samples immediately after Lipitor was approved, but before it was formally launched.

D. All these pre-marketing efforts resulted in Lipitor achieving a 3 percent of all new cholesterol-lowering prescriptions.

E. The combined salesforce of Warner-Lambert and Pfizer numbering 2,200 was the largest to promote a statin brand in the US. They targeted about 91,000 key prescribers – physicians within the cardiology area, interns and general and family practitioners who were known prescribers of cholesterol-lowering drugs.

F. Lipitor has achieved a 29 percent share of voice, the highest among all statin drugs in the market in the launch year.

G. The combined salesforce of Warner-Lambert and Pfizer implemented a very aggressive sampling program. They distributed 7.3 million samples of Lipitor to physicians in the first year of launch.

H. The company had its moment of luck. The year of Lipitor's launch was also the year when FDA allowed prescription drug advertising, targeting consumers. The Direct-to-consumer-advertising (DTCA) began in 1997. Warner-Lambert benefited from this significantly. The company spent tens of millions dollars on DTCA urging patients to *Know Your Numbers* and then showing patients discuss how Lipitor helped them get their cholesterol numbers below guidelines goals.

I. Pfizer acquired Warner-Lambert by a hostile takeover in 2000 and gained total control of Lipitor.

J. Pfizer conducted focus groups with doctors and unearthed key selling points that its competitors missed. The company found that doctors were scared of the dosages of statins. This helped significantly in highlighting the simplicity of Lipitor's dosage.

K. Lipitor had achieved an extensive insurance coverage and Medicare-eligibility which have improved its access considerably.

L. Pfizer continued research on Lipitor and conducted more than 400 clinical studies including more than 80,000 patients costing about a billion dollars. These studies have shown how Lipitor helped patients with heart problems and associated risks such as stroke and heart attacks.

Success Right From the Start!

Lipitor has been a spectacular success right from the start. First synthesized by Dr. Bruce Roth, a chemist at Warner-Lambert in 1982,

Lipitor entered the market with the FDA approval in 1997 as a fifth-in-class statin drug. Since then Lipitor never looked back. Nicknamed, Turbostatin, for its superior cholesterol-reducing ability, Lipitor passed the coveted $1 billion in the launch year itself. Within three years Lipitor became the largest-selling statin drug and later became the first-ever prescription drug to pass the $12 billion mark in annual sales. What is more, Lipitor became the largest-selling prescription drug in history with a lifetime sales of $140.75 billion from its launch till its patent expired in 2012. Five years after losing its market exclusivity, Lipitor continues to be a valuable asset to Pfizer with annual sales of $1.9 billion in 2017.

Lipitor's *How* Wins Over Mevacor's *Where*!

The key to Lipitor's unprecedented success was its basic strategic approach. While the pioneer among statins - Mevacor chose the position of *Where* to compete, Lipitor, a late entrant, and a fifth-in-class drug chose the *How* to compete position. The difference between the positions - Where and How was crucial. By selecting the *Where* position, Mevacor decided rightly for a pioneer on defining the market. By definition, defining the market means creating the market for a particular product class, and that would also pave the way for competition to enter. While focusing on *where* to compete was essential it should not have been the exclusive focus ignoring *how* to compete. Merck was not ready with all its vital clinical research data when it launched Mevacor. The company was still conducting its 4-S Study (The Scandinavian Simvastatin Survival Study). Merck did not spend adequate time and effort to educate the doctors and the public initially about its product and what it could do to improve their heart health. Merck rushed its Mevacor into the market and then began their disease awareness and education campaign.

Pfizer chose an altogether different strategy. The strategy of *How* to compete. Being a late entrant into the statin market, Pfizer focused on how to reach more doctors and how to gain their approval for prescribing Lipitor. How to make Lipitor communication more effective. The company's head-to-head trials with its significant competitors was a part of the How to strategy. More importantly, Warner-Lambert was ready with its clinical data establishing the superiority of Lipitor over its competitors before it launched Lipitor. It had also trained its sales force adequately on how to convert doctors prescribing other statins to prescribing Lipitor.

Brilliant Campaign, Frayed Execution

Pfizer launched a brilliant Direct-to-consumer (DTC) advertising campaign for Lipitor just as the first generics of Simvastatin (Zocor) were entering the market. The company released for a full week full color, full-page advertisements in the New York Times in June 2006. The objective was to protect Lipitor prescriptions from being substituted with Simvastatin generics.

The advertising campaign featured Robert Jarvik, the medical investigator-cum-entrepreneur credited with the invention of the Jarvik Artificial Heart. The advertisements showed Jarvik rowing a boat. In the advertisements towards the close, Jarvik looking straight into the camera says: *I take Lipitor. For me, there is no substitute*. The Jarvik - Lipitor advertisements taught patients to be cautious about the probable generic substitution for Lipitor by physicians, pharmacists, and insurers.

The campaign revolved around authenticity. For the first time, the celebrity endorser was a real doctor and not an actor who played the role of the doctor in a prescription drug campaign. The campaign became highly visible and at the same time highly controversial. Choosing Jarvik as the celebrity brand ambassador for Lipitor boomeranged. Because Robert Jarvik was not a cardiologist. Although he completed an undergraduate course in medicine from an offshore medical school, he never completed a residency program and was not licensed to prescribe and practice. Critics also argued that Jarvik claimed credit for inventing the artificial heart but the concept and technology behind the invention predate his work. Furthermore, a middle-aged rower from Seattle, Dennis Williams who bore a close resemblance to Jarvik announced that he had served as Jarvik's body double in the video shoot of the Lipitor that showed Jarvik rowing the boat. Jarvik's admission later that he did not use Lipitor until after he had been hired as a Pfizer spokesperson implying that his advertising message of Lipitor being responsible for his cardiovascular health as untrue.

All these had a very adverse impact on the credibility of the campaign. Later, Pfizer replaced the rowing advertisement with Jarvik jogging along with his son. However, for a marketing campaign based on the importance of authenticity, these revelations were intensely damaging. Later in 2007, there was a congressional hearing where the portrayal of Jarvik as a spokesperson and the positioning of Lipitor as a superior to generic statins were explicitly linked in.

Pfizer withdrew Jarvik from the Lipitor advertisements but stayed on with its campaign stating that *Lipitor is Lipitor*, with the underlying message of inimitableness.

Whistle Blowing Case

Dr. Jesse Polansky, former director of outcomes management strategy at Pfizer, who was responsible for reviewing some of the marketing materials for Lipitor and other products filed a lawsuit on Pfizer regarding the unethical marketing practices of Lipitor seeking compensation as a whistleblower. His main allegations against the company were:

▸ Pfizer gave unrestricted education grants. These grants were a part of the marketing plans of Lipitor, with a clear objective of creating a medical platform supporting Lipitor's new positioning.

▸ Pfizer wanted to extend Lipitor use beyond the indications found on the table by targeting people at moderate risk of developing heart disease or having a heart attack. People with moderate risk did not need Lipitor therapy.

▸ Pfizer programs included deliberate misinformation promoting the idea that kidney-disease patients may need to be treated with statins.

Here is what Pfizer had said in response to all the allegations:

We believe this case has no merit. Furthermore, after reviewing the allegations in the complaint, the government declined to intervene in their action. Pfizer does not condone the off-label promotion of its products. We believe our sales and marketing practices are solely based on our prescription information approved by the FDA.

Defending Against Generics

Pfizer implemented a raft of initiatives to stem the loss of market share and revenue of Lipitor, its most valuable asset to generic rivals before its patent expiry. The US accounted for around 55 percent of the $10.7 billion worldwide sales of Lipitor. Pfizer made significant efforts to capitalize on brand loyalty and emotional attachment of patients and prescribers with Lipitor, which is unusual in prescription drug marketing. Pfizer took many measures to encourage prescribers and patients to stay with the Lipitor brand even when generics are available.

Some of the more important initiatives of Pfizer are:

▸ Pfizer signed a series of discounted deals with Pharmacy Benefit Managers (PBMs) and health insurers including reduced copays for Lipitor.

▸ Pfizer also took an unusual step of setting up its own mail-order service to supply Lipitor to patients who have been taking Lipitor for years and wanted to stay with Lipitor and are reluctant to switch to generics.

▸ Pfizer Licensed a generic version (authorized generic) of Lipitor to Watson Pharmaceuticals

Pfizer's initiatives to minimize the generic loss have helped the company significantly. Even after six years of its patent expiry, Lipitor achieved sales of $1.9 billion in 2017. Lipitor is a classic example of launch excellence and marketing excellence.

Lessons

Christopher Bowe identified three important lessons learned from the Lipitor success which are valuable to all pharmaceutical marketers in his Harvard Business Review article, *Say farewell to Lipitor but don't forget its lessons* on November 18, 2011. He very aptly observed that getting bigger through mega-mergers has not proven to make big Pharma accomplish better at their core task of producing innovative products. The case of Pfizer (despite the unprecedented success of Lipitor) validates that. Here are the Lessons:

1. *Resist the lure of strategies that depend on a single source of power*. Pfizer was a much different company when the acquisition bug bit it in 1999. It was smaller but intensely aspirational and even obsessed with getting even with the bigger Merck, the industry leader at the time. Pfizer's primary motivation of acquiring Warner-Lambert, the owner of Lipitor and with whom it had a co-marketing alliance is to gain the total control and ownership of Lipitor and become bigger. A decade later, in retrospect, that motive seems to have been based more on hubris than on setting the company on a sustainable path to continued success.

2. *When a strategic distraction occurs,* don't add more distraction. Lipitor's spectacular success and the Warner-Lambert acquisition seem to be a one-trick pony with limited prospects for organic growth. To fuel further growth, Pfizer engineered another large-scale merger with Pharmacia in 2003 to gain control on Celebrex, an anti-arthritic drug that was thought to be very promising at the time. Later in 2009, Pfizer acquired Wyeth to form the world's premier biopharmaceutical company. All these acquisitions caused disruption and distraction as Pfizer struggled to integrate them.

3. *Acquisitions should fund innovation, not replace it*. All the oceans of money that Lipitor generated over its lifetime (over $140 billion) did not help to keep the Pfizer share price stable over the years. The company's share was at its peak in June 2000, five months after the Warner-Lambert deal was

announced. In 2011, Pfizer's price fell 60 percent below its historical peak, and the shareholder value suffered. The company could not protect its share price from a broad decline and stagnation, despite huge cash generation that fueled dividends and other returns.

Pfizer, due to its heavy dependence on one drug for revenues and beset with distracting acquisitions, was unable to innovate on its own. In the pharmaceutical industry, the key rationale for high prices for branded drugs is that they fund innovation and not acquisitions. Innovation brings value, acquisitions not necessarily so.

(Source: Adapted from articles: 1. Matthew Leafstedt, Amy Marta, Jitendra Marwaha, Philip Schalwig and Reka Shinkle, *Lipitor: At the heart of Warner-Lambert - Case prepared for class room discussion in Professor Allan Afuah's Corporate Strategy Class,* University of Michigan Business School, December 1999; 2. Christopher Bowe, *Say farewell to Lipitor but don't forget its lessons,* Strategy: Harvard Business Review, November 2011; 3. Associated Press, *It took a brilliant marketing campaign to create the best-selling drug of all time,* Business Insider, December 28, 2011)

Pharmaceutical Marketing Practices: Good and Bad

Declining Reputation

Pharma's reputation has been going down these days. Pharma-bashing too has become a popular game. The public perception of the pharmaceutical industry is the lowest it has been in recent history. Consider for example the case of Merck, the company which was Fortune Magazine's most admired company in the US for an unprecedented seven years in a row. Paradoxically, it was the same Merck, the marketer of Vioxx a product that experienced one of the most well-publicized drug recalls and final withdrawal. Several books such as *Bad Pharma* by Ben Goldacre, *The truth about the drug companies* by Marcia Angell, *Hooked* by Howard Brody described several areas controversy such as unethical marketing practices, and lack of transparency. Magazines such as Forbes have devoted stories calling the industry, 'Pill Pushers,' and detailing how pharmaceutical companies have 'abandoned and science for salesmanship.'

Good Practices

The behavior and practices of pharmaceutical companies determine whether their reputation is going north or south. In other words, what you do determines your reputation. Not very long ago, the pharmaceutical industry enjoyed an excellent reputation and even the admiration of all the stakeholders and the general public. It is because of their significant contribution to society through their breakthrough discoveries in medicines that conquered many fatal diseases. Here are some of the more critical good practices that Pharma engages in :

▸ The industry plays a significant role in discovery and development of new medicines.

▸ Responsible education of healthcare professionals (in particular physicians).

▸ The understanding of the real value of drugs for appropriate patient populations. The recent advances towards personalized healthcare by many specialty pharmaceutical companies.

▸ The dramatic improvement of patients' quality of life by improving diagnosis and compliance.

▸ The continuous use of clinical research to support the true value addition of drugs.

▸ Building up evidence concerning the needs and wants of patients to the R&D community and allocating more resources to the appropriate research projects.

▸ Planning and implementing patient-centric strategies from bench to bedside.

▸ Pharma companies have established R&D centers solely to work on cures for neglected diseases. Pharmaceutical companies are devoting resources to find treatment for malaria, trypanosomiasis (sleeping sickness), dengue fever, the Chagas disease that plague the developing world. Many of these companies are working along with the Gates Foundation, the United Nations' International Children's Emergency Fund (UNICEF) and the World Health Organization (WHO) on these projects.

▸ Companies such as GlaxoSmithKline have been running the African Malaria Partnership for a decade to implement behavioral change programs to aid prevention of malaria in vulnerable areas.

▸ The industry has been known for its philanthropy too. In annual surveys of the most generous companies, pharmaceutical companies dominate the list.

Pharma's Bad Practices

Pharmaceutical companies have been receiving their share of criticism in recent years not only concerning their alleged profiteering but also for their behavior that led to the excessive profits.

Pharmaceutical industry's marketing practices have been particularly facing severe criticism. The areas which face criticism more often are:

- Excessive incentives for sales reps
- Using their medical liaisons for promoting products
- Excessive incentives for Key opinion leaders (KOLs), physicians for prescribing the drugs
- Physician engagement practices. Campbell et al. in 2007 wrote in an article, *A national survey of physician-industry relationships* published in New England Journal of Medicine, that out of 3,167 physicians surveyed, 94 percent of physicians had free food in their office; 28 percent received consultancy fees for lectures or clinical trial recruiting; 35 percent received reimbursement for attending continuing medical education programs (CME) or professional meetings. This is only illustrative of the nature of physician engagement with Pharma.
- Off-label promotions
- Lack of transparency and deception over outcomes and scientific evidence for marketed products
- The pharmaceutical industry spends more money on marketing than on research and development, and it is this marketing expenditure that drives drug prices very high. In 2014, the Global Data reported that Johnson & Johnson, Pfizer, and Novartis were spending almost double their R&D expenses on marketing while others such as Roche and Lilly nearly equal amounts on both marketing and R&D.
- Bribery. Transparency International in 2011 reported that the pharmaceutical industry ranked seventh out of 19 industries that use bribery to speed up administrative processes in 30 countries around the world. GlaxoSmithKline's bribery charges in China and Kickbacks to pharmacies in the US by Novartis are widely known.

Factors Associated With Reputational Damage

It is these unethical marketing practices that have been responsible for bringing the reputation of the pharmaceutical industry down and not the marketing of prescription drugs *perse*. Lea Prevel Katsanis, a marketing professor, in her insightful book, *Global Issues in Pharmaceutical Marketing* suggested the following factors associated with reputational damage:

1. The pharmaceutical industry is an industry that is more inward-looking and resistant to change with self-reinforcing beliefs about its marketing practices.

2. In-experienced marketing managers, who manage brands and learn their skills on-the-job without sufficient formal training.

3. A lack of accuracy and balance in the presentation of marketing messages. The effects of this message multiply as it is repeated in multiple channels.

4. The use of direct-to-consumer-advertising (DTCA) and the way it trivializes drug therapy.

5. The belief that if a particular marketing activity is legal, then by definition, it must also be appropriate. Pharmaceutical companies have a 'no apologies' approach regarding their marketing activities.

6. The perception of high drug prices as a consequence of sizable marketing budgets. The public, in particular, believes that pharmaceutical companies spend more on marketing than on research to develop new drugs and this marketing activity results in higher prices.

7. The effects of physician engagement with the industry resulting in a potential bias towards prescribing the drugs.

8. The inaccurate reporting of medical news and the blurred lines between legitimate news and marketing messages.

9. The perception that the pharmaceutical industry sets its own agenda to determine the disease treatment policies.

10. The public distrust of the industry as a result of the negative publicity given to off-label drug marketing.

The 'TARES' Test

How can the pharmaceutical industry change its behavior so that it can improve its reputation by stamping out the unethical marketing practices? Situational factors and organizational culture are the most critical determinants of ethical behavior in an organization. In a corporate setting, the influence of one's peers and the top management is even more important than one's belief system. Introducing an ethical framework such as TARES Test may be one way to change behavior and imbibe good marketing practices. While there are many ethical frameworks, TARES Test is a straightforward, self-explanatory and yet introspective in nature.

The TARES Test provides a useful framework for establishing values and measuring whether or not they are explicitly followed for marketing and advertising, but the general principles may be applied at an individual and an organizational level as well. The TARES framework provides a view of ethics both in macro-ethical and micro-ethical contexts. Micro-ethical context is looking at a particular piece of persuasive communication or an advertising message as unethical or ethical. Looking at how the company as a whole must examine the compelling communication or an advertising message and its effect on the target audience is macro-ethical context. Marketers must put the interest of their target audiences before their narrowly defined self-interest, which may be increased in sales and market share for example.

The TARES Test combines five principles, hence the acronym: *Truthfulness, Authenticity, Respect, Equity, and Social Responsibility*. It also suggests the application of a Golden Rule, a concept which forms the foundation of equity. The following table presents an illustrative TARES Test questionnaire that helps in evaluating an ethical framework and even an ethical mindset.

The TARES Test

The TARES Test
Truthfulness
1. Is communication true and truthful?
2. Have I presented selected information?
3. Have I withheld information needed to make an informed decision?
4. Have I distorted information by using improper comparisons?
Authenticity
1. Does this action affect my integrity?
2. Would I recommend this product to my loved ones without reservation?
3. Are my motives self-serving or do they benefit others?
4. Would I be proud if others were to find out my behavior?
Respect
1. Do my actions respect the rights and dignity of others?
2. Have I provided enough information to meet the needs of physicians and patients?
3. Will physicians and patients benefit from following the advice in my communication?
4. How I can be more responsible in my behavior towards physicians and patients?
Equity
1. Have I targeted vulnerable audiences based on the content of my communication?
2. Are my persuadees (target audience) able to assess the claims I make in my communication fully and rationally?
3. Does the audience know that I am persuading them rather than informing them?
4. Should I engage in this type of persuasion?
Social Responsibility
1. Do I respect the welfare of all?
2. Do I harm individuals with my action?
3. Do I encourage public dialogue based on truthful information?
4. How can I serve the interests of society?
Source: *Global Issues in Pharmaceutical Marketing* by Lea Prevel Katsanis

Here are a few cases that illustrate some of the good and bad marketing practices by leading pharmaceutical companies providing the pharmaceutical marketer valuable insights into what to do what to avoid.

Marketing through Manipulation and Misinformation!

Parke-Davis, one of the leading American pharmaceutical firms patented gabapentin (Neurontin) in 1977 and obtained the US FDA approval in 1993 as adjunctive therapy for partial complex seizures. Neurontin became a significant blockbuster for Parke-Davis, which later became a division of Warner-Lambert by an acquisition. In 2000, Pfizer acquired Warner-Lambert.

Sales of Neurontin rose from the US $95 million in 1995 to nearly $3 billion in 2004, after which its patent expired and lost most of its sales to the generics that flooded the market. How Neurontin became a three-billion-dollar molecule is a story that is stranger than fiction and tells us that success at any cost is indeed very costly! Here is a brief account of what happened:

The Early 1990s

Parke-Davis was facing severe challenges in the early 1990s. The patents of the company's blockbuster drugs had expired. The R&D pipeline too was nothing to write home about. The stock market had downgraded the firm's stock. The company was in a desperate need of something good to sell. The company hired a marketing consultant, Richard Vanderveer, a man with considerable knowledge in pharmaceutical marketing research and strategy. He helped the company institute a micro-marketing program.

Micro-marketing Program

Micro-marketing program is about targeting individual physicians with tailored information that resonates with them as individuals. The communication is target-specific or physician-specific taking into account the needs of individual physicians. It, therefore, would be of high interest to doctors unlike a carpet-bombing approach, where the company presented the same data and information to all the physicians.

Around the same time, the company also hired Anthony Wild, who had considerable experience in the sales and marketing side of the pharmaceutical industry. He knew the task at hand when he joined Parke-Davis and was well aware of the critical nature of his assignment. He had a compelling need to succeed.

The 'Wild' Era

The company was banking all its hopes for future survival and growth on the two new drugs pending approval with the US FDA. One was Lipitor (atorvastatin), cholesterol-reducing drug and the other was Rezulin (troglitazone) for treating type 2 diabetes.

Wild chalked out a survival plan for himself as well the company. He identified three products among the existing product mix of Parke-Davis, which were not selling well, but had great potential. These products were - Neurontin (approved as adjunct therapy in epilepsy), Accupril (quinapril), an anti-hypertensive drug, and Loestrin, a low-estrogen birth control pill. He planned to raise the sales of each of these three brands to reach a 15 percent market share in their respective therapeutic categories. What is more, he wanted to invest the profits generated by these three products in the promotion of the new two drugs once the company receives the approval from the FDA. He proposed his plan to the top management and got their approval.

Wild had set out to change the culture at the company. He focused on improving the somewhat fatalistic approach at the company to a highly confident one. His message to the sales force? "Believe in yourself." He focused on three principal areas of change:

A. From a risk-averse or low-risk stance to a high-risk, rich-rewards mindset

B. Removing all the caps or restrictions on sales force incentives and making them very attractive

C. Relentless focus on increasing the sales of Neurontin

Focus on Expanding Indications for Neurontin

Although the primary approval for Neurontin was in the adjunctive therapy of partial-complex seizures, the sales force was hearing favorable comments from doctors, who had experimented with off-label uses of the drug to treat neuropathic pain, bipolar disorders, attention deficit disorders, migraine, restless legs syndrome, alcohol and drug withdrawal and as a monotherapy for seizures (instead of an adjutant). There was no reliable evidence proving Neurontin's benefits in treating these conditions. It was all anecdotal.

Conducting clinical trials for new drug application was the only way to establish the efficacy of Neurontin in all these conditions. Clinical trials were expensive, and there was no guarantee that they would succeed. Moreover, Neurontin was coming off patent in four years. Therefore, the considerable investment in clinical trials would not be viable. The sales force, although charged with the new incentive system and all revved up, seemed helpless in expanding the sales. How could they increase the sales without overtly promoting its off-label use, which was illegal?

The company found its answer in the medical liaisons division. The primary responsibility of medical liaison is to provide a fair and balanced scientific information regarding the clinical trials, drug's uses, side effects, adverse reactions and help physicians understand the state-of-the-science and up-to-date information on the treatment modalities. They should not engage in any way in persuading physicians to prescribe their products. The medical liaison executives are usually are MDs or PhDs and should have the domain expertise comparable to physicians they visit to maintain a peer-to-peer status.

The company knew that it was illegal to promote its products and solicit prescriptions through its medical liaisons team but still went ahead. The company, in the process, committed many unethical and even illegal actions. Here is a very brief account of their so-called innovative marketing practices and what they did:

1. The company started hiring medical liaisons directly out of the sales department. They were all trained in sales techniques to generate prescriptions that the company needed very badly at the time.

2. They also started incentivizing the medical liaisons by compensating them in part, on the basis of sales.

3. The medical liaisons had to work with the regular pharmaceutical representatives of the company and had no communication with the medical research division. The company gave their medical sales liaisons a list of doctors for 'cold calls' based on the size of the doctors' practices and their potential to prescribe Neurontin. Also, the company provided them with a package of monetary incentives to offer physicians for participating in the Parke-Davis programs.

4. Although it is illegal for a drug company to pay physicians to prescribe a drug, it is not unlawful technically, to pay them for being individual consultants. Parke-Davis paid thousands of physicians to become such consultants. It is not a mere coincidence that all the physicians who received money from the company had one thing in common. They were all heavy prescribers of Neurontin, particularly for treating neuropathic pain.

5. Parke-Davis at the time implemented a program called, *Preceptor program* in which, physicians who allowed a company representative to a visit that included discussions of patients. As a part of the Preceptor program, representatives often had an opportunity to meet actual patients and influence the physicians often to prescribe Neurontin for off-label uses to treat these patients.

6. Besides, the company established a Parke-Davis speaker's bureau and paid high-prescribers of Neurontin thought leaders to go out and spread the word. However, there was no

substantial clinical data. They only had data from their less rigorous case studies based on their clinical experience where they used Neurontin. The physicians were paid for these case studies on a case-by-case basis to write up each patient history and their response to Neurontin.

All these marketing practices had led to the blatant off-label promotion of Neurontin. In April 1996, John Ford, the Parke-Davis Executive articulated the company's expectations at a recorded marketing managers meeting. He said:

I want you out there every day selling Neurontin. Look, this isn't just me, It's come down from Morris Plains (Headquarters) that Neurontin is more profitable than Accupril. So we need to focus on Neurontin. We all know that Neurontin is not growing for adjunctive therapy (It's the approved indication). Besides, that's not where the money is. Pain management, now that's the money. Mono-therapy, that's the money. We don't want to share these patients with everybody. We want them on Neurontin only. We want their whole drug budget, not a quarter, not a half, the whole thing. We can't wait for them to ask, we need to get out there and tell them out front. Dinner programs, CME (Continuing Medical Education) Programs, consultantships - all work great, but don't forget the one-on-one. That's where we need to be, holding their hand and whispering in the ear, Neurontin for pain, Neurontin for monotherapy, Neurontin for bipolar, Neurontin for everything. I don't want to see a single patient coming off Neurontin before they've been up to 4,800 milligrams a day. I don't want to hear that safety crap either - every one of you should take one just to see there is nothing. It's a great drug.

The scale and magnitude of this change in Tony Wild's Parke-Davis were not only stunning but also illegal. While the change energized the marketing team significantly, the legal downside too was substantial. As was mandatory, in April 1996, the company conducted a program to educate medical liaisons about the prevailing legal environment governing their role. A former FDA official and a company lawyer held a seminar on the subject. The seminar was in two parts, and only the first part was videotaped. The FDA official and the lawyer said to the team:

If you get caught violating the FDA rules, you're on your own and acting without the company's knowledge or permission. You must have a physician information request (PIR) for each call. You must provide a fair and balanced presentation. You cannot close or sell. You can't promote a drug off-label. You cannot promote a drug pre-approval. You must keep an accurate record of your activities. You cannot solicit an inquiry.

After this, the video camera was turned off and the second part of the seminar began. The second part of the presentation was candid and to the point. The former FDA official gave them tips on how to circumvent the system without getting caught. He told the team what the company expected from them explicitly. He said:

We expect you to do your job out there and stay focused on sales. Don't worry about this (the first part of the seminar). If you are cold calling with a sales representative,have him fill out the physician information request form, so you are covered. You're not out there to help the competitors, and the doctors know it. So don't worry about being balanced in your presentation. Look, without sales, there is no Parke-Davis. We all have to sell at some level. Be careful about this. Just don't leave anything behind. Above all, don't put anything in writing.

The medical liaisons very soon almost became an integrated part of the sales and marketing department. The company gave them the same pep talk and offered the same incentives as it did for the sales teams. The company promised them an all-expense-paid cruise to the Bahamas if the company achieves the sales goals for Neurontin and Accupril. A marketing executive told them:

The only way we will make it (to the Bahamas) is if you as a group take ownership of the task and get out there and aggressively move market share. You have to be aggressive.

Don't take no for an answer. If the rep does not close, you close. If the rep is seeing the wrong doctors, you see the right ones. If a high-prescribing practice is not using Neurontin, get in there, do your thing, then ask why. I don't care, but you're wasting your time and our money if you don't ask for the new prescription when you are through.

Medical sales liaisons (MSL) soon dominated the Neurontin team. They were contacting more and more high-prescribing physicians as per the micro-marketing strategy. The physicians were prescribing Neurontin for treating many of the off-label uses such as bipolar disorder, neuropathic pain, and others. They focused on incentivizing these doctors and engaging and making them a part of the Neurontin family. As a result of all these activities, Neurontin achieved explosive growth reaching from the modest US $98 million in 1995 to the whopping US $3 billion in annual sales in 2004.

Finally, all these unethical and illegal promotional activities of the company in promoting Neurontin had come to light because of a whistleblower, who was a recruit in medical sales liaisons. David Franklin, a post-doctoral fellow in microbiology from Harvard University joined the medical sales liaisons at Parke-Davis on April 1, 1996. He attended the now infamous seminar that the former FDA official and the company lawyer gave the new trainees in medical sales liaisons on April 16, 1996. A senior marketing executive repeatedly told Franklin to go out and sell Neurontin for off-label uses, which was contrary to the briefing that he received at the time of training. Franklin was disenchanted, disappointed and confused with these conflicting messages. They were in total contradiction to what he perceived the medical sales liaison job would be and the way it had turned out. He left Parke-Davis within three months, collected data and evidence about the firm's illegal marketing practices in promoting Neurontin and filed a suit against the company. Later Pfizer acquired Warner-Lambert, and thus Parke-Davis also became a part of Pfizer in 2000.

After protracted hearings and a detailed investigation into the allegations filed by Franklin, Pfizer pleaded guilty to its illegal marketing practices and agreed to pay $430 million to resolve all the criminal and civil liabilities. The following table presents a timeline of events that describe the rise of Neurontin and the fall of the company concerning its unethical marketing practices.

Illegal Marketing of Neurontin: A Timeline

Period	Event
1977	Parke-Davis obtains a patent for its gabapentin.
1993	US FDA approves gabapentin under the brand name Neurontin as adjunctive therapy for partial-complex seizures.
1995	Neurontin records US $98 million in annual sales.
April 1, 1996	David Franklin, a post-doctoral fellow in microbiology from Harvard University joins Parke-Davis in Medical Sales Liaison (MSL).
April 16, 1996	David Franklin and his peers get a briefing from Parke-Davis on FDA regulations and about their responsibilities as medical sales liaison officers.
April 22, 1996	A senior marketing executive a week later repeatedly tells David Franklin to go and promote the drug - Neurontin for off-label uses, which is contrary to the briefing Franklin had at the time of training.
August 1996	Franklin leaves Parke-Davis and files a suit against the company stating that it is indulging in illegal marketing practices such as the off-label promotion of its drug - Neurontin and making false claims to elicit payments from the Federal government. The case put under seal, deferring action pending government review.
December 1999	The government lifts the seal and litigation resumes.
2000	Pfizer acquires Warner Lambert along with its Parke-Davis division.

Table Contd...

Period	Event
October 2000	The FDA approves Gabapentin (Neurontin) for adjunctive treatment of partial seizures in children of 3 - 12 years.
May 2002	The FDA approves Gabapentin (Neurontin) for post-herpetic neuralgia in adults.
2004	Annual sales of Neurontin reach almost US $3 billion.
May 13, 2004	Pfizer (Warner-Lambert) pleads guilty and agrees to pay US $430 million to resolve criminal charges and civil liabilities.

(Adapted from Greg Critser's book, *Generation Rx: How Prescription Drugs Are Altering American Lives, Minds, and Bodies*, Houghton Mifflin and Company, New York, 2005)

The Vioxx Fiasco!

Merck discovered Vioxx (rofecoxib), a Cox 2 selective inhibitor by a team led by P. Prasit at Merck-Frosst in Montreal, Canada. Merck acquired Charles E. Frosst in 1965. FDA approved Vioxx in May 1999.

Vioxx was an anti-inflammatory drug used to treat arthritis and acute pain without stomach irritation caused by other non-steroidal anti-inflammatory (NSAID) drugs. Merck promoted Vioxx aggressively using direct marketing to doctors, private clinics, and hospitals through advertising campaigns both in print media and television. The drug was also endorsed by celebrities, who were former athletes such as Dorothy Hamill and Bruce Jenner. Merck also offered Vioxx to hospitals and doctors at discounted rates. As a result, Vioxx had emerged as one of the best selling drugs in the treatment of arthritis and acute pain within one year of launch.

Termed as Super Aspirin, Merck promoted Vioxx as a cure for everything from arthritis pain to menstrual cramps. The company projected It as a pain reliever, which was a boon for patients who have arthritis. What is more, Vioxx relieved pain without gastrointestinal problems caused by older generation painkillers. Merck spent about $160.8 million in promoting Vioxx in 1999. It soon emerged as one of the fastest selling drugs in the world. Vioxx quickly became a blockbuster drug for the treatment of pain associated with both osteoarthritis (OA) and rheumatoid arthritis (RA).

However, even as the prescriptions and sales were increasing rapidly for Vioxx, so were the concerns of side effects associated with it. Although Vioxx was relatively gastro-safe, as it did not cause any gastrointestinal side effects, you cannot say the same thing about its cardiovascular side effects. Medical experts were raising doubts about the cardiovascular risks associated with Vioxx's long-term usage almost since its launch. In the initial years, Merck disagreed with the various medical studies that indicated cardiovascular risks until its internal investigation stated the risk.

In Merck's VIGOR clinical studies published in 2004, there was a five-fold increase in myocardial infarction among patients taking Vioxx compared to patients taking naproxen. In September 2004, clinical trials showed that Vioxx increased the risk of myocardial infarction and stroke. Immediately, Merck voluntarily withdrew Vioxx from the market on September 30.

The stock market reacted violently to Merck's withdrawal of Vioxx from the market wiping out about to $28 billion of the company's value of the stocks in a matter of few months.

Launched in May 1999. Withdrawn on September 30, 2004. During the short life of Vioxx, it had about 105 million prescriptions in the US. More than 84 million people had taken the drug during this period across the world, and at the time of recall, about 2 million people were taking it. Soon after the recall, Merck's share prices fell by 27 percent from $45.07 to $33 per share wiping out $28 billion in market value. Vioxx had been the fastest moving drug in Merck's portfolio at the time of recall. What a fall! How did it happen? The timeline of events leading to the precipitous fall Vioxx is in the following table.

The Rise and Fall of Vioxx: A Timeline

Period	Actions and Activities
November 1998	Merck completes a clinical trial testing their Investigative New Drug (IND) on 5,400 subjects and seeks US FDA approval.
January 1999	Merck launches Vioxx Gastrointestinal Outcomes Research study (VIGOR) with more than 8,000 participants. Half of the participants take Vioxx and the other half take naproxen, a painkiller and NSAID of an older generation. The clinical trial is designed to see whether Vioxx is safer for the gastrointestinal system than naproxen.
May 1999	FDA approves Vioxx making the drug available by prescription in the US.
October 1999	The VIGOR Study's Data and Safety Monitoring Board (DSMB) meets for the first time, and notes that Vioxx patients have fewer ulcers and less gastrointestinal bleeding than patients taking naproxen. It looks as if the study will be a success for Merck.
November 1999	The VIGOR Study's Data and Safety Monitoring Board (DSMB) meets again, and focuses on heart problems. The panel finds that 79 patients out of 4,000 taking Vioxx have serious heart problems or have died, compared with 41 patients taking naproxen. They note that while the trends are disconcerting, the number of events are small and to continue the study.
December 1999	The safety panel observes that the risk of serious heart problems and death among Vioxx patients are twice as high as in the naproxen group. The panel, while recommending the continuation of the study, decides that Merck needs to develop a plan to analyze the study's cardiovascular results before the study ends.
	When recommending the continuation of the study, the Safety panel said that it could not tell if Vioxx was causing the heart problems or if naproxen, acting like a low-dose aspirin protected people from them, making Vioxx just look risky in comparison.

Table Contd...

Period	Actions and Activities
January 2000	Merck hesitates at developing the analysis plan. The company wants to wait and combine the cardiovascular results of VIGOR with the results from other Vioxx studies. But, Dr. Michael E. Weinblatt, the safety panel Chair and a rheumatologist from Brigham & Women's Hospital at Boston pushes for immediate analysis. Merck agrees to analyze heart problems reported by February 10 - at least a month before the last patient leaves the study. Events reported later won't be included in the initial analysis.
February 2000	Dr. Michel E. Weinblatt files out a disclosure form that says he and his wife own $72,975 of Merck stock. He also agrees to a new contract involving 12 days of work over two years, at the rate of $5,000 per day.
March 2000	Merck gets the results of the VIGOR trial.
May 2000	Merck submits VIGOR study paper to the New England Journal of Medicine (NEJM) for publication. The data includes only 17 out of 20 heart attacks Vioxx patients had.
July - November 2000	A. A memo from Merck statistician Deborah Shapiro to Merck scientist Alise Reicin (both are listed authors of the NEJM paper) refers to heart attacks 18, 19, and 20 suffered by patients taking Vioxx during the study. B. Merck tells the FDA about the heart attacks 18, 19, and 20. C. VIGOR study authors submit two sets of corrections to their NEJM manuscript, without mentioning the three additional heart attacks D. NEJM publishes the VIGOR study results, still with no mention of the three additional heart attacks in the Vioxx group. The published results also leave out many other kinds of cardiovascular adverse events.

Table Contd...

Period	Actions and Activities
February 2001	The FDA holds an advisory meeting on VIGOR trials. It publishes complete VIGOR data on its website, including the additional heart attacks and data on other cardiovascular events.
August, 2001	Cardiologists - Debabrata Mukherjee, Steven Wissen, and Eric Topol publish their meta-analysis in the Journal of American Medical Association (JAMA), based on complete VIGOR data that the FDA has made available.
January 2002 to August 2004	Numerous epidemiological studies point out that Vioxx increased the risk of cardiovascular problems.
September 2004	A. Merck withdraws Vioxx after its colon-polyp prevention study – APPROVe shows that the drug raises the risk of heart attacks after 18 months. By the time Vioxx is withdrawn from the market, an estimated 20 million Americans have taken the drug. B. The decision resulted in a huge loss of $28 billion in market value for Merck. C. The number of lawsuits blaming Vioxx for the deaths of patients who were taking the drug also start mounting.
July 2005	NEJM editor-in-chief, Dr. Jeffrey M. Drazen tells NPR that the journal had been hoodwinked by Merck and that the authors of the VIGOR study should have told the Journal about the additional heart attacks.
November / December 2005	A. NEJM issues an *Expression of Concern* writing that, inaccuracies and deletions in the VIGOR manuscript Merck submitted to the Journal calls into question the *integrity of data*. The Journals asks the study authors to submit a correction to the Journal. B. The first Federal trial on Vioxx lawsuits begins in 2005 in New Jersey court.

Table Contd...

Period	Actions and Activities
March 2006	VIGOR study authors respond to NEJM's expression of concern stating: *our evaluation leads us to conclude that our original article follows appropriate clinical trial principles and does not require a correction. The three additional heart attacks in question occurred after the study's respecified cutoff date for reporting cardiovascular problems.*
May 2006	A. Outside analysis of data sent to the FDA from Vioxx APPROVe study shows that the cardiovascular risks from Vioxx began shortly after patients started taking the drug. The data also indicated that the risks from Vioxx remain long after patients stop taking the drug. B. Merck disagrees with the analysis and maintains that patients are not at risk unless they had taken the drug for more than 18 months. This point is very important for Merck as it could cost the company billions of dollars. Many of those suing the company say that they took the drug for less than 18 months.
June 2006	A. The seventh trial against Merck begins. Out of six cases that have already gone to trial, Merck has won three and lost three. B. Research published in the medical journal, Lancet estimates that 88,000 Americans had heart attacks from taking Vioxx and 38,000 of them died.
November 2007	Merck announces that it will pay $4.85 billion to end the thousands of lawsuits over its painkiller Vioxx. The amount paid into a settlement fund is believed to be the largest settlement ever.

Vioxx withdrawal had cost Merck very dearly in loss of revenues, market capitalization and above all reputation. What is paradoxical about the whole Vioxx fiasco is that Merck was banking on a drug that is gastro-safe, compared it with a drug, Naproxen that is cardiac-safe but has serious gastrointestinal side effects like many NSAIDs. In the bargain it has got a gastro-safe drug all right, but with severe and even fatal cardiovascular side effects. As

Dr. Wayne Ray, Epidemiologist at Vanderbilt University, aptly observed, *"A heart attack in exchange for an ulcer is poor treatment."*

(Source: Adapted from Source: Snigdha Prakash, Vikki Valentine, *The Rise and Fall of Vioxx: A Timeline*, NPR, November 10, 2007)

The Rise and Fall of Baycol

The US FDA approved Bayer's new statin drug - cerivastatin (Baycol) just four months after the launch of Lipitor (Atorvastatin). Baycol was discovered by a group of Bayer scientists led by medicinal chemist Rolf Angerbauer and biologist Hilmar Bischoff in Wuppertal, Germany in the late 1980s. It was only the second optically pure synthetic statin on the market (Lipitor was the first). Baycol was extremely potent, almost 100-fold more potent than Mevacor (Lovastatin), the grandfather of all statins.

Statins are generally known to cause rhabdomyolysis, a disorder in which muscle cells break down, overwhelming the kidneys with cellular waste and leading to kidney failure. This condition rarely occurs in case of the five statins (Mevacor, Zocor, Pravachol, Lescol, and Lipitor) before Baycol and almost never fatal. With Baycol, however, reports of severe rhabdomyolysis were about 15 - 60 times more frequent as with other statins. During initial clinical trials involving approximately 3,000 patients, no serious adverse events were observed with initially approved doses of 0.2 mg and 0.3 mg. Two years later, after the FDA approved two more strengths - 0.4 mg and 0.8 mg of Baycol tablets, it is observed that there was a correlation between the high dose and the incidence of rhabdomyolysis.

Bayer priced Baycol so competitively that some overconfident physicians initially overlooked the higher rhabdomyolysis rate. Baycol's prescriptions soared. As the patient population grew exponentially, so did the number of serious adverse effects.

A Baycol fatality tended to occur in patients taking higher doses of the drug and in those, who are also taking fibrates, especially gemfibrozil (Lopid), the popular fibrate drug of Parke-Davis. Bayer somehow paid no heed to the telltale signs of increased adverse effects that were dose-related and acted inadequately and a little too late. The company kept on revising their prescribing information labeling, including contraindications and package inserts.

Before its fall, Baycol, however, had become the third largest pharmaceutical product for Bayer with a forecasted sale of $ 1-billion. Bayer was aspiring to reach a peak annual sales of $ 2.5-billion. The company was even planning to invest $ 125-million in clinical trials involving over 20,000 patients to strengthen Baycol's efficacy claim and gain approvals for further indications.

The excessive focus on efficacy and inadequate attention towards safety concerns seem to be responsible in a more significant measure for the fall of Baycol, one of the most potent statins. The following table - The Rise and Fall of Baycol: A Timeline explains it all.

The Rise and Fall of Baycol: A Timeline

Timeline	Events
April 1997	Bayer Launches Cerivastatin, its new molecule in the statin-class under the brand names Baycol and Lipobay first in the United Kingdom in April, 1997.
February 1998	Bayer launches Baycol in the United States in February 1998 in two strengths - 0.2 mg and 0.3 mg dosages, 0.3 mg being the starting dose. The US is the largest market for statin drugs accounting for about 60 per cent of worldwide statin sales.
May 1999	Bayer obtains the FDA approval on 24th May 1999 for a 0.4 mg strength of Baycol tablets, which became the new starting dose. This new 0.4 mg dose allowed Baycol to compete in the biggest LDL-C efficacy segment of the US market, accounting for about 50 per cent of statin prescriptions. Bayer priced its 0.4 mg tablet the same as its 0.3 mg tablet.
July 1999	Bayer's clinical trial of Baycol 1.6 mg strength reveals a high incidence of severe C K (creatinine kinase) elevation partly connected with symptoms. Bayer discontinues the project, does not publish the results. The 0.4mg tablet of becomes Baycol's most prescribed US dosage rising from 31 per cent to 78 percent of total prescriptions of the drug in one year.

Table Contd...

Timeline	Events
December 1999	Bayer requests for labeling change and gets the FDA nod resulting in a bolded contraindication regarding Baycol with gemfibrozil concomitant treatment.
June 2000	A. Bayer executives discuss issues arising out of the increasing cases of rhabdomyolysis associated with Baycol in the US because of the high proportion of cases of concomitant medications with gemfibrozil and conclude that everyone understands the nature of the contraindication of Baycol with Gemfibrozil. B. Internal analysis of confirmed FDA-reported US cases of rhabdomyolysis suggested that the reported rate for Baycol monotherapy was 20 times higher and for concomitant therapy, and 855 percent higher than for Lipitor. C. The director of medical research suggested that the leaflet mentioning the contraindication of Baycol with gemfibrozil should not be distributed before the approval of Baycol 0.8 mg, which is round the corner as prior distribution of the leaflets with this contraindication might delay the approval. D. Even the consultant at Bayer, a former FDA employee cautioned that there is a problem that is dose-related and it may be difficult to convince the regulatory authorities that the risk/benefit ratio of the 0.8 mg dose is low enough to be approved.
July 2000	A. Bayer obtains the approval for 0.8 mg dosage strength of Baycol. The U.S. labeling indicated that *caution should be exercised when titrating ...to 0.8 mg dose of Baycol.* B. Bayer maintains consistency with its past pricing policy and prices Baycol 0.8 mg tablets significantly below Zocor's equivalent dosage strength so that it can continue to claim: *with Baycol, you get premium power not premium price* C. Bayer steps up its detailing effort for the 0.8 mg launch and captures 24 percent of all Baycol's prescriptions.
August 2000	After the approval of 0.8 mg strength of Baycol, Bayer submitted an application for a package insert change that would inform patients that they should not take Baycol if they were taking gemfibrozil.

Table Contd...

Timeline	Events
December 2000	A. Bayer's drug safety and regulatory team proposes that they ask the UK MCA (Medicines Control Agency) to strengthen the statement to a contraindication with concomitant use of Baycol with gemfibrozil. B. The global head of strategic marketing at Bayer was not in favor of this move as it might delay the introduction of 0.8 mg strength in other international markets. But their director of global safety at the time, Ernst Weidmann prevailed and the team included the contraindication with gemfibrozil.
May 2001	A. With Baycol-associated fatalities on the rise and the reports that safety concerns associated even with Baycol monotherapy at 0.8 dose, Bayer felt that current prescribing information is inadequate to discourage the starting dose of 0.8 mg. The company did two things immediately. B. One is that they stopped the shipping of 0.8mg samples of Baycol to physicians in the US C. They got the approval from the FDA and updated prescribing information emphasizing that the starting dose should be 0.4 mg. D. They prepared a 'Dear Healthcare Professional' letter to inform HCPs of these changes and to remind them of the gemfibrozil contraindication.
June 26 2001	Bayer makes the following changes to Baycol's E U (European Union) prescribing information: A. Contraindication to the concomitant usage of Baycol and gemfibrozil B. Restriction of the maximum dose to 0.4 mg and reinforcement of the importance of dose titration Bayer and its marketing partners communicate these changes to all HCPs in EU member states through 'Dear Doctor' letters
July 13 2001	Bayer informs its US sales force about the recent development in the EU and briefs them stating that: *A. Competitive counter detailing has occurred in recent weeks and we fully expect the competition to try to spin this information as proof that Baycol is getting a 'Black Box' warning or is being pulled out from the U K market.* B. While sales reps should be prepared to respond to physicians' questions about this issue, they should not be the first to initiate the discussion.

Table Contd...

Timeline	Events
	A. Bayer also briefed their sales force on how to respond to the issue. Their first response should be: *This is old news to us in the U.S. because, as you know, the US placed the same contraindication into labeling back in 1999, but the EU is just now implementing this.* B. The company urged their US sales force to continue their sales pitch focused on their power and safety messages…Their brief was to *continue delivering the messages you want to hear.*
August 2001	Bayer decides to suspend marketing of Baycol 0.8mg in the U.S. and proposes to the FDA regarding a Black Box warning for 0.4 mg. The final Black Box warning that FDA suggested was: *Concomitant treatment with Baycol and gemfibrozil is contraindicated due to a significantly increased risk of potentially fatal rhabdomyolysis over the risk with either drug alone…the maximum daily dose of Baycol must not exceed 0.4 mg due to a significantly increased risk for potentially Fatal rhabdomyolysis at higher total doses.*
August 7 2001	Bayer decides to withdraw Baycol from all markets except Japan. It was not withdrawing Baycol from Japan, because gemfibrozil was not available in Japan.
August 23 2001	Bayer announces withdrawal of Baycol from Japan market as gemfibrozil was soon entering the Japanese market.

The Aftermath

By the time Bayer recalled Baycol in August 2001, at least six million people worldwide had taken the drug including 700,000 Americans. More than 100 deaths were attributed to Baycol therapy, and many lawsuits ensued. Bayer's share price plummeted 26 percent by 2003. The effects of Baycol dealt the German pharmaceutical major, responsible for the discovery of Aspirin and Cipro (ciprofloxacin, an antibiotic) a significant blow. The fall of Baycol was responsible in a significant way for the closure of their research and development center in the United States at West Haven, Connecticut.

(Source: Reinhard Angelmar, *Marketing case: The rise and fall of Baycol*, Journal of medical marketing, January 2007)

Prozac: A Classic Example of Marketing Excellence!

In 1999, Fortune magazine added Prozac to its Products of the Century list, putting it in the company of Penicillin, Band-Aid, Radio, Television, and the World Wide Web. In response to this, Garry Tollefson, then president of neuroscience products of Eli Lilly, which discovered and developed Prozac commented: *The recognition by Fortune underscores the critical role that Prozac has played in elevating the awareness of major depression as a disorder of the brain, the importance of seeking medical evaluation and the existence of safe and effective treatment.*

Eli Lilly introduced Prozac (Fluoxetine) for the treatment of depression in the United States in 1987. Prozac had crossed the coveted $1 billion mark in sales and achieved a blockbuster sales in 1992. Prozac had achieved more than sales and prescriptions. By 1994, Prozac's name recognition had attained the familiarity of Kleenex and the social status of spring water according to an oft-quoted Newsweek article. There is more. Twenty-five years after the introduction of Prozac, the name had entered the cultural lexicon and helped define how people think of mental illness. How did Prozac achieve all this?

What is behind the spectacular success of Prozac is Lilly's strategic marketing excellence. Right from the brand name, it gave to its first-in-class selective serotonin reuptake inhibitor (SSRI) fluoxetine. Prozac. A name that is created by the internationally renowned branding firm, Interbrand. A name that aimed to distance the drug from everything typically associated with antidepressants - strong chemicals, side effects. Eli Lilly hired Interbrand to find a zesty, communicable name that cuts through the clutter for the blandly titled chemical compound–fluoxetine hydrochloride. The company chose Prozac because *Pro* connoted positivity and professionalism and *Zac* action.

The marketing success of Prozac was so spectacular that its marketing strategy became the standard operating procedure for subsequent psychiatric drug campaigns. Here are some of the key action steps that the company took for promoting Prozac:

A. A few months before the launch of Prozac, Ken Cohen, a marketing manager at Eli Lilly convened a series of educational meetings involving about 150 of the company's leading psychiatrists and senior executives. This marketing move of grooming key opinion leaders (KOLs) as prominent spokespersons when a company was launching a new drug to bolster its acceptability within the larger medical community, had become a standard practice in the pharmaceutical industry.

B. Lilly hired teams of medical representatives and meticulously prepared them to familiarize doctors with the therapeutic benefits of Prozac. The company knew if representatives were to be persuasive in changing physicians' prescribing habits, the reps would have to be more than just informed – they should have a fervent belief and one-hundred percent conviction in their product.

C. Personal relations with physicians are crucial to success, and the reps need to develop a rapport with physicians.

D. Prozac was considered to be a clean drug targeting serotonin levels in the brain, in contrast to the current medications like tricyclic compounds, which were not selective or target-specific and hence had many unwanted side effects. Commenting on this theme and Prozac's advantage, one psychiatrist put it succinctly when he said: *instead of using a shotgun, you're using a bullet!*

E. The once-a-day dosage of Prozac increased treatment compliance, and this was a significant advantage. Besides, research by Eli Lilly showed that between 75 to 80 percent of depressed patients responded well to Prozac. To increase the number of patients, who are currently not seeking treatment seek the medical help is possible only by raising awareness of depression and possible therapy among physicians and patients. You can expand the prescriber and prescription bases, only when you promote the product to primary care physicians (doctors in family practice, and internal medicine) and not just to psychiatrists. The company decided to position the drug to primary care physicians in addition to psychiatrists. To achieve this, Lilly planned a strategy of developing a comfort level among PCPs regarding treating depression. PCPs, who are the gatekeepers of medicine have the potential to drive prescriptions upward. The company, therefore, funded a program, wherein key opinion leaders were sent out to large PCP conferences and other medical meetings to share their expert knowledge and experiences of Prozac. Drug reps fanned out to PCP office across the country to make the sales calls.

F. Lilly also made use of two more channels in optimizing its promotion. Sampling to induce trial among new patients and medical journal advertising to sway more doctors towards prescribing Prozac for newly diagnosed patients with depression.

G. Lilly launched a massive direct-to-consumer program to increase the awareness of depression as a treatable disorder as depression at the time remained a severely under-diagnosed and undertreated illness. According to the estimates, two out of every three depressed patients did not receive treatment. Lilly targeted those who were reluctant to seek professional help for their symptoms and thus the campaign attempted to appeal to a substantial number of people. The objective of the campaign was simple: *To encourage people suffering from depression to get into treatment.*

Introduced in 1987, Prozac immediately revolutionized the treatment of depression. By 1996, Prozac had been prescribed to more than 17 million Americans and had achieved $2.36 billion in sales worldwide. It accounted for about 29 percent of Eli Lilly's total revenues. But, then success brings with it competition. Huge success brings huge competition. That's what had happened to Prozac. There were two Prozac-like (SSRI) drugs chasing Lilly's Prozac. Pfizer's Zoloft had become the second largest selling antidepressant with $1.7 billion, closely followed by GSK's Paxil with $1.45 in annual sales. These competitive threats spelled urgency for Eli Lilly as its stakes were high in the antidepressant market with Prozac accounting for close to a third of the company's total revenues.

Eli Lilly responded to these mounting pressures from competition and slowing pace of growth by launching a major advertising campaign in print media targeting patients directly, not physicians. The print ad campaign by Leo Burnett Company in Chicago used weather imaging to amplify its message symbolically such as – dark clouds giving way to bright sunshine – from a Sun that is somewhat evocative of the happy face symbol, that urged everyone to have a nice day in the 1970s – to promote Prozac, the antidepressant treatment that had come to symbolize how consumers in the 1990s try to cure their ills with pills. The company released its print ad campaign in twenty popular magazines and journals such as Family Circle, Good Housekeeping, Sports Illustrated, Cosmopolitan, Men's Health, Newsweek, Time, Parade Magazine, and Entertainment Weekly and more. There was a gender bias tilting towards women readership in selecting the journals and magazines as research indicated that women accounted for 60 percent of doctor visits and were twice as likely as men to request for a specific brand of medication. There were two main reasons why Lilly chose the print media for its DTC campaign:

A. Firstly, the limitations placed by the US FDA on DTC television ads. Regulations in force at the time prohibited pharmaceutical companies from drawing an explicit connection between a medical condition and medication. Print ads did not have such restrictions and therefore a better way for Lilly to convey its message to consumers.

B. Secondly, a print advertisement gave consumers more time to reflect than a 30-second television spot, which was ideal for Lilly's campaign purposes.

Lilly's print campaign had one main communication objective as Mike Grossman, Leo Burnett's Director of Public Relations explained. It had to assist people in their depressed stupor to raise their hand for help. They might not recognize their condition or know, that help is out there. The campaign, therefore, had to overcome the stigma that surrounded depression and other mental illnesses. The advertising copy was carefully crafted to describe the symptoms of depression in a non-threatening way:

> So you may have trouble sleeping...feeling unusually sad or irritable... Find it hard to concentrate ...lose your appetite...lack energy or have trouble feeling pleasure...

The ads also sought to dispel some of the prevalent misconceptions and fears about depression:

> It isn't just feeling down. It's a real illness with real causes...some people think you can just will yourself out of depression...That's not true.

Behind the print ad campaign of Eli Lilly, there was a lot of qualitative consumer research. The company talked to 900 consumers in great depth, spending intensive time with depressed patients seeking treatment. One finding from this research partly explains why depression remained such an under-diagnosed and under-treated illness. Some of the respondents, who came from a boomer generation said that their parents asked them: *Why don't you pick yourself up?*

Not only the copy, even the visuals resonated with depressed patients, who did not seek treatment for their illness earlier. It is because patients' illustrations of their own feelings about depression and recovery inspired the visual elements in the campaign ads. The campaign clearly intended to connect depressed readers or their family members and friends on an emotional level. The simple yet powerful symbols of darkness and light were developed to be inclusive.

The original ad was a three-page magazine spread that featured sharply contrasting images portraying the darkness experienced by a person suffering from depression and the visual on the second (facing) page showing the light that a patient felt when the illness abated. The first page consisted of a gray cloud on a black background accompanied by a copy line that says: *Depression hurts*. The opposite page was a vibrant blue with a highly stylized drawing of a yellow Sun captioned with the campaign's signature line: *Prozac can help*.

There was copy beneath the visuals that describes the symptoms of depression in a non-threatening way. The final paragraph encouraged readers to seek medical help if their symptoms matched those described in the ad and closed by stating that:

> *Prozac has been prescribed for more than 17 million Americans. Chances are someone you know is feeling sunny again because of it. Prozac. Welcome back.*

In the months following the publication of the initial ad, Lilly released two companion ads. Each featured the same text, and all thematically similar. One of the new ads substituted a broken vase and a vase holding flowers for the gray cloud and the yellow Sun of the original advertisement. The other, which ran only in November and December 1997, displayed a limp Christmas tree on one page and a sturdy uptight tree on the opposite page. The creative inspiration for these images came from the focus groups that Lilly conducted with depressed patients. The dual metaphorical images of darkness and light accurately expressed to the target audience (depressed patients and their families and friends) what depression and a return to health felt like. Lilly also sought input from doctors and mental health advocacy groups before releasing the original ad to the public.

The DTCA (Direct-to-Consumer-Advertising) campaign encouraged the reader to muse actively over the symptoms. As Gary Mitchell, a professor at the Indiana University of Medical Center observed the ad provoked the readers with a question like: *You are on Paxil, and you see the Prozac ad and ask yourself, Why am I not on that drug?*

The campaign also drew some negative responses too from some columnists and consumer advocacy groups. That the drug companies were creating demand through consumer advertising and this could be a problem and that physicians would prescribe drugs their patients ask for. At the same time, there was praise from a great many doctors and mental health alliances. They appreciated the campaign's efforts to educate a more significant number of individuals, who suffered undiagnosed and untreated, from the often debilitating depression.

Prozac's launch and overall marketing effort can only be described as excellent, even unprecedented. Because it has become a standard operating procedure for all brands that were introduced in the Central Nervous System (CNS) therapeutic area. The following table presents important milestones in Prozac's journey.

Key Milestones in the Development of Prozac: A Timeline

Milestones	Activity
1975	Fluoxetine generic name approved.
1976	Fluoxetine IND submitted to the US FDA, Phase I trial initiated.
1978	Phase II trial initiated.
1979	First indication of anti-depressant effect.
1981	Phase III trials initiated.
1983	NDA submitted to US FDA.
1985	FDA advisory committee unanimously endorsed fluoxetine.

Milestones	Activity
1986	Fluoxetine (Prozac) was approved and launched in Belgium for the treatment of depression.
1987	Prozac was approved and launched in the United States for the treatment of depression.
1992	Annual sales of Prozac reached US $1 billion in the United States.
1994	A. New indication approval for Prozac. FDA approved Prozac for the treatment Obsessive Compulsive Disorder (OCD) in the US. B. Prozac attained the name recognition of *Kleenex* and social status of *Spring Water* in the United States, as quoted in a Newsweek article.
1996	Another New indication approval for Prozac. FDA approved Prozac for the treatment of *bulimia nervosa* in the US.
1997	Eli Lilly launched its first-ever print ad campaign for Prozac in about 20 popular magazines in the United States.
1999	Prozac named as one of the Products of the Century by Fortune magazine putting it in the company of Penicillin, Band-Aid, Radio, Television, World Wide Web.
2000	Over 38 million patients have been prescribed Prozac according to estimates.
2001	Prozac's market exclusivity expired in the United States.

Prozac had not only become trendy with its marketing but also set the trend for the future brands to follow. Prozac's marketing strategy had many firsts to its credit. Right from naming the brand to a systematic grooming and development of KOLs to become its spokespersons, focusing on Primary Care Physicians(PCPs), Listening to depressed patients to understand their perceptions and built it into a meaningful, memorable DTCA campaign–with all these activities, Eli Lilly had set a standard which are being followed and practiced by many pharmaceutical firms even today.

(Source: Adapted from: 1. Stuart Elliott, *A new campaign by Leo Burnett will try to promote Prozac directly to consumers,* the New York turies, July 1, 1997, and 2. Bali Sunset, *Prozac print campaign, Prozac print campaign case studies*, October 15, 2008).

The Rise of the Weekend Pill!

The third-in-class drug, Cialis (tadalafil) for treating erectile dysfunction turned out to be a very bright student overtaking the first-in-class drug, Viagra of Pfizer, which was not only the market leader but also which had revolutionized the treatment for the condition it created. How it achieved such a remarkable success is an exciting story. But first about the origins of Cialis.

Cialis: The Origin

Glaxo Wellcome, the British drugmaker began studying a new molecule, tadalafil for cardiovascular problems in the early 1990s with its 50-50 joint venture partner ICOS Corporation, a biotechnology company based in Bothell, Washington. The clinical trials took an unexpected turn when the ICOS researchers discovered that the drug was causing erections among the participants of the trail. Glaxo did not want to continue the partnership as it was not its therapeutic area of focus and wanted to focus on other drugs. Glaxo exited from the joint venture in 1996.

In 1998, Eli Lilly, which was actively looking for a new molecule to overcome its Prozac's patent expiry blues stepped in and agreed to form a 50-50 partnership with ICOS and carry the late-stage trials on the molecule and eventually market the product.

The US FDA approved Eli Lilly and ICOS Biotech's tadalafil under the brand name Cialis for the treatment of erectile dysfunction on November 21, 2003. Cialis was the third entrant after Pfizer's Viagra

(1998), and Bayer's Levitra, which was approved just two months before in August 2003 in the rapidly growing erectile dysfunction therapeutic area. Viagra had already been enjoying a blockbuster drug status for four years when Cialis was approved. How do you compete with a brand like Viagra which had created not only the erectile dysfunction market but also revolutionized it?

It would not be wise to compete head-on with such a firmly entrenched brand like Viagra and the recent entrant Levitra of Bayer and co-marketed by GlaxoSmithKline. That too, with a me-too drug status. Because all the three pills treated erectile dysfunction and all the three drugs belong to the same drug class. There are, however, some differences. The primary value propositions of both the competitors, Viagra and Levitra surrounded efficacy and safety. Not only that, both had an effective duration of action of less than five hours. Here lies the significant difference between Cialis and its two competitors. While Cialis is safe and effective like its competitors, it had a longer duration of action. Its window of time could last as long as thirty-six hours! In fact, it is this long window of time that won Cialis the sobriquet, *The Weekend Pill*!

Positioning Cialis

Could Eli Lilly use this huge difference of more prolonged duration of action between Cialis and its two competitors as a positioning strategy to market Cialis? The company conducted several consumer focus group discussions to test this. Paula Garret, a marketing executive of Eli Lilly for Cialis narrates an exciting experience in a New York Times article.

> *In one of the focus group study, the participants, who were wives of the persons with erectile dysfunction, watched a TV ad clip attentively with a man's gentle voiceover that said: Introducing Cialis. You can take Cialis anytime and have up to 36 hours to respond to your partner without planning or rushing. The moderator asked participants a simple question to gather consumer insights about Cialis. She asked, "Tell me specifically what is it you like about Cialis?" Paula Garret was observing all*

this from the other side of a one-way mirror. She found that suddenly on hearing this question, a sixty-year-old woman jumped out of her seat, whooping and raised her arms like she was doing the wave at a ball game and cried out, "Thirty-six hours, Yeah!" That is the most spontaneous response or reaction that you can ever get for any product! That was the decisive moment for positioning Cialis.

The critical question facing the Cialis team was how to position the product. Cialis was different from its competitors in two ways. One is that whereas Viagra and Levitra were effective for four to five hours, Cialis lasted up to 36 hours making it much more convenient for customers to use. The second difference is that Cialis has a more favorable side effect profile. Physicians at the time considered efficacy and safety as the two main criteria in prescribing a drug for erectile dysfunction. Duration was relatively very low in importance, say at about ten percent as compared to seventy percent for efficacy and safety regarding weightage.

The Lilly team debated a lot over the positioning of Cialis. Should the company center its marketing strategy around safety and efficacy which are the main criteria for prescribing? Or should they try to establish duration as a new criterion? The marketing team decided to emphasize its significant differentiator. Duration – being able to choose a time for intimacy and romance in a 36-hour window in its launch campaign. The company had set the price of Cialis higher than competitors to underscore its superiority. The rest was history. In 2012, Cialis passed Viagra's $1.9 billion in annual sales to claim the leadership position in the erectile dysfunction market vindicating its positioning decision.

The participants in another focus group study of Viagra users were given the competitive features of both Viagra and Cialis and were asked to sort out many objects into collections representing the two drugs. Here is what a Business Week article reported on the experiment:

The participants assigned red lace teddies, stiletto-heeled shoes and champagne glasses to Viagra, and while assigned fluffy bathrobes, and down pillows to Cialis. The marketing team realized that this was the primary point of differentiation: Viagra for Sex and Cialis for Romance. This new insight regarding messaging and its longer duration of action as the key differentiator drove all the subsequent advertising campaigns which had become very effective.

Big Opportunity

Whatever differential advantage the drug may have, it is still a monumental task for a new drug to take the lead away from the first drug to market, that too a drug as well established as Viagra. Eli Lilly, therefore, embarked on a monumental research effort surveying thousands of men who have erectile dysfunction and their partners to unearth advertising opportunities. Here are some of the more significant opportunities that came up as a result of its marketing research:

- An estimated 30 million Americans were suffering from at least some sexual dysfunction
- Pfizer had persuaded over half of them (16 million approximately) to try Viagra
- Nearly half of the people who tried Viagra did not renew their prescriptions

These research findings showed Cialis how big the opportunity was in the erectile dysfunction therapeutic area, despite the incumbent's blockbuster performance. Here was the simple math:

Lilly Could persuade the 14 million people suffering from sexual dysfunction to try Cialis. It. The target patient pool or population was a massive 22 million. Cialis found a chink in Viagra's armor!

The Cialis Difference

Cialis had two distinct advantages over Viagra. Cialis can be taken with food or drink as it does not alter its absorption rate. Whereas with Viagra food intake can alter its absorption. The second advantage of Cialis over Viagra is the most significant. It stays in the body as long as thirty-six hours giving it a huge window of opportunity of staying in the romantic mood longer without anxiety. With Viagra, the pill reminds you of your failures every time you have sex. This is because when you take Viagra, you know that the effect wears off in four to five hours.

Cialis comes in two versions. One version is approved for daily use, and the other version lasts for thirty-six hours or as the weekend pill as the French call it. When you take the daily use pill, it is more like taking an anti-allergic pill when you brush your teeth in the morning and not preparatory one before making love. Therefore, with Cialis, it is basically denial, men's favorite sexual emotion - in the pill form.

The Advertising Strategy

Eli Lilly launched its first TV spot for Cialis during the Super Bowl in 2003, which featured a couple in the surf on a beach holding hands across their own bathtubs. The ad quickly became a recognizable symbol for the brand. Over the years, the Cialis bathtub couples evolved and went into new locations, were featured In different iterations and with varying levels of prominence, but were never entirely left out. They were always present. The bathtubs are used almost as mnemonic.

Why bathtubs? Because they symbolically represent freedom. Freedom to choose when, so they can relax and not worry about it. Lilly had arrived at the bathtub concept based on the insights it gained from consumer research. They had found that a relaxed mind free of performance anxiety was the most sought-after need of men with erectile dysfunction and their partners. The idea of relaxing and not rushing is Cialis' core differentiation in the erectile dysfunction category, with its time-release formula working for 36-hours. The bathtubs were a hit right from the beginning. Surprising as it may seem, the concept of bathtubs in the Cialis ad was not a planned, research-based creative concept. The idea struck the director of the original Cialis ad at the last minute on a creative whim, and he added the bathtub storyboard while on the set for the first ad. The concept resonated with the brand managers and audiences and generated lively online discussions. Cialis bathtubs were an iconic marketing success. There were many conversations among the patients regarding the Cialis ad as the one with people in the bathtubs in the waiting rooms of physicians across the country.

Another distinct feature of Cialis ads that separate them from the competition is that their advertising speaks to women even though they are not directly targeted to women. They influence the partners of men who have erectile dysfunction. Cialis ads talk about the right moment. The right moment appeals to the partner as well as men who suffer from the condition. The Cialis ad asks men the key question that says it all: *If a relaxing moment turns into the right moment, will you be ready?*

Above all, the Cialis ad uses fear as its primary motivator. However, it is not the same as the fear of ability – can-you-do-it kind of fear. It is about the fear of preparedness – will-you-be-ready-when-the-time-is-right kind of fear. This shift from the ability to preparedness makes the fear less threatening. This whole approach of Cialis advertising does two things at the same time:

A. It presupposes the existence of drugs like Viagra and Levitra and

B. Implies their limitations and suggests that they are inadequate, fall short and not up to it

The Viagra - Cialis dichotomy was reinforced in one-on-one interviews with partners of men with erectile dysfunction. The Viagra women (whose partners were on Viagra) confessed that they felt undue pressure, almost like the ones being under the gun to perform. It felt like that there were three of them in the bed! Me, him and the pill. On the other hand, these women said that from what they had heard about Cialis, they could be more natural and won't have to have sex until both of them were in the mood. Armed with these insights, Eli Lilly and the agency eventually narrowed their advertising themes down to two in early 2002.

Choose the moment

You can't hurry love with the tagline: *When a tender moment turns into the right moment, you will be ready.*

The Cialis ads were not only a big hit but also effective. Cialis after achieving a blockbuster status in 2007, went on to generate $17 billion in sales during its patent life, which now extends at least through September 27, 2018. Some of the more critical milestones in the development and rise of Cialis are presented in the following table - Cialis: The Rise of the Weekend Pill - A Timeline.

Cialis: The Rise of the Weekend Pill - A Timeline

Timeline	Activity or Event
The early 1990s	A. Glaxo Wellcome began a study of tadalafil compound for cardiovascular diseases with ICOS corporation. B. ICOS researchers discovered that the drug caused erections of participants during the trial and the experimental drug took an unexpected turn.
1996	Glaxo Wellcome discontinued the agreement with ICOS midway through the trial as the experimental drug took an unexpected turn, deciding to focus on other drugs.
1998	Lilly stepped in and agreed to pay ICOS an upfront fee of $75 million and entered into a fifty-fifty partnership for marketing and selling the drug when the it was entering into late-stage trials.
2003	The US FDA approved tadalafil under the brand name Cialis for the treatment of erectile dysfunction.
2007	A. Cialis achieved the coveted blockbuster status with over $1 billion in annual sales. B. Eli Lilly bought out its partner's interest in Cialis for $2.3 billion. ICOS closed down its operations afterwards, unable to launch another drug.
2011	The US FDA approved Cialis for another indication, Benign Prostatic Hyperplasia (BPH).
2012	Cialis overtakes Viagra's $1.9 billion in annual sales to achieve the leader ship position in the erectile dysfunction market.

Counter Attack by Competitors

As Cialis was making rapid progress, its rivals were not standing still. They were stepping their marketing efforts with thousands of their sales reps working hard to derail the strategy of Cialis. The reps of Pfizer and Bayer were warning doctors often while hosting expensive meals, that while Cialis may be effective for as long as 36 hours, its side effects too might last that long. They also insisted that their own research showed that most men with erectile dysfunction know well ahead of time when they might have sex, so the hours that Viagra or Levitra provides them was usually sufficient.

Cialis' Reinforcement Strategy

Not resting on its laurels, Eli Lilly continued to reinforce the strategic marketing of Cialis by getting additional approval for indication and managing its life cycle. Lilly had obtained the US FDA approval for an additional indication – benign prostatic hyperplasia (BPH) for Cialis in 2011. It is estimated that about half of the people who have erectile dysfunction are likely to develop BPH.

In a move to minimize the impending post-patent expiry decline in sales, Lilly had settled with many generic manufacturers who are ready with their generic versions, on a unit-dose patent set to expire in 2020.

Cialis is one of the best-known products in Eli Lilly's 145 Plus-year history along with the antidepressant Prozac and its portfolio of insulins. Although, Lilly did not invent the drug itself (ICOS developed it somewhat accidentally). It has been managing it very successfully to make it one of the top blockbusters in the world pharmaceutical industry.

Lessons

The marketing strategy of Cialis provides at least three valuable lessons to marketers in general and pharmaceutical marketers in particular.

A. How to successfully differentiate your product from the competition

B. How to position your product effectively

C. How to reinforce your 'Me-different' position to achieve market leadership.

A. *How to successfully differentiate your product from the competition*: Cialis was not the first-in-class drug. It was a third-in-class drug. It had an opportunity to study the earlier drugs. Longer duration of action as a product benefit was absent with the two drugs that were already in development and subsequently in the market. Cialis had developed two versions – one for daily use and the other for the longer duration of action. The one that can stay effective in the body for as long as thirty-six hours. This is a huge difference, but not perceived as such at the time. Because physicians at the time did not give much importance to the action of duration. They gave it only a 10 percent weightage, whereas they gave for efficacy and safety a total of 70 percent weightage. However, it is a huge difference and an important one. The only thing is that it was not perceived as necessary at the time. The task for Cialis was how to make its crucial difference of 36-hour action more important to physicians. In other words, how to redefine their criterion for buying-in? That brings us to the next step, positioning the product.

B. *How to position your product effectively*: Cialis had considered many positioning options. Should it center its marketing effort around the current, established purchasing criteria of physicians such as efficacy and safety and highlight its superior, more favorable side effect profile? Alternatively, should it attempt to establish its 36-hour long action as the new criterion? The marketing team at Eli Lilly decided to emphasize the benefits of its 36-hour action. Being able to choose a time for intimacy and romance in a 36-hour window meant that the fear of failure is removed and ensured a relaxed, no-hurry mood to facilitate spontaneity. They backed up this theme with brilliant advertising and TV spots that resonated with their audience.

C. *How to reinforce your 'Me-different' position to achieve market leadership*: Having arrived at a superior 'Me-different' positioning strategy, the company had set a higher price for Cialis than its competitors to underscore its superiority. This bold move proved to be the winner later.

(Source: Adapted from articles - 1. Chris Wienke, *Male sexuality, medicalization and the marketing of Cialis and Levitra*, Sexuality & Culture, Fall 2005, Vol. 9, No. 4, pp 29-57; 2. Niraj Dawar, *When marketing is strategy*, Harvard Business Review, December 2013; 3. Michael Arndt, *Is Viagra vulnerable*? Bloomberg, October 27, 2003)

Glaxo, The House that Zantac Built

Glaxo Holdings is the house that Zantac built. In 1989, Zantac became the best selling drug in the world accounting for more than half of Glaxo's $4.4 billion in revenues. Zantac was launched in the United States in 1983, after its hugely successful 1982 launch in Europe.

Glaxo Holdings PLC of Great Britain had a reputation as a somewhat conservative if not stodgy organization till the late 1970s. However, its anti-ulcer drug, Zantac, a me-too new drug product that became the market leader, made Glaxo a global contender in the highly competitive pharmaceutical industry.

In 1983, when Zantac was launched in the United States, Glaxo was ranked sixteenth in the world pharmaceutical industry; by 1992, it became number two! During that time, Glaxo's market value grew four-fold, from $4 billion to 36 billion!

Zantac's excellent sales contrast with its relatively ordinary medical performance. For all its achievements in the marketplace, Zantac was not a first-in-class drug. It was a me-too copy of SmithKline's pioneering antiulcerant drug Tagamet (cimetidine).

In the late 1970s, Glaxo was effectively UK-based. The purchase of Meyer Laboratories Inc. in 1978 gave the company a foothold and an R&D base in the United States. Glaxo's sales from the US Initially and until the launch of Zantac were relatively insignificant. In the first half of the 1980s, more than two-thirds of Glaxo's sales revenues were from Europe, Africa, and the Middle East. Zantac's launch in the US changed all that. The company came into the top gear and moved onto a new growth trajectory.

A Brief History of Anti-ulcer Drugs

One of the significant new products in the 1970s was the discovery of cimetidine, the first histamine-2 receptor antagonist for the treatment of ulcer disease. James Black and his team of scientists at the British Laboratories of SmithKline & French (GlaxoSmithKline now) discovered cimetidine. Cimetidine was launched as Tagamet late in 1976, at a symposium of the Royal College of Physicians. By 1981, Tagamet was achieving sales of nearly $300 million in the United States.

In the late 1970s, Glaxo's scientists too had been working on histamine-2 receptor antagonists, which are analogs of cimetidine (Tagamet). The anti-ulcer market thanks to Tagamet was growing rapidly. Glaxo scientists were working on improving cimetidine by overcoming its existing limitations and side effects. Glaxo in the process discovered ranitidine, which it named as Zantac.

Launched in 1981 in the United Kingdom, and in Italy, Zantac had the following advantages over Tagamet:

  A. Zantac needed to be taken only two times a day whereas Tagamet had to be taken four times a day.
  B. Zantac had fewer side effects as compared to Tagamet.

Glaxo had made great use of its advantages over Tagamet in its promotional campaigns in copybook style. Zantac's phenomenal success had catapulted Glaxo from a medium-sized British pharmaceutical company into the top ranks of world pharmaceutical industry. To the enviable Second position by 1989.

To get Zantac into the vast and lucrative US market, Glaxo mounted a classic two-stage operation in textbook style. In the first phase between 1983 and 1989, Glaxo forged a co-promotion strategy with the Swiss Pharma Major, Hoffman-La Roche. In the second Phase from 1990 to 1994, Glaxo rapidly consolidated the success of Zantac by building its own marketing workforce in the United States to sell what was by then an established product.

Key Elements of Zantac's Strategy

Glaxo decided to market Zantac not as a Tagamet monopoly breaker but as a significant evolutionary advance in the treatment of peptic ulcer and other acid peptic disorders. It was somewhat unusual for a second product in the drug class. It was a major strategic decision that guided all others in Zantac's winning game plan.

Paul Girolami, Glaxo's Chairman, and Managing director himself assumed the responsibility of developing the launch marketing plan for Zantac. He began with the focus on the physicians' needs. He knew that an anti-ulcer drug's ability to relieve the patients' pain and its ability to heal the ulcer (healing rate) were the two prime characteristics that influence the physicians' selection of anti-ulcer therapy.

Questioning Tagamet's safety was a neat line of attack. Glaxo had a very aggressive positioning strategy and attacked its rival where it was more vulnerable. Particularly so, when Glaxo could not prove that Zantac was better. It had not been used widely enough for its side effect profile to emerge. However, by the same logic, it could not be disproved. Glaxo made very skillful use of this information and conveyed it as a decisive advantage to all key stakeholders such as physicians, patients, and payors. Although Tagamet had proven its safety in trials and over time in use, it had certain side effects such as nausea, diarrhea, drowsiness, decreased sperm count, gynecomastia, and drug-drug interactions. These side effects of Tagamet had proved to be Zantac's window of opportunity. Also, Glaxo turned Tagamet's weaknesses into Zantac's strengths, using aggressive advertising to give information-hungry gastrointestinal physicians the evidence they needed to prescribe Zantac.

Girolami and his marketing team decided to alleviate selected side effects through product refinement and then attack Tagamet on those side effects. Tagamet could not deny them. Zantac, as a result of product refinement, did not have them. Zantac launched an aggressive marketing program highlighting their product superiority.

Glaxo had priced its second-in-class drug, Zantac at a 20 percent premium over its rival, the first-in-class drug and market leader Tagamet, which was unheard of in the industry.

Co-marketing of Zantac with the Swiss Drug Major, Hoffman-La Roche, in the United States was another masterstroke in Zantac's strategy. Its primary purpose was to reach the critical mass regarding appropriate sales levels for Zantac, and co-marketing alliances were a necessity since Glaxo had a relatively small field force at the time of Zantac launch. Roche at the time had an under-utilized sales force with the patents of its commercially successful products, Valium and Librium running out. With this, more than 1,200 detail men started promoting Zantac's superiority to all gastroenterologists and PCPs across the country leading to a rapid increase in prescriptions and sales. Under the co-marketing agreement, Roche would detail and sell Zantac under the Glaxo brand name. Glaxo would pay Roche 40 percent of sales revenue for five years.

Glaxo had also used the co-marketing strategies in France with Formin and in Germany with Cascan. Co-marketing had helped the company in reaching the critical mass needed for Zantac regarding sales volumes and market share very rapidly.

Continuous and accelerated product development was another vital element in Zantac's strategy. In fact, Zantac was an outcome of product development. Glaxo tweaked the Tagamet molecule and improved its side-effect profile considerably and extended its action of duration. It had also used parallel processing to cut the developmental time in half. Glaxo did not stop after discovering ranitidine with these perceptible and patentable therapeutic advantages. It continued its development. When Tagamet responded to Zantac's attack on its dosing frequency with its twice-daily dosage version, Zantac continued to improve its dosing frequency to once-daily. Zantac seized the product development initiative from its rival, Tagamet. Further, Glaxo continued with many line extensions for Zantac regarding different strengths, dosage forms such as liquid, pediatric dosage forms such as Baby Zantac, and injectables. The pioneer, Tagamet although responded to most of these but a bit late.

The Birth of A New Indication - GERD

The GERD indication approval for Zantac in 1986 was probably one of the essential features of its strategy. It offered Zantac a significant advantage. GERD was created by Glaxo, which grouped many symptoms related to gastrointestinal disorders such as heartburn, acid reflux and called it Gastro Esophageal Reflux Disorder. Before the FDA's approval of treating GERD with Zantac, heartburn did not seem to warrant a prescription drug. It was perceived to be well managed by over-the-counter remedies. Glaxo had elevated the medical importance of GERD condition by presenting it as an acutely chronic disorder with an underlying physiologic etiology and its potential for serious longer-term consequence if left untreated.

Glaxo created an Institute for Digestive Health (GIDH), which sponsored its research and equated GERD with more serious gastrointestinal diseases simply by discussing it in the same context. One of the missions of the institute is to raise public awareness about issues relating to digestive health. Branding of GERD not only shifted the public perception about the dangers of chronic acid reflux, but it also put Zantac in the spotlight as the best overall solution. It also implied that acid blockade rather than acid neutralization is necessary as it attacks the root of the condition before it manifests itself and does the damage.

The GERD indication approval enlarged the market considerably. Because GERD is a condition that occurs more commonly and in a relatively larger population. It is also treated by primary care physicians more often and not just by gastroenterologists. Besides, Zantac was the only product that received FDA approval for the treatment of GERD for quite some time. Tagamet got approval for the treatment of GERD almost five years later, in 1991, GERD accounted for nearly two-thirds of Glaxo's annual $2 billion sales of Zantac.

Last but not least, overcoming the traditional marketing mindset was also a crucial factor for Zantac's success. Pharmaceutical companies at the time used to think of themselves as highly specialized, hanging in on their target markets of doctors and hospitals, pharmacists and wholesalers as if they were packaged goods consumers. When it came to marketing Zantac, the company thought differently. Zantac's marketing strategy had evolved from close studies of the marketing tactics of some of the leading consumer goods success stories such as McDonald's, Nutrasweet, and Perrier.

Glaxo had used an extensive range of marketing techniques across multiple channels to promote Zantac. The company had conducted many educational symposia, issued numerous consumer awareness bulletins, public service announcements via radio and television, Journal advertisements. Glaxo had also introduced many formulations of Zantac for different age groups and medical practice settings and extended many therapies for long-term maintenance. All these initiatives had not only gained a more significant market share for the company but also successfully expanded the market for anti-ulcer drugs.

Racing for the Anti-ulcer Market

The anti-ulcer drug market as we know today had started in 1977 with the introduction of SmithKline & French's Tagamet in the United States. Until the entry of Zantac in 1983, SmithKline did not have to bother about competing for market share in the histamine-2 receptor antagonist market as it had one hundred percent of the market to itself under its patent status. The goal of marketing for Tagamet was to convince more and more physicians of its therapeutic benefits and improve the rate of adoption of its new therapy.

When Glaxo introduced Zantac in 1983, the monopoly of Tagamet had become a duopoly. There was an additional marketing goal. Tagamet had to preserve its market share against Zantac among those doctors, who were currently prescribing Tagamet. Zantac detailers too had a twin objective before them. They had to convince the doctors who had not yet taken up the new therapy to take up Zantac for treating their patients with duodenal ulcer and take a share from the current prescribers of Tagamet by convincing them about Zantac's superiority over Tagamet and consequent therapeutic benefits to their patients. Thus the marketing rivalry had begun in the anti-ulcer drug market between Tagamet and Zantac.

Two more competitors in the histamine–2 receptor antagonist market, Pepcid of Merck, and Axid of Eli Lilly entered in October 1986 and April 1988 respectively. The competitive noise had increased. So did the market expansion with more players drumming up their versions of the H2 receptor antagonist story in treating acid peptic disorders. In 1989, a new class of drug for treating GERD and ulcers, Prilosec (omeprazole, discovered by Astra of Sweden and marketed by Merck in the USA) was also approved by the FDA further intensifying competition. The following table presents important milestones of the race for the anti-ulcer drug market.

Racing for the Anti-ulcer Drug Market: Key Milestones

Timeline	Event or Activity
August 1977	US FDA approves Smithkline's Tagamet (cimetidine) for the short-term treatment of duodenal ulcer
April 1980	US FDA approves Tagamet for the long-term maintenance treatment of duodenal ulcer
December 1980	US FDA approves Tagamet for the treatment of gastric ulcer

Timeline	Event or Activity
July 1983	US FDA approves Glaxo's Zantac (ranitidine) for the treatment of duodenal ulcer
July 1984	Glaxo's Zantac captures 25 per cent of Tagamet-Zantac market within one year of its launch
May 1986	US FDA approves Zantac for the treatment of GERD (Gastro Esophageal Reflux Disorder) an indication created by Glaxo
October 1986	US FDA approves Merck's Pepcid (famotidine) another histamine-2 receptor antagonist for the treatment of duodenal ulcer
January 1988	Zantac overtakes Tagamet in total sales
April 1988	US FDA approves Eli Lilly's Axid (nizatidine)
September 1989	US FDA approves Merck's Prilosec (omeprazole discovered by Astra, Sweden and marketed by Merck in the United States) a first-in-class proton pump inhibitor drug for the treatment of GERD
March 1991	A. US FDA approves Tagamet for the treatment of GERD B. Zantac becomes the first-ever drug in the world to reach $1 billion in sales
June 1991	US FDA approves Prilosec for the short-term treatment of duodenal ulcer
May 1993	The market shares of the four histamine 2 receptor antagonists were: Zantac 55 percent; Tagamet 21 percent: Pepcid 15 percent; Axid 9 percent
1994	Zantac becomes the best selling drug in the world with almost $4 billion in annual sales

Zantac continued to race past its competitors in the anti-ulcer drug market. Zantac was genuinely prodigious in its performance right from its birth throughout its life cycle. It had many firsts to its credit. It was the first-ever prescription drug to cross the coveted $1 billion mark in global sales. Also, it was the first-ever prescription drug to pass the $4 billion mark in worldwide sales.

Speaking about Zantac's phenomenal success, Martin Preuveneers, Director for International marketing remarked in 1992: *The sales of Zantac were very close to those of Jaguar and just a little more profitable.*

(Source: Adapted from: R. Berndt, Linda T. Bui, David H. Lucking Reiley, and Glen L. Urban, *The roles of marketing, product quality, and price competition in the growth and composition of the US anti-ulcer drug industry*, University of Chicago Press, January 1996).

Gardasil - Marketing Success or Missed Opportunity?

In 1976, Herald Zur Hausen, a German scientist, who was a professor emeritus and virologist discovered that human papillomavirus (HPV) causes cervical tumors. He won the 2008 Nobel prize for physiology and medicine for this discovery. Merck spotted an opportunity in this discovery and decided to develop a vaccine for HPV. The company, accordingly, put a microbiologist, Katherine Jansen in charge for knitting together several technologies necessary to make the vaccine a reality.

Merck developed a vaccine, Gardasil against human papillomavirus (HPV) successfully and got the approval of the US FDA in June 2006. Gardasil protects against four of the more than thirty types of sexually transmitted human papillomavirus (HPV). The FDA cleared it in record time. It took only six months for Gardasil from application to approval. Most vaccines take three years or more.

Merck lobbied every opinion leader, women's group, medical society, politicians and went directly to the people. The company brought unprecedented attention to its vaccine by generously funding many women's groups, medical experts, doctors, lobbyists and political organizations interested in the disease area.

Merck knew from the beginning that education about the vaccine was going to play a critical role due to a lack of understanding about human papillomavirus (HPV) even among physicians let lone patients and the general public. Besides, there was a controversy that vaccination against sexually transmitted infection (STI) such as HPV might lead to teen promiscuity. Anticipating a fair amount of public resistance against a vaccine for against sexually transmitted infection (STI), Merck decided to position Gardasil differently. The company positioned the Gardasil as the vaccine to prevent cancer arising out of HPV infection. Because, research studies showed that HPV infection could cause cervical, vaginal, anal, throat and penile cancers. Experts also were of the view that the best to time to vaccinate against the virus is at ages 11 and 12 when the children have the most robust immune response.

Merck launched massive disease awareness and educational programs even before the FDA approval of Gardasil. The company started with a teaser campaign – *Tell Someone*. In doing so, Merck began the process of positioning a vaccine that protects primarily against a common sexually transmitted infection instead as a potent vaccine against cancer. Merck followed up its teaser campaign with a series of advertising campaigns addressing women's lack of familiarity with the virus and its consequences. The television advertisements featured women talking directly into the camera exclaiming: "Cancer caused by a virus... I didn't know that!"

Tell Someone campaign encouraged viewers to share the knowledge with other women and sharing was critical in getting the word out. The initial advertisements appeared to be banking on the fear of cancer in promoting Gardasil, the new HPV vaccine. The messaging focused on cancer prevention rather than the less comfortable and socially not-so-acceptable topic of sexually transmitted infection.

Merck, in its strong direct-to-consumer-advertising awareness campaigns, launched both unbranded and branded campaigns in the most famous women's magazines and prime time television programs. Here are some of the more interesting advertisements:

▸ The advertisements always featured teen and pre-teen girls jumping rope, shooting hoops, and playing the drums - while pledging to be One Less...cervical cancer statistic. These young girls look into the camera and declare: *Each year in the US, thousands of women learn that they have cervical cancer. I could be One Less*.

▸ The advertisements also featured images of mothers and daughters, and close with a call for action – *Get Vaccinated*. It is a powerful message calling for a positive response.

▸ Merck very cleverly sequenced its advertisements, which began with " Tell Someone," moving to One Less (in the cancer statistic) and moving to "I Choose." It then launched an ad that initially said, " Make the Connection" (between HPV and cancer) and subsequently changed to "Make the Commitment."

▸ One commercial began with a woman saying: *I have cervical cancer from an infection - human papillomavirus*. (photos of her as a young adult and preteen flash by) *Who knew HPV would lead to certain cancers? Who knew that there was something that could have helped protect me from HPV, when I was 11 or 12, way before I would be even be exposed to it*? It ends up with a version of herself as a child looking from a birthday cake festooned with candles and asking plaintively: *Did you know Mom - Dad*?

▸ Later, when the company got approval for Gardasil for boys, the advertisements featured a young man and ended with him asking the same haunting question.

▸ Many celebrities participated in the so-called public service announcement promotions of Gardasil. Merck discontinued these promotions subsequently. Some of these unbranded campaigns did not mention Merck's Gardasil. Instead, they aim for a tender spot – the parents' concern for doing right for their children.

Educating the Educators

Merck launched a massive *Educate the Educators* session to inform physicians, targeting mainly gynecologists about their new vaccine, Gardasil. However, the company did not focus its discussion on the epidemiology of the virus, or any of the existing treatment options, which most of the participants would be using in their daily practice. The entire focus of Merck right from the FDA's approval seemed to be on reducing the mortality due to cervical cancer.

The promotion of the vaccine and the management trial data stressed that the need was for a cancer vaccine, not for a vaccine to prevent a highly transmissible and a highly prevalent STI. The emphasis seemed to be on how to minimize parental resistance to the vaccine.

Enhanced Coverage

One of the main reasons for Gardasil's commercial success lies in the fact that it could enhance its coverage. More than 95 insurance plans – covering 94 percent of insured individuals have decided to reimburse Gardasil. The Centers for Disease Control and Prevention added the vaccine to its 'vaccines for children contract' making it available for Medicaid-eligible, uninsured, under-insured, or native American children upto the age of 18.

Market Performance

How did Gardasil perform in the market? Not only the vaccine was on a fast track for approval, but also rapidly achieved the blockbuster status within the first full year of launch bypassing the US $1.4 billion mark. Consider these facts for example:

A. Merck's Gardasil was the most expensive vaccine at launch costing $350 for one course of three injections.

B. In 2009, the US FDA approved Gardasil for vaccinating boys and young men. What is more, the vaccine got its approval in 120 countries around the world within five years of its first approval, in 2011.

C. In 2014, 40 percent of girls and 22 percent of boys had gotten the three-shot course of Gardasil according to Centers For Disease Control and Prevention (CDC).

D. In 2014, The US FDA approved a nine-valent Gardasil vaccine to protect against the infection in five other HPV strains responsible for 20 percent of cervical cancers.

E. Gardasil passed the US $2.17 billion-mark annual sales in 2016.

Lessons

Merck, one of the most respected pharmaceutical companies in the world is known for excellence in product launches, life cycle management and in building and growing disease franchises over the years. Gardasil is one more feather in its cap. Merck followed the best practices in every department of the game in launching and building a new pharmaceutical brand. Consider the actions and activities that the company undertook in case of Gardasil Promotion:

▸ Built substantial clinical evidence proving the safety and efficacy of Gardasil with many clinical trials.

▸ Launched unbranded and branded disease awareness campaigns directly to patients, and all the critical stakeholders and educating the educators' programs for physicians well before launching Gardasil.

▸ Created powerful, emotional advertising that is at times controversial, with a compelling call to action, Lobbied heavily among all the concerned groups such as women's groups, gynecologists, politicians, patient groups. Generously funded all the relevant groups for convincing the necessity of a cancer vaccine such as Gardasil.

▸ Enhanced coverage by convincing almost all the insurance companies (94 percent) to reimburse Gardasil.

Did Merck maximize the opportunity for its first-in-class vaccine for a highly prevalent condition? Is there anything that Merck could have done better. Samantha D. Gottlieb, author of *Not Quite A Cancer Vaccine: Selling HPV and Cervical Cancer*, Rutgers University Press (2018) cogently argues in her book as to how Merck missed an opportunity in marketing Gardasil. Merck had an incredible opportunity before launching Gardasil. Merck had achieved something very significant in developing a vaccine that protects against a sexually transmitted infection (STI) that can slowly progress into cancer. Instead of empowering women to reduce their health risks associated with HPV, the company has through its advertising campaigns chose to manipulate women by playing on their ignorance or confusion about their healthcare.

Even after a thorough analysis, a few questions remain.

Merck had an option to position Gardasil either as a vaccine against STI caused by HPV or as a vaccine for preventing cancer that is likely to be caused by HPV at a later date. Merck chose to promote Gardasil for prevention against cancer. The company anticipated considerable resistance by parents and women's groups for a vaccine that will prevent STI caused by human papillomavirus. The company was still reeling under the pressures following the Vioxx fiasco and its related legal settlements regarding criminal and civil suits. The company could not afford another controversy or social resistance.

Could Gardasil have become a more prominent brand if it were to choose a different positioning? The Positioning of a vaccine against STI?

(Source: 1. Laurie McGinley's article, *Do the new Merck HPV ads guilt-trip parents or tell hard truths? Both*, Published in The Washington Post, August 11, 2016, 2. S. D. Gottileib's article, *Vaccine promotion in the hands of a corporation: The missed opportunity of Merck's marketing of Gardasil*, Corporations and Health Watch, June 1, 2010)

BiDil: Rational Medicine or Racial Medicine?

BiDil, approved by the US FDA is the first-ever drug with a race-specific indication. It has fueled the controversy over the meaning of race and ethnicity. It also raised questions whether this approval should be seen as an advance or a setback in the struggle to address disparities in health status associated with race.

BiDil combines two generic drugs – isosorbide dinitrate and hydralazine hydrochloride, which are known to benefitting patients with heart failure irrespective of race or ethnicity. However, the fixed-dose combination of these two drugs, BiDil was approved for treating congestive heart failure (CHF) specifically in a single racial-ethnic group, African Americans. The push to bring these drugs as a race-specific treatment was motivated by peculiarities of the US patent law and willingness to exploit race to gain a commercial and regulatory advantage.

Understanding the science underpinning BiDil requires a brief historical review and a discussion of the scientific data. African American patients are more likely to die of heart failure compared with whites. There are several explanations for this. Consider the following for example:

- ▸ Delay in diagnosis and treatment
- ▸ Limited access to coronary care
- ▸ High prevalence of high-risk individuals with hypertension
- ▸ Diabetes and dyslipidemia and other risk-related behavioral factors such as physical inactivity, and smoking

Furthermore, there was one explanation that focuses on the impaired availability of nitric oxide, which is thought to contribute to the structural remodeling of the left ventricle that increases the rate of death and complications in heart disease. It was also proposed that African American patients may have a disproportionately lower nitric oxide bioavailability. Isosorbide dinitrate acts as a nitrate donor and hydralazine as an antioxidant, and so together they might ameliorate the long-term effects of heart failure.

In the 1970s, Dr. Jay Cohn, a heart specialist at the University of Minnesota in Minneapolis, USA started his research work on using vasodilation and hydralazine and nitrate therapy to treat heart disorders. The studies that he conducted in 1973 and 1978 paved the way for further testing of a novel approach to treat heart failure.

In the 1980s, Cohn was the lead cardiologist on the two vasodilator-heart failure trials (V-HeFT I and II) conducted to determine the efficacy of combination therapy of isosorbide dinitrate and hydralazine in heart failure. The result of V-HeFT I showed that the combination had a significant beneficial effect in treating heart failure in the black patient population.

Later, V-HeFT II was conducted with its results published in 1991. It was a comparative clinical trial of isosorbide dinitrate and hydralazine with enalapril. Its results showed that mortality was significantly lower in the enalapril arm. A retrospective review of the trial data, however, found that white patients had disproportionate benefit from enalapril, whereas the subset of African American patients appeared to receive substantially more benefit from the isosorbide dinitrate-hydralazine therapy. At this point, no one had tested the hypothesis that isosorbide dinitrate and hydralazine, added to a regimen that already included an angiotensin-converting enzyme (ACE) inhibitor, might provide benefits to patients with congestive heart failure.

BiDil's NDA for the treatment of heart failure was rejected by the FDA in 1997 when it was first filed without a race indication. FDA said no to the use of BiDil to treat heart failure in general population as it found the data was insufficient and evidence inconclusive.

Following the rejection of the FDA, researchers sought to resuscitate the drug as a racial medicine by sizing on the data from the original clinical trials to make a case to the FDA that the black patients responded better to the drug than the white patients. However, many epidemiologists and other critics remain unconvinced by this data.

NitroMed, the USA-based company had acquired a New Drug Application (NDA) and intellectual property relating BiDil based on the new data published in the Journal of Cardiac Failure (September 10, 1999). The new data, which was based on a retrospective review of a comparative clinical trial of isosorbide dinitrate and hydralazine. The data showed that a combination of isosorbide dinitrate and hydralazine benefited the African-American patients substantially during the trial. NitroMed acquired the dossier from Dr. Jay Cohen of the University of Minnesota, who had conducted the V-HEFT I and II trials.

The African American Heart Failure Trial (A-HEFT) was conducted to test this hypothesis and it was sponsored by NitroMed, a Charlotte, North Carolina, the USA-based company that develops and commercializes pharmaceutical products. Only African-American patients were enrolled in the trial. About 1,000 patients were randomized to a fixed-dose combination of isosorbide dinitrate and hydralazine (BiDil) or a placebo added to their existing medication. Sixty- nine percent of the patients were on ACE inhibitors at baseline. Although follow-up was planned for 18 months, the trial was stopped early, because there was excess mortality in the placebo group. Based on these impressive findings, the FDA advisory panel recommended on June 16, 2005, that BiDil be approved specifically for the treatment of heart failure in African-American patients.

NitroMed amended the NDA and sought approval for BiDil in the treatment of congestive heart failure (CHF) specifically for the African-American patients. The US FDA approved BiDil for the treatment of heart failure in black patients. It is interesting to note that the patent of BiDil for use among the general population expired in 2007, but the new patent for use among black patients remains valid till 2020.

Strategic Lobbying

NitroMed, the maker of the drug BiDil lobbied for the drug's approval by the FDA soliciting the support of black interest groups such as Association of Black Cardiologists (ABC), Congressional Black Caucus (CBC), The National Association for the Advancement of Colored People (NAACP). After the approval, NitroMed used the support it gained from the black interest groups and community members to make BiDil as a unique grassroots pharmaceutical to African Americans.

In December 2005, NitroMed formed a strategic alliance with the NAACP to address healthcare disparities. NitroMed gave a $1.5 million grant to NAACP to develop health advocacy programs within the organization. The support showed for the drug by the NAACP, and many members of the African American community swayed the FDA Advisory Committee, and the drug was approved in 2005.

Marketing BiDil

NitroMed launched nationally in the US in mid-July 2005 in bottles of 180 tablets at a wholesale acquisition cost of US $1.80 per tablet. The company made the product available one month before the launch in pharmacies, and the doctors started receiving samples a few weeks before the launch. Michael D. Loberg, the chief executive officer of NitroMed, said at the time of BiDil launch:

> NitroMed is pleased to be able to make BiDil available within one year of the African-American Heart Failure Trial (A-HEFT) being halted and within only two weeks of FDA approval. This speaks to NitroMed's sense of urgency and to the importance of BiDil patients who need it.

What is more, NitroMed launched a patient assistance program called NitroMed Cares to lower health care disparities by providing BiDil free of charge to low-income patients without health insurance coverage. NitroMed used the support it received from the advisory groups and the community organizations to launch a unique marketing campaign targeted at African American consumers. BiDil thus has become a pioneer not only in its status as the first race-based drug but also because of the unprecedented support of the African American advocacy and community groups, and a unique niche marketing campaign.

African American trade and entrepreneurship magazines widely celebrated BiDil as a racially targeted marketing success story. In 2004, Target Market News, which covers news and trends in marketing to African Americans named BiDil among its top 25 news stories in African American marketing for that year!

It was estimated that there were 39.7 million African-Americans in the US, roughly making up 13.4 percent of the population according to a report released by the US Census Bureau in May 2006. There were studies done that showed that this segment of the population was more prone to heart diseases than the average population. NitroMed projected that BiDil sales would touch $120 million in the first year and within a few years would cross the coveted $1 billion in annual sales. However, BiDil could achieve a mere $4.5 million in 2005 falling far short of expectations. NitroMed even launched a direct-to-consumer advertising campaign (DTCA) in September 2006 for BiDil.

The sales of BiDil, however, did not show any progress. BiDil sales were a fraction of their original projections. The sales of BiDil were $12.1 million in 2006; $15.3 million in 2007; and $14.9 million in 2008. In 2009, NitroMed declared that:

> *The company had never been profitable and expected the* future revenues from *BiDil to fall significantly* based on *declining prescriptions, an unwillingness of third-party payers to provide reimbursement and a reduction in their sales force and promotional efforts.*

NitroMed stopped the marketing of its BiDil but continued to make the drug available. In 2009, the healthcare investment company, Deerfield Management acquired NitroMed for about $36 million.

The forty plus year-long, spectacular journey of the first-ever race-based drug, thus came to an insignificant end.

Lessons

The most important lesson that BiDil teaches us is that market protection alone is not enough. While market protection is vital for a drug's commercial success, it is not sufficient. NitroMed sought and obtained market protection for the use of its drug, BiDil in black patients, that patent protection seems to have done little work in the actual marketplace because it did not command a price premium compared to separately prescribed generics.

The patent may have prevented competitors from introducing a generic version of BiDil for use in African American Patients, but it did not stop the physicians, patients, and payers from using the two generic drugs (active ingredients of the fixed-dose combination of BiDil) separately. The business strategy of NitroMed would have been successful if BiDil's active components were not generics.

Another valuable lesson is that payer collaboration, and insurance coverage are crucial for a drug's commercial success. Several insurance companies did not cover BiDil as cheaper generics of the two separate drugs were available. The copays were hefty where insurance coverage was available. The separately prescribed generics were available with considerably lower copays.

Cardiologists and patients were not as enthusiastic as the African American advocacy and other community groups in welcoming or even accepting BiDil. There was more political and social support to BiDil than the support from the scientific community.

(Source: Adapted from: 1. Howard Brody, M.D, PhD., and Linda M. Hunt, PhD., *BiDil: Assessing a race-based pharmaceutical*, Annals of Family Medicine, 2006 Nov 4 (6) 556-560; Britt M. Rusert, PhD., and Charmaine D.M. Royal, PhD., *Grassroots marketing in a global era: More lessons from BiDil*, The Journal of Law, Medicine & Ethics, 2011 Spring; 39 (1): 79-90)

The First Rationally Designed Small Molecule Drug of Novartis Wins the 'Prestigious Prix Galien Foundation's' Discovery of the Decade Award in 2016!

Novartis took decades to develop Gleevec, but it later broke several records. Many people may not know that the planners at Novartis were trying to kill the imatinib (Gleevec) molecule in its development because of low sales forecasts. They forecasted that the product would peak at $50 million. However, Daniel Vasella's vision changed that and Gleevec went on to become a blockbuster with $4.69 billion in global sales in 2013. Daniel Vasella, the Chief Executive Officer (CEO) of Novartis at that time was a physician by qualification. He looked at the drug under development and the sales forecasts and had the guts to trust his guts. He told the team:

> As a scientist, I can see a breakthrough in Gleevec and therefore this is a standard that we will be using. We will look at this thing, and will only move to the clinic things that can change the status quo, and that will cause physicians to abandon what they have been doing, and embrace the new therapy.

The rest became history. Gleevec came to be considered a wonder drug that has transformed some blood cancers into chronic illnesses rather than death sentences. Here is how it all began.

The Journey of imatinib (Gleevec)

Gleevec was the result of more than thirty years of cellular research in CML. The identification of the Philadelphia chromosome in the 1960s was the first instance of a genetic abnormality that causally linked it to cancer. The Philadelphia chromosome was associated with the formation of an abnormal hybrid BCR-ABL gene, which coded for an enzyme (tyrosine kinase) with increased activity. This, in turn stimulated the growth of leukemia cells.

In the 1980s, Novartis started a research program on BCR-ABL kinase blockers. It took a decade to develop a compound, but it had a weak efficacy. Two years later, Nicholas Lyndon, a biochemist working at Ciba-Geigy (Novartis now) developed imatinib (Gleevec), which was found to be a potent and specific inhibitor.

Brain Druker, an oncologist at the Oregon Health and Science University, was hoping to find a treatment for CML that unlike chemotherapy could kill cancer cells but leave healthy cells intact. He hypothesized that if patients could be treated with a drug that blocks BCR-ABL, it is possible to kill only the cancer cells and not the healthy cells as healthy cells do not have BCR-ABL. Later, he started collaborating with Nicholas Lyndon searching for the drug. Dr. Druker and Nicholas Lyndon after searching many compounds finally identified a compound - STI-571 that was capable of killing cancer cells better than all other compounds. The compound was later named imatinib (Gleevec).

In 1998, Dr. Druker and his colleagues tested imatinib in Phase I clinical trial partially funded by the National Cancer Institute (NCI). The drug killed cancer cells in most of the patients with CML. Furthermore, five years later, 98 percent of patients from the trial were without remission. Thus Dr. Druker was instrumental in using Gleevec to treat Chronic Myeloid Leukemia (CML). The first clinical trials started in 1998, and the FDA cleared the New Drug Application (NDA) on a fast track and approved it in May 2001.

Gleevec created a new class in bio-oncology - the signal transduction inhibitors. It was indicated for the treatment of chronic myeloid leukemia (CML) after the failure of interferon-alpha therapy. In 95 percent of the CML patients, an abnormal Philadelphia chromosome was found; a transduction between chromosome 9 and 22 formed an abnormal hybrid BCR-ABL gene, which coded for an enzyme (tyrosine kinase) with increased activity. This, in turn, stimulated the growth of leukemia cells. Gleevec was a potent inhibitor of tyrosine kinase with only mild side effects. It took time to develop Gleevec, but it later broke several records in obtaining the regulatory approvals. Consider the following for example:

- Gleevec had the fastest-ever FDA approval time. It was approved in just 72 days in the US.
- It was approved in record time even in the European Union and Japan.
- Clinical trials took close to three years, which is half as long as the standard development time. Clinical trials started in August 1998, and US FDA approved the drug in May 2001.

Global Niche Market

Although Gleevec addressed a high unmet need, its target patient population was very small. CML patients accounted for 20 percent of all leukemias worldwide. The disease prevalence was 20,000, and the incidence was about 5000 cases per year in the United States. The patient population in the European Union too was more or less similar. Japan had about 1,200 cases annually. The number of physicians who treated the disease also was very small as the treatment required a double-specialty – Hematology and Oncology. There were only about 5,000 double-specialists at the time.

The New Gold Standard

The only curative therapy for CML when Gleevec was launched was bone marrow transplant but was limited to 15 to 25 percent of patients because of age and donor availability, very high costs and mortality rates. Interferon-alpha marketed by Roche and Schering-Plough was the gold standard, but it did not cure CML and had severe side effects.

Gleevec with its significantly superior efficacy and a better safety profile quickly became the new gold standard.

Data-Driven Positioning

Gleevec's positioning highlighted its unique targeted nature and its outstanding clinical data. Its promotional message was:

Precise targeting of the molecular abnormality that leads to CML.

So the key points were:

- A. Outstanding hematological response
- B. Unprecedented cytogenetic response, and
- C. Well tolerated, Convenient, Once-daily Oral Therapy

The promotional strategy of Novartis was evidence-based. There were only fifteen opinion leaders who were dual-specialists at the time in the entire world. Many of them were trial investigators for Gleevec and knew its outstanding efficacy.

The evidence of Gleevec's superior efficacy was reinforced further by a pre-launch access program through clinical trials covering about 7,000 patients worldwide.

Patients Drive Demand!

The most significant feature of Gleevec's marketing is that the patients drove its demand! As soon as the patient activists learned about the interim data showing dramatic efficacy in the article published by the American Society of Hematology, they aggressively lobbied for early access and fast-track approval of Gleevec. Patient advocacy groups such as Leukemia & Lymphoma Society, internet-positive patients and others who had their websites facilitated global networking and petitioned the company and regulators for early approval. The result? The fastest FDA approval in just 72 days!

Innovative Pricing Strategy, Broader Access

Gleevec's innovative spirit was not restricted to science alone. It had also followed an innovative pricing strategy and gained broader access. The company worldwide had set a price of $2,200 per month, and the treatment might continue indefinitely for patients who responded. Gleevec tried to show its cost-effectiveness compared with the standard care. Novartis came up with an innovative Global Assistance Program that not only addressed the lower income group but also to patients in the middle-income group. The details of its offering in the United States were:

A. Drug-free of charge to anyone earning less than $43,000 per year

B. Drug cost capped at 20 percent of income for those earning between $43,000 and $100,000 per year

The innovative pricing strategy of Novartis had achieved two objectives. Firstly, it reinforced the share of voice that Gleevec gained by its significantly superior clinical profile. Secondly, it earned the company an extensive and favorable press coverage.

Five More Indication-Approvals

Gleevec tablets received the US FDA approval to treat patients with five rare, potentially life-threatening disorders. It was the first time that a regulatory authority had approved simultaneously one targeted medicine for so many disorders. Gleevec was previously approved for the treatment of Philadelphia chromosome-positive CML and gastrointestinal tumors (GIST). The new approvals are for one solid tumor condition and four diseases of the blood.

Prestigious Award

Novartis has been awarded the prestigious 2016 Prix Galien Foundation, USA award - Discovery of the Decade for the best pharmaceutical product for Gleevec. Gleevec's discovery marked for the first time in the history of cancer treatment that scientists were able to identify a chromosomal abnormality and then develop the drug that would target that specific protein. Prix Galien award is considered as the pharmaceutical industry's Nobel Prize for excellence in scientific innovation that improves the state of human health. Roland Mehl, the French pharmacist, first established it in 1970. The award was inaugurated in the United States in 2007 to recognize the technical, scientific and clinical research skills necessary to develop innovative medicines. The Discovery of the Decade is a special once-in-ten year recognition for industry achievement in medical innovation.

How do you describe a breakthrough drug like Gleevec and its unprecedented success? Dr. Jason Fong, the nephrologist described it best when he said:

The cancer drug known as Gleevec is the unquestioned superstar of the genetic approach to treating cancer. It is the LeBron James, Michael Jordan, and Wilt Chamberlain all rolled into one.

The spirit of Gleevec is best captured in the words of Dr. Druker, one of the key persons behind the discovery of Gleevec in an interview with Claudia Driefus for the New York Times on November 2, 2009:

For a lot of people, Gleevec was simply too good to be true. But these once-dying patients were getting out of bed, dancing, going hiking, doing yoga. The drug was assuring.

(Source: Adapted from: 1. *Building Global Biobrands: Taking Biotechnology to Market* by Francoise Simon and Philip Kotler, Free Press - A Division of Simon & Schuster, New York, 2003; 2. NIH - National Cancer Institute, *How Imatinib transformed leukemia treatment and cancer research*, Updated April 11, 2018; 3. Claudia Driefus, Science: *Research behind the drug Gleevec - A conversation with Dr. Druker*, The New York Times, November 2, 2009; Dr. Jason Fung, Gleevec's false dawn, Medium, November 1, 2017)

Disease Branding

Disease Branding

Disease branding or branding of a condition has been gaining importance in pharmaceutical marketing for some time now. Pharmaceutical marketers and healthcare practitioners are taking it to a new level of sophistication. Branding a condition is gaining prominence as it helps both the Pharma brand managers and clinicians stay focused on the same theme, and structure of the problem and solution surrounding a disease condition. In other words, it keeps them both on the same page.

Origins of Disease Branding

When did the branding of condition or disease begin? How did the pharmaceutical industry get the idea of branding a disease? You can get the answers for these questions and understand from where the Pharma industry got the idea of branding a disease from a 1928 book, *Propaganda* by Edward Bernays. Many consider Bernays as the father of public relations in America. Carl Elliot narrates the interesting case that throws light on the origin of disease branding in his book, *White Coat and Black Hat*.

Pharmaceutical Industry Learns the Art of Disease Branding From The Father of Public Relations in America!

Edward Bernays believed that public relations business was less about selling things than about creating conditions for things that sell themselves. He put this idea into practice when he was working for Mozart Pianos. He did not place advertisements in the newspapers for Mozart Pianos to market them like all marketers do. That would have been commonplace. He came up with a different idea. He convinced the reporters of the leading magazines to write about a new trend that the wealthy and sophisticated people at the time were doing. The sophisticated people at the time were putting aside a special music room in the home for playing music. Bernays believed that once a person had a music room, he would naturally think of buying a piano. As Bernays wrote, "It will come to him as his own idea."

Just as Bernays sold his pianos by selling the music room, pharmaceutical marketers now sell their cures by selling the diseases that they treat. The buzzword is disease branding.

How do you brand a disease or condition? It is pretty straightforward. First, you need to define a particular condition and its associated symptoms in the minds of physicians and patients. Second, you need to predicate and offer the best treatment for that condition.

The concept of branding a disease condition is by no means new. The first-ever disease branding effort dates back to the 1920s when Warner and Lambert (Pfizer now) successfully branded a condition – Halitosis (Case 76). The landscape for branding a disease has become more complicated today. It includes pharmaceutical companies, external thought leaders, support groups and patient communities. The success of branding a condition depends on how you can build consensus among the diverse groups that matter both internally and externally. When done appropriately, the disease branding follows the structure of a lock and key story, where the lock is the problem or the disease and the key is your product, which is a solution for the problem condition.

Dual Advantages

Branding a disease offers significant benefits to the company both internally and externally. Internally, the activity rallies the support of the entire team by motivating them and creates a sense of ownership among all the members. The product too can better own the customer perceptions about current and evolving disease states and define new patient segments. The product can also reinforce its position by meeting the currently unmet needs and by providing greater therapeutic benefits.

Externally, the branding effort of a company-sponsored activity helps forge better relationships with the thought leaders while they are engaged in debating and shaping the new therapeutic approaches with the physician community. The brand, as a result of all this significant initiative and effort, creates a leadership status as the owner and driver in the new category.

Three Strategic Approaches

How do you brand a disease or condition? Three principal strategies help you create a disease condition and align it with your product:

A. Elevating the importance of an existing condition

B. Redefining a current condition to reduce a stigma

C. Developing a new condition to build recognition for an unmet need.

Five Questions

Vince Parry, president and chief branding officer at Parry Branding Group, a leading Pharma branding consultancy company, suggests five questions to find out whether disease branding is right for you in his article, *The art of branding a condition* in Medical Marketing & Media on May 1, 2003:

1. Does your product uniquely impact a disease condition? Does it work via a new pathway or at a new site of action? Does it address an underlying cause and attack the root of the problem or relieve symptoms that would benefit from redefining (branding) the disease to highlight the difference?

2. Are there any stigmas or social concerns about the condition your product treats, that would hinder a physician-patient dialogue?

3. Does your product have significant benefits for a condition with little or no awareness?

4. Are there competitive efforts to reposition your product as beneficial in only a niche condition that is not perceived as an essential health risk?

5. Are you seeking a niche within a crowded therapeutic category?

Benefits of Disease Branding

Detractors criticize disease branding as empty profiteering. However, the truth is that disease branding does provide certain benefits. Consider these for example:

▸ New understanding of diseases that have been around for many years

▸ Awareness of little-known conditions

▸ A more positive (or less negative perception) of a disease

▸ Seeing old diseases in new ways

▸ Removing frustration, and confusion about certain old disease conditions by understanding the underlying pathology and new approaches to treat them

▸ New understanding leading to more awareness and cognizance of seriousness and legitimacy

▸ Eliminating stigmas surrounding certain disease conditions

To brand a disease is to shape its public perception to make it more palatable to potential patients. Not very long ago, people regarded many conditions such as bad breath, panic disorder, reflux disease, erectile dysfunction, bipolar disorder, overactive bladder, attention deficit hyperactivity disorder (ADHD), premenstrual dysphoric disorder (PMDD), restless legs syndrome (RLS) and many others as rare, until a marketing campaign transformed the trend.

Here are some of those classic cases where disease branding has been used with significant success.

Pharma's First Shot at Disease Branding!

Warner-Lambert's Listerine offers a classic example of a solution looking for a problem. Humans had bad breath from time immemorial. Ancient peoples had spent centuries searching for a cure for bad breath. Finally, a pharmaceutical company created a medical condition out of bad breath, offered treatment and made huge profits.

Warner and Lambert invented Listerine in the 1880s. Listerine was named after Dr. Joseph Lister (1817-1912), who was considered as the father of modern antiseptics. Listerine was originally marketed for a variety of conditions such as dandruff, foot cleaning, and even for floor-cleaning. Later, people used to apply it to wounds or areas that were likely to be infected. They used it as a surgical antiseptic and not as a mouthwash like we do today. The company later found that Listerine would work very well in killing germs in the mouth. The company also moved Listerine from a prescription-only-medicine (POM) to over-the-counter (OTC) status. Although the sales gradually moved up, that was not enough for the founder, Jordan Wheat Lambert. He wanted more. Finally, his son came up with a brilliant idea. He found a new name for bad breath – Halitosis. The company adopted the word from the Latin word, 'Halitus,' which means bad breath. The word, 'Osis' makes it sound more medical. The new name for bad breath made people with bad breath believe that they had a condition that is treatable. Bad breath had a stigma surrounding it. People were shy to speak about it and were even avoiding social contacts. Friends and relatives, who notice it also would keep quiet and maintained a safe distance. Also, bad breath had its own negative consequences ranging from social casualties such as lack of career advancement to divorce. Nobody believed that bad breath could be treated. Warner-Lambert changed it all by creating awareness - and anxiety - and a severe-sounding medical condition, Halitosis.

The new name for bad breath, Halitosis quickly transformed the social stigma and given confidence to people that they can treat it with Listerine. They felt confident marching into the drug stores and nowhere else since the advertisements stressed that "Your closest friends won't tell you about the problem," and asking for the cure. The creative advertising for Listerine not only increased the awareness of the condition among the public but also made Listerine a household name.

Listerine ran many advertisements in many newspapers and magazines talking about the sad unmarried Edna, who remained a single as she watched her friends getting married. It's not that she wasn't a great gal! It's just, she had this condition (bad breath)! Here is one of the most successful and memorable ads of Listerine with a very persuasive copy:

> Often a bridesmaid...Never a bride! Most of the girls of her set were married...but not Eleanor. It was beginning to look, too, as if she never would be. True, men were attracted to her, but their interest quickly turned into indifference. Poor girl! She had not the remotest idea why people dropped her so quickly...and even her best friends wouldn't tell her.
>
> No Toothpaste Kills Germs Like Listerine... Instantly. Listerine antiseptic does for you what no toothpaste does. Listerine instantly kills germs, by millions. Stops bad breath (halitosis) instantly, and usually for hours on end.
>
> Far and away is the most common cause of bad breath is germs. You see, germs cause fermentation of proteins, which

are always present in the mouth. And research shows that your breath stays sweeter longer, the more you reduce germs in the mouth.

Toothpaste with the aid of a toothbrush is an effective method of oral hygiene. But, no toothpaste gives you the proven Listerine Antiseptic Method - banishing bad breath with super-efficient germ-killing action.

Listerine Antiseptic Chemically Proved Four Times Better Than Toothpaste. Is it any wonder Listerine antiseptic in recent clinical tests averaged at least four times more effective in stopping bad breath odors than the chlorophyll products or toothpaste brands it was tested against?

Every night… before every date, make it habit to use Listerine, the most widely used antiseptic in the world. Listerine Antiseptic Stops Bad Breath 4 Times Better Than Any Toothpaste.

There are many companies today that medicalize problems and brand disease conditions to solve them. However, Listerine was medicalization's first and most famous success story!

(Source: Adapted from articles 1. Laura Clark, How halitosis became a medical condition with 'cure', Smart News, Smithsonian Magazine, January 29, 2015, and; 2. Esther Inglis-Arkell, The medical condition invented by Listerine, Science History, iOS9, We Come From the Future, January 27, 2015)

The Mother of all Disease Awareness Campaigns!

You develop a new drug that meets the currently unmet need and market it. That is a simple, straightforward view of drug development and marketing as we know. Sometimes, the process of drug development and marketing as we know and understand may be entirely different in practice. Picture this, for example: A pharmaceutical company scientists develop a drug with a range of physiological effects, none of which are very much helpful. Marketers, therefore are driven to identify and promote a disease for the drug to treat, which is drug development in reverse order. It might mean co-opting a relatively rare illness and think of ways and means of expanding its borders to increase the prospective patient pool.

Merck's promotion of amitriptyline (Elavil) in the 1960s offers a classic example of this strategy. Amitriptyline was a new antidepressant useful in the treatment of clinical depression. However, in the 1960s clinical depression was regarded as a rare condition offering minimal scope in marketing it profitably as an antidepressant.

The solution is rather obvious. Increase the frequency of diagnosis. Expand the patient pool. Merck came up with the idea that had set a trend of increasing the disease awareness. The mother of all disease awareness campaigns that were to follow later. What did Merck exactly do? Merck bought fifty-thousand copies of a book by Frank Ayd called, *Recognizing the Depressed Patient* and sent them free of charge to general practitioners all over the country. Prescriptions for Elavil (amitriptyline) increased dramatically following this strategic attempt to increase the frequency of diagnoses. It is despite the fact there was another antidepressant, imipramine available since the mid-1950s in the market.

The sales of antidepressants were never depressing since then. From a few million dollars in the 1960s the market for treating depression has grown to multi-billion dollars in the next thirty years.

The key to selling antidepressants became clear, and it was to sell clinical depression.

(Source: Adapted from Carl Elliott's book, *White Coat, Black Hat*)

The Birth of A New Condition - GERD!

In 1986, When Glaxo (GlaxoSmithKline now) launched Zantac for ulcers, it faced the challenge of broadening its reach into the heartburn market. Heartburn, at the time, did not seem to warrant treatment, not certainly a prescription drug. The heartburn sufferers were managing their condition with many available over-the-counter remedies.

To enter the large heartburn segment for expanding the usage of its Zantac, Glaxo had to elevate the medical importance of heartburn to an acutely chronic disorder with an underlying physiological etiology and the potential for severe longer-term consequences if one does not treat it. The company launched a well-coordinated initiative to achieve this. The term heartburn, coined decades ago by antacid brands suggested that the mechanism of action in the treatment of indigestion is acid neutralization, which is precisely what antacids do. However, research in the 1980s suggested that chronic heartburn could further be described as a malfunction of esophageal sphincter - a more serious disorder that can lead to the erosion of gastrointestinal tissue over time.

Glaxo and Zantac worked to rebrand chronic heartburn as a more serious medical concern that you cannot afford to ignore. Glaxo coined a new term for heartburn and many other associated symptoms and grouped them into one condition, Gastro-Esophageal Reflux Disorder (GERD) thus giving heartburn the status of a medical condition warranting treatment. Through this rebranding of the condition, Glaxo could put Zantac in the spotlight as the best overall solution. It suggested that you should stop the problem at its root, which is the blockade of acid and not at its symptom level which is neutralizing the acid.

Glaxo created the Glaxo Institute of Digestive Health (GIDH), which served as a platform for education and awareness of digestive diseases. The GIDH sponsored research awards in the area of gastrointestinal health and discussed Gastrointestinal Esophageal Reflux Disorder (GERD) in the context of other, more serious gastrointestinal (GI) diseases. The company engaged with powerful third-party advocates such as the American College of Gastroenterology (ACG) and fielded a massive public relations effort called Heartburn Across America.

The result? Glaxo doubled the number of physicians who were leaders in gastrointestinal (GI) health, which in turn helped the company to drive the annual sales of Zantac to a whopping US $2 billion. What is even more interesting about this is that about two-thirds of this revenue is from the prescriptions for GERD!

Upjohn's Efforts in Disentangling of Panic Disorders from Anxiety Disorders Pay Handsome Dividends!

The development of Xanax in the 1970s and the creation of the condition Panic Disorder in DSM III (Diagnostic and Statistical Manual for Mental Disorders III Edition) offers an excellent example of the condition-branding strategy.

In anxiety and depression, as the illnesses are rarely based on measurable physical symptoms, they are open to conceptual definitions. Over the years, the increasing number of identified emotional conditions has resulted from breaking the problems into different conditions to better access treatment options. Pharmaceutical companies funded the research as well as publicity of many of these newly coined disease-conditions.

In the Diagnostic and Statistical Manual of Mental Disorders - II (DSM-II), panic disorder fell into the broad category of anxiety neurosis. Patients experiencing panic attacks, as there was no clear branding of the condition at the time, often visited cardiologists thinking their problem was a heart condition. Cardiologists too, labeled those complaints as cardiac complaints and the patients' hypochondriacs, due to a lack of physical pathology.

Dr. David Sheehan, a pioneering thought leader in the field of panic disorders, helped characterize the conditions and push for a new way to diagnose and treat it. Upjohn, the makers of Xanax (alprazolam), helped fund this early research. His research helped characterize panic disorder as a condition and paved the way to diagnose and treat it. Furthermore, Upjohn had given an unrestricted grant to the National Institutes of Mental Health (NIMH) to organize a three-day thought leader conference that resulted in a published consensus on the diagnostic criteria for panic disorder and how best to treat it. As a result, in 1980, the DSM-III lists panic disorders as a new diagnostic category.

Upjohn had a very clear strategy for the development of alprazolam (Xanax) in the 1970s. According to Dr. David Sheehan, the company's strategy was to take advantage of the medical profession's confusion in the classification of anxiety disorders. The company wanted to create a perception that the drug (Xanax) had special and unique properties that would help capture market share and displace diazepam from the top position. There was in fact, nothing unique in this regard about Xanax. Benzodiazepines were all good for panic disorder. However, only Upjohn got the US FDA approval for its Xanax in the treatment of panic disorder in doses up to 6 mg daily (equivalent to 20 - 120 mg of Diazepam).

Xanax was the first to receive panic disorder as an exclusive indication and thereby maintained its leadership position in anxiety disorders. Upjohn aggressively marketed its Xanax in panic disorders. The company had undertaken publication of research articles in all the relevant scientific journals, arranged speaking tours to cardiologists to raise their awareness of the heart-brain connection in the minds of panic-disorder patients. It is perhaps no coincidence that the incidence of panic disorders has grown over 1,000-fold since the 1980s!

(Source: Adapted from Vince Parry's article on *Branding a condition*, Medical Marketing & Media, May 2003)

Pfizer Eliminates the Stigma Surrounding Impotence with an Acronym!

There are some conditions, which are medically relevant with considerable social stigma and embarrassment surrounding them. The stigma surrounding these conditions is often worsened by a plethora of over-the-counter (OTC) remedies, whose low-brow promotional efforts push patients further into hiding. Male impotence is one of those conditions. It has long existed as a medical condition, but even the medical profession in the past associated it with disability linked to physical trauma or more often with a loss of libido. The patriarchal society always looked down upon the persons with this condition as inadequate contributing to the low self-esteem of the sufferers. Even the remedies over the years were often invasive and their implementation indiscreet.

Pfizer redefined this embarrassing medical condition by renaming it as 'erectile dysfunction' (ED) and eliminated the stigma surrounding it. Furthermore, with its brilliant and hugely successful effort of linking the newly named condition with its new drug, Viagra (sildenafil citrate), Pfizer showed the millions of patients who have male impotence that it is treatable. The term 'erectile dysfunction' (ED) changed the focus of the condition from being associated with lack of potency or male virility to the more enlightened concept of a physical loss of function that is reversible. Like other recognizable conditions such as GERD (Gastro Esophageal Reflux Disease), OAB (Over Active Bladder), the company captured the condition of male impotence in an acronym - ED. ED makes it suitable for direct-to-consumer promotion and functions as an easy password between physician and patient to initiate a formerly difficult conversation. ED gave a kind of empowerment to its sufferers.

The simple, discreet and empowering brand personality of ED, has met its match Viagra, which is an elegant and effective solution for this redefined condition.

(Source: Adapted from Vince Parry's article on *Branding a condition*, Medical Marketing & Media, May 2003)

Eli Lilly Fields A Second Brand of the Same Drug for A Branded Condition!

The Diagnostic and Statistical Manual for Mental Disorders (DSM) first mentioned Premenstrual Dysphoric Disorder (PMDD) in 1987. The 1993 edition, which was DSM IV repackaged and renamed the condition giving it a new life. PMDD is a severe form of premenstrual syndrome (PMS).

In June 1999, with its patent of Prozac about to expire, Eli Lilly organized a roundtable discussion inviting the PMDD subcommittee members to build a consensus regarding the diagnosis and treatment of PMDD and to get the approval for its Prozac. Approval for Prozac for treating PMDD would give a seven-year extension for Prozac. For getting approval, Lilly needs to establish that PMDD is a real condition and Prozac is the right treatment.

Shortly after the roundtable discussion, an article, " Is premenstrual dysphoric disorder a distinct clinical entity?" appeared in the Journal of Women's Health and Gender-Based Medicine, and emerged as the state-of-the-science. This was the outcome of the roundtable discussion. The authors, probably recalling their own description of earlier research (before DSM IV) as sparse and poor, claimed that later evidence proved PMDD to be a real condition and Prozac to be an effective treatment. However, only a small number of articles were post-DSM IV Research, and they did not provide any substantial evidence that post-menstrual mental illness exists. Most of the article constituted promotion of Prozac by reporting that Prozac improves symptoms of women with a premenstrual dysphoric disorder (PMDD).

The FDA's Psychopharmacological Drugs Advisory Committee (PDAC) met on November 3, 1999. Eli Lilly representatives brought PMDD Subcommittee member Jean Endicott, the first author of the roundtable article to speak. There was a consensus among the PDAC members at the end of the meeting that PMDD is a clinical entity that is well defined and has accepted the diagnostic criteria.

In July 2000, the US FDA granted Interneuron Pharmaceuticals Inc. based in Lexington, Massachusetts the approval for Sarafem (fluoxetine) in the treatment of the premenstrual dysphoric disorder (PMDD). Lilly received the US and global patent application rights for marketing Sarafem under an agreement with Interneuron Pharmaceuticals. Sarafem is the first and only prescription medication indicated for PMDD. Eli Lilly sponsored a pre-launch activity to build awareness for the new condition, recasting diagnosis to conform to the new criteria. The result was a fascinating integration of PMDD awareness and Sarafem brand strategy.

Lilly decided on a dual brand strategy for its fluoxetine - Prozac for depression and Sarafem for PMDD. The additional brand - Sarafem will give it a distinct identity, which will help with its educational efforts for the mostly under-recognized condition, PMDD. It would also reduce confusion about the differences between depression and PMDD. Prozac is primarily associated with depression and women with PMDD are not depressed. So Lilly needed a new name to effectively distinguish the new patient group (potential PMDD sufferers) from Prozac's association with depression.

Lilly's marketing team did create a distinct personality for their new brand of fluoxetine for treating PMDD. First, the name itself. Sarafem. 'Seraphin' in Hebrew means 'Angel,' a word with feminine overtones befitting the target patient group. Its packaging too amplified the feminine associations. The Sarafem tablet came in a pretty pink-and-lavender shell. The company created a wonder cure aura around the brand for this distinctly female condition - premenstrual dysphoric disorder.

Eli Lilly followed a multichannel marketing strategy to promote Sarafem. Its advertising messages flooded airwaves immediately after the FDA's approval of Sarafem for the treatment of PMDD. The following advertisement illustrates the kind of advertising effort that the company had put: The ad shows a woman who has lost her keys growing increasingly frustrated. The voiceover breaks through:

> *Think it's PMS? It could be PMDD - premenstrual dysphoric disorder. You know these intense moods and physical symptoms the week before your period. Sound familiar? Call to get free information about PMDD and treatment your doctor has to relieve its symptoms. Why put up with this another month?*

In addition to its direct-to-consumer advertising, Lilly had launched a marketing campaign targeting psychiatrists, gynecologists, and mental health providers and sent them promotional materials such as flyers, free samples, an invitation to Lilly Talks, and visits by their pharmaceutical representatives. The massive promotional effort had spread the word around the medical community quickly increasing the diagnoses of PMDD. When the diagnoses soar, can sales be far behind? They too soared.

(Source: Adapted from an article by Caplan, Paula J, Premenstrual mental illness: *The truth about Sarafem (premenstrual dysphoric disorder and the usage of Sarafem (Prozac) as treatment*, The Network News, May 2001)

Positioning A Brand by Creating A Disease!

What would you do if you had a drug that relieves some of the annoying symptoms of a disorder that is not very common and patients do not seek even treatment because they are embarrassed to share their condition? Drop the drug and move on to the next drug-candidate in the development phase? Many marketers might do that. Drop the drug from marketing because it is unviable. But not Neil Wolf, the group vice president of Pharmacia (now Pfizer). He was different and thought differently and spotted a tremendous opportunity. Here is what he did with a little-known disorder and their drug to treat it.

Pharmacia found that its new drug, tolterodine (Detrol) was useful in treating urge incontinence. However, there was just one major problem. The market for incontinence in the United States was very small - about $40 million with generic Oxybutynin having annual sales of $29 million. The disease prevalence was very low around 5 - 15 percent mainly affecting the elderly patients of 65 years and above. When it came to the pharmacotherapy of the condition, only about a fifth of the patients of this small segment of the patient population were treated with prescription drugs. Therefore, it was a significantly under-diagnosed and under-treated condition.

What is the solution? Neil Wolf, the group vice president, who later steered the global launch of Detrol came up with a brilliant strategy. Broaden, and expand the market. More importantly, own the understanding of the market in all possible dimensions such as clinical, epidemiological, psychometric and economic to create a commercial opportunity that was attractive enough. Pharmacia had to convert a niche product into a mass market opportunity. The company had to:

A. Increase the diagnosis and treatment of incontinence
B. Expand the appropriate patient population beyond urge incontinence

To increase the diagnosis and treatment of incontinence, raise awareness of the disease – urge incontinence, which is not currently perceived as a disease as it was thought to be a consequence of aging. Change that perception and make the patients and physicians understand that urge incontinence was a disorder and was treatable with medications. In other words, create a disease in the minds of the patients and physicians that urge incontinence was a treatable disorder. And then, position Detrol as the treatment for that disorder. However, first, change the name and definition of urge incontinence to *Overactive Bladder*.

Why change the name? The name – overactive bladder is highly intuitive and marketing-oriented as compared to the earlier names – incontinence or detrusor instability. Detrusor is a muscle that controls the process of storing and releasing urine by its contraction and relaxation. The name – overactive bladder – immediately suggests a picture of something you can recognize and associate with. What is more, experts say that the name change helped in making the condition more acceptable for public discussion? The patients were able to bring it up with their doctors without embarrassment. Meanwhile, those doctors were encouraged to screen patients for this condition and to keep them on their medication once it was diagnosed.

To create and increase awareness about the condition – overactive bladder among physicians was the next significant step that Pharmacia took. As early as in 1996, Pharmacia identified two major key opinion leaders, Alan Wein of the University of Pennsylvania and Paul Abrams of the University of Bristol in England for its new drug under development, tolterodine (Detrol), which is found to be useful in the treatment of incontinence. These two well-known KOLs held their first conference on overactive bladder in London in June 1997. Wein And Abrams later came to be known as the godfathers of overactive bladder disorder. Pharmacia, which had been doing pioneering work on overactive bladder drugs, sponsored the conference.

Pharmacia's public relations work too had been exemplary. In December 1997, six months after the first conference on overactive bladder, the leading journal of the Urology field – *Urology* published a special supplement on overactive bladder with about thirty articles on the condition. Wein and Abrams wrote the introduction in which they talked about a promising new drug, Detrol manufactured by Pharmacia.

The US FDA approved Detrol on March 25, 1998. By 1999, the International Continence Society (ICS) was writing a new definition of overactive bladder, which expanded the number of people who met the diagnostic criteria. Pharmacia's groundwork in illness inflation was beginning to pay off. Disease inflation is an effort driven by drug companies to create or expand the definition of conditions that are part of everyday life and to create treatment guidelines for drugs designed for those conditions.

In 2001, Pharmacia sponsored the National Phone Survey, which asked a variety of questions about urinary habits of Americans. The survey asked 5,204 adults questions that included how often they needed to urinate, whether they had to get up at night and whether they felt the urgency.

The company wanted the condition - overactive bladder not only to be recognized by both patients and primary care physicians but also create an environment where they own the condition.

Pharmacia got what it wanted from this survey. The results produced a striking number: Nearly 17 percent of adults in the United States - about 33 million people - were deemed to have overactive bladder disorder. So a massive new market for Detrol was born.

Pharmacia, through its significant efforts at KOL-level, Phase IV research activity, and active participation at the first ICS (International Continence Society) was able to change the earlier name of the disorder of overactive detrusor to the overactive bladder at the Overactive Bladder Consensus Conference in July 1999. The new definition is:

OAB (overactive bladder) is a medical condition referring to the symptoms of frequency, and urgency, with or without urge incontinence when appearing in the absence of local pathological or metabolic factors that would account for these symptoms.

Accordingly, Detrol tablets are useful in the treatment of patients with symptoms of urinary frequency, urgency or urge incontinence. A case of the disease that is tailor-made for the capabilities of the drug!

Now that the indication had been defined as it was intended, the next logical step in Pharmacia's game plan was to create an environment where primary care providers perceive overactive bladder as a serious condition and not a consequence of aging. Also, to make it easy to screen, diagnose and treat OAB. Later, in January 1999, the company followed it up with a DTC campaign in print medium increase screening and diagnostic rates. The copy of the print ads was somewhat like this:

If you think you have an overactive bladder... Let your doctor know how symptoms affect your life...Your doctor needs to know about more than your symptoms. He or she should also know how it affects your life. If you recognize even one of these signs, fill out the questionnaire and discuss it with your doctor:

A. Do you to the bathroom so often at night that it interrupts your sleep 2 or more times?

B. Do you go to the bathroom so often that it interferes with the things you do (usually more than eight times in 24 hours)

C. Do you always have to know where the bathroom is because of frequent, strong sudden urges to urinate?

D. Do you sometimes not make it to the bathroom in time?

E. Do you wear pads to protect your clothes from wetting?

These are some of the typical signs of overactive bladder. Occasionally, some may be associated with other more severe conditions. If you have any of these symptoms be sure to contact your doctor.

Pharmacia not only established overactive bladder as a serious condition and not just a consequence of aging not only among patients and physicians but also among all other key stakeholders such as payers, regulators. Last but not least, the company established superiority over oxybutynin, the existing treatment option for urge incontinence. As a result of all this marketing blitz, Pharmacia achieved greater than 90 percent unrestricted access for Detrol among managed-care lives.

Time Line for Detrol Positioning and Creating the Overactive Bladder Condition

With a well thought-out, creatively crafted strategy, Pharmacia made a little-known, under-diagnosed, and under-treated niche-condition like urge incontinence into a mass-market opportunity by converting it into the overactive bladder. The following table presents a snapshot of what the company had achieved with Detrol in less than five years.

Timeline	Activity
1996	Pharmacia begins its activity to develop and engage key opinion leaders to educate physicians and patients about its new drug under development, Detrol (tolterodine), which is useful in the treatment of incontinence.
1997	Alan Wein of the University of Pennsylvania and Paul Abrams of the University of Bristol in England hold their first *Overactive Bladder* conference in June. The conference is sponsored by Pharmacia.
1997	*Urology*, the leading medical journal of the field publishes a special supplement on Overactive Bladder with about thirty articles on the condition in the month of December.
1998	US FDA approves Detrol.
1999	The international Incontinence Society expands number of people who meet the criteria with its new definition of Overactive Bladder
2001	Pharmacia sponsors a National Phone Survey among 5,204 adults asking a variety of questions about urinary habits of Americans.
2002	Neil Wolf, group vice president, who was in charge of the global launch of Detrol makes a slide presentation on how the company tried to promote their new drug.

Detrol's Marketing Success

How did Detrol achieve such remarkable success with an insufficient, insignificant opportunity? By broadening disease definition and simplifying screening and diagnosis, Pharmacia expanded the patient population, and it differentiated Detrol from Oxybutynin.

Marketing Criteria	1997	2001
New Prescriptions	1.5 million	4.6 million
Treated Patients	3.6 million	12.7 million
Detrol Sales	-	400 million
Detrol Prescriptions (Market Share - %)	-	50.2

In sum, Pharmacia created a disease (Over Active Bladder) out of almost nowhere (urge incontinence, which was thought to be a consequence of aging, and not a disorder) and positioned its new drug, Detrol to treat the new disorder, OAB!

(Source: Adapted from 1. Kiristina Flore, John Fauber, and Math Wynn, *Drug Firms helped create $3 billion over active bladder market*, MedPage Today and Milwaukee Journal Sentinel, October 15, 2016; and 2. Neil Wolfe, Group Vice President, Pharmacia, *Positioning Detrol (Creating a disease) presented to PMRG, October 7, 2002*, published by Pharmacosesias on SlideShare, December 6, 2009).

A Disorder Made to Order!

SmithKline Beecham (Glaxo SmithKline now) received approval for its Paxil (paroxetine hydrochloride) from the US FDA in May 1996 for the treatment of panic disorder and obsessive-compulsive disorder (OCD). The company was lagging behind in the antidepressant market, where Pfizer's Zoloft was the market leader. SmithKline wanted to bridge the gap and move rapidly in the market. The company was in search of a new indication that would help it grow quickly.

Glaxo SmithKline hired Cohn & Wolfe, a public relations firm specializing in the pharmaceutical industry, well-known for its unconventional ways of marketing. The company wanted Cohn & Wolfe to lay the groundwork for the introduction of Paxil. They identified a new condition, social anxiety disorder (SAD), which was under-diagnosed and under-treated at the time. Diagnostic and Statistical Manual of Mental Disorders IV (DSM IV) listed Social anxiety disorder for the first time replacing the earlier term – generalized social phobia. DSM IV defined social anxiety disorder as "marked and persistent fear of one or more social or performance situations in which the person is exposed to unfamiliar people or possible scrutiny by others."

The task before SmithKline and Cohn & Wolfe, their public relations firm became clear. The company obtained approval from the US FDA for Paxil in the treatment of social anxiety disorders in 1999. Once the company got its approval of Paxil for SAD, SmithKline turned its attention to the task of promoting the disease itself. To promote social anxiety disorder as a severe condition. They had to convince shy people that they suffer from social anxiety disorder and need treatment. They formulated and followed advertising and public relations blitz campaign with multiple activities. Consider these for example:

1. By early 1999, the PR firm created a slogan, *"Imagine being allergic to people"* and wallpapered bus shelters nationwide with pictures of a SAD-looking man vacantly playing with a teacup. The copy read: *You blush, sweat, shake - even find it hard to breathe. That's what Social Anxiety Disorder feels like.* The posters did not refer to Paxil or SmithKline. Because if you make any reference to the brand or the company that makes it, you need to mention all the risk factors and side effects. Therefore, the posters bore the insignia of a group called the Social Anxiety Disorder Coalition and its three non-profit members, the *American Psychiatric Association* (APA), The Anxiety Disorders Association of America and the Freedom from Fear advocacy organization.

2. The coalition was not a grassroots alliance of patients suffering from anxiety disorders or other mental illnesses. SmithKline assembled it quickly and its PR firm, Cohn & Wolfe handled all the media inquiries on behalf of the group.

3. Cohn & Wolfe did not stop with posters. The firm also created a video news release, a radio news release and a Matte (a bylined article that smaller newspapers often run unedited) release. The PR agency gave a press packet that stated: *SAD affects 13.3 percent of the population or 1 in 8 Americans and the third most common psychiatric disorder in the United States after depression and alcoholism.* However, this information contrasts with what the DSM cites. According to DSM, *studies show that between 3 and 13 percent of people may suffer the disease at some point in their lives, but that only 2 percent experience enough impairment or distress to warrant treatment.*

4. A few months after the FDA approval of Paxil for SAD, SmithKline launched a series of advertisements touting its efficacy in helping the patients of social anxiety disorders in braving dinner party situations and public speaking occasions.

5. SmithKline also had psychiatrists as paid consultants for conducting SAD trials for Paxil and for making TV appearances.

6. Cohn & Wolfe, the PR agency also supplied journalists with expressive patients for putting a face on the disorder. PR firms handpick patients, give them media training and send them on promotional tours to help publicize a disease condition.

7. GlaxoSmithKline also recruited celebrities like Ricky Williams, the NFL (National Football League) running back, to give interviews to the press about their own social anxiety disorder.

8. Also, the company hired academic psychiatrists working on social anxiety disorder and sent them out on the lecture circuit in the top 25 media markets.

The results of the massive advertising and public relations thrust by the company were remarkable. In the two years before SmithKline received the FDA approval for Paxil, there were hardly about fifty references to social anxiety disorder in the popular press. In May 1999, the month when the FDA approved Paxil for social anxiety disorder, hundreds of stories about the condition – SAD appeared in the US publications such as the New York Times, Vogue and Good Morning America and several television news programs.

By 2001, Paxil had become the seventh most profitable brand in America. Cohn & Wolfe had picked up an award for the best PR campaign of 1999. In less than two years, GlaxoSmithKline took a once-considered-rare psychiatric condition and helped it transform into a major epidemic called social anxiety disorder, claiming that 1 in 8 Americans suffers from it. In the process, this transformation pushed Paxil's sales to US $3 billion a year!

(Source: Adapted from Article: Brendan L. Koerner, *Disorders made to order*, Mother Jones, July/August issue 2002)

Pfizer, PSTD, and Zoloft!

In 1980, the American Psychiatric Association added post-traumatic stress disorder (PTSD) to the third edition of its Diagnostic and Statistical Manual of Mental Disorders (DSM). PTSD, in fact almost exclusively had been associated with combat veterans and victims of violent crime. Pfizer, however, had set out in 1999, to change that convincing Americans that PTSD could, in fact, afflict almost anyone after getting the US FDA's approval for its Zoloft (sertraline) in the treatment of PTSD.

Pfizer had left no stone unturned in raising the awareness for the condition, PTSD. Here are some of its more significant actions in this regard:

1. Pfizer funded the creation of the PTSD Alliance and staffed it with its public relations firm, The Chandler Chicco Agency, which ran it from its offices.

2. One of the essential functions of the alliance was to build a network of journalists and thought leaders in PTSD. The alliance connected journalists of the mainstream media with PTSD experts like Jerilyn Ross, President, and CEO of Anxiety Disorders Association of America, whom the Pharma majors such as Pfizer as well as GlaxoSmithKline heavily subsidized.

3. Shortly after the Zoloft's campaign in PTSD, media mentions of PTSD grew substantially. The New York Times, for example, ran a story with statistics provided by Pfizer on childhood PTSD quoting that minors who experience the sudden death

of a close friend or a relative will develop the disorder. Even other papers and magazines carried articles highlighting the studies promoted by the alliance. The studies indicated that 1 in 13 Americans would suffer from PTSD at some point in time.

4. On September 26, 2001, The PTSD Alliance stated from its office at Pfizer's PR firm, Chandler Chicco, that post-traumatic stress can affect anyone who has witnessed a violent act or experienced natural disasters or other unexpected catastrophic, or psychologically distressing events such as September 11 terrorist attacks.

5. In October 2001, Pfizer had spent US $5.6 million, which was 25 percent more than its average ad spend per month on advertising Zoloft's benefits in treating PTSD.

Pfizer's massive public relations effort combined with its promotion to physicians, contributed significantly to pass the US $2.3 billion mark in Zoloft's annual sales.

(Adapted from Article: Brendan I. Koerner, *Disorders Made to Order*, Mother Jones, July/August 2002)

Merck Creates A Market for A Bone Disease, Fields its New Drug, Fosamax and Makes it the Market Leader!

Merck had in-licensed an early-stage new chemical compound alendronate (Fosamax) in 1988 from Instituto Gentili, an Italian pharmaceutical and biotechnology company for further development and commercialization. The company obtained the US FDA approval for Fosamax, which was a first-in-class (bisphosphonates) compound for the treatment of osteoporosis in 1995.

Osteoporosis has been a serious problem affecting millions of women, and therefore the potential market for Fosamax was enormous. Fosamax could become a blockbuster drug. However, the problem was Fosamax had a very poor sales uptake in the first two years. The company came up with a three-pronged strategy:

1. Expanding diagnosis
2. Obtaining multiple indications
3. Developing new formulations

Expanding Diagnosis

How Merck had gone about expanding diagnosis is an exciting story involving some out-of-the-box thinking. However, before that, a brief of overview of the market scenario surrounding osteoporosis at the time.

Osteoporosis is a disease that causes bones to become brittle and break more easily. It mostly affects elderly women, and a fall can be devastating with breaking a hip. One in five elderly women who break a hip will die within a year.

Osteopenia is different from Osteoporosis. Think of it as a midpoint between having healthy bones and Osteoporosis. WEB MD says that Osteopenia is when your bones are weaker than normal but not so far gone that they break easily, which is the hallmark of Osteoporosis. Your bones are usually at their densest when you are about thirty. Osteopenia, if it happens at all, often occurs after age fifty.

The story of Osteopenia is also the story of how the definition of what constitutes a disease evolves, and the role that drug companies can play in that evolution.

Osteopenia as a condition was hardly known in the early 1990s. Only a handful of people would have heard even about the word – Osteopenia. Merck's strategy of expanding the diagnosis had played a significant role in transforming Osteopenia from the status of a rarely heard-word into a diagnosis for which millions of women swallow pills to slow the progress of the condition further to Osteoporosis. The whole process of diagnosing Osteopenia began at a meeting of a group of renowned experts on Osteoporosis in 1992 in Rome, under the auspices of the World Health Organization (WHO) to arrive at a consensus on diagnosing and measuring Osteoporosis. The group of experts created a category of Osteopenia mostly because they thought it might be useful for public health researchers who like clear categories for their studies. They never thought that people would come to think of Osteopenia as a disease in itself to be treated when they created it!

How did Osteopenia transform from a category for public health researchers to a condition that millions of women want to get treated for? That brings us to Jeremy Allen, the man who measured the bone.

Jeremy Allen retired from IMS Health, an American company engaged in providing healthcare information and technology to the healthcare industry worldwide in 1991 and had set up a consulting business in the US. In 1995, he was approached by David Anstice, the president of Merck, who was also his former colleague at IMS

Health before he took the position at Merck, with a proposition: Fosamax the first-in-class drug for osteoporosis with a tremendous market potential was not getting enough prescriptions and sales. Figure out this problem and fix it.

How do you generate more prescriptions for Fosamax seemed an obvious question. Get more diagnoses. How do you get more diagnoses of Osteoporosis? More bone scans, of course!

However, in America, in 1995 there was just no way of getting more scans done. The machines that measured bone density were scarce. There were only huge tabletop machines to measure the bone density, and the scans were costing between $200 to $350 per test. Besides, there were just a couple of hundred testing centers across the US, which made it even more difficult to access.

To sell Fosamax, Merck had to necessarily increase the number of scans because without a bone densitometry test no diagnosis was possible. To expand diagnosis, the company had to do two things:

A. Place machines that could measure bone density in doctors' offices across America, and
B. Bring down the price of bone scans

To achieve these two objectives, Merck and Allen had gone about changing the way the American Healthcare system measured bone. They started an institute, Bone Measurement Institute, a non-profit organization with the purpose of serving the public good. Although six of the most respected Osteoporosis researchers were on its board, the institute was essentially a one-person show with Allen as its sole employee. His desk at the Merck's office was the office of the Institute too.

Merck needed smaller, more affordable and even portable machines to measure bone density so that doctors can do the tests in their offices. These machines were called peripheral machines, and they measured the bone density in the forearm, heel, wrist or fingers than the hip and spine. There were very few manufacturers who made these peripheral machines as the demand was low, because they did not measure the hip and spine. However, these machines were the perfect fit for Merck's strategy, which aims to keep as many machines as needed in doctors' offices and to reduce the cost of bone scans. Being small in size, they would not take up much office space, and cost only a fraction of the big central machines.

Merck started a campaign to increase the manufacture and promotion of the peripheral machines. The company even took an equity position in a company to begin manufacturing the peripheral machines essentially to demonstrate its strategic intent. The big dominant players who manufactured the huge central machines that measured the hip and spine were hostile to these peripheral machines. There was also criticism and resistance to the peripheral machines stating that it was not a good basis for diagnosis and would lead to just bad medicine.

However, Merck was hellbent on taking up the cause of spreading the peripheral machines and make the prices of bone density tests affordable. Merck bought one of the companies that manufactured peripheral machines and showed how low the price could become, primarily to get everyone's attention. What is more, to prove that peripheral machines were not inferior, Merck took a position that the peripheral bone density scans had a good correlation in providing adequate information about the risk of hip and spine fractures and backed it by many studies. What is more, Merck partnered with diagnostic equipment manufacturers Hologic and Lunar corporations to finance the rollout of bone-mineral testing machines even in far-flung areas that are thinly populated.

Strategic Lobbying

Merck worked hard to get the smaller machines into doctors' offices and did not stop with that. Merck funded the required trials and helped peripheral machines with submissions to get through the FDA process. Merck also conducted massive education campaigns about the availability of the new, inexpensive peripheral machines. Fosamax sales force distributed the promotional literature highlighting these machines' usage and prices to doctors during their visits. Furthermore, Merck created a leasing program so that doctors could finance the purchase of a machine, large or small.

The Birth of A Diagnosis

Perhaps the most important and notable strategic moves of Merck was to change the very economics of measuring the bone reimbursable by Medicare. In 1997, the Bone Measurement Institute and other interested organizations successfully lobbied to pass the Bone Measurement Act, legislation that changed Medicare reimbursement rules to cover bone scans. Merck funded several of the organizations that have lobbied for the bill.

As a matter of strategic coincidence, in 1997, Merck got clearance from the FDA for a new lower dose of Fosamax, a 5-milligram tablet for those women diagnosed with Osteopenia. Most of the machines that Merck helped place in doctors' offices across the US, the ease of diagnosis, and the new legislation that made bone scans reimbursable expanded the diagnosis of Osteopenia and Osteoporosis phenomenally. The new peripheral machines made the diagnosis so simple that they generate a report with three distinct colors: Green, Yellow, and Red; Green meant normal, Yellow meant Osteopenia, and Red indicated Osteoporosis.

The very mention of the word Osteopenia on a report and the color-coded diagnosis had a profound effect on millions of women that it was a disease. When you have a condition, you should get it treated, and there is treatment now for Osteopenia. So you can maintain bone health with that.

What is more, Merck ran commercials advertising drugs to prevent Osteoporosis. Interestingly, those commercials didn't feature humped grannies but young-looking women. The focus was on Osteopenia, which had a larger patient pool. Finally, through a process of testing and advertising a cultural consensus took hold. Osteopenia simply became a condition that was seriously considered for treatment. A diagnosis was born!

Proof of the Pudding

Merck's efforts to expand diagnoses of Osteoporosis and Osteopenia were a phenomenal success. The proof of the pudding is in the eating. Consider these statistics:

▸ Medicare claims for bone scanning exams increased from 77,000 in 1994 to more than 1.5 million annually by 1997. New Medicare benefit was standardized in 1998.

▸ The sale of peripheral machines went up more than 500 percent over the same period. The Bone Densitometry centers had grown from 2000 in 1995 to 7,500 in a short period.

▸ The cost of a bone measuring test dropped to less than $30 per test from over $200.

▸ Fosamax became a blockbuster with $1.04 billion in 1999. It took close to four years for Fosamax to achieve its first billion-dollar mark. It reached over $2 billion in annual sales in 2002 and $3.2 billion by 2004.

Multiple Indications

Merck had also obtained approval for three new indications in addition to the initial 1995 approval of Post-Menopausal Osteoporosis (PMO) treatment of (10 mg) and Paget's disease (40 mg). The details of the new indications are presented in the following table.

New Indication Approval by the US FDA	Date of Approval
PMO Prevention 5 mg (Osteopenia)	2nd Quarter, 1997
Glucocorticoid-induced Osteoporosis (5/10mg)	3rd Quarter, 1999
Male Osteoporosis (10mg)	4th Quarter, 2000

New Formulations

The most effective growth strategy of Fosamax had been the development of a once-weekly Fosamax formulation of 35/70 mg.

The FDA approved it in November 2000. It had the same price as the daily tablets and immediately cannibalized the sales of the regular formula. However, It had grown overall sales of Fosamax. Fosamax once weekly was a breakaway success taking more than 80 percent of franchise sales within the first two years. The gastrointestinal side effects that were present with the daily dose had considerably eased with the once-weekly formulation of Fosamax. The original molecule patent expired in 2008, Fosamax OW (once-weekly) formula patent would be valid till 2018. Fosamax Once-weekly thus had the power to prevent the generic erosion in no small extent. Besides, on April 17, 2005, Merck gained the FDA approval for a Fixed-Dose-Combination (FDC) of alendronate sodium plus cholecalciferol (Vitamin D3) under the brand name Fosamax Plus D for the treatment of osteoporosis in post-menopausal women and to increase bone mass in men. Fosamax Plus D too helped Merck to consolidate its osteoporosis franchise.

Effective Lifecycle Management

Merck had managed the Fosamax timeline well despite challenges. It had launched new indications and formulations well before patent expiry. It had its share of challenges such as:

- ▶ Low diagnosis and treatment rates
- ▶ Low long-term compliance
- ▶ Low franchise equity in women's health
- ▶ Delayed consumer marketing opportunity to raise awareness (Branded DTC advertising did not start till 2001)

At the same time, Merck also had a big opportunity when the doubts were cast on Hormonal Replacement Therapy for menopausal women. Merck seized the opportunity with its DTC advertising. It had also increased the sales force emphasis on obstetric and gynecology therapeutic areas.

Merck did exceedingly well in developing the market for osteoporosis and in creating a condition called osteopenia out of virtually nowhere. Merck did an excellent job of maintaining its dominance within the bisphosphonates class.

Lessons

Merck created a market for bone disease remarkably, expanded the market through increased awareness, fielded a drug to treat it and even made it a market leader. However, Merck did not create an enduring osteoporosis franchise, the disorder that it expanded so dramatically. Here are the key lessons:

1. Identify the unmet needs and shape your market around them. Merck identified a substantial unmet need in osteoporosis and osteopenia. In fact, osteopenia was unheard of before Merck began its awareness programs and campaigns.

2. Begin your market-shaping activity long before the launch. Most brand teams start their marketing activities months before the launch. The most effective companies begin the market shaping work during the clinical development work once they see the initial promise of the drug to transform both the disease perception and the product profile long before launch. Merck invested in an intensive campaign to educate physicians (gynecologists mainly) and the American public (especially the middle-aged women) about osteoporosis and the availability bone-mineral testing. Merck's efforts resulted in expanding the potential market from 1.3 million per year in the US to 16 million women at risk in a short period.

3. Involve and engage as many stakeholders as necessary to raise the awareness of the disease condition and how the product is best suited to treat it. Merck co-sponsored media campaigns with the National Osteoporosis Foundation.

4. Go beyond the conventional partnerships such as patient advocacy groups and physicians in meeting the unmet needs. For Fosamax, Merck partnered with diagnostic equipment manufacturers Hologic and Lunar corporations to finance the rollout of bone-mineral testing machines in far-flung, sparsely-populated areas.

5. Expand indications and develop new formulations to extend market exclusivity and patient segments, which will increase sales both in the short and long-term.

6. Improving the access and insurance coverage are vital to make your new drug a blockbuster. Merck worked hard to bring down the prices of bone scans. The company along with other organizations got legislation, Bone Measurement Act that makes bone scans reimbursable.

(Source: Adapted from Alix Spiegel's article, *How a bone disease grew to fit the prescription*, NPR, December 21, 2009; and Building *Global Biobrands: Taking Biotechnology to market*, by Francois Simmons and Philip Kotler)

Two Stories: How ADHD was Sold and How Two Brands Dominated the ADHD Market!

Attention Deficit Hyperactivity Disorder (ADHD) was virtually unknown in 1956, when the Swiss Pharma major, CIBA-Geigy started marketing Ritalin (methylphenidate), the drug that is most widely used for ADHD today.

It was only in 1980 that the American Psychiatric Association (APA) in their publication, the third edition of the Diagnostic and Statistical Manual of Mental Disorders (DSM-III) included Attention Deficit Disorder (ADD) for the first time including the subtypes – ADD with hyperactivity and ADD without hyperactivity, and ADD residual type.

Attention deficit disorder (ADD) - the condition for which, Ritalin (methylphenidate) is most commonly prescribed was formerly called hyperactivity, as reflected in its alternative acronym: Attention Deficit Hyperactivity Disorder (ADHD). Its diagnosis is based on problems with attention, focus, impulsivity, or overactivity at school or home.

In 1990, ten years after the condition was first mentioned in the DSM III, about 900,000 children, and adults were diagnosed ADHD. And less than a decade later, the number of diagnoses swelled to five million. The growth of this magnitude in ADHD diagnoses suggested a problem of epidemic proportions.

The sharp rise in ADHD diagnosis was directly tied to another startling statistic–a 700 percent increase in the amount of Ritalin (methylphenidate) produced during the same period. An increase in this proportion was not only unprecedented, but also alarming for a single drug particularly when it was considered as a controlled substance.

In later years, the sales of stimulant medications for treating the ADHD have soared from about $1.7 billion in 2002 to a whopping $9 billion in 2012 according to IMS Health.

ADHD: A Historical Timeline

How did the number of diagnoses and the sales of ADHD medications had shown such phenomenal growth? What factors contributed to this? Before we explore further into the causes and reasons behind this enormous growth, let us quickly take a quick look into the historical timeline of ADHD and how it came to be what it is now. adhd-brain.com presents the timeline of ADHD history:

- In 1902, Sir Frederick Still, the well-known English pediatrician made the first descriptions of children with symptoms like ADHD and thought that the children with these symptoms had a defect of moral control.

- In 1908, Alfred Frank.Tredgold, an influential writer and medical expert in the early decades of the twentieth century in Great Britain, described high-grade feeble-minded children who likely had a form of mild brain damage that caused them to have ADHD-like anti-school behavior.

- In 1937, Dr. Charles Bradley, a Rhode Island physician, whose serendipitous discovery that the use of benzedrine in children with behavior problems resulted in an improvement in performance in a residential as well as school setting. Investigations from his work later led directly to the current pharmaceutical treatment of ADHD.

- The year 1952 marked the publication of the first edition of the Diagnostic and Statistical Manual of Mental Disorders by the American Psychiatric Association (APA). It does not mention ADHD like disorder.

- In 1957, hyperkinetic impulse disorder was used to describe for the first time to describe children with ADHD symptoms.

▶ Herbert Freed and Charles A Peifer studied the use of Thorazine (chlorpromazine) on hyperkinetic, emotionally disturbed children in 1957.

▶ In 1963, Dr. Carmen Keith Conners, an American psychologist best known for establishing the first standards for the diagnosis of attention deficit hyperactivity disorder (ADHD) published a study on the effects of Ritalin (methylphenidate) in emotionally disturbed children.

▶ In 1966, minimal brain dysfunction syndrome became a popular term to describe children with various combinations of impairment in perception, conceptualization, language, memory, and control of attention, impulse or motor function.

▶ In 1967 and 1968, National Institutes of Mental Health (NIH) gave many grants to researchers to study the effectiveness of stimulants on children with ADHD symptoms.

▶ In 1968, the American Psychiatric Association (APA) published the second edition of Diagnostic and Statistical Manual of Mental Disorders (DSM-II) and included the disorders - hyperkinetic reaction of childhood or adolescence and organic brain syndrome.

▶ In 1969, Dr. Keith Conners published the first Conner's Rating Scale, which eventually led to revised editions of the Conner's Rating Scales for parents and teachers.

▶ The Washington Post published a story describing how 5 to 10 percent of all school children in Omaha and Nebraska were receiving stimulants like Ritalin to control their behavior, even though the statistics referred to in the story were a subset of students who were in specialized programs. However, the story seemed to imply that 5 to 10 percent of all students in Omaha were on stimulants. Also implied in the article was that many parents were being coerced to put their children on a stimulant. This fueled a major controversy around the overuse of medications in students and over diagnosis of ADHD.

▶ In 1970 and 1971, the Comprehensive Drug Abuse Prevention and Control Act created a separate class for drugs that had the highest potential for abuse and addiction. As a result stimulants such as methylphenidate were added to Schedule II class, placing tight controls on their prescribing and refills.

▶ The Rehabilitation Act of 1973 added ADHD as a qualification for additional help and services at school for children with ADHD to help them succeed.

▶ In 1975, the anti-Ritalin movement gained momentum. Several books were published to reinforce the belief that ADHD is not a real diagnosis and hyperactivity is caused by food allergies and additives and not inherited. Further, it was a condition created by drug companies to make more profits.

▶ In 1980, The Association for Academic Psychiatry (AAP) published the first statement about ADHD and Medication for hyperkinetic children, which says that in addition to consideration of non-drug therapy situations where such an approach is appropriate, that there is a place for stimulant drugs in the treatment of hyperkinetic children.

▶ Also in 1980, the American Psychiatric Association (APA) published the third edition of Diagnostic and Statistical Manual of Mental Disorders (DSM-III), which included for the first time, Attention Deficit Disorder (ADD) including the subtypes - ADD with hyperactivity; ADD without hyperactivity; and ADD residual type.

▶ In 1981, Dr. Russel A Barkley, professor of clinical psychiatry at medical university of South Carolina, USA wrote the first of 17 books about ADHD - *Hyperactive Children: A Handbook of Diagnosis and Treatment.*

▶ In 1987, APA published the DSM-III-R. This edition changes the name of ADD to ADHD but does not name subtypes.

▶ Also in 1987, the American Academy of Pediatrics published a special report: Medication for the treatment of children with Attention Deficit Disorder containing guidelines and indications for drug therapy in its treatment naming several stimulant drugs and tricyclic antidepressants as being potentially useful.

▶ In 1993, Dr. Russel A Barkley started publishing, The ADHD Report Newsletter.

- In 1995, Dr. Joseph Biederman published one of the first hundreds of medical studies about children with ADHD.

- In 1996, AAP published an updated report: Medication for children with attention disorders, which stressed that drug therapy should be combined with appropriate management of a child's environment and curriculum.

- In 1999, NIMH (National Institutes of Mental Health) published results from a 14-month study known as the Multimodal Treatment of ADHD study (MTA Study); it involved 570 children with ADHD at six sites in the United States and Canada. It showed that medication alone was more effective than psychosocial treatments alone, but their combination was more beneficial.

- In 2000, APA published DSM-IV-TR naming three types of ADHD - including ADHD combined type; ADHD inattentive type; and ADHD predominantly hyperactive/impulsive type.

- Also in 2000, the AAP published its clinical practice guidelines including the diagnosis and evaluation of children with ADHD giving clear clinical guidelines for pediatricians and parents on the assessment and treatment of children with ADHD.

Adults: The New Frontier of ADHD

Undoubtedly, the children's market for ADHD has been very profitable for the drug industry. However, it is still limited. However, there is a much larger market for adult ADHD. But, how should a doctor diagnose adult ADHD? Eli Lilly, the makers of Concerta (methylphenidate) sponsored the efforts of some academic ADHD specialists at Harvard and New York University to create a diagnostic ADHD questionnaire that could be used in adults. Later, the World Health Organization (WHO) endorsed a slimmed down version of the questionnaire. Big Pharma then spent considerably on public awareness campaigns of the illness. Consider these highly influential campaigns narrated by Alan Schwarz in his book *ADHD Nation* for example:

▸ Dr. Ned Hallowell, ADHD guru and child psychiatrist on an episode of ABC's The Revolution in 2012 along with the host of the show, Ty Pennington performed a quick ADHD exam on an adult member of the audience. After the test he concluded: *So you passed the test. Welcome to the illustrious club (of ADHD). It's a good news diagnosis... there is medication, which people are so afraid of, but they should not be. Medication works about 80 percent of the time. And when it works, it works like eyeglasses! ...You can suddenly see!*

▸ Later, Dr. Hallowell with the same level of enthusiasm that goes beyond the evidence said in an interview with Gwyneth Paltrow's lifestyle website, GOOP: *If you are an adult reading this, and you feel you are underachieving, learn more about ADHD. It could be the answer you've been looking for - for years. Diagnosis and treatment would replace frustration and underachievement with success... The diagnosis of ADHD and the treatment that follows, if done properly, truly can change a life, at any age, from the frustration and underachievement to one of triumph, fulfillment, and joy.*

Can you think about promoting the diagnosis and treatment of serious mental illness by promising a solution to all life's problems? Of course, that is how you effectively sell a product.

Globalization of ADHD

ADHD diagnoses and prescriptions skyrocketed in the US. The trend of increasing diagnoses and prescriptions for ADHD in other parts of the world too have been growing significantly if not to the same extent as in the US. Between 2007 and 2012, methylphenidate prescriptions increased by 50 percent in the United Kingdom. In 2013, the global consumption of methylphenidate increased to 2.4 billion doses, a 66 percent increase from the year before. The United States, however, accounts for more than 80 percent of global consumption.

Peter Conrad, and Meredith R. Bergey, medical sociologists both, vehemently criticize the medicalization of ADHD in their paper on *the impending globalization of ADHD: Notes on the expansive and growth of a medicalized disorder* in Social Science & Medicine, in December 2014. Here is the gist of what they said in their article:

▸ The principal concern of the authors is that the ADHD is being medicalized. Children of different age groups who may be merely naughty or high-high-spirited are being misdiagnosed with ADHD and are wrongly being treated with powerful medications such as Ritalin.

▸ Five major causes are driving the global expansion of ADHD and its subsequent medicalization: drug industry lobbying; the influence of US-based psychiatry; the adoption of looser criteria for diagnosis; the influence of ADHD patient advocacy groups; the growth of information on the internet.

▸ In the past, drugs for ADHD were heavily marketed in the US, which is getting saturated. The drug companies, therefore are looking for the greener pastures and expanding into the international markets for aggressively promoting their ADHD medications. The markets they have been targeting are – Western Europe, Japan, Mexico and Brazil among others.

That is how ADHD as a medical condition requiring treatment with stimulants and non-stimulants has evolved into a multi-billion dollar market. The ADHD market is expected to experience significant growth in seven markets such as the US, France, Germany, Italy, Spain, the UK, and Japan to reach $13.9 billion by 2024 according to Global Data, a research and consulting firm. Two brands mainly have contributed to the phenomenal growth of the condition and the market. They are Ritalin of Ciba-Geigy (Novartis now), the Swiss drug major and Adderall of Shire Pharmaceuticals, a leading global biotech company with Dublin, Ireland as its headquarters.

Big Pharma Sponsors Biederman Studies

Dr. Joseph Biederman, unequivocally the most published psychopharmacology maven for ADHD had conducted many clinical studies on the effectiveness of psycho-stimulant drugs in the treatment of attention disorders. Pharmaceutical companies sponsored most of these studies. The findings of these studies gave credibility to the treatment of ADHD with stimulant drugs by giving three essential messages:

1. The disorder was under-diagnosed.
2. Stimulants were effective and safe.
3. Unmedicated ADHD led to significant risks for academic failure, drug dependence, car accidents, and brushes with the law

Ritalin and Adderall through their brilliant marketing efforts first marketed ADHD as a condition and then offered their brands as a solution to treat the problem of ADHD. Ritalin started it all and Adderall reinforced it with all its might and had been reaping rich rewards from the ADHD market. The story of Ritalin and Adderall marketing, therefore, is also the story of marketing ADHD. Ritalin first.

How Ritalin (methylphenidate) Marketed ADHD

Before we go into the details of how Ritalin rode the market with ADHD, an interesting tidbit about how Ritalin got its name. Leandro Panizzon, a chemist at Ciba (now Novartis), synthesized methylphenidate in the early 1950s. He shared his invention with his wife, Rita, who tried the medication on herself. Rita enjoyed tennis and to the couple's delight methylphenidate had an excellent effect on her tennis game. Leandro named the new drug in honor of his wife. He named the new drug Ritalin.

Ciba began marketing Ritalin in 1956 in the United States for a wide range of adult psychiatric disorders. However, the evidence was emerging that it might be useful in improving the behavior of disturbed children as they were then called. In 1963, child psychiatrist Leon Eisenberg and the child psychologist Carmen Keith Conners who were then working at the Johns Hopkins hospital published a landmark article based on their clinical studies that showed methylphenidate improving the behavioral symptoms in children.

The diagnostic label, attention deficit hyperactivity disorder did not exist yet. However, the article. *The effects of methylphenidate on symptomatology and learning in disturbed children* by Eisenberg and Conners in The American Journal of Psychiatry in November 1963 had put the drug on child psychiatry map.

Journalist, Alan Schwarz in his hard-hitting book, *ADHD Nation: Children, Big Pharma and the Making of an Epidemic*, narrated an episode that explains how the involvement of Ritalin and indeed the Big Pharma began in selling ADHD, following the famous methylphenidate clinical trial by Eisenberg and Keith Conners. Here's the story:

> *Some weeks after the publication of Conner's and Eisenberg's paper in the American Journal of Psychiatry, the authors received a man in a suit who showed up at Eisenberg's office. The visitor gratefully glided a slip of paper across his desk as Conners was looking on saying, "for further studies." The visitor was a representative from Ciba, and the note was a check for $5,000. Eisenberg tucked the check into a desk drawer, warned Conners to "watch out for these guys" and never spoke of the day after that.*

That's how the long and enduring engagement of Ritalin in the marketing of ADHD began. Since that $5,000 check from Ciba, Schwarz says that pharmaceutical money has irrigated the channels running through every corner of the ADHD ecosystem, feeding researchers, patient advocacy groups, celebrity spokespeople, and advertisers.

In the late 1960s, when the direct-to-consumer advertising was not allowed in the US, Ciba found a smart way of persuading the parents to test and treat their children for ADHD. They distributed pamphlets to parents through the teachers in the schools their children were studying. Ciba representative in that district provided these pamphlets to the schools. The pamphlet contained a logo of the company Ciba on the backside. One of such brochures read:

Parents should be aware that these medicines (stimulants such as methylphenidate) do not drug or alter the brain of the child. They make the child normal.

Targeting the Teachers

Targeting the doctors, nurses and patients is a normal and established practice for pharmaceutical companies. Pharma companies had started targeting teachers for marketing their ADHD medications even before the direct-to-consumer advertising was approved in the US. As teachers have some concern and play an important intermediary role in the diagnosis and treatment of ADHD, pharmaceutical companies had designed many ways to reach and influence them. Novartis, the manufacturer of Ritalin, created an educational website that has specific content for teachers. On one page entitled If Parents Ask, for example, Novartis suggests responses teachers might make to concerned parents:

Make it clear to them that it is important for them - and their child - to understand and follow the doctor's medical advice about medication and other therapies for ADHD. ADHD is a serious condition that may require the child to be on medication and undergo counseling for a longer duration.

Further, the site incorporates links to the company, or directly to Ritalin (medication produced by the manufacturer) for a discussion on the diagnostic process, and references to the legislation regarding the access to medication. Another pharmaceutical company, Shire Pharmaceuticals (manufacturer of Adderall) has an annual toll-free *Ask The Experts ADHD hotline*. Experts provided for this hotline include teachers, school nurses, doctors, and advocates. The suggested topics include the management of ADHD in the school.

Furthermore, in 1997, Novartis collaborated with the National Association of School Nurses in the US to run a nationwide campaign in which 11,000 school nurses provided with a resource kit containing information on ADHD and its treatment, and various support organizations. The company extended the collaboration further to produce a resource to curb the misuse of psycho-stimulant medication providing links to Novartis Pharmaceuticals.

Sixty-plus and Still Counting...

It has been sixty-two years since Ritalin was launched and the drug continues to have a significant presence in the treatment of ADHD. Even though there have been many competitors since its patent expired eroding its sales and profits, the importance of methylphenidate is very much present. Notable among the competitors is Adderall, which is marketed by Shire Pharmaceuticals. In fact, it is Adderall that took the mantle and eventually the leadership position in expanding the ADHD market when Ritalin lost its market exclusivity. Here's the timeline of methylphenidate that reinforces its continued importance in ADHD treatment.

Methylphenidate (Ritalin) Timeline

1955	Ritalin (Novartis)
1982	Ritalin SR (Novartis)
1999	Metadate ER (methylphenidate extended release - Cell Tech Pharmaceuticals)
2000	Methylin ER (Methylphenidate extended-release - Novartis)
2000	Concerta (Methylphenidate - Janssen Pharmaceuticals)
2001	Metadate CD (Cell Tech Pharmaceuticals)
2002	Ritalin LA (Novartis)
2005	Focalin XR (dexmethylphenidate – Novartis. Licensed from Celgene)
2006	Daytrana (methylphenidate patch – Noven Pharmaceuticals)
2012	Quillivalant XR (Liquid Methylphenidate – Next Wave Pharmaceuticals)
2016	QuilliChew (Methylphenidate chewable tablets – Pfizer)

Adderall, the New Leader

The loss of exclusivity of Ritalin opened the doors of fortune for the company that could invent a new drug to treat ADHD, get approved and patented, then unleash it on the awaiting market. As Schwarz notes, *this is par for the course for the big Pharma: when a patent dies, a new brand drug must rise - even if the new one is not one iota better.* Enter Adderall. How it entered the market and later conquered is a curious and interesting story.

The story of Adderall starts with a decades-old weight loss drug called Obetrol. The US FDA withdrew its approval for this drug as early as 1973. Rexar, a small pharmaceutical company kept on selling it for weight loss even into the 1990s without approval. Rexar was not selling much of Obetrol, but interestingly a pediatrician in Utah was writing an unusually high number of prescriptions of the drug. He was using it for ADHD.

Around the same time, Roger Griggs, a high school football coach, started a small pharmaceutical company named Richwood Pharmaceuticals. Griggs became interested in Obetrol and therefore acquired the company. He asked one simple question: *Could the United States with its notoriously short memory, be ready to try amphetamine again*? Of course, it would, with the right marketing.

Griggs acquired Rexar and started marketing Obetrol with a new brand name. It is interesting to know how Griggs arrived at the brand name. He acquired Rexar suspecting that Obetrol might treat ADHD although it was not tested, but because a pediatrician in Utah was prescribing a lot of it for ADHD. Also, he knew that ADHD was found in 3 to 5 percent of the children at the time. It was indeed a significant opportunity. He took 'ADD' (from Attention Deficit Disorder) and fiddled with some suffixes: All for ADD, ADD for All - Adderall! Griggs later recalled that it was meant to be a kind of inclusive thing.

 He went ahead and marketed Adderall for ADHD without the FDA approval. The drug was not even tested for its efficacy in treating the condition. FDA very soon halted the marketing of the drug. In response, Richmond Pharmaceuticals started a trial and submitted a new drug application (NDA). The company was not sure whether its application would be approved by the FDA or not. As luck would have it, Griggs received a phone call from a well-connected Washington lobbyist, who told him that a US senator was furious that his son could no longer obtain Adderall. And sure enough, the FDA approved the Adderall new drug application. Later, Griggs sold his company, Richwood Pharmaceuticals to Shire Pharmaceuticals. Shire marketed both ADHD and Adderall with equal vigor.

Shire Markets ADHD and Adderall Aggressively

Shire spared no effort in marketing the ADHD condition with its key brand Adderall. It had conducted disease awareness and education campaigns, engaged multiple stakeholders, and heavily advertised in print and television. It also had a considerable online presence through its websites for information and education of teachers and parents in addition to healthcare professionals. Here are some of the important marketing and advertising initiatives that the company has been taking over the years:

▶ Gathered hundreds of doctors at many meetings sponsored by the company, where a specialist physician (child psychiatrist or child psychologist of repute) paid by the company explained the value of Adderall in treating ADHD.

▶ Massive personal selling effort to engage physicians frequently with communication inputs such as posters, visual-aids highlighting the benefits such as better grades and behavior that Adderall could offer. Shire representatives used to visit at the time all psychiatrists in their respective areas once every two weeks for promoting of Adderall.

▶ Sponsored ADHD patient advocacy groups such as CHADD (Children and Adults with ADHD) to spread awareness of the condition.

- Has been sponsoring online ADHD self-assessment tests to drive diagnoses up. Shire sponsored, for example, a quiz, Could you have ADHD? On the website, everydayhealth.com. Shire advertised about the quiz sometime in 2011 featuring the celebrity singer Levine of Maroon 5, which resulted in about 570,000 people taking the test according to Medical Marketing & Media.

- Partnered with TV personality, Ty Pennington, a popular television host and later Maroon 5 star, Adam Levine to spread awareness of Adult ADHD in their campaign, *It's your ADHD - Own it.*

- Sponsored a medical education video portraying a physician making a diagnosis of the disorder in an adult in a six-minute conversation, after which the doctor recommends the medication.

- Shire once subsidized 50,000 copies of a comic book that tries to demystify the disorder and uses Superheroes to tell children: *medication may make it easier to pay attention and control your behavior.*

- Shire paid the CHADD, the ADHD advocacy group $ 3million from 2006 to 2009 to have the group's bi-monthly magazine, Attention distributed to doctors' offices nationwide.

- Shire targeted parents also in its Direct-to-consumer advertisements. The company carried a wrap-around advertisement for Adderall XR in the People magazine cover of September 2005 that showed a mother hugged her smiling child holding a sheet of paper with a "B+" written it. The advertisement read: *Finally! School work that matches her intelligence.*

- Shire designed compelling advertising messages, even if misleading, based on Dr. Joseph Biederman's (a prominent child psychiatrist at Harvard) studies it sponsored. One of the advertisements says: *Adderall XR improves academic performance.*

Attention Continues

That is a brief account of how attention deficit hyperactivity disorder (ADHD) has evolved and continued to grow. Recently a few non-stimulant drugs too have entered the market. These are – Straterra (atomoxetine) by Eli Lilly; Kapvay (clonidine) by Shionogi.

The two major players who are primarily responsible for the phenomenal growth of ADHD as a condition are Ritalin of Novartis and Adderall of Shire Pharmaceuticals. Ritalin started it all in 1956 and Adderall took the mantle once Ritalin lost its market exclusivity. Ritalin has been an enduring brand in the treatment of the condition for over sixty years now. Methylphenidate (Ritalin and many other brands of methylphenidate) continue to play an essential role in the treatment of ADHD. The sixty-plus Methylphenidate, which is a senior citizen of the ADHD-medication community is still fit as a fiddle!

(Source: Adapted from articles - 1. Adam Gaffney, *How ADHD was sold*, The New Republic, September 23, 2016; 2. Vincent Iannelli, M.D, *A history of medication timeline of ADHD*, VeryWell Mind, September 05, 2018, www.verywellmind.com; 3. *ADHD History, www.adhd-brain.com*)

Blue Ocean Strategy

Blue and Red Oceans

W. Chan Kim and Renée Mauborgne used blue, and red oceans as a metaphor for describing the market universe in their highly acclaimed book, *Blue Ocean Strategy*. Red Oceans are all industries in existence today - the known marketplace. In Red Oceans, industry boundaries are defined and accepted, and the competitive rules of the game are known. The companies in the Red Ocean market space try to outperform their rivals and grab a more significant share of the product or market demand. The prospects for profits and growth are reduced in red oceans as the market space gets crowded. Cutthroat competition turns red oceans bloody hence the metaphorical name red oceans.

Blue Oceans, on the contrary, denote all the industries that are not in existence today - the unknown market space untainted by competition. Blue Oceans provide ample opportunities for rapid growth and profits as there is no competition. Competition is irrelevant as the rules for the game are waiting to be set. Blue Ocean is an analogy to describe the wider, deeper potential of market space that is not yet explored. The following table presents the key differences between Red Ocean and Blue Ocean market spaces at a glance:

Table 8.1 Red and Blue Oceans: Key Differences

Red Ocean Strategies	Blue Ocean Strategies
1. Competing in existing market space.	Create uncontested market space.
2. Beat the competition.	Make the competition irrelevant.
3. Make the value/cost tradeoff.	Break the value/cost tradeoff.
4. Align the whole system of a company's activities with a strategic choice of differentiation or low cost.	Align the whole system of a company's activities in the pursuit of differentiation and low cost.

(Source: Blue Ocean Strategy, Harvard Business Review, October 2004)

Value Innovation

The bedrock of the blue ocean strategy is value innovation. What is value innovation? Value innovation is creating a value simultaneously for both the buyer and the company. It was Charles W. L. Hill, a professor at Michigan State University, who proposed the concept of value innovation first. He claimed that Porter's Five Forces Framework for competitive analysis was inadequate because differentiation can be a means to achieve low cost. Instead, he suggested that a combination of differentiation and low cost may be necessary for firms to achieve a sustainable competitive advantage. The core idea of a blue ocean strategy too is to create a leap in value for both the company and its sellers by breaking a tradeoff between differentiation and low cost.

Later in 2004, W. Chan Kim and Renée Mauborgne, both professors at INSEAD business school in France have come out with the Blue Ocean Strategy that explains the what, why and how of creating Blue Ocean strategies in today's predominantly Red-Ocean marketplace. The core idea here too is based on value innovation. Value innovation is creating value simultaneously both for the buyer and the company. You create a Blue Ocean when you raise the value (in product, service or delivery) for the market, while simultaneously reducing or eliminating features or functions that are less valued by the current or future market (customers). The essence of value innovation is best captured in the statement of Akio Morita, Chairman of Sony Corporation when he pioneered the concept of value innovation in the personal music industry with the introduction of Walkman:

> Carefully watch how people live, get an intuitive sense as to what they might want and then go with it. Don't do market research.

This careful observation created a new, uncontested market space in 1979, with the introduction of Walkman. Henry Ford's Model T Car offers another classic example of how the value innovation created a blue ocean in the automobile industry at the time. W. Chan Kim and Renée Mauborgne clearly explain how Henry Ford used the value innovation to create an uncontested market space for his Model T Car in their Harvard Business Review Article of October 2004 on Blue Ocean Strategy:

Henry Ford Creates A Blue Ocean

The automobile industry was small and unattractive at the end of the 19th century. It was crammed with over 500 automakers competing in the crowded market for handmade luxury cars. The average price of the car was around the US $1,500. Only the very rich could afford it. The industry, as a result, was so unpopular that it led to even an anti-car activist movement. The anti-car activists tore up roads, ringed parked cars with barbed wire and organized boycotts of car-driving businessmen and politicians to demonstrate their protests.

Henry Ford did not want to swim in this Red Ocean. Instead of trying to beat the competition for a slice of the share in this heavily contested market, he reconstructed the industry boundaries of cars and horse-drawn carriages, which were competing in the same space of local transportation. Horse-drawn carriages were the primary means of local transportation across America. The major advantage of the horse-drawn carriages over the automobiles was that they could easily negotiate the bumps and dirt roads that were present everywhere in America, which the automobiles at the time could not.

Henry Ford understood the market situation enough to break away from competition and unlock the enormous untapped potential demand. He built Model T Car and called it for the multitude (not only for the rich) constructed with the best materials. Ford built a car like the horse-drawn carriage meant for everyday use. Model T came in just one color, black and there were few optional extras. It was durable and reliable and designed to travel effortlessly on dirt roads in rain, snow or sunshine. People could learn to drive it easily.

The pricing strategy too was different. Ford did not look at the automobile industry for a price point; he looked at the horse-drawn carriages, which cost $400 on average. In 1908, the first Model T cost $850. In 1909, the price dropped to $609, and by 1924 it was down to $290. The mass production with its pioneering assembly-line operation of Model T made the price drops possible.

Ford Motor Company transformed the industry boundaries, achieved value innovation, created an uncontested market space and made the competition irrelevant. Ford created a Blue Ocean!

How to Formulate a Blue Ocean Strategy

Understand that Blue Ocean is a journey and not a destination. It challenges everything you thought you know about strategic success in the marketplace. It provides a systematic approach to making competition irrelevant. To formulate a Blue Ocean strategy, you need to take a critical look at yourself, your business, your path. The 'Pioneer - Migrator - Settler Map' (PMS Map) can help you as a diagnostic tool to start your first step of taking stock of where your products and services fit into your industry.

The PMS Map

The Pioneer - Migrator - Settler Map is a diagnostic tool shows how your revenue-generating products and services fare in their contribution to the future growth of the company. The map helps you to determine if you are in the Red Ocean fighting for your life or enjoying the tranquility of the deep blue waters of the Blue Ocean where there is no competition in sight. You can organize the key products in the three categories and display them by size even. Once you analyze and understand the current positions of your products and services regarding their relative positions on the PMS Map, you would be able to move them to the more desirable stages from where they are now. Here is a brief description of what these labels - Pioneer, Migrator, and Settler stand for:

A. The Pioneers are products that offer unprecedented value with high-profit growth potential. They are unique products and virtually free from competition. They have the entire market for themselves.

B. The Migrators are products with exceptional value but not innovative. These products sit on the boundaries of the Red and Blue oceans. They may offer some value and potential for profit growth if you make some changes.

C. The Settlers are products that follow the industry norms with little or no differentiation. They are not innovative and not much different from the competition and therefore, do not offer much potential for profit growth. Also, these products face a shrinking customer pool. Settlers are primarily in the Red Ocean space.

The PMS Map

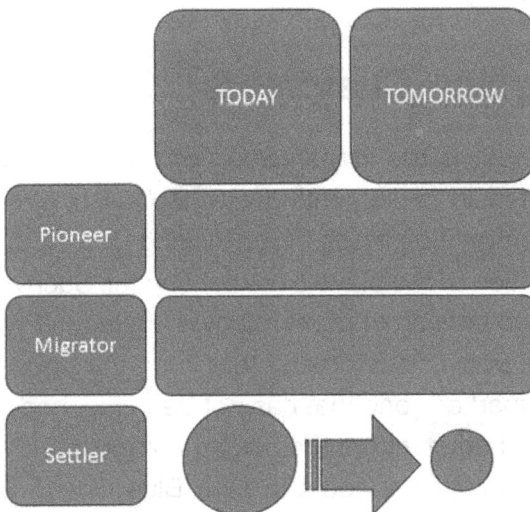

Figure 8.1 The PMS Map

Blue Ocean Strategy: Key Questions

Blue Ocean Strategy is a shift in mindset. You need to expand your mental horizons and shift your understanding to find out where the opportunity lies. You need to ask a fundamentally different set of questions. The answers to such questions would then enable you to perceive the fallacies and limitations of long-held beliefs and conventional thinking and the consequent boundaries that we impose on ourselves. Here are the necessary steps involved in migrating your products which are currently settlers (swimming in the bloody Red Ocean) to the status of pioneers (enjoying the tranquility of the vast, deep Blue Ocean space with no competition in sight):

1. Get a clear idea about the current state of play in your industry.
2. Find out and uncover the hidden pain points that limit the current size of the industry and discover an ocean of non-customers.
3. Find out how you can reconstruct your market boundaries and explore blue ocean opportunities
4. Select the right Blue Ocean move, conduct rapid market test and launch.

Identifying Non-Customers

Last, but not least is the identification of non-customers. It is the most crucial step in implementing a Blue Ocean Strategy. In Red Oceans, the competition leads to a shrinking pool of the customers for whose attention all the players are fighting for. Such a competition naturally leads to erosion of profit margins. Instead, if you can find a market (a large pool of customers) that is on the boundaries of our existing target market - one that has not been reached, then we can open up a new market where there is no competition. W. Chan Kim and Renée Mauborgne suggest in their Blue Ocean Strategy that there are three tiers of non-customers:

1. The first tier consists of existing customers, who are looking to leave the industry. We need to find out their pain points responsible for this decision.
2. The second tier consists of those, who consciously decide against your product or service. What are they looking for?

What should we do to meet their latent needs and to remove their pain points in our current offering?

3. The third tier contains people who are in distant markets. What are the key differences between our existing markets and those distant markets? How can we transform the boundaries of both - our current markets and those distant markets?

Eventually, Blue Oceans turn red, when more players enter their space. The companies must, therefore, continuously explore to find the Blue Ocean opportunities or uncontested market spaces to stay at the top of the game. Pharmaceutical markets are Red Ocean markets. The industry offers its Blue Ocean periods for those companies who can create uncontested spaces every time they are at their innovative best. Successful pharmaceutical companies are continually exploring the market space to create their Blue Ocean strategies.

The following four cases show how some of the world's leading pharmaceutical companies have created uncontested market spaces with their Blue Ocean strategies for their products and reaped rich dividends.

Novo Nordisk's Blue Ocean Strategy

How do you create a blue ocean strategy? By challenging the conventional wisdom in any given industry. By challenging the prevailing mental model. By rediscovering the market needs in markets that are mature and saturated. By shifting the way of looking at customer needs from the functional to the emotional. Companies, who look at various customer groups, can gain new insights into how to design their value proposition to focus on a previously overlooked set of customer needs.

That is what exactly Novo Nordisk had done with its Novopen. Novo Nordisk, the Danish insulin producer, broke away from the competition and created a blue ocean by shifting the industry's longstanding focus on doctors to the users - patients themselves.

Insulin is used by diabetic patients to regulate their blood sugar levels. Historically, the insulin industry, like the pharmaceutical industry focused its attention on the key influencers: doctors. It is the doctors, who prescribe insulin to their patients and therefore, the industry sharpened its attention and efforts to produce purer insulin in response to doctors' quest for better medication. The innovations in purification technology had improved dramatically in the 1980s, and there was minimal scope to develop it further. Novo Nordisk, the leader in the insulin industry, had already created the first human monocomponent insulin that was chemically the exact copy of human insulin. The competition was rapidly catching on.

Novo Nordisk saw that it could break away from competition and create a new market by shifting the industry's longstanding focus on doctors to the users. By focusing on patients, Novo Nordisk found that most diabetic patients were uncomfortable about using syringes to administer insulin injections. Considering a diabetic needs to inject himself three or four times a day, the use of the syringe is a very daunting prospect. Moreover, there was the social stigma attached to the idea of using a needle and vial in public. Novo Nordisk thus broke through a prevailing mental model by making a shift from a functional to an emotional (and social) need. It led to the creation of the Novopen, a drug delivery device that is patient-friendly for the diabetics. Rajiv Narang and Devika Devaiah narrate this exciting story of how exactly this had happened in their book, *Orbit-shifting Innovations: The dynamics of ideas that created history*:

> *In January 1981, Sonnich Fryland, the marketing director, Novo Nordisk called John Rex, the head of packaging and Ivan Jensen, a doctor into his room. Fryland removed his fountain pen from his pocket and asked whether it would be possible to produce a device that looked like a fountain pen, that could be used and which could hold a week's supply of insulin and administer two units of insulin at the touch of a button. The pen had to be simple and discreet and preferably look like, well an actual fountain pen.*

That is how Novo Nordisk seized the blue ocean opportunity of Novopen, launched in 1985. Novopen, the first user-friendly insulin delivery solution, was designed to remove the hassle and embarrassment of administering insulin. The Novopen resembled a fountain pen; it contained an insulin cartridge that allowed the patient to carry comfortably, in one self-contained unit, roughly a week's requirement of insulin. The pen had an integrated click mechanism, making it possible even for blind patients to control the dosing and administer insulin.

Novo Nordisk continued to dominate the blue ocean it had unlocked. The company pursued a continuous innovation program. It introduced in 1989, Novolet, a pre-filled disposable insulin injection pen with a dosing system that provided users with even greater convenience and ease of use. In 1999, the company brought out the Innovo, integrated electronic memory and cartridge based delivery system. Innovo was designed to manage the delivery of insulin through built-in-memory and to display the dose, the last dose, and the elapsed time - information that is critical for reducing risk and eliminating worries about missing a dose.

Thus, Novo Nordisk had shifted the industry landscape and transformed the company from an insulin manufacturing and marketing company to a diabetes care company. The company had always been a dominant player in the insulin market. The difference today is that about 70 percent of the company's total turnover comes from diabetes care, an offering that originated mostly in the company's thinking regarding users rather than influencers. In other words, from the blue ocean that it had created.

(Source: Adapted from Rajiv Narang and Devika Devaiah's book, *Orbit-shifting Innovations: The dynamics of ideas that created history*)

The Little Blue Pill's Astonishing Dream Run!

Viagra, launched in America twenty years ago, is the most ubiquitous pharmaceutical brand name in the world today. Type it into Google, and a search throws up more than four million references; ten times more than Prozac and 20 times as many as Botox, its nearest competitors.

Indeed, the takeoff Viagra was one of the fastest that a new drug has ever seen. Almost immediately after its launch in the United States, it was being prescribed at the rate of 10,000 a day. This was unprecedented for a prescription drug. In Atlanta, urologist, Dr. John Stripling had reportedly written about 300 prescriptions on the day Viagra was available.

Accidental Discovery

For all the great success that Viagra achieved, its discovery was accidental and not a result of focused research. Two British scientists – Peter Dunn and Albert Wood at Pfizer created sildenafil Citrate, a new chemical entity (NCE). They believed that the drug would be useful in treating high blood pressure and angina. However, as they were employees of Pfizer at the time, they are not allowed to discuss the status of the invention.

In 1994, Dr. Nicholas Terret and his colleague Peter Ellis found that sildenafil can be very effective in enhancing the flow of blood to the penile region in patients suffering from erectile dysfunction. They discovered that sildenafil increases the muscle relaxing effects of nitric oxide, a chemical that gets released during sexual stimulation. This relaxation of the muscle in the penis allows a higher rate of blood flow and aids in producing an erection. Dr. Nicholas Terret was named in the British patent for sildenafil citrate.

Pfizer completed several trials of sildenafil citrate, but none of them provided any hope of treating heart diseases. However, Ian Osterloh, a researcher observed an interesting side effect of the drug during the trials. Volunteers of the trail were reporting increased erections several days after taking the drug. An interesting coincidence was that around the same time, other studies were revealing more information about the biochemical pathways involved in the erection process. This helped the Pfizer team of scientists to understand how the drug might amplify the process of erection. Dr. Simon Campbell, a Pfizer veteran submitted a research proposal for a further investigation into this and handed over the project to another research team. Although Dr. Simon Campbell did not invent sildenafil citrate, which later became Viagra, he is called the father of Viagra because he laid the seed and started the project. He was later Knighted. Viagra indeed was a serendipitous discovery!

Viagra in the Media

Thousands of stories were written in the popular press about Viagra between September 1996 and the product's eventual launch in the late March 1998. No other prescription drug brand received as much media attention as Viagra did. Jay Baglia, Assistant Professor in the department of communication studies at San Jose University at the time describes in his well-researched book, *The Viagra Adventure*, four phases of media coverage during the period starting from September 1996 to October 2002. Viagra was frequently introduced in these articles through the use of emphatic epithets. Here are some of the more important ones:

> ▸ Eighteen months before its launch, Viagra was characterized as the *Ultimate erection* aid in a Newsweek article by Geoffrey Cowley titled, *Attention Aging Men*

- ▸ The New York Times called Viagra, *A Wonder of the Modern Age; The New Miracle Drug and; The New National Drug of Choice*

- ▸ Newsweek Followed its earlier article with *The Potency Wonder Drug*

- ▸ The US News & World Report called Viagra, *The Sexual Potency Drug*

All these monickers imply that this technology is something we have all been waiting for. Also, Douglas Martin's article in the New York Times, *Thanks a Bunch Viagra: The Pill that Revived Sex, or At Least Talking About It*, suggested that Viagra's availability got people talking about sex generally and got men to visit their doctors. After generations of taboo, of refusing to talk about sexual failure, erectile dysfunction had become a subject that one can discuss openly. Erica Jung, the author, summed up best this great transformation that media had brought about when she said: *Impotence was the great secret. Now suddenly you can't go to a dinner party without people talking about erection!*

Marketing Excellence

Viagra is a classic example of marketing excellence in action. Pfizer's first strategic masterstroke was its embarkation of the rebranding of impotence itself. Impotence suggested, literally a lack of power, a referendum on a man's masculinity and humanity. Pfizer instead of talking about impotence chose to speak of Viagra regarding male enhancement. It adopted the medicalized language of erectile dysfunction and offered a straightforward and convenient medical solution. Furthermore, the company made the condition look like a common condition through its marketing communication - *that half of men over 40 are affected with 'ED.' How can something that is so common be shameful?*

The second brilliant marketing move was to hire Bob Dole, a former presidential nominee, a war veteran and an elder statesman as Viagra's spokesman. With this, Pfizer was able to bring a gendered notion of power and patriotism to Viagra marketing and make the sexual function a metaphor for a kind of masculine dignity. Bob Dole appeared on a Larry King Live Show in 1998 to discuss his own struggles with erectile dysfunction and his battle with prostate cancer. He even talked about the effect the battle had on his body even after the battle was won - and told the viewers about the medical solution he had found for the malady. The company later used Bob Dole in a TV ad, which had instantly become iconic. Dole, however, did not talk about Viagra itself in the ad. The little blue pill in all this talk of heroism was merely implied.

The third winning move that Pfizer made in its marketing was that it successfully attempted to reclaim the notions of potency from the ideas of impotence, which it had almost antiquated. The company recruited celebrities from the sports world such as the NASCAR driver Mark Martin, the soccer legend Pele, the baseball player Rafael Palmer to star in ads to accomplish this. The ads featuring these sports celebrities emphasized men being classically manly: speeding, winning, overcoming. The taglines used for these ads were: *Love life again* and *Step up to the plate. The ads always signed off with an - Ask your doctor.*

Viagra Advertising

How did Pfizer come up with such great ads that resonated with its target audience? Pfizer followed the same principles and procedures that it would follow for its drug discovery program. To unearth an ad or a TV commercial that would resonate with its audience, it developed a screening system that would parallel its drug discovery program. Pfizer's vice president for consumer marketing, Dorothy Wetzel explained:

> *Just as the Pfizer research and development screened thousands of different components to find the one that makes a difference, we are trying to apply the same process to our communication development; getting multiple agencies to develop ideas and screen it down to the one killer communication.*

After relying on metaphorical ads featuring older men using horses to get their trucks out of mud or figuring out how to get the factory works unclogged, Viagra tried a more direct and bold approach: having a woman encourage men to get treatment for erectile dysfunction. The new TV ad spot from BBDO shows a forty-something woman with a British accent and slinky dress, saying:

You know what, plenty of guys have this issue...If ED is stopping what you started, ask your doctor about Viagra...

This ad is almost an endorsement from the women for Viagra.

The competition for erectile dysfunction scripts was heating up if ad spends of 2014 were any indication. Two erectile dysfunction drugs were among the top ten in ad spends. Eli Lilly took the top spot for ad spend in 2014. It was the number one spender with $272 million followed by Viagra at number four with an ad spend of $232 million.

With a US sales of $1.14 billion and a worldwide sales of over $2 billion in 2016, after eighteen years since its approval, Viagra had a dream run indeed! The following table presents a timeline of Viagra's dream run.

Viagra's Dream Run: A Timeline

Timeline	Activity
1989	Prizer scientists in Great Britain, Peter Dunn, and Albert Wood created a drug called sildenafil citrate that they believed would be useful in treating high blood pressure and angina.
The 1990s (Early)	Sildenafil showed little or no hope of treating high blood pressure and angina in the trials. However, an interesting side effect was observed during the clinical trials. The volunteers in the trials reported increased erections several days after taking the drug.
1991	Dr. Nicholas Terret is named in the British patent for sildenafil citrate (Trade name Viagra) as a heart medication. Terret is often considered as the father of Viagra.

Table Contd...

Timeline	Activity
1996	Pfizer patents sildenafil in the United States.
March 1998	The US FDA approves Viagra for treating erectile dysfunction. In the following weeks, US pharmacists dispense more than 40,000 prescriptions.
May 1998	Viagra gets unprecedented media attention: A. Time magazine's cover story quotes the Penthouse publisher Bob Guccione as saying: *We believe Viagra will free the American male Libido.* B. On CNN's Larry King Live show, former presidential nominee, Bob Dole admits that he took part in experimental trials of Viagra calling it a great drug.
June 1998	Newsweek calls Viagra *the hottest new drug in history — almost anywhere in the world.* At the time Viagra was being marketed only in the United States, Mexico, Brazil and Morocco, but Newsweek reports growing black market sales in other countries.
December 1998	A. Pfizer hires Bob Dole, a former Presidential nominee for a television campaign aimed at raising awareness of male impotence. B. The Washington Post reports that CIA was using Viagra to gain friends in Afghanistan. While CIA had a long history of buying information with cash, the growing insurgency had prompted the use of novel incentives and creative bargaining to get information.
July 1999	The popular TV show, *Sex and the City* airs *The Man, The Myth, and Viagra* in which, character Samatha dates a wealthy Alderman, who uses the *little blue pills*. In the next season, Samantha takes the *little blue pills* herself to enhance her sexual experiences.
2000	Dr. Sanjay Kaul presents research at the 49th Annual Scientific Session of the American College of Cardiology that suggests 522 patients died while taking Viagra in the first year the drug was on the market. However, there was no implication of a cause-and-effect relationship.

Table Contd...

Timeline	Activity
August 2003	The US FDA approves Bayer Corporation's vardenafil Hydrochloride (Levitra) to treat erectile dysfunction.
November 2003	The US FDA approves Lilly Icos' tadalafil (Cialis) to treat erectile dysfunction.
2011	A Federal Judge extends Pfizer's US patent for Viagra, making sure that generic versions of Viagra cannot come to market until 2020.
April 2012	The US FDA approves a new erectile dysfunction drug called avanafil, which will be sold under the brand name of Stendra. Stendra, which is taken as-needed basis 30 minutes before the sexual activity is a product of Vivus, a small pharmaceutical company headquartered in Campbell, California.
2013	A. Cialis of Eli Lilly overtakes Viagra for the first time in global sales. B. Teva settles Viagra patent litigation with Pfizer and enters into an agreement to market generic version of Viagra from December 2017.
2014	Viagra plans ahead and gets ready to face the impending genericization in 2020: A. Introduces a *singles* pack B. Launches a massive DTC campaign C. Goes on line for selling Viagra as a prescription drug, which is first for a Big Pharma company
2015	Mylan settles a patent litigation related to Viagra with Pfizer and gets ready to launch generic Viagra in the US in December 2017.
2017	Pfizer gets Pharmacy (P) approval for its Viagra Connect 50 mg film-coated tablets by MHRA in the United Kingdom in November 2017. Pfizer can market Viagra Connect directly to consumers through pharmacists without prescriptions.

Pfizer Gets Ready for Viagra's Genericization

Competition for Viagra was heating up with new entrants such as Levitra (co-marketed by Bayer and GlaxoSmithKline in the US) and Cialis (Eli Lilly). The Viagra patents too were nearing their expiries in some markets. The drug makers were flooding television, radio, magazines, newspapers, and even the mailboxes with their advertising messages. The drug makers were sponsoring sports like golf and auto racing. Levitra and Cialis had even tried the Super Bowl advertising. They paid more than $4 million each for 60-second commercial spots during the game in February 2012. Finally, Cialis had overtaken Pfizer as the market leader with a world sales of $1.9 billion at the end of 2012. Pfizer had been actively planning to counter competition and protect its market share from the impending generic erosion. Some of the more important moves that Pfizer undertook were:

1. Launching of a generic version of Viagra in New Zealand under a different brand name - Avigra in 2011. Avigra was made available in New Zealand at a competitive price to those men who want to remain on it. Avigra, the second brand of Pfizer's Viagra retails for about half the price of Viagra Classic. The price was more than other generics, but the discount was significant enough to tempt consumers, who are sensitive to price.

2. Pfizer attempted to rethink the typical drug starter pack of three tablets in a box that was almost the industry practice. Instead, it drew inspiration from Z-Pack (5 tablets in a box) and departed the norm. Why this change? The Viagra team recognized the importance of the first experience for all people suffering from ED. They knew that clinically, it might take a few tries for the people to get the full effect of the drug. To ensure that the people with ED should get the full effect with the first starter pack, they increased the number of tablets.

3. Publication of *Voices*, a custom publication service of Viagra for the waiting rooms at doctors offices in the United States to improve awareness and knowledge about the condition ED.

Voices covered important personalities from sports, entertainment, and members of Earth, Wind & Fire - weighing in on the importance of taking charge of their health. *Voices* also attempted to dispel the myths surrounding erectile dysfunction. Men could pick up *Voices* in the doctors' offices, and the other patients would not necessarily recognize that it is a Viagra piece.

4. Introduction of chewable form Viagra in Mexico in 2012 before its patent expiry under the brand name Viagra Jet.

5. Introduction of Viagra in single packs to help men with erectile dysfunction to treat their condition when they need it. Pfizer conducted an online survey of 200 men, and 16 percent of them reported that they were taking Viagra outside the home. The company introduced the single packs to refresh an aging brand making purchasing more convenient.

6. Entering into an agreement with two leading international generic manufacturers, Teva and Mylan in the US for bringing out their respective generic versions by end 2017. Both Teva and Mylan would pay a certain amount as royalty on the sales of their generic versions under the agreement.

7. Selling of Viagra, the prescription drug online in 2012. In a first for the drug industry, Pfizer decided to make Viagra available online. Patients still needed a prescription to buy Viagra online, but they no longer had to face a pharmacist to get the drug. Pfizer offered three free pills with the first order and 30 percent discount on the second order. This bold move blew up the drug industry's distribution model. Pharmaceutical companies do not sell their products directly to patients. Instead, they sell their products in bulk to wholesalers, who then distribute them to pharmacists, hospitals and doctors' offices.

8. Launching of an OTC version of Viagra, in the United Kingdom under the brand name, Viagra Connect.

9. Introduction of a frequent user *Value Card* offering a free seventh prescription from each six, a customer refills.

10. Introduction of mobile texting for Viagra discounts. In what seemed to be the first for a pharmaceutical company, Pfizer's

new TV commercial of 2017 for Viagra encouraged patients to text a keyword from their mobile phones to receive special discounts. The ad opened with the now familiar woman in a dark blue dress, who asked: Guys, want to save 50 percent on a year-long supply of Viagra for ED? A mobile phone close up then takes over the screen with the promotion and text keyword "VSAVE," and she explains in voiceover how to get the discount.

Viagra Connect

Pfizer got a Pharmacy (P) approval in November 2017 to market its 50 mg film-coated sildenafil tablets by Medicines and Healthcare Regulatory Authority (MHRA) in the United Kingdom. These tablets were to be sold under the brand name; Viagra Connect through pharmacists directly to the consumers without a prescription. Pharmacy (P) is an over-the-counter approval where pharmacists can dispense medicines without prescriptions in the UK. Viagra Connect was retailed at £19.99 for a four-tablet pack and £34.99 for eight tablets. The reclassification of Viagra Connect from prescription-only medicine (POM) to pharmacy (P) status increased safe access to sildenafil and ensured that patients got good, accurate advice if it's right for them.

Viagra Connect went on sale in the UK in the third week of April 2018 and is available in pharmacies without prescriptions, unlike standard Viagra medication.

To support the launch of Viagra Connect, Pfizer unveiled extensive training for the product on March 12, 2018. This largest-ever program for pharmacists includes e-learning modules, face-to-face sessions, and regional meetings. Pfizer is providing all the participating pharmacists tips on managing conversations. This is important because pharmacists need to become familiar with the indications and contraindications and how to counsel those seeking sildenafil as conversations may involve teasing out some sensitive information.

Digital training that is available to the participants includes videos, interactive content and print-and-keep resources. The site also includes a Viagra Connect Checklist. Tailored content is also available to pharmacy assistants, who may be the first point of contact for men presenting to the pharmacy with erectile dysfunction symptoms.

The training was free of charge for pharmacists and pharmacy staff including access to 23 regional training events with two places allocated for pharmacy on a first-come-first-serve basis.

The Viagra Connect DTC Campaign

To overturn the stigma surrounding erectile dysfunction and to increase the patient traffic for its new over-the-counter Viagra Connect to the pharmacies in the UK, Pfizer launched a new direct-to-consumer (DTC) campaign. These ads were created by Tony Malcolm, Josh Pearce, and Sean Johnson at Y & R (Young & Rubicam), London. The purpose of this ad campaign is to raise the awareness of erectile dysfunction in the UK and communicate the normality of the condition among men. The copy of ads creatively deliver the messages that erectile dysfunction is a common condition that can be treated without the need for a prescription. There were three ads released, and the copy of each ad is presented below:

Copy of the Sport-focused Ad

4.3 million men in the UK experience erectile problems. That's a lot of men. That's enough men to fill every major British football stadium. In fact, that's more men than people who went to a rugby match last year. That's more men than all the people who go to the gym every day, even. So a lot of men will be glad to know that Viagra Connect is now Available without prescription.

viagraconnect.co.uk   Viagra Connect

Copy of the Travel-Focused Ad

4.3 million men in the UK experience erectile problems. That's a lot of men. That's 49,000 buses worth, in fact. That is more

men there than are cabs in the whole of the UK. That's more men than there are cars in London. More men than people who cycled to work yesterday. More men than people who will use the tube today. More men than all the red buses in the world. More men than there are flights out-of-the UK in a whole year, even. So a lot of men will be glad to know that Viagra Connect is now available without a prescription.

viagraconnect.co.uk   Viagra Connect

Copy of the News-focused Ad

4.3 million men in the UK Experience erectile problems. That's a lot of men. That's more men than there are words in this newspaper. In fact, that's twenty-five times more Men than there are words in the English language. More men than all the words in all the novels of Charles Dickens ever wrote, even. So a lot of Men will be glad to know that Viagra Connect is now Available without prescription.

viagraconnect.co.uk   Viagra Connect

These ads have used very creatively the incredibly large number of 4.3 million to communicate compellingly how common the erectile dysfunction is, and that help is available just for the asking. It was the first phase of the creative campaign, and more ads would follow. A media strategy supported it by Wavemaker, which includes social and content partnerships and public relations (PR) activity by Burson Cohn & Wolfe.

Success Beyond Compare

The success of Viagra cannot be viewed in financial terms alone. It had been a phenomenal success no doubt, but there is more to Viagra's success than meets the eye. Than just sales and profits alone. Viagra did make sales and profits, plenty of them. In fact, Viagra became a darling of the Wall Street. After introducing Viagra in 1998, and Pfizer became the fifth most profitable corporation in the world by 2002. Such was the commercial success of Viagra. However, then, there is more to Viagra.

Lynne Luciano, in her book, *Looking Good: Male Body Image in Modern America*, writes of ED as a circular malady:

> *The more it was talked about, the more of it there was. Something similar had happened with Viagra - while it arrived on the market at the tail end of the 1990s, it eclipsed both Penicillin and the Birth control pill to become the most talked about the drug of the century!*

Viagra, the brand name drug as we know it, may no longer be the market force it once was. However, even then, there is no question that its impact on two decades of conversations about modern sex and de-stigmatization of erectile dysfunction has been incredible.

Finally, what can you say about Viagra and how do you explain its phenomenal success? As Jamie Reidy, an early salesman of Pfizer's game-changing drug, in his book, *The Hard Sell: The evolution of a Viagra salesman says: This isn't a pill. It's a revolution!*

Lessons

The marketing of Viagra offers many valuable lessons for pharmaceutical marketers. Firstly, It provides a blueprint for medicalizing a lifestyle condition - impotence, that was almost considered taboo to discuss in public and was embarrassing to talk even with physicians. Pfizer had changed it all with its marketing, advertising, and public relations strategies. Lisa Stockman of Inventiv health put it succinctly when she said: *"No matter what anybody said or did, Impotence had little chance of being thought of as a medical condition. Erectile Dysfunction did."*

The brand and marketing teams at Pfizer realized that the current perception of impotence could limit the drug's impact, both on the lives of needy patients and the bottom line. The solution was to launch a focused educational effort before the launch of Viagra. The result? The Pfizer's educational effort went down in pharmaceutical marketing history as the first and most effective medicalization campaign.

It was not an easy task. Pfizer had to give the reluctant physicians a reason to have a conversation about the condition. That meant linking erectile dysfunction to the things familiar to physicians and the things they were traditionally concerned about such as diseases like diabetes and cardiac problems. The conversation started something like this: *"Doctor, you should be asking about ED, because it often happens eighteen months before a cardiac event."*

Pfizer followed the same approach even for its media campaigns. The company subtly explained and tried to show the impact of ED on men, regarding emotional well-being and depression, beyond the effect on sex lives.

Secondly, Pfizer showed a way to create a therapeutic category. Impotence was thoroughly stigmatized as both a condition and a word. By recasting impotence as erectile dysfunction, Pfizer was able to dodge the toxic attitudinal predisposition towards the condition.

Thirdly, Pfizer showed the industry how to get the best out of DTCA campaigns for Viagra. Pfizer was not the first to use a celebrity endorsement for its disease awareness campaigns. However, it ushered in the era of the celebrity spokesperson. When the long-term senator, former presidential candidate, and an honored war veteran, Bob Dole appeared in a Viagra commercial in 1998, he revolutionized the way such personalities participated in pharmaceutical campaigns. This had encouraged pharmaceutical companies to aim higher in their pursuit of celebrity endorsers and advocates. Here is a message Bob Dole delivered in a TV commercial that resonated with its target audience: *"It is a little embarrassing to talk about ED, but it's so important to millions of men and their partners that I decided to talk about it publicly."*

Fourth, Viagra's media strategy shows us how to obliterate the media's reluctance to cover embarrassing health-related stories. The media and public relations teams at Pfizer sat down with physicians and scientists and spent much time before the launch. Their counsel mainly helped in underpinning the medical and psychological impact of ED. The media that was once reluctant to do any story on impotence made an about turn to push Viagra into pop culture and the family living room conversation. A record two-billion impressions within a month and 865 million audience impressions within 48 hours of FDA approval of Viagra were recorded as per a report in Medical Media & Marketing article.

Pfizer rallied the entire troops and encouraged everyone charged with the marketing of Viagra to push the creative envelope. The lesson here is how to engage and involve every member of the team in the launch and promotion of new products.

Perhaps, the most important of all lessons is that how Pfizer had created a blue ocean for Viagra in lifestyle drugs by going beyond the boundaries of the pharmaceutical industry at the time. Pharmaceutical marketing practices traditionally revolve around functional and emotional orientation in their product offerings. Pfizer had created a lifestyle enhancement and an emotional orientation by recasting a highly stigmatized condition like impotence as erectile dysfunction. A new category was born. Pfizer created a blue ocean for Viagra. Viagra reigned the blue ocean space it created for itself for almost twenty years and is still managing a leading position if not a leadership position.

Viagra had shown that when companies are willing to challenge the functional-emotional orientation of their industry, they can often create a new market space. A new blue ocean.

(Source: Adapted from articles: 1. Dominic Utton, *Viagra: The rise of erectile dysfunction drug set to be sold over-the-counter*, Express, the house of the Daily and Sunday Express, November 30, 2017; 2. Brittaney Kiefer, *Pfizer tackles erectile dysfunction taboo In a new campaign*, Campaign, April 18, 2018)

Requip's Success Recipe: Brand A Disease, Market A Treatment!

Karl A. Ekborn, a Swedish neurologist, first described a condition, known as Ekborn's Syndrome in the mid-1940s. Sensory symptoms and motor disturbances in the limbs mainly during rest characterize the syndrome. Earlier descriptions of such a condition date back to the 17th century. Thomas Willis, the English anatomist, and physician who lived from 1621 to 1675, first described these symptoms. Restless Legs Syndrome is the new name for the Ekborn syndrome. National Institute of Neurological Disorders and Stroke at NIH (National Institutes of Health) describes restless legs syndrome (RLS) as:

> RLS is a neurological disorder characterized by unpleasant sensations in the legs and an uncontrollable urge to move when at rest to relieve these feelings. The sensations are described as burning, creeping, tugging, or like insects crawling inside the legs. These sensations are known as abnormal (paresthesias) or unpleasant (dysesthesias) in medical literature.

GlaxoSmithKline's (GSK) marketing of Requip offers a classic example of disease branding. Requip (ropinirole) is a drug used for treating Parkinson's Disease. GSK found that the drug is also useful in treating a hitherto little-known condition called Restless Legs Syndrome (RLS). FDA approved Requip for the treatment of RLS in 2005.

Clinicians saw Restless Legs Syndrome (RLS), until a few years ago till GSK started its awareness campaigns, as an unusual, somewhat mysterious condition. It was characterized by a crawling sensation in the legs, often more severe at night, which could be relieved by movement such as walking. It was not a common affliction. Not until GSK got approval from FDA for its Requip in the treatment of RLS. Getting approval for your drug for a lesser known, infrequently occurring condition is one thing and marketing a drug profitably for that condition is quite another.

How do you market your drug, although approved for treating a little-known condition? GSK thought out a clearcut strategy. The strategy of creating a market for this little known, under-diagnosed and under-treated condition called RLS. GSK, the second largest pharmaceutical company at the time in the world made good use of public relations and its marketing muscle to promote awareness among doctors and patients about RLS.

GSK started its awareness campaigns on Restless Legs Syndrome months before FDA's approval in medical journals targeting doctors. On getting the approval for Requip, Glaxo soon issued a press release titled, "New survey reveals common yet under-recognized disorder–restless legs syndrome is keeping Americans awake at night!" The Requip public relations campaign went on to suggest that problems such as insomnia and depression might be symptoms of restless legs syndrome, which tormented as many as one in ten Americans.

After the public awareness campaign and the FDA approval, Requip experienced substantial growth. In the process, the company created a blue ocean that it was expected to own for a long time.

However, GSK's marketing effort and its initial success for Requip in RLS had drawn criticism from various quarters. Critics felt that RLS was a concocted disorder and that the company had resorted to disease mongering to promote the sale of the drug. There was also some criticism that GSKs marketing of RLS had many conflicts of interest such as using patient advocacy groups (PAGs) and key opinion leaders (KOLs) to further its marketing agenda.

The NBC Nightly News aired on January 31, 2007, a story on Restless Legs Syndrome disorder and why GlaxoSmithKline, the world's second-largest pharmaceutical company, had so heavily advertised its drug, Requip (Ropinirole hydrochloride) for this disorder on the news channel. Some critics viewed this as a mere publicity stunt. The RLS disorder, which was perceived as an uncommon condition, soon became a household name after GSK started its marketing effort to increase public awareness.

GSK also started direct-to-consumer advertising (DTCA) campaigns after the FDA's approval of Requip for RLS. Initial ads were brand awareness advertisements and unbranded campaigns. These were later followed up with branded ads.

GSK also used the key opinion leaders (KOLs) such as sleep specialists to raise awareness about RLS and its scope for Requip among general practitioners (GPs). The company's overall marketing efforts in raising awareness through multiple channels got a lot of media attention creating publicity for the disorder (RLS) as well as the drug (Requip).

The Wall Street Journal commented on the overall marketing efforts and success of Requip in 2006 when it stated:

> Behind Requip's sales boom is Glaxo's marketing machine, which has persuaded many consumers and physicians to accept restless legs syndrome or RLS, as a real condition warranting treatment.

Apart from criticism, GSK's marketing efforts also got praise from some quarters such as marketing experts, doctors, and patient advocacy groups. They were particularly appreciative of the unbranded campaigns that strove to increase awareness about the disease. Some doctors and patient advocates praised GSK for raising the profile of the disorder, which was under-diagnosed and under-treated.

How did restless legs and Reequip happen? GlaxoSmithKline believed that Requip held much promise in the treatment of restless legs syndrome. It hit upon the idea of marketing Requip for RLS after observing that some doctors were prescribing the drug off-label to treat this condition, RLS. On March 31, 2003, GSK started the RLS promotion with press releases about a research paper that was presented at the 55th American Academy of Neurology (AAN) meetings at Honolulu, which described the early results of using ropinirole for the treatment of RLS. FDA approval and marketing blitz followed approval. GSK had put all its marketing might behind Requip in RLS through multichannel marketing involving personal selling, CMEs by KOLs and thought leaders, unbranded and branded DTC campaigns targeting all key stakeholders such as doctors, patients, and payers.

What are the results of all this marketing effort behind Requip? The company observed that the number of patients treated for RLS grew from an estimated 3,80,000 in 2006 to 2.2 million in 2015. The market size, too for this little-known condition or disorder in 2005 had increased from a few million dollars to the US $1.7 billion by 2015.

GSKs response to all the negative criticism such as disease mongering, and conflict of interest about its marketing of Requip was best summed up by David Stout, Head of Pharmaceuticals, GlaxoSmithKline Plc, when he said:

You need to talk to the patients. Things like restless legs syndrome can ruin people 's lives. It is easy to trivialize things when you don't have them. If people did not want the treatment, they would not seek them.

With GlaxoSmithKline's marketing might and a firm conviction of its effectiveness behind it, Requip literally ran on its Restless Legs (syndrome)!

(Source: 1. Carl Elliott, *White coat and black hat*, Beacon Press, 2010; 2. *GlaxoSmithKline's marketing strategy for Requip: A case study in product life cycle management*, ICMR: 3. Jeanne Whalen, *How Glaxo marketed a malady to sell a drug*, The Wall Street Journal, October 25, 2006)

Mankind Pharma: Changing the Rules of the Game!

For a long time, the game of pharmaceutical business has been running on a rulebook primarily filled with unwritten rules. Rules such as:

1. The pyramidical structure of the business comprises factors such as the type of therapy, doctor specialization, drug pricing, with leading companies at the top and majority of the firms competing fiercely in the middle.
2. Pareto's principle is at work in pharmaceutical marketing too, with almost all the companies competing for a share of the mind of the top twenty percent of the doctors, who are specialists and are practicing in metros and tier-1 cities.
3. Specialty focus regarding therapy area as well physician specialty are crucial for success.
4. There is value at the top of the pyramid.

Changing the Rules of the Game!

The pharmaceutical industry in India too, has been governed by these somewhat unwritten rules. At least till Mankind Pharma started its operations. Ramesh Juneja, the founder of Mankind Pharma and his brother Rajeev Juneja, who has been heading the marketing operations since its inception in 1986, changed the rules of the game unknowingly. They knew that to start a pharmaceutical company and compete with established players in metro cities and Tier One cities would be next to impossible. They would not even get a second glance from the specialists and super specialists. They also knew from their experience as medical representatives and first-line sales managers in the pharmaceutical industry that the large and mid-size pharmaceutical companies focused their entire attention on top prescribers in metro cities and Tier One cities. Remember the Pareto principle (20 percent of your customers account for 80 percent of your market) and neglected general practitioners and doctors in small towns.

The Juneja brothers asked a seemingly innocent question. Everyone is thinking that there is value only at the top of the pyramid and focusing there. It is very crowded, and it is impossible to compete in that space for a start-up company. What if there is value at the bottom of the pyramid? Can we unlock it? It is eminently possible to compete in this rather 'no-competition zone'. They focused their total attention on the so far un-served, and under-served market of general practitioners and all other doctors. The doctors welcomed Mankind Pharma with open arms and rewarded them with their prescriptions making the company the Number one regarding the number of prescriptions written in India in 2014 as per IMS Health Report.

Rapid Growth

Coming into existence in 1986, Mankind Pharma became a corporation in 1991. The company has been highly-customer centric since its inception. The company's real growth phase started in 1995. For the next ten years or more, the company has been growing at a break-neck speed of 30 percent per year as compared to the industry's 12 percent. How did Mankind Pharma achieve this extraordinary success? What is its secret sauce? Here it is in the words of Rajeev Juneja himself when he spoke to the press on different occasions:

You become creative when there is scarcity. When you have less money, no experience, no name, no background, it makes sense to tap doctors in small towns and villages. The top doctors in the metros would not have given us a second chance. The idea is to create a presence in small towns and villages and then work our way up to cities.

The Company's Secret Sauce!

The essence or the secret sauce of Mankind's strategy has been:

A. To unlock the value at the bottom of the period. The company told its medical representatives to tap as many doctors as possible and generate prescriptions. Mankind has the most extensive physician coverage in the Indian pharmaceutical industry.

B. To market their products at affordable prices. Mankind Pharma priced its products to patients at prices that are lower by 40 - 60 percent as compared to the competition. The company followed Walmart's business model in marketing its products. Walmart strives to consistently lower purchasing and operating costs and then pass those savings to consumers. Like Walmart, Mankind strives to keep its overheads and all other manufacturing and operating costs low and offers the savings to patients. The company follows a penetrative pricing strategy. Mankind bombarded the Indian pharmaceutical market with low priced drugs – up to 50 percent cheaper than prevailing prices, which made competition sit up and take notice of this new entrant. That is why and how the company can deliver quality products at affordable prices.

C. The company has also entered the OTC (Over-the-counter) drugs and invested over Rs. 350-crore on advertising over a period of six years to tap the OTC market and to improve brand recognition. The company today has become well known with successful brands such as Manforce (Condoms), Unwanted 72 (Emergency contraceptives), and Unwanted (Home Pregnancy kits). OTC drugs account for about 8 percent of Mankind's total sales.

The strategy is working. Mankind today has become a behemoth of a company with its revenues of around Rs. 5,000-crore and a total employee strength of about 14,000. What is noteworthy of

Mankind's achievement is the fact that its entire growth has been organic except for two acquisitions. The company acquired Magnet Labs in 2007 to enter the CNS (Central Nervous System) disorders and three years later in 2010, acquired Longifene, a UCB brand for improving appetitive in children.

What Next?

The critical question is can Mankind continue its growth spurt? Can the company maintain the high growth rate that it has been used to for such a long time? Mankind seems to be determined to grow faster than the fastest competitor and grab market share to reach the top in the coming years. The company is not complacent and does not take itself for granted. The company recognizes and realizes the challenges ahead and crafted a strategy accordingly. What brought Mankind up to here will not take the company to where it wants to go. What is needed is changing of the gears. The game changer needs a new game plan. The essential elements or growth drivers of Mankind's new game plan are:

1. Increase the company's presence in chronic therapy segment. Chronic therapy segment is growing at a higher rate of 14 percent than acute therapies which are growing at 9.6 percent. Magnet Mankind is already making rapid strides in the segment.

2. Push OTC segment further. It has already started contributing to the profitability of the company.

3. The domestic market alone cannot provide the opportunities to grow at the current rate. Expanding into the international markets and increasing exports is vital to continue the company's frenetic pace that has become a habit. The company plans to enter the global markets in a phased and focused manner. To focus on South East Asia, Africa, CIS, and Latin America in the first phase and then graduate to the developed markets. The company plans to sell certain APIs (active pharmaceutical ingredients) in the developed markets such as the US.

4. Even in export markets, Mankind will follow its winning strategy of unlocking the value at the bottom of the pyramid. The company will target smaller towns and cities in the export markets too and offer differentiated products and not me-too products, as most of these export markets are already crowded with me-too products.

5. Move into drugs for life-threatening diseases such as cancer. The company is planning to enter the oncology segment with a penetrative pricing strategy. Mankind intends to price its oncology drugs too at 40 - 60 percent cheaper than its competitors. The strategy is to approach the oncology segment with Mankind prices.

6. Foray into diagnostic space, which is growing rapidly with an investment of Rs. 305-crore over a period of four years. Pathkind is the name of the proposed diagnostic arm of the company's business. Pathkind aims to reach out to the masses in tier 2 and tier 3 cities in India to provide easily accessible diagnostic services at affordable prices. The company is planning to open 12 large labs, 20 rapid response labs and 150 collection centers in U. P. and Uttarakhand states of India in the first year. The company's planning to go pan India with 1300 collection centers and130 labs in the next five years.

In its second phase of rapid growth strategy, Mankind is banking on higher growth from international markets. In fact, that is what has happened to all successful Indian Pharma majors ever since India became a signatory to GATT and a member of WTO. All the leading Indian pharmaceutical companies have started getting a significant share of their revenues from international markets. Because India accounts currently for about 5 - 6 percent of the total world Pharma market and there is a limit to what a company can exploit if it chooses to compete only in the domestic market.

Mankind is working on building the required competencies such as international marketing, formulation development and competing in metro cities and tier-one cities. The company's impeccable track record since its inception indicates that there is every reason to believe that Mankind might as well change the rules of the game for the second time around!

(Source: Shabana Hussain, *Mankind Pharma: Formulating strategy to enter the big league*, www.forbes.com, May 8, 2014)

The Pricing Strategies

Price and Pharma Marketing Mix

In a highly regulated industry like pharmaceuticals in India, can the price be considered an element of the marketing mix? When the government fixes the prices, conversion norms, packaging norms for all essential drugs and formulations, does the pharmaceutical marketer have an option? Is there a choice, really speaking?

Of course, there is a choice, however, restricted it may be. Price may not be the most critical variable in the marketing mix of the pharmaceutical industry in India. However, it is important enough. One has to make the most of all the options available. One has to exploit the residual degrees of freedom to the optimum. A brief discussion of pricing concepts, objectives and strategy would be helpful in this regard.

Pricing is a strategic decision. Many factors influence the decision regarding what pricing strategy to use and when to use it. Some of these are:

1. Price sensitivity of different market segments
2. Market position of product and the firm (image, market share and so on)
3. State of the life cycle the product is in
4. Economies of scale in production
5. Channels of distribution
6. Pricing moves by the competition
7. The composition of the product-line and product-mix of the firm (number of product packs in controlled categories I and II and the decontrolled categories. This categorization of controlled and decontrolled categories is specific to the Indian pharmaceutical market)

Understanding these factors that influence pricing decisions is essential for the pharmaceutical marketer, for it would enable him to formulate realistic and profitable pricing strategies for his products.

Pricing Objectives

You must have clearly defined objectives for price setting. The top management sets pricing objectives typically. Pricing objectives usually revolve around and are related to market share, return on investment, profit, price stability. Since prices of pharmaceuticals are primarily regulated and controlled, the scope of pricing objectives is somewhat restricted. Improving the efficiency of operations both in manufacturing and marketing, therefore, assumes greater importance than ever before. Adequate return is what everyone talks about while on the subject of pricing. What is a fair return? How much is enough? That's difficult to say. It depends. It depends on many factors like economies of scale, cost leadership, etc. Profit is what is left over after meeting all the costs and expenditure. That is why it is called the bottom line. All pricing objectives have one thing in common. A sound, healthy bottom line. Some of the critical goals of pricing are:

1. Maximization of profit. Specific objectives for short term and long term. Short-term objectives should not jeopardize the long-term goals.
2. Sustained growth over an extended period.
3. Should obtain a predetermined rate of return over an extended period.
4. Achieving market leadership.
5. Should allow the firm to be ahead of the competition regarding innovation.
6. To increase market share.
7. Meeting competitive price levels.
8. To achieve a higher degree of market penetration.
9. To recover the investment faster.
10. Minimizing risks.

Pricing Decisions

Usually, there are two situations around which, almost all pricing decisions revolve. They are:

A. Setting the price for the first time, as when you launch a new product, a new pack, or new dosage form. In case the new product falls into the controlled Categories of I and II, the choice of pricing is restricted to the extent of specified (Maximum Allowable Post Manufacturing Expenses) MAPE, i.e., to pricing it at the uppermost limit of MAPE or below. In case a leader or ceiling price exists for that particular product, the choice is once again limited to whether to price it at par with the leader or ceiling price or below that, to be more competitive. If the proposed new product belongs to the decontrolled category, the choice of pricing is relatively broader. The government, however, can bring any product into the controlled categories any time it chooses to.

B. The second situation for price setting involves the existing products. Changing circumstances necessitate a price change for some of the current products. For example, the government can bring the products hitherto failing in the decontrolled category into a controlled category. Another example is that you are likely to be forced to bring down your prices when your main competitors lower their prices considerably.

Bases for Pricing

There are four commonly used bases for approaches towards pricing a product. They are:

1. Cost based pricing
2. Demand-based pricing
3. Competition based pricing
4. Market-based pricing

Cost-based Pricing

Cost-based pricing is an accountant's approach. As the name implies, it is the total cost of the product, plus an allocation for overheads plus a predetermined percentage to provide for an adequate return (profit margin) that determine the cost-based pricing. The Toal of all these gives you the selling price. It is very much like the pricing formula suggested in DPCO. In addition, DPCO fixed the cost norms (conversion and packaging norms) and MAPE (maximum allowable post-manufacturing expenditure) for all formulations and bulk drugs belonging to Categories I and II.

The primary advantage of cost-based pricing is that it can help to indicate the minimum price levels. The disadvantages of cost-based pricing are that it:

A. Does not take into account the fluctuations in input costs as a particular level of demand and production determine the cost-based pricing. It has been the main disadvantage with the DPCO, which does not take into account the escalation of input costs.

B. Ignores the market factors like demand and competitors' actions. That is why the pharmaceutical manufacturers stopped voluntary price reductions after DPCO 1969. The formula for pricing suggested as per DPCO 1969 was a cost-based approach with an added restriction – predetermined conversion and packaging norms.

C. May lead to wrong pricing decision as overhead cost allocation based pricing can be misleading.

Demand-based Pricing

It is an economist's approach towards pricing. The economist's theory of pricing and elasticity of demand states that:

A. Demand will fall as price increases

B. Demand will rise as price decreases

This approach to pricing, therefore, takes into account the likely effect that different prices may have on the demand for a product. Under this method, you are required to calculate the break-even points at different selling prices and different volume forecasts. After evaluating the impact of price on volume, you try to arrive at the most profitable price volume ratio. To arrive at this, you must be able to forecast with a reasonable degree of accuracy the number of units of a given product you could sell at different price levels.

One significant advantage of market demand-based pricing is that it takes the market realities into account while pricing a product. This method is, therefore, useful in pricing products profitably in a market that is price sensitive and demand elastic.

Since pharmaceuticals in general and ethical drugs, in particular, are not price-sensitive this may not be a very appropriate approach for the pharmaceutical marketer.

Competition-based Pricing

In so far as the pharmaceutical industry is concerned, competition-based pricing is perhaps the most commonly used method. The options that are available to the marketer are:

A. You can set prices can above competitors'
B. You can set prices can at par with competitors'
C. You can set prices can below competitors'

It is important to estimate your competitors' costs when considering their prices for formulating your pricing strategy. Determining the costs of competitors is relatively easy in the Indian pharmaceutical industry since The Drug Price Control Order (DPCO) fixes the norms for conversion and packaging. They are the upper limits, and it is possible that some of your competitors may have achieved greater efficiency levels, incurring less cost than the prescribed norms. It is, therefore, more important to know the real costs of the competitors and whether they have achieved cost leadership. For example, if a manufacturer of a formulation happens to be one of the largest manufacturers of the bulk drug used in that formulation this a distinct advantage.

Price Comparison

In the Pharmaceutical industry, price comparison could be on the unit basis, the daily cost of therapy or the total cost of the treatment. You can obtain the prices of competitors from published sources like the Indian Pharmaceutical Guide, price lists of respective companies, MIMS, IMS or AWACS Pharma Track reports among others. You have to analyze the prices at all the four levels, namely, consumer (maximum retail price), the retailer (price to the retailer), wholesaler and the special hospital price, so that you can have a clear idea regarding trade margins, discounts, given by various competitors.

Market-based Pricing

Market-based pricing deals with the judgmental or subjective elements or pricing. The judgments, of course, will have to be based on an analysis of specific facts. This basis of pricing is judgmental in the sense that it deals with the perceptions of customers regarding the value satisfaction, or the bundle of benefits that the product might offer. The key word is perception, and the critical factor is the perceived value. This perceived value could be a result of:

- ▸ Performance of the product as experienced by customers and consumers
- ▸ Reputation and image of the firm
- ▸ Quality of service delivered

An accurate assessment of a market's perception of your product is crucial for success in market-based pricing. Market research is an essential and invaluable tool for assessing the perceived value of your product by the market. It also helps you avoid the pitfalls of overpricing and underpricing.

Overpricing may be because you have taken for granted your perception a high value (of your product), instead of the market's perception. Perceived value by definition is a qualitative judgment made by the consumer regarding your product vis-a-vis competition, based on his experiences.

Underpricing is the result of underestimating the real value of your product of charging less than you could.

Pricing Strategies

What is the right pricing strategy for a product? Admittedly, there is no formula for arriving at a single pricing strategy that suits all products and all markets. The choice of a right or ideal pricing strategy depends on many factors like the objectives, the type of product and its value perceptions, the market segment it belongs to and the extent of competition. The three commonly used pricing strategies are:

1. Skim the Cream Strategy

The skim-the-cream strategy aims at the top end of the demand curve. It sets the price at the top of the acceptable price range. You can use the skimming strategy:

▸ On a new product during the introductory and early part of the product lifecycle to recover the high R&D costs faster. Since it is easier to reduce prices if a need arises than to increase prices, you use the skimming strategy. You are erring on the right side and playing safe when you use a skimming strategy. The disadvantages of the skimming strategy are that:

▸ It increases vulnerability since it attracts competition

▸ The higher price may result in low unit sales, which may not suit the plant output and may result in underutilization of capacities

2. Penetration Strategy

As the name suggests, a penetration pricing strategy aims at greater and deeper market penetration by pricing at the lower end of the spectrum. Thus penetration pricing strategy takes a diametrically opposite approach to the skimming strategy. This strategy can be profitable only when the sales volumes are large. Penetration strategy is helpful in the growth and maturity phases of the product lifecycle.

Furthermore, this is a highly competitive strategy as it preempts competition. You can also use it as an entry barrier. Penetration strategy can help build the sales of a product even in the long-term by widening the customer base due to lower prices.

Penetration strategy is not without disadvantages. The first and foremost disadvantage is that the payback period is more extended for a new product. It is due to low-profit margin. Secondly, if the product has a very short life cycle, this pricing strategy could be disastrous. Thirdly, it is often tough to increase prices substantially, if the initial price set is very low. The psychological disadvantages that follow such revision can be very difficult to overcome.

3. Marginal Cost Pricing Strategy

Simply stated, marginal cost is the cost of producing one more unit. The cost of producing one more unit implies that the cost of producing the extra unit consists only of the variable costs since current sales volumes already covered fixed costs. It should be adequate even if you make a small profit on the additional sales because this small profit would not have been there had you not obtained the extra business. By getting an additional order at a small profit, you are improving your capacity utilization, which would have been otherwise idle. That is why many companies use the marginal costing approach towards pricing, particularly for highly competitive business situations like large institutional tenders, where a lower price is always an advantage. The principal use of marginal cost-based pricing, therefore, is not as a pricing tool but to answer the question - should you accept this order?

This type of pricing strategy is also used often where production capacities are high, and high volumes of sales are essential to keep the fixed costs low and where the demand is price elastic.

Pricing Management

Pricing management in the pharmaceutical industry involves decisions related to setting prices for new products, implementing price changes according to the changes in governmental policies (DPCO amendments), monitoring the costs of company's own products as well as those of major competitors, analyzing prices of competitors, quantity discounts, free goods and bonus offers , etc.

Bonus offers or free goods on selected products, mainly seasonal products like cough and cold preparations, antidiarrhoeals among others, are a common practice in the Indian pharmaceutical market. Introductory bonus offers on new products too is a common practice to achieve adequate stocking at the retail level before the company commences promotion to doctors.

Many companies, who have piled up inventories and need a sales spurt to liquidate them, offer Bonus offers. Pharmaceutical marketers also use bonus offers frequently as sales promotional tools to boost their sales of OTC (over the counter) drug brands, since a retail chemist can help push the sales of non-prescription drugs.

What should be the bonus offer? How many free issues on the purchase of how many units of a given product? It has been the practice in the pharmaceutical industry to provide free units of a product under a bonus offer, rather than a percentage discount. The reasons are obvious and even elementary. One is that it costs less for the manufacturer to give free units, whereas the monetary value for the retailer is retained and not reduced. Secondly, the manufacturer would be reducing his inventories at a faster rate. Thirdly, the firm can exert a greater stock pressure at the retail level.

Regarding the number of free issues to be given for a product on bonus offer, it depends on factors like:

- The Image and reputation of your product and the firm
- The extent of competition and their likely moves
- The price of your product
- The marketing objectives of your product
- The nature of the market in which your product is competing, for example, whether its demand is price elastic?

Customers' Reactions to Price Changes

It is essential to understand the likely reactions of your customers towards price changes. Some of the critical responses of customers towards the price changes in general are:

A. When you reduce the price, they may think that you are downgrading the product or even deleting it subsequently, if they perceive your product as a premium product

B. Conversely, if you increase the price, they may think that you are improving the product. It probably explains the reason why there seem to be never-ending claims such as New-Improved Formula, Improved Flavor, and Taste and so on. The discerning observer will notice an inevitable price increase every time a company makes such a label claim. It is not to say that these claims are not justified or untrue, the primary purpose of these claims is to desensitize customers price towards price increases.

In case of a price increase, a retailer may reduce his stock holding, delay his payments, or may substitute other brands in case of OTC products. More often than not, he may stock up more before the effective price increase.

An understanding of the psychological aspects of pricing will be helpful for the marketer in planning and managing pricing strategies effectively.

Price Communicates!

You can use price as a very useful marketing communication tool. In its purest form, price communicates the exchange value of a particular product. Price can be, however, used to signal status, quality, low purchase risk, and other ideas. Research indicates that consumers are inclined to use price as a cue to quality in evaluating brands. This tendency to equate price with quality is unusually high, where a perceptible difference in quality between bands exists. In ethical drugs, consumers believe that the higher price reflects hidden attributes in the brand.

In the case of new products that are less familiar to consumers, price becomes a powerful cue in evaluating the quality of a brand. In other words, the consumer is left with little or no choice regarding attributes to assess an unknown or unfamiliar brand. There are no established brands or even the companies in a given product category. How does he go about evaluating a brand before deciding to purchase or not? The price here becomes a powerful cue to quality.

In case of new products, entirely new products, markets can use price as a communications cue for their products since these new products have no traditional cost and therefore are likely to be assessed by the consumers mainly by their initial prices.

Marketers quite often use a skimming strategy to price their new products. We have already discussed that skimming refers to both strategy of setting a high price to catch the upper portion of the demand curve and its disadvantages. By reinforcing the price as a communications cue of the product's quality, and by careful and creative use of the elements of its marketing mix like the pack, the product itself and its promotion, the firm can further strengthen the consumer's beliefs about its quality. Here is a case where a large multinational pharmaceutical company has used price and reinforced it as a reliable communications cue, both in international and Indian markets, to emerge victorious in the global anti-ulcer market.

How Glaxo Won the Anti-Ulcer Market!

Glaxo (GSK now), the British pharmaceutical giant, had developed ranitidine and launched it under the brand name Zantac in many countries. SKF's (GSK now) Tagamet was reigning supreme in the anti-ulcer market with an annual sales of over US $ 950-million and was aiming to become the first-ever prescription drug to cross the US$ 1-billion. However, Zantac of Glaxo shattered all those dreams for it was Zantac, which became the first-ever prescription drug to pass the US $ 1-billion mark.

How did Glaxo win with Zantac? Glaxo obtained a higher price for Zantac compared with Tagamet of SKF, which was the first of H2 antagonists and the market leader (skimming strategy to recover the high R&D investment faster). To reinforce the communications cue of quality and superiority that the relatively high price of Zantac offered, Glaxo launched a prestige campaign and differentiated their anti-ulcer drug Zantac and positioned it as a superior product – in fact, a Super Tagamet in the doctors' minds.

In India too, Glaxo followed the skimming strategy for their Zinetec brand of ranitidine, when they launched it in 1986. The company priced it very high, almost one hundred percent above the prices of many a competitor.

The company very aggressively pursued a promotional strategy aimed at desensitizing the customers to the high price and reinforcing the quality cues that the high price offered. These included seminars, lecture sessions for doctors in class I towns and metro-cities, by eminent gastroenterologists from all over the world, persuasion by a team of highly proficient and well trained medical representatives, samples, gifts, an attractive premium looking pack and a differentiated product in the form of a specially coated tablet (all other formulations were plain tablets). Consequently, Glaxo achieved brand leadership for Zinetec in the very first year of its introduction.

The company had to drastically reduce the price of Zinetec consequent to the DPCO 1987, to almost half of its introductory price. The company followed a penetration strategy (it had virtually no choice) and made the most of it, by making customers perceive it as enhanced value for their money.

The reduction in price, however, did not affect the quality image of the product since the doctors and dealers are aware that the price reduction was not voluntary but a result of a government order (DPCO 1987).

Glaxo, by following a skimming strategy for their Zinetec in India, not only recovered the development costs faster but could also afford the heavy promotional expenditure in establishing it as a market leader. When the company was forced to reduce the price of Zinetec, Glaxo valiantly pursued an aggressive market growth strategy, thereby increasing its sales volume considerably. The result was a formidable leadership position in the Indian anti-ulcer market with over 20 percent market share, growing at an impressive 18 percent (1988).

Mankind Pharma Storms into Indian Pharmaceutical Market with its Penetrative Pricing!

When the entire pharmaceutical industry in India is complaining of drug price control, Mankind Pharma, like a true contrarian followed a penetrative pricing strategy. Penetrative pricing strategy is a marketing strategy used by businesses the world over to attract customers to a new product or service. However, to use it as a strategy for the whole company's pricing policy or philosophy is not seen in the pharmaceutical industry. In the retail business, Walmart and Costco, the supermarket giants in the US followed the policy of penetrative pricing and achieved the leadership position. No pharmaceutical company has used a penetrative pricing strategy across the board. What is Mankind's pricing strategy? To offer the patients (consumers) all their products at prices that are lower by 40 to 60 percent lower than the major players in the industry.

The result? Mankind Pharma today has reached the top of the pharmaceutical league table in India with the maximum number of prescriptions to its credit. The company currently occupies the fifth position in terms of sales value, in the Indian pharmaceutical industry. An unprecedented achievement indeed!

Psychological Effects of Pricing

There is more to the effects of price on demand than the price-demand relationships, or price-quality connotations. There are many observable yet unsatisfactorily explained, if not inexplicable phenomenon of price on demand. In fact, some of them are diametrically opposite to the traditional explanations or views of the economists. They are:

Quantum Effect in Pricing

It is an observable fact that increases in prices up to some point do not result in a loss of sales volume but increases beyond that point produce a sharp decline in sales. This particular point at which the rapid drop in sales occurs is called the quantum point. Consumers do not show any resistance or sensitivity to prices up to the quantum point but appear to be hypersensitive to even moderate increases in prices beyond the quantum point. Bata, the leading shoemaker in India, is an excellent example of this quantum effect in pricing. The almost proverbial Bata prices are typically at the right side of the quantum point.

For example, you can price a new antibiotic capsule (assuming that it is in the decontrolled category) at Rs. 4.65, 4.75, 4.80 and in fact, up to Rs. 4.95 without any drop in sales. However, a price of Rs. 5.05 could lead to a sharp decline in sales volume. In this case Rs. 5 is the quantum point.

Price Perception in Reverse Direction

As the name implies, consumer perceptions regarding the price work sometimes in a reverse direction. In other words, as consumers perceive lower prices higher than the higher prices. For instance, consumers may view a price of Rs. 4.95 as Lower than a price of Rs. 4.45 for a 10-gram jar of pain-relieving ointment. How does this happen? You can explain this phenomenon regarding reference points. Round figures serve as reference points and tell the consumer that the price of Rs. 4.95 is five paise less than Rs. 5 and the price of Rs. 4.45 is 45 paise more than Rs. 4. Thus the higher price may appear lower and lower price higher because of their relationship to their reference points.

Just Price Standard

Another observable phenomenon, which you cannot explain satisfactorily is the *just price* standard. Consumers seem to develop a *just price* in their minds, which serves as a *just price* standard for evaluating brands. Prices falling within this *just price* standard are acceptable to consumers. If you price your product above this fair price standard, it will result in low sales. Prices below this standard are likely to reflect poor quality.

Cost Price Standard

Knowledgeable consumers often think that they can judge a manufacturer's cost of a product and develop a fair price estimate based on their judgment of the manufacturer's cost plus a reasonable profit. It is useful in case of industrial buyers more often.

Understanding the psychological effects of pricing will help the marketer in gaining insight into all aspects of pricing. These, in turn, will enable him to formulate strategies to desensitize the consumer to price and to find ways to overcome the price barrier.

Desensitizing the Consumer to Price

Overcoming the price barrier or desensitizing the consumer to price requires some basic understanding of consumer behavior and also of the underlying factors that are responsible for increasing this sensitivity to price. It is possible to identify the desensitizing factors once you understand the character of this sensitivity to price changes.

Remember that sensitivity to price changes is greater where:

- There is no variance in point of sale effectiveness
- Service after the sale is not important
- Personal selling is not involved

- There is little or no product differentiation
- Unit price is high

In the pharmaceutical industry sensitivity to price changes is relatively low because the products are differentiated. Furthermore, personal selling is a significant differential and a medical representative, who is a more effective persuader, can often overcome the difference in price by convincing the doctor about the value for money that his product offers as compared to others.

The image of the company is another differential, though it is not as significant a differentiator as personal selling is, in the pharmaceutical industry. Multinationals seem to have a better image as producers of better quality products compared to their Indian counterparts. It may be a result of the halo effect of the significant R&D effort of multinationals on their Indian subsidiaries. The Indian sector, too, has been asserting its strong presence in this area during recent years. It is evident from the spectacular progress made by some Indian companies like Sun Pharma, Cadila, Ranbaxy (Sun Pharma now), Cipla, Torrent among others.

The significant action implications for the pharmaceutical marketer in understanding the sensitivity of customers and consumers to price changes are:

A. To communicate the quality image of the company both in words and deeds.

B. To strengthen the personal selling effort by giving better training inputs and developing the sales force to become more competent and more persuasive.

C. To create perceptible product differentiation, not merely by adopting a cosmetic change, but by instituting a systematic product development process.

Predatory Pricing: An Emerging Trend

Predatory pricing is the illegal activity of setting prices to eliminate competition and create a monopoly situation. Predatory pricing is also called undercutting. Usually, firms that are practicing predatory pricing strategy keep their prices very low to make it unattractive for competitors. However, there seems to be a new type of predatory pricing that is rearing its ugly head. It is predatory pricing in a reverse direction. Here the pricing strategy followed is to keep the prices very high, in fact even to socially unacceptable levels and yet keep competition at bay. When you can price your product so high, that must be attracting more competition, isn't it? That is a logical question. But, then the modus operandi or the business model of these modern pharmaceutical predators on the prowl beats the logic. Their business model looks somewhat like this:

A. *Source a Sole-Source Drug:* Acquire a drug that had come off patent and yet remained a single source drug, which means that there is no imminent competition.

B. *Ensure that it is a Gold Standard:* Check that the single-source drug that you acquired or about to acquire is considered a gold standard for the condition it treats. If it is a gold standard treatment, the physicians will continue to prescribe it even if the price is increased. The perceived efficacy standard and the essential nature of the drug determines the level of price increase that it can absorb.

C. *Select a Drug that has a Smaller Market:* A smaller market means that it is relatively unattractive for competitors to enter. However, ensure that the drug has smaller, dependent patient populations, who are too small to organize an opposition to the price hike.

D. *Closed Distribution:* Make sure when you acquire the drug that meets all these criteria, that it has a restricted distribution system and not readily available from any other sources. When the drug is not available through the usual channels, it creates another entry barrier for competition.

Once you acquire a drug that meets all the criteria mentioned above, the firm is ready to practice its predatory pricing strategy, which is in reverse direction. The predatory pricing is pricing the product or service keeping it so low that it becomes an entry barrier to competition. The new predatory pricing is to create entry barriers into their carefully chosen markets and then hike prices exorbitantly to maximize profitability. Consider the following cases for example:

Predatory Pricing in Pharmaceutical Industry

Daraprim (pyrimethamine) was developed in the 1950s to treat toxoplasmosis, a relatively common parasitic infection. Turing Pharmaceuticals acquired the drug in the US from Impax Laboratories in August 2015 and immediately raised the price from $13.50 a to $750 for a single pill. That is predatory pricing for you, and it made the CEO, Martin Shekril, the most hated man in America. Compare for example the price of a single tablet of Pyrimethamine in India, which is between $0.06 and $0.10.

While the price hike of Daraprim acquired notoriety because of its CEO and the fraudulent methods that landed him in prison, there are some other companies, which followed similar predatory pricing strategies, if you can call them strategies. Yes, predatory pricing seems to have become a new strategy. It is all about acquiring old, neglected drugs, often for rare diseases and turning them into costly specialty drugs. It is this trend that is disturbing. Consider these examples of predatory pricing:

1. Valeant Pharmaceuticals acquired in 2014, Isupril (isoproterenol) and Nitropress (nitroprusside sodium) both of which are used to treat heart-related ailments from Marathon Pharmaceuticals. Valeant raised the price of Isupril by 525 percent and the price of Nitropress by 212 percent.

2. Rodelis Therapeutics acquired cycloserine, a drug used in the treatment of drug-resistant tuberculosis and raised it by 2,100 percent. Later, after learning about the price hike as well as the company's failure to provide services to patients that would

help them stay on the drug, Purdue Research Foundation, who sold the drug to Rodelis asked the company to return the cycloserine rights.

3. Horizon Pharmaceuticals acquired Vimovo (esomeprazole and naproxen Sodium), pain medication and raised the price by 527 percent.

The concern here is that there are some predator marketers like Martin Shekril scouring for drugs like Daraprim that don't have active generic rivals (as the market for such drugs is too small for a generic drug company to view it as profitable). It is not a question of merely acquiring a drug and raising its price after acquiring the drug. Instead, the issue is that these drug companies are strategically searching for drugs that can sustain massive price increases. It is a nefarious motivation and there lies the moral fault.

(Adapted from Fritz Alhoff's article, *Daraprim and Predatory Pricing: Martin Shkreli's 5000% Hike* on Law and Biosciences Blog, Stanford Law Schools (SLS), Blogs, Stanford Law School)

Awareness Campaigns, Lobbying, Legislation, Competitors' Stumbles and Exorbitant Price Hikes Make A Blockbuster!

Can you believe that a company which did not know whether to keep a product that it acquired ended up taking it in-house, build a multi-pronged marketing strategy to market and made it a blockbuster, a go-to product for patients with severe allergies? Well, the company is Mylan, and the product is their auto-injector device, EpiPen. Here is how it all happened.

Epinephrine (also known as adrenaline) is a hormone that the body produces to increase blood flow to the muscles in its response to fight or flight. Jockichi Takamine, a Japanese chemist, was one of the first people to discover and isolate epinephrine. Soon after the discovery, scientists figured out a way to produce it in large enough quantities and how to use it in different medical settings. In 1906, scientists synthesized epinephrine for the first time. Doctors continued to investigate how adrenaline worked and used it in for over a hundred years now. It has been studied extensively with over 12,000 studies referencing it. It has heralded many areas of emergency medication. Epinephrine is used in hospitals across the world and is on the World Health Organization's (WHOs) essential medicines list. It only costs a few dollars a vial in the developed world and much less in the developing world.

In the 1970s, Sheldon Kaplan a biochemical engineer invented a way to self-inject epinephrine, called ComboPen. Initially, it was the US military that used the ComboPen to protect their soldiers in the event of chemical warfare as it was easy to use in an emergency situation.

Shortly after, Kaplan and others found out that they could use ComboPen to deliver epinephrine in emergencies to treat severe allergic reactions without the presence and help of healthcare providers. The US FDA approved in 1987 the EpiPen as we know now. Meridian Medical Technologies, now a subsidiary of Pfizer, owned the product.

Later Merck KGaA, a German drug company acquired the product. In 2007, Mylan bought the generics business of Merck KGaA and became the owner of the EpiPen. What is interesting is that Meridian continues to manufacture EpiPen for Mylan even today. In 2007, when Mylan acquired EpiPen, its annual sales were around the US $200 million. In 2015, EpiPen's global sales passed the coveted one-billion-dollar mark. How did Mylan achieve this? Here are some of the significant strategic steps that the company took:

A. Mylan Specialty, the marketer, and distributor of EpiPen auto-injector launched many an allergy and anaphylaxis awareness campaigns, both unbranded and branded with celebrities, who have been either living with or caring for someone who is living with severe allergic conditions. The company ran more recently a *Face your risk campaign*, an ultra-realistic commercial about someone having an allergic reaction to peanut butter. Mylan had spent a billion dollars to raise awareness of the need for EpiPen in the eight-year period from 2009 to 2016.

B. Mylan had also invested in a massive lobbying effort and was able to get legislation passed in 48 states allowing schools to have undesignated EpiPens for emergency use.

C. Mylan has increased the price of a pack of two EpiPen auto-injectors exorbitantly from $93 in 2008 to $608.61 in 2016.

Mylan today has a virtual monopoly of the epinephrine market in the US with over 90 percent share of the market. While these are the three main reasons for its phenomenal sales growth of Epipen, its price increase has been the most controversial and drew criticism from all corners of society. In response, the company increased its copay coupon system and doubled the discount to $300 on a two-pack EpiPen auto-injector. The company even announced sometime back that it would introduce a cheaper version of EpiPen at half the current price.

The phenomenal sales success is due to a combination of many factors such as awareness campaigns, lobbying leading to legislative changes, competitors' inability to field an approvable alternative and exorbitant price hike of 500 percent - some acceptable and some not acceptable.

Lessons

Mylan followed the classic marketing strategy behind every blockbuster drug meticulously. These are: impactful disease awareness campaigns, lobbying to get the legislation to empower schools to provide EpiPen auto-injectors in time to treat medical emergencies due to severe allergic reactions among others.

Perhaps the most important lesson is that one should not exploit their monopoly situation and price it irresponsibly to maximize profits at the expense of patients.

(Source: Lydia Ramsey's article, *The strange history of the Epipen, the device developed by the military that turned into a billion-dollar business,* published in Business Insider India on August 28, 2016)

'Me-too' Pricing Strategy for 'Me-too' Products

In branded-generic pharmaceutical markets such as India, the general practice has been to set the prices by competitive parity. There are, however, a few exceptions to this. In the absence of any perceptible product differentiation, one probably feels safer for pricing his product by competitive parity.

Periodical Review

A periodical review of prices and costs is essential for it will help identify the improvement areas. Comparison of your actual manufacturing costs with the conversion and packaging norms fixed by the government will also throw open the gates of opportunity. How can you optimize your manufacturing costs? How can you increase your productivity? The answers to these questions will enable you to strive and achieve cost leadership, which is crucial for winning in the marketplace. Your focus should be on cost-effectiveness rather than on cost control. A periodical review will help you in preparing an action plan to achieve this.

Pharma and Social Media

What is Social Media?

Social media generally refers to Internet-based tools that allow individuals and communities to gather and share information, ideas, personal messages, images, and other content. It also facilitates real-time collaboration with other users. Social media is referred to as Web 2.0 and Social networking. Social media includes blogs, social networks, video and photo-sharing sites, wikis and many other media. Here is an example showing some of the media grouped by purpose and functions. The list is only indicative and not exhaustive by any means:

A. Social networking (Facebook, MySpace, Google Plus, Twitter among others)
B. Professional Networking (LinkedIn)
C. Physician Social Networks (Sermo, Quantia MD, Doximity, Docplexus)
D. Media sharing (YouTube, Flickr)
E. Content production (blogs, Blogger, WordPress, Tumblr, and Microblogs such as Twitter)
F. Knowledge / Information aggregation (Wikipedia)
G. Virtual reality and gaming environments (Second Life)

Social Media Marketing

Social media marketing in the pharmaceutical industry combines a wide variety of social media tools and platforms to establish conversations with physicians, patients, and other stakeholders. These online conversations help pharmaceutical companies build relationships with customers. You can spread brand messages through the electronic word-of-mouth.

While traditional marketing media was more of a monologue, social media has created an opportunity for engaging in a dialogue and conversation with consumers. Consumers can express their questions and concerns about enabling the brand to build a relationship. Social media users in the process generate much content. In fact, they post over 30 billion comments to Facebook and more than two billion tweets on Twitter every month. What is more, about twenty percent of this vast generated content mentions a specific drug or disease. When one in every five conversation pieces is in the pharmaceutical and healthcare space, can Pharma afford to remain a silent spectator?

Physicians on Social Media

While the exact numbers vary, most studies indicate that about 80 percent of physicians use social media for personal interactions as well as professional communication and research. Physicians' social media usage seems to follow a typical 1-9-90 pattern. Approximately 1 percent of physicians using social media are content producers creating and publishing original content to other healthcare professionals and ePatients. They provide this information on blogs, forums, and information-sharing websites. A further 9 percent of physicians engage with others on social media by commenting on posts and participating in online discussions and chats are sharing useful information and links to other members online. The remaining 90 percent of physicians consume information. They use the internet and social media to find and read information that is relevant to their patients and practice.

Patients Are in Control

More and more patients are turning to many sites such as *Patients Like Me* and other patient and disease communities online to research their symptoms and arrive at a self-diagnosis before visiting their physicians. The availability of extensive healthcare information on the social web is impacting the relationship between patients, physicians, and brands. Increasingly, doctors, today are facing the self-diagnosing patients who have already researched their symptoms seeking prescriptions for conditions they think they have. The patients may even post reviews of their experiences in case of pushback by their doctors. Patients today are taking greater responsibility than ever for their health.

Insights From Social Media Conversations

Patients seem to be more forthright and descriptive in their online conversations about their disease conditions and feedback on treatments as they afford greater privacy than in-person consults. These conversations are beneficial for Pharma Marketers as they provide a richer understanding of how patients perceive the current product or service offerings and what their unmet needs are. With insights gained from this deep understanding, marketers can develop better, more relevant marketing materials including packaging, educational and promotional tools aimed at physicians and patients.

Challenging Regulatory Environment

Pharmaceutical companies as they are operating in a highly regulated industry, face many challenges such as how to handle incomplete and misinformation about their products both offline and online. According to the US Federal Drug Administration (FDA) Guidance on how Pharma should use social media, pharmaceutical companies should provide fair and balanced information about their products in their social media posts. They need to include the side effects, adverse reactions, and contraindications in their product information.

Furthermore, FDA clearly stated that it wouldn't be taking a lenient approach towards either tweets or sponsored links. Social media posts even in sites with limited character-spaces such as Twitter need to incorporate full and balanced information about their products. It is not enough to provide links in the post to your web pages for detailed product information. Pharmaceutical companies face serious penalties by the FDA if they don't make the proper disclosure. Drug firms must be careful not to mislead consumers on Twitter. Otherwise, they will open themselves for liability. Kim Kardashian's Instagram post is a classic example of what happens when you don't follow the regulations governing social media. The following cases illustrate this:

How Kim Kardashian's Instagram Post Got the Drug Firm that Makes 'Diclegis' into Trouble with the FDA.

In July 2015, Kim Kardashian, a leading supermodel with a massive following on social media posted to her 45 million followers on Instagram and 35 million followers on Twitter, about Diclegis, a prescription drug brand of a morning sickness tablet manufactured by Rosemont-based Pharma company, Duchesnay in the US. Here's a transcript of that post:

> OMG. Have you heard about this? As you guys know my #morning sickness has been pretty bad...I tried changing things about my lifestyle like my diet, but nothing helped, so I talked to my doctor. He prescribed me #Diclegis, and I felt a lot better, and most importantly, it's been studied, and there was no increased risk to the baby. I'm so excited and happy with my results that I'm partnering with Duchesnay USA to raise awareness about the morning sickness. If you have morning sickness, be safe and sure to ask your doctor about the pill with the pregnant woman on it and find out more ... www.diclegis.com; www.diclegis Important Safety Information.com

Well, this is not a typical post by an average morning sickness sufferer, who recommends a product online. Kim Kardashian is a celebrity with a massive online following and is paid to endorse the brand. The FDA took objection to this post as it failed to mention relevant information like the drug's side effects, adverse reactions, and contraindications. The social media post is false and misleading in that it presents efficacy claims for 'Diclegis,' but fails to communicate any risk information. The FDA demanded that

Duchesnay immediately cease its 'misbranding' of the drug of the drug and has given time until August 21 to respond to the Agency. The company withdrew the social media posts. Here's what Dean Hopkins, general manager of Duchesnay said in this regard:

> *In the original post, which we developed with Kim, we provided her with a link to risk information and limitation of use for Diclegis. However, the post did not meet the FDA requirements for communicating important product information.*

Kim Kardashian had posted a long corrective ad on August 30, 2015.

('Source: Adapted from an article by Levi Sharpe, *Kim Kardashian's Instagram is only the latest victim of FDA campaign,* Popular Science, August 12, 2015')

Facebook-Share Function Gets a Warning From The FDA!

Novartis, one of the global Pharma majors, got approval from the US FDA on October 29, 2017, and launched Tasigna (Nilotinib) for the treatment of chronic myeloid leukemia with resistance or intolerance to existing therapies.

In 2010, Novartis used a Facebook share function as one of the marketing tactics for promoting its leukemia drug, Tasigna on individual consumers' profile pages and news feeds. The company shared through this functionality a short description of the drug, relevant visuals, and website links on an individual's Facebook profile page and upon his or her approval of the posting, some specific networking newsfeeds. The FDA found this objectionable as it did not present the risk information about the drug in these postings. The agency's primary concern was that these postings could imply that the drug was effective in treating all types of leukemia patients, while in fact, the medication was effective only in a narrow subset of leukemia patients, for which it got approval. The company duly withdrew the Facebook share function.

Suprenza's False Claims Ring an Alarm!

Suprenza's case is an example of how false and misleading pharmaceutical advertising in digital media can land the company in trouble.

The Citius pharmaceutical company obtained approval from the US FDA in June 2011, for its Suprenza (phentermine chloride) a prescription drug for use as an adjunct for the short-term in the regimen of weight reduction based on exercise, behavioral modification in the management of exogenous obesity.

The landing page of Suprenza's website, www.leanonsuprenza.com contained an image of an attractive woman, holding the lettered blocks of the word, 'LEAN' and eye-catching efficacy claims such as: *Stay on course for success with Suprenza Lean Program*. The web page conspicuously omitted all the relevant information regarding side effects, contraindications and risk factors. There was no information substantiating the product claims. The site only revealed one warning about the risk of simultaneously using Suprenza with other drugs for weight loss. It ignored all other warnings and precautions. There was no information regarding the approved indications and required body mass index (BMI) for starting the treatment.

On June 9, 2014, the FDA sent a warning letter to the company urging the company to stop violating the FDA rules and to respond with a plan for discontinuing such promotional materials promptly. The letter stated that the information presented on the website was false and misleading as it did not contain any risk and safety information. The letter also noted that it was a clear violation of the Federal Food, Drug, and Cosmetic Act.

Citius promptly removed the website from the internet search. The company moved it to a new website, www.suprenza.com and eliminated its Lean program. Later, Citius Pharma withdrew Suprenza to focus on the company's core assets.

FDA Guidance on Social Media: Implications for Pharma

What it means for pharmaceutical companies is that they won't be able to send a series of tweets containing the full benefit and risk information of a product, but will instead need to provide the entire information in a single tweet.

How Can Pharma Comply with the FDA Guidance on Social Media?

Pharmaceutical companies need to connect with patients and physicians on social media to offer reliable information about their products and about improving health and wellbeing. However, how can they comply with the FDA regulations while providing this information and control the conversations on various social media platforms and ensure delivery of fair and balanced information? Henniger Bullock and Collen Tracy Jones suggest a five-way approach to achieve this in their Law 360 article of April 21, 2017, *5 Social Media Pitfalls in the Pharmaceutical Industry.*

1. **Set A Clear Internal Policy:** Develop a clear policy that includes a centralized social media hub such as a company-sponsored website, twitter handle, facebook page among others, for posting messages on behalf of the company. Create a concrete social media advertising policy and clearly define who may engage with social media on the company's behalf. Ensure that all employees understand their role on social media whether it is in their personal or official capacity and how they need to conduct themselves on social media sites. The legal department must clear the content for regulatory compliance.

2. **Create A Controlled Environment:** When its consumers (patients) and customers (HCPs) are frequently on social media, can Pharma afford to shy away? Pharma should embrace social media but maintain control of it. By creating a company website or a company-initiated chat area, a

pharmaceutical company can create a controlled environment and foster relationships with patients and communicate useful, fair and balanced information about its products and services.

3. **Create A Compliance Strategy:** It is not enough if you define the roles of engagement and rules of conduct on social media for your patients in your social media policy. You need to ensure compliance. Put in place a compliance strategy and a monitoring system to ensure total compliance.

4. **Comply With All HIPAA Act Privacy Laws:** Pharmaceutical companies need to do more than comply with the FDA Guidance on social media. They need to comply with HIPAA (Health Insurance Privacy, Portability and Accountability Act). Complying with patient privacy laws is equally essential. Therefore, educate all employees on patient privacy laws and how they are related to business. Remember, even an individual posting of a patient's picture is a privacy violation. Create a social media working group to discuss any concerns and issues.

5. **Keep Future Litigation in Mind:** Ensure that you prepare a carefully coordinated message and have it approved. Ensure compliance with the standards and policies governing social media before embarking on a social media campaign.

Pharma Must Embrace Social Media

Although there are many regulations over how pharmaceutical companies should conduct themselves on social media that are challenging, Pharma must find a way to comply with them and participate actively in social media as it offers many opportunities. Pharma must embrace social media. Consider these reasons for example:

A. More and more patients are using social media today as a significant source of information and an integral part of their healthcare research journey. Typically, their journey begins when they notice their symptoms leading to their searching social channels often before their visit to a physician or simultaneously with their visit to the doctor. The second phase of online search follows the diagnosis to seek more information about their condition from credible sources, and people like themselves. Patients, who share their stories on social channels become a significant source of information to those actively seeking their perspectives. This information at times could be unbalanced and even irrelevant.

B. The information on social media may not always be from reputable and accredited sources. It may be marginally accurate at best and significantly harmful at worst.

It is crucial, therefore, for Pharma companies to provide balanced and credible information on social media where their patients are seeking meaningful information and help them in getting balanced, accurate information that is essential for their wellbeing.

6 Ways Pharma May Use Social Media

Dr. Kevin Campbell, an internationally recognized cardiologist, suggested six ways in which pharmaceutical companies can use social media in an interview with Joanna Belbey, a columnist with Forbes magazine. He said that Social Media is an ideal channel for pharmaceutical and device companies to educate, market, listen to and connect with customers. Pharma firms can do all this while complying with the guidelines of industry regulators. Here's a summary of what he suggested:

1. **Education:** Pharmaceutical firms may offer disease-specific, unbiased educational information on broad topics to consumers. The purpose of such educative information is to help patients understand their disease state better so that they can engage with their healthcare professionals better for improved outcomes.

2. **Marketing:** Pharma can use social media as another channel to share press releases on new products, clinical trial results, community service, significant contributions to charities and their primary commitment to developing new and better treatments.

3. **Connecting with Physicians:** Social media is an efficient and effective means of connecting with physician customers. It is also less expensive than the sales force costs. Through social media, Pharma can engage with a large number of physicians at one time with its own best and brightest scientists and researchers. It is also an excellent opportunity to ask questions and have a dialogue with each other than being 'detailed-to'by a sales representative, which is merely a regurgitation of a memorized script of a new study. The physician would have already read it in all probabilities.

4. **Connecting with Patients:** Pharma can use social media to create patient support groups and communities. These groups allow the patients with common interests and need to connect with each other and discuss their conditions, treatments, and experiences.

5. **Clinical Trials:** Social media can become a powerful tool to enroll patients in clinical trials. Clinical trial enrollment is one of the most significant barriers to complete a clinical trial.

6. **Listening:** Social media can be a big help for Pharma in gaining insights into the unmet needs of the patients through social listening. These insights can be of immense use to Pharma in developing its communication strategies to physicians and even in directing the future course of their product development.

The following case offers an excellent example of how Janssen Pharmaceuticals used social media to create a patient awareness program.

Janssen's *Me Without Migraine* Patient Awareness Campaign!

Around 80 million Indians suffer from a Migraine, but only about a quarter of them seek treatment and only half of them complete the treatment. It is because a migraine manifests as a headache and the similarity ends there. A migraine is different from regular headaches. Most people are not aware of this difference. Janssen Pharmaceuticals recognized the need for an awareness of the migraine condition among patients and decided to help them in differentiating between a migraine and a regular headache. Once the patients know the difference, they can seek the treatment from a doctor. Even many of the HCPs too, initially give many painkillers before they diagnose it as a migraine.

The company gained the patient insight that patients are not quite themselves when they get a headache. To increase the awareness about a migraine among patients and HCPs, Janssen launched an integrated multichannel campaign called, *Me Without Migraine*, covering field force involvement, patient education at doctor's clinic, digital and social media channels for disseminating medical information that is easy to understand.

The company launched the campaign with an SEO-optimized website as the first step with several resources such as:

▸ A migraine test to help the patients distinguish between regular headaches and migraines

- ▸ Locate your doctor tool, for locating a neurophysician or a migraine specialist nearby by entering their Pin code and filtering by radius
- ▸ Migraine Diary for patients to keep track of episodes and share the details with their doctor
- ▸ Migraine myth buster, to address commonly held beliefs about migraines

The company created compelling content and shared it across different media platforms such as Facebook to drive traffic to their website. Facebook page of the campaign communicated the interesting and informative messages in an easy to use manner with visuals and videos. Also, articles in blogs and magazines, forums and interviews with doctors engaged the patients and pushed them to the website. The company reinforced its online campaign with mass media and digital PR. Greatly enthused with this novel and innovative campaign, the field force actively promoted their products and increased their prescription share in less than a year.

Me without Migraine campaign was a phenomenal success. The digital reach of the campaign was over 14 million people with over 200,000 thousand people getting engaged through Facebook over a ten-month period. The Facebook page for the campaign has over 50,000 likes. Two years later, in 2018, the Facebook page of *Me Without Migraine* has over 147,447 followers and 147,661 likes. What is more, over 100,000 people that is half-of-visitors to the campaign's Facebook page took the migraine test during the campaign period.

Janssen Pharma, a division of Johnson & Johnson has won the Digital Pioneer award in 2016, while the campaign itself won two awards at DigiPharmaX – Business World awards ceremony, namely, Best Pharma Social Media and Best Digital Community Building. The campaign also won the Gold at SABRE Awards, South Asia 2016 in the Healthcare category.

Lessons

Me without migraine campaign by Janssen teaches us of the importance of a patient-centric approach. It also shows us about the importance of seeking to understand first and foremost in creating a social media campaign to improve awareness. It is not enough to promote awareness. You need to do more. You need to engage them, help them in understanding the condition, and manage them.

A social media campaign is not just about creating a facebook page, a twitter handle, a LinkedIn profile, an Instagram account, and others. You need to engage with the patients individually and collectively. Remember, engagement is commitment. Commitment to help. Commitment to assist. Commitment to share.

You need to provide the tools and techniques to cope and overcome their condition. You must become a partner and source of support in fighting their condition.

(Source: Adapted from Dinesh Chindarkars' case study on *Janssen creates patient awareness around migraine* in Medicinman, August 2016 and www.mewithoutmigraine.com and the facebook page *me without migraine*.)

Content is King!

The internet is the starting point for most people researching health information. Digital Pharma reported that over a 12-month period, 72 percent of internet users mentioned in a survey that they looked online for information on health. Pharmaceutical companies can take advantage of this opportunity for creating informative and engaging content on health information related to their therapeutic areas and brands.

Who and what rules the internet? Content, of course! Content is the king when it comes to marketing online. Content is the fuel that drives your digital marketing activities such as Search Engine Optimization (SEO). Content is what gets you noticed in social media. It is content that gives you something of value to offer your customers in emails and paid search ads.

Creating content that is not promotional in nature, but educates and inspires instead, gets you noticed. Content that offers valuable and relevant information ensures that your customers stay tuned in. The key to good content, therefore, is that it avoids being overtly promotional and it is useful or valuable to the customer. Because, if the content is not relevant to the consumer whether it is the patient or HCP, they go elsewhere. They are looking to understand the condition and the treatment options available to them. Therefore, you need to give the information they need to decide on a language they fully understand, through the medium they want and when they want it. Quality of content is crucial to engaging them on their terms. The good quality content aims to create a two-way engagement rather than delivering a one-way sales pitch. Once you generate good quality content, you need to market it effectively. How do you market your content? Content marketing as defined by the *Whatis* website is:

> *Content marketing is the publication of material designed to promote a brand (or service) usually through a more oblique and subtle approach than that of a traditional push advertising. The essence of good content marketing is that it offers*

something the viewer wants such as information or entertainment. Content marketing can take a lot of different forms including Youtube videos, and articles. It shouldn't seem like marketing in some cases, in fact, it should only be identifiable as marketing because the advertiser is the content provider.

Pharmaceutical marketers need to provide engaging content that meets the needs, wants aspirations and goals of all their key stakeholders, namely, patients, HCPs, providers, and payers. Meeting the needs and interests of the target audience is crucial for success. Pharma should create different content for each of its customer segment in a way that speaks directly to their particular issues. A one-size-fits-all approach is outdated now. The fundamental questions to ask and answer are:

▸ Who is your target audience? Are they patients, general practitioners? Specialist physicians?

▸ What information do they want?

▸ What issues do they have and how can you solve them?

Remember that to be engaging content should be interactive, interesting, informative and shareable. Your content should not seem like a marketing strategy or appear to be promotional. Content, however engaging it may be, cannot promote itself, unless at least you share it on social media.

The key to a successful and sustainable content strategy for a pharmaceutical company hinges on developing a trusted relationship using the content. Moreover, trust is an emotion based on credibility. It can be built only on aligned values. Pharmaceutical marketers need to be very objective in developing their content and focus more on establishing credibility than on grabbing attention. Of course, you need to grab attention and sustain it, but reliability is more important in building a trusting relationship. In healthcare, it is even more critical. You can draw attention and build trust only when you have a strong point of view based on facts in your content. Otherwise, it would be a series of mere facts that anyone can find with a google search. In sum, your content must resonate with all your key customers - patients, physicians, and payers. All of them should feel that the pharmaceutical company understands their values and beliefs and that it is not just educating them to a prescriptive solution.

Robert Rose, the chief strategist at Content Marketing Institute and co-author with Joe Pulizzi of the book, *Managing Content Marketing*, advised that:

> *Content marketers should start thinking of themselves as media companies – with a clear point of view. Their goal is to develop an audience for their content. However, they have to balance that with how, when and where they will show their distinct an unique point of view.*

Gamification

You can find gamification everywhere today - from boardrooms to classrooms and even on social media. Over the last few years, gamification has gained general acceptance and recognition in many areas such as marketing, healthcare, business, politics, and technology design. Pharmaceutical industry too has been embracing this recent trend in healthcare gamification to meet the ever-increasing challenges in creating value and brand building. Initial research and case studies provide evidence that gamification improves both patient compliance and health outcomes.

Five Key Elements

Gamification uses the mechanics of gaming to engage users and solve problems in a non-game context. There are four critical elements in a gamification strategy:

1. Reward or recognition for the players' achievements.
2. A goal and a sense of purpose.
3. Rules and a framework for participation that motivate participants to tackle challenges strategically.
4. Continuous challenge. Achieving each next step should be harder but not too hard. The best option is that level one

prepares the user for level two. There should be a flow that will keep the users fully engaged.

5. The feedback that tracks the players' status informing them how close they are to reaching the end goal.

How Gamification is Beneficial

1. Gamification can promote therapies. By creating interactive, educational health content, gamification can be utilized to encourage new and existing treatments.

2. Gamification can increase engagement between Pharma, HCPs, and patients. HCPs' use of interactive technology to communicate with their patients is gradually growing. With gamification, Pharma can provide responsible, educational, health content and improve health awareness among patients. Consider the case of Sanofi-Aventis, which has successfully used gamification as a strategy to improve patient adherence.

3. Gamification allows showing patients first hand how their condition is affected by their daily habits and choices.

4. Gamification helps in creating and regulating virtual patients by inserting actual medical record information.

5. Gamification can facilitate physician education. Physicians are interested in improving health outcomes of their patients in less time. Pharma companies can help achieve this by implementing gamification. Here's how Sanofi, the international drug major used gamification to increase awareness and adherence among patients (Case 99).

Sanofi Has Got Game!

1. Sanofi's *GoMeals* mobile app is an excellent example of gamification in pharmaceutical marketing. *GoMeals* is a set of applications developed for Sanofi-Aventis, the US by Intouch Solutions, a specialized digital Pharma marketing agency.

   Sanofi designed *GoMeals* for people living with diabetes to promote its diabetes drug Apdria. The app available for the web as well as for smartphones encourages users to make healthy choices regarding nutrition as the name *GoMeals* suggests. The app comes with features for eating healthy, staying active and tracking blood glucose levels. *GoMeals* allows patients to see how their daily habits regarding nutrition and exercise impact their diabetes.

   GoMeals uses the game design elements providing users clear reports on calorie-intake from their meals, calories burnt from their exercise and physician activity and glucose readings.

2. Sanofi-Aventis with Vancouver-based Ayogo has developed *Monster Manor*, a game that rewards children with Type 2 diabetes for checking their blood glucose regularly. The app uses short mini-games that add up to unlock features and characters. It automatically sends the results to the parents' smartphones. The parents can give 'kids-rewards' to the children directly through the app.

3. Sanofi Diabetes, a division of Sanofi-Aventis has launched in the UK another mobile game called *Mission T1D* to educate and teach children as well as their parents, caregivers, and friends about Type 1 diabetes.

School is the background of the game. When players complete levels and get points, they unlock short practical messages about living with Type 1 diabetes and longer shareable educational videos. The videos cover essential topics such as:

- ▸ What is Type 1 diabetes?
- ▸ Everyday life with diabetes
- ▸ What is hypoglycemia and how to help
- ▸ What is hyperglycemia and how to help
- ▸ How to have a healthy diet with or without Type 1 diabetes

The entire program can run on a PC and a smartphone designed to be used either by individuals or in a classroom setting.

Sanofi has undoubtedly made a pioneering effort in developing these apps for diabetes and in engaging patients as well as HCPs.

(Source: Mobile Health News)

More Apps

Pharmaceutical companies are realizing the importance of gamification as yet another tool to engage their key stakeholders such as patients and HCPs mainly and have been developing more and more apps. Here are some examples of successful apps:

1. *Respimat* inhalation demonstration by Boehringer Ingelheim designed for HCPs. The app provides medical information on the next generation device and facilitates physicians training patients on how to use Respimat. The app enables inhaler interaction, a critical issue, offers hands-on experience with an intuitive interface and is available at no additional cost.

2. *Back-in-Play by* Pfizer. Designed as a game, this app aims to boost knowledge of a little-known disease, ankylosing spondylitis. Through this, patients in Europe learned about this condition that causes inflammation in their spine and pelvic joints.

3. Boehringer Ingelheim's *HealthSeeker* is a game that helps those with diabetes make better lifestyle choices about their condition and overall wellness.

4. Bayer created the diabetes *Didget* game for use with Nintendo's DS handheld game system, to encourage children with diabetes to regularly test their blood glucose levels. Players receive rewards for testing consistently. Bayer's Didget blood glucose meter fits in with the Nintendo's handheld game system and allows children with diabetes to play Knock-'em-down, the World's Fair Board Game, which inspires pediatric patients to keep up with their testing schedule.

5. Johnson & Johnson's *Care4Today* is designed to improve adherence to treatment regimens through reminders to take medication, refill prescriptions and visit healthcare providers. The mobile adherence program can be used for any prescription or OTC medication or nutritional supplement, including but not limited to the Johnson & Johnson group of companies.

6. Janssen designed *Sorted App* is for patients with attention deficit hyperactivity disorder (ADHD) in the UK The app acts as a daily organizer to help patients create, categorize, and prioritize daily tasks with a point-scoring element to motivate the users. Janssen's leading product for ADHD is Concerta XL. The company developed the app with the concurrence of Physicians In the UK. The app utilizes the functionalities of iPhone such as its calendar, reminders, and voice memos. The app's targeted for people above 12 years.

7. Sun Pharma's *RespiTrack App* is a mobile application that connects doctors with their asthma patients. The app's focus is to improve treatment compliance and minimize instances of non-adherence and dropouts in the asthma treatment regime. *RespiTrack* allows complete monitoring of asthma attacks, symptoms, medications prescribed by the physicians. It enables patients to record time, place, duration and triggers of attacks along with medication details on the mobile app. The patient can easily send this data to his physician through over-the-air mode on a weekly or monthly basis. A review dashboard in the app provides a snapshot of all parameters for monitoring over a period. What is more, through *RespiTrack*, a doctor can access his patient's details through a personalized tracker module, which syncs with the patients' app. This module allows doctors to access patients' ailment history, attack patterns, symptoms, medication patterns, and reports. A doctor can remotely view patient reports and also connect with him through an integrated messaging app.

A research study by Research2Guidance (R2G) observed that between 2008 and 2016 the top Pharma companies had 65 apps in the Apple and Google Play app stores on average compared to 1 or 2 apps from other health app publishers. However, even the Pharma companies with the most downloaded apps have accrued 6.6 million downloads since 2008, had less than a million active users. Why is the rate of adoption slower in case of Pharma as compared to other healthcare and fitness apps?

Slow Rate of Adoption

If gamification offers so many benefits why is it that there are relatively fewer downloads for Pharma apps as compared to other healthcare apps? Here are the possible reasons:

A. Many of the Pharma apps have highly targeted audiences like HCPs.

B. People with specific disease states.

C. Pharma apps tend to target local markets, say in three or fewer countries, which makes them unlikely to compete on download numbers with fitness, health or diet tracking apps that appeal to a broader segment of the market.

Engagification, not Gamification!

While gamification has a positive impact on participant engagement, message recall, and patient outcomes, there is one problem. It is the name itself - gamification. When you say that you are going to gamify the participants' interaction with your content, the term - gamification lends itself to trivializing the most serious experience related to improving health and wellbeing. Patients, physicians and other stakeholders of the pharmaceutical industry still cling to the idea that games should not be part of the conversation in such a severe realm as healthcare. In Pharma marketing, it is crucial to steering the discussion away from the word Game – and towards terms like engagement, retention, adherence. Therefore, do not call it a game. Call it an app. Extending the same thought, your strategy is not gamification. It is engagification!

Research tells us that people spend about three billion hours on an average per week playing online games. Gamification has vast potential for Pharma, especially in areas such as medication adherence, and medical education.

Pharma and Social Media:
The Indian Scenario

The global pharmaceutical industry in general and Indian pharmaceutical industry, in particular, has been a laggard in its adoption of social media. D. Yellow Elephant, a leading digital marketing consultancy firm researched 40 pharmaceutical companies in India across ten critical digital parameters ranging - across websites, social network platforms, and applications and published a study titled, Indian Pharma Digital Health Report 2015. The study revealed that only 9 out of 40 - less than 25 percent of the companies managed to score 50 out of 100 on these parameters.

Presence Vs. Engagement

What has emerged out of this study is a pattern of presence vs. engagement by Indian pharmaceutical companies on social media. While Pharma companies in India are present and registered on most social media platforms, only a few of them are active. Here is a summary of some key findings:

A. LinkedIn: Only 14 companies were present

B. Google+: Two companies have a presence while one of the 40 companies was active

C. Facebook: 8 out of 40 companies had an India-specific page

D. Twitter: 29 percent of the companies have a presence, but only 16 percent are active

E. YouTube: 24 percent of the companies have a presence

F. Blog: 12 companies had a blogger presence

Patients on Social Media

Patients in India have a better adoption rate than the Pharma industry to social media. Consider these facts:

▸ 47 percent of people consulted a doctor based on an online search.

▸ 60 percent of people discussed the information they found on the web with their doctor.

▸ As high as 69 percent of people said that they did not find India-specific information on the web.

These indicate the low engagement of Pharma with patients on social media and amplify the need to improve their presence.

Physicians on Social Media

Physicians too, in India are increasingly taking to online media. Medical professionals are using online media for many activities ranging from knowledge updates to peer interactions. Docplexus, India's largest community of doctors conducted a survey recently among 12,635 doctors that revealed the following insights towards the online behavior of physicians in India:

▸ 83 percent of the doctors surveyed agreed that online learning is beneficial as it overcomes geographic constraints

▸ 71 percent found it easy to gain knowledge from online key opinion leaders (KOLs)

▸ 78 percent preferred video content (KOL interviews, webinars, surgical videos) as they are easy to grasp

▸ 72 percent feel that it is easy to source drug-related information online

▸ 26 percent used online media for networking with peers

▸ 75 percent of doctors spend a maximum of 5 minutes online, and only 10 percent spend 10 minutes or more of their time on online activities. Pharmaceutical marketers, therefore, should create online content that is concise, clear and devoid of complexities

▸ Mobiles and laptops are the most preferred devices of doctors. 78 percent of medical professionals accessed online media through mobiles and laptops

▸ There seem to be three peak surf times for doctors - at 10 am when they check into their offices; at 2 pm, after the morning rush of patients is over; and from 9 to 10 pm before signing off for the day

Pharmaceutical marketers now armed with these insights can plan their online strategies more effectively.

Digital Initiatives of MNCs in India

Unlike their counterparts in the domestic sector, some of the more progressive MNC pharmaceutical companies are taking initiatives to exploit the emerging opportunities in the digital era. Here is a partial list of MNCs in India and their digital marketing initiatives:

Abbott Healthcare

As a consumer healthcare company, Abbott over the past few years has built a digital ecosystem for a doctor and consumer education comprising mobile apps and technologies such as augmented reality and virtual reality over ten therapy areas including heart health, liver health, vertigo management, thyroid, women's health among others. Besides the company has also created a one-of-a-kind initiative – Knowledge Genie that provides Indian physicians with a single platform-access all kinds of medical information. Doctors stay updated with the latest advancements in their specialties to ensure the best clinical outcomes.

GlaxoSmithKline

GlaxoSmithKline, India believes that pharmaceutical companies will have to hone their digital skills because a significant portion of their customers will operate in that space in the years to come. As of now, at least 20 to 30 percent of GSK's customers are already in the digital world, says Annaswamy Vaideesh, managing director of GSK, India. The company is already leveraging many digital platforms such as webinars, video chats, information portals and so on. It has also equipped its 3000-strong field force with iPads to improve the quality of interactive presentations to the physicians.

Furthermore, GSK has invested about Rs. 10-crore in India for designing its digital platforms. The company has also developed a cloud-based application, which enables direct communication between practicing physicians and the company's medical department. The company has also hired about 20 doctors to respond to medical questions from physicians. Furthermore, Glaxo is also test-marketing with a software company in a rural setting to improve access to health care in remote areas. The company is pulling out all the stops to become and stay digitally savvy.

Pfizer

Pfizer has pioneered several digital initiatives towards enhancing customer engagement and providing result-driven outcomes. The rep-triggered-Email (RTE) campaign is one example. The company has launched a multi-therapy area HCP portal, Inquimed, on which 18,000 doctors have already registered. Also, the company's webcasts, Meet the Expert (MTE) have seen an attendance of approximately 9,000 doctors across different specialties.

Janssen

Janssen Pharma has been active in the digital marketing space with a few initiatives. The company's awareness campaign for increasing migraine awareness, *Me without Migraine* is familiar to all its stakeholders in India. It has won many awards for its campaign. Many patients don't realize they have a migraine, confuse it with a headache and continue taking painkillers. For the first time, Janssen has launched a campaign in migraine space across digital (website, Facebook, Twitter and a launch video) and non-digital channels (in-clinic promotion, PoP activities, and corporate outreach programs). The campaign has achieved within a year 40,000 followers on its Facebook page and almost 22,000 people visiting its website every month.

Sanofi

Sanofi in India has equipped its sales force with iPads for delivering engaging detail talks to physicians across the country. The company is also toying with the idea of developing a messaging application, which will give flexibility and convenience to seek a meeting with the company's medical representatives.

These few examples illustrate that multinational companies understand the advantages of digital marketing better than their counterparts in the domestic pharmaceutical sector. It may be due to their experience in the other markets which are more developed and have become digitally savvy. They also realize that when the UCPMP is made mandatory, which seems to be around the corner, most of the companies, which are practicing the transactional marketing methods will have to mend their ways and resort to ethical and science-based marketing. Digital marketing can provide the much-needed power to engage all stakeholders in an ethical, transparent manner.

Social Media and Indian Pharma

Aman Gupta, managing director of D Yellow Elephant, said that looking at the data, Indian Pharma sector – whether Indian companies or global players – lag behind their international counterparts by at least 5 - 7 years. Indian drug majors use of social media is considerably low resulting in their negligible presence on social media. Social media presence of the top five Indian drug firms illustrates this (Tables 10.1 and 10.2).

Table 10.1 Social Presence of Top
Five Indian Pharma Companies in March 2017

Company	Facebook	Twitter	YouTube	LinkedIn
1. Cipla	26,475 Followers	1,681 Followers 1,593 Tweets	402 Subscribers 72 Videos	1,05,802 Followers 253 Updates
2. Dr. Reddy's	1,72,558 Followers	3,845 Followers 3,561 Tweets	180 Subscribers 19 Videos	1,31,607 Followers 380 Updates
3. Sun Pharma	15,434 Followers	3,284 Followers 528 Tweets	47 Subscribers 12 Videos	1,12,120 Followers Only 1 Update
4. Lupin	3,762 Followers	2,090 Subscribers 212 Tweets	Absent	21,181 Followers Only 1 Update
5. Aurobindo Pharma	469 Followers	Absent	127 Subscribers 2 Videos	30,387 Followers No Updates

(Source: moneycontrol.com The information is as on March 6, 2017)

Table 10.2 Social Media Buttons on Home
Page of Top Five Indian Pharma Companies in 2017

Company	Social Media Buttons
1. Cipla	Facebook Twitter YouTube LinkedIn
2. Dr. Reddy's	Facebook Twitter YouTube LinkedIn
3. Sun Pharma	Twitter LinkedIn
4. Lupin	None
5. Aurobindo Pharma	None

(Source: moneycontrol as on March 6, 2017)

Less than half of India Pharma giants have a token presence in online media. Most seem to have given up after dabbling with networking platforms for a short while. Cipla had created CiplaMed, an online resource for doctors to keep themselves updated. However, the portal is yet to include interactive features such as blogs and discussion forums. Only a few companies such as Biocon have an active blog page named Bio-conversation. Some other companies have featured dynamic blog pages on their websites in other countries, but not in India.

All these findings show the reluctance of the pharmaceutical companies in India in engaging with their stakeholders on digital platforms. Indian pharmaceutical industry seems to be sitting still on the fence when it comes to social media marketing. It could be due to any of the following reasons:

A. Indian pharmaceutical market is predominantly branded generic with 90 percent of products being branded generics or generic-generics. There is very little new scientific information that a branded-generic firm can provide to physicians, which they do not know already.

B. Many pharmaceutical companies seem to think that a transactional approach to marketing is the way to go and take the shortcut. They also seem to believe in substantial price discounts, high-value gifts, sponsorships, and even cash payments for getting prescriptions for their products and investing in those things rather than on technology, innovative marketing, training, and development. Customer relationship management (CRM) to them has an entirely different meaning.

The branded-generic firms in India today, may not be perceiving a pressing need to engage physicians differently and through online channels, even as access to physicians in India, is decreasing, The do not seem to consider it a serious issue yet. However, it could be a serious issue, when the Department of Pharmaceuticals (DoP), which is determined to make the UCPMP Code mandatory and puts an end to the current transactional marketing model. The industry that is focusing on a promotion mix that mostly comprises of freebies, sponsored seminars, foreign junkets, even payments for prescriptions, would have to change its tacks of tactics suddenly. Social media marketing, which is ethical, and transparent is the only way to build a sustainable way of building enduring relationships with all stakeholders of the industry. That's what vision is. Seeing the future before it arrives. Companies with foresight are the ones who would take to social media before others do.

Social Media, Public Relations and Crisis Management

The public relations is to help stabilize the environment by developing messages and public relations strategy, which results in prompt, honest, informative and concerned communications with all essential audiences - internal and external, explains Professor and founder of Bernstein communications, Jonathan Bernstein.

A crisis is a significant threat to operations or reputations that can have negative consequences for the organization and its stakeholders. Crisis management is about dealing with the risk of potential damages that a crisis can inflict on on an organization and its stakeholders and even industry. A crisis can create damage in three areas, namely, public safety, financial loss, and reputation loss.

Crisis management is a process to prevent or lessen the damage a crisis can inflict on an organization and its stakeholders. You can divide It into three phases:

1. Pre-crisis: The pre-crisis stage is connected with prevention and preparation.
2. Crisis response: The crisis-response phase is when management is facing a crisis.
3. Post-crisis: The post-crisis phase looks for ways to better prepare for the next crisis and fulfills commitments made during the crisis, including a follow-up that is necessary.

13 Golden Rules of PR Crisis Management

Forbes Agency Council members suggested 13 Golden Rules for managing a public relations crisis effectively. Don't take them lightly as they are deceptively simple and self-explanatory. Stick to them firmly, and you are well-equipped to handle any crisis that you may have to face:

1. Take Responsibility.
2. Be proactive. Be transparent. Be accountable.
3. Get ahead of the story. Don't wait till you formulate a complete strategy.
4. Be ready for social media backlash.
5. Remember to be human.
6. First apologize, then take action.
7. Monitor, plan and communicate.
8. Seek first to understand the situation.
9. Listen to your team first.
10. Develop a strong brand culture. Remember, you can develop an organization with a strong brand culture only when you treat your customers and employees (internal customers) with respect.
11. Turn off the fan. When you-know-what hits the fan, the first rule of crisis management is to turn off the fan, says Kim Miller of Ink Marketing. Don't fuel the fire. Step back, put yourself in the shoes of the customer and ask, If this happened to me how would I feel? And then decide the course of action. It ensures that we do the right thing.
12. Avoid knee-jerk reaction. Freeze all external communication until you can assess what is going on, suggests Coltrane Curtis of Team Epiphany.
13. Be Prepared.

Social Media in Crisis Management

Managing a crisis in the social media era is very challenging even to the most seasoned public relations professionals. News spreads faster, in fact instantaneously. Things can escalate in a matter of minutes. At the same time, social media can be your most dependable ally in managing a crisis if you use it wisely. Here are three ways to use social media for crisis communications.

1. Provide timely updates on what you are doing to manage the crisis and help the people affected by it to all your key audiences.

2. Monitor the conversations and listen actively. Remember social media is not about just posting your messages and updates. It is about engaging. Tracking and listening to your customers allows you to understand what they are saying about your company and your actions.

3. Address your customers' concerns. When you listen and track conversations on social media you will be able to understand your customers' concerns better and address them effectively. Thus social media can help you manage the crisis and avert it. It can also help you in preventing a crisis from happening again.

Here is a case of how Johnson & Johnson managed its Tylenol crisis in an exemplary manner (Case 100) before the evolution of social media. The principles and practices that the company followed are very useful and relevant even today.

Tylenol Scandal and Crisis Management

The Crisis

Tylenol, the leading OTC painkiller drug in the United States faced a tremendous crisis in October 1982. Tylenol was the market leader with a dominant 37 percent of the OTC analgesic market at the time. An unknown suspect(s) tampered Tylenol capsules and put 65 milligrams of deadly cyanide into them. The tampering occurred once the product reached the shelves. They were removed from the shelves, infected with cyanide and returned to the shelves.

The poisoning of the Tylenol capsules resulted in seven deaths in Chicago. The company, Johnson & Johnson immediately after this incident lost a significant chunk of its market share, which became 7 percent.

How The Company Responded

McNeil Consumer Products, a subsidiary of Johnson & Johnson, which markets Tylenol responded immediately in the most appropriate and even an exemplary manner.

The company following a principle of protecting people first and property second conducted an immediate product recall from the entire country, which amounted to about 31 million bottles worth more than $100 million. Although Johnson & Johnson knew they were not responsible for the tampering of the product, they assumed responsibility for public safety first and recalled entire stock from the market. They stopped all advertising for the product.

Later, in 1986 when a woman was reported dead from cyanide poisoning in Tylenol capsules, Johnson & Johnson removed all of the capsules from the market. The company had come up with a campaign to re-introduce the product and more importantly restore the confidence of the consumers in the product. Here is how they did it and Tylenol won its leadership back.

The company reintroduced Tylenol capsules in a triple-seal tamper-resistant packaging and called them caplets and promoted the tamper-proof concept of the packaging that was the first of its kind.

They offered a $2.50 discount coupon on the purchase of the product to motivate consumers to buy the product. They (the coupons) were available in the newspapers as well as by calling a toll-free number.

Besides, the company made a new pricing program that gave consumers up to 25 percent off on the purchase of Tylenol caplets to recover any stock loss from the crisis. To restore confidence in the product, over 2,250 salespeople made presentations to the medical community.

Living up to the Mission Statement

How did Johnson & Johnson do what it did so brilliantly to manage such a massive crisis? By living up to their Credo, written in the mid-1940s by Robert Wood Johnson, who stated that the company's responsibilities were to the consumers and medical professionals using its products, employees, the communities where its people work and live, and its stockholders.

The company's responsibility to its publics first proved to be its most efficient and effective public relations tool. It was the key to a brand's survival. Tylenol is a brand to reckon with even today!

(Source: Adapted from Interactive Media Labs, College of Journalism, Crisis Management, University of Florida)

Key Insights, and Practical Lessons

A careful study of the hundred cases discussed in this book are most likely to spark our imagination and help us to plan, launch, build and manage our brands. The insights gained from studying these cases provide practical lessons and enable us in almost preparing templates for pharmaceutical marketing excellence. Here is an executive summary of actionable insights that one can gain and the practical lessons that are eminently implementable.

1. All the great launches have one common feature. They all have excelled at shaping the product and shaping the market. Gardasil of Merck very effectively changed the perception of human papillomavirus from a sexually transmitted viral disease to a causal factor in cervical cancer. To shape the product and market, we need to start early on in the development process. We need to start the marketing planning process as soon as we get the promising clinical evidence of our Phase III clinical trials for registration.

2. We must find and create an edge that will differentiate our product from the existing competition. This will require innovative approaches to unveil insights into customer and stakeholder needs and behaviors that competitors do not have. Cialis, for example, invested heavily in developing deep customer insights to create a strong positioning against the well-established Viagra. It changed the rules of the game by making the not-considered-important-enough advantage of its longer duration of action as the most significant advantage for patients with erectile dysfunction.

3. How to position your product effectively? Cialis has considered many positioning options. Should it center its marketing effort around the current, established purchasing criteria of physicians such as efficacy and safety and highlight its superior, more favorable side effect profile? Alternatively, should it attempt to establish its 36-hour long action as the new criterion? The marketing team at Eli Lilly decided to emphasize the benefits of its 36-hour action. Being able to choose a time

for intimacy and romance in a 36-hour window meant that the fear of failure is removed and ensured a relaxed, no-hurry mood to facilitate spontaneity. They backed up this theme with brilliant advertising and TV spots that resonated with their audience.

4. Differential positioning is even more important in highly crowded branded-generic markets. Consider how Livogen capsules, Fefol, Betnesol injections, and Incidal have won in the Indian pharmaceutical market with their creative positioning strategies.

5. Communication strategy plays a very critical role in conveying your brand's distinct identity, which is the essence of your differentiation. Let's look at Rocephin's brand communication for example. It was the essence of simplicity. While all its major competitors were talking about severe problems like life-threatening infections, Rocephin was refreshingly different and talked about the most desirable positive outcomes such as safe discharge from the hospital and owned the position of 'wellness' in the minds of the prescribing physicians.

6. We need to unearth, find and fill an unmet need for a targeted patient population. Like GlaxoSmithKline did with their Requip. Requip filled a relatively unknown condition that was under-diagnosed and under-treated such as restless legs syndrome (RLS) and positioned Requip as its perfect solution.

7. Consider how Merck identified the unmet needs and shaped the market around them. Merck identified a substantial unmet need in osteoporosis and osteopenia. Osteopenia was unheard of before Merck began its awareness programs and campaigns.

8. We have to start the product launch planning activity early. How early is too early? For research-based Pharma companies, the launch phase begins as soon as it publishes the clinical data from its Phase III registration trials. All the significant new product launches have one thing in common.

Whether it is Lipitor, Januvia, Fosamax and others, they all started preparing for the launch very early. Beginning the process of preparation early on gives us an opportunity to put in place the success principle for launching new products suggested by McKinsey, the leading international strategic management consultancy firm: Shape the product, shape the market and shape the company.

9. Begin your market-shaping activity long before the launch. Most brand teams start their marketing activities months before the launch.

10. Think portfolio! It is crucial to achieving a leadership or dominant position in a given therapeutic area is vital for long-term success. The life of products in general and pharmaceutical products, in particular, is very limited in today's hyper-competitive world. The life (market exclusivity) of a pharmaceutical product is only twenty years. When you consider its life in the marketplace (after launch) is even lesser by eight to ten years as it takes that much time for a developing a new pharmaceutical product. Therefore, it is vital to own a disease condition by building a leading brand and fielding successive product candidates to maintain leadership forever. That is what every pharmaceutical marketer dreams and strives for. Consider for example how Eli Lilly has been maintaining a leading position in the diabetes area with its franchise. The case of Eli Lilly's diabetes franchise illustrates and illuminates as to how to manage a therapeutic franchise. The critical success factors for developing and sustaining a therapeutic franchise are: early development of multiple indications, new dosage forms, and formulations; and to launch the new patented molecules before the patents on the first brands expire as it allows for switching patients to the company's successive (new) brands. That is the route to building a therapeutic franchise and leadership.

11. Prilosec is another excellent example of what proactive planning, distinct identity, and creative promotion can do to a brand and even the therapeutic franchise. Prilosec could field

a successive anti-ulcer drug - Nexium well before the patent expiry of its predecessor - Prilosec and switch its patients effectively.

12. Johnson & Johnson had also tried very hard to sustain its position in the antipsychotic area. Xylocaine and Lidocaine too, offer a classic example in extending their therapeutic leadership. It is axiomatic that a product launch always takes place in a portfolio context. To maximize the value of the franchise, the launch must take into account existing brands and work forward to those in the pipeline.

13. Building and maintaining therapeutic leadership is important and possible even in branded generic markets. The case of Ranbaxy (Sun Pharma now) in the Indian urological market illustrates this.

14. Be Aware that awareness is crucial. We cannot argue about the importance of awareness. Creating and improving awareness of a disorder or a disease condition that is less-known or taken-for-granted is vital for your product success. It is through creating and enhancing awareness of a disorder and what your product can do to improve it that you can shape a market, shape your product and indeed shape even the company. Look at what Pfizer's awareness campaigns of Viagra have accomplished. Remember that your (new) product success is highly dependent on the appropriate perception of the target disease.

15. Consider the case of Eli Lilly's Prozac for example. When fluoxetine entered the market in the 1980s, major depressive disorder was a term reserved for psychiatrists in hospitals. Prozac and its peers helped to reposition depression by classifying its milder and more prevalent forms. They improved the disease awareness and understanding considerably with their brochures such as *depression: what you need to know* and with the media attention followed by their campaigns with celebrities that were undergoing treatment. Today, the public awareness of depression is much broader and consequently the increase in diagnoses and treatment rates.

16. The marketing of Viagra provides a blueprint for medicalizing a lifestyle condition, male impotence which was almost

considered a taboo to discuss in public and was embarrassing to talk even with physicians. Pfizer changed it all with its marketing, advertising, educating and public relations strategies. The company created an acronym that almost became a password ED (erectile dysfunction) for discussions and conversations regarding a highly stigmatized condition till then.

17. Celebrity advertising accelerates the awareness process. It increases awareness rapidly. When the long-term senator, former presidential candidate, and an honored war veteran, Bob Dole appeared in a Viagra commercial in 1998, he revolutionized the way such personalities participated in pharmaceutical campaigns. This had encouraged pharmaceutical companies to aim higher in their pursuit of celebrity endorsers and advocates. Here is a message Bob delivered in a TV commercial that resonated with its target audience: *"It is a little embarrassing to talk about ED, but it's so important to millions of men and their partners that I decided to talk about it publicly."*

18. Gardasil of Merck created highly powerful, emotional that is at times controversial advertising with a compelling call to action.

19. Educational campaigns to physicians, patients, and all the stakeholders hold the key to success. The most effective companies begin the market shaping work during the clinical development work once they see the initial promise of the drug to transform both the disease perception and the product profile long before launch. Merck invested in an intensive campaign to educate physicians (gynecologists mainly) and the American public (especially the middle-aged women) about osteoporosis and the availability bone-mineral testing. Merck's efforts resulted in expanding the potential market from 1.3 million per year in the US to 16 million women at risk in a short period.

20. We need to involve and engage as many stakeholders as necessary to raise the awareness of the disease condition and how the product is best suited to treat it. Merck co-sponsored media campaigns with the National Osteoporosis Foundation.

21. Highly effective companies go beyond conventional partnerships such as patient advocacy groups and physicians in meeting the unmet needs. For Fosamax, Merck partnered with diagnostic equipment manufacturers such as Hologic and Lunar corporations to facilitate the rollout of bone-mineral testing machines in far-flung areas in the United States. Merck also partnered with the diagnostic giant Siemens in many countries for enabling in-clinic testing of diabetes for HbA1c in a patient-centric move. This move saved a visit to the diagnostic center to test, collect the report and revisit the physician. Novartis for example engaged teachers and parents and educated them about the need to test and treat the children for attention deficit hyperactivity disorder (ADHD) very effectively.

22. Key stakeholder engagement is vital for marketing a product successfully. Every pharmaceutical company tries to engage their primary stakeholders such as physicians, patients and other healthcare providers. Many of the winning companies in these cases have engaged the key stakeholders such as payers effectively. Engaging payers effectively improves the access of the drug significantly. Merck achieved a 94 percent reimbursement level with almost all the insurance companies for Gardasil.

23. Market protection or exclusivity alone is not enough. That's what the case of BiDil teaches us. Ability to command a price premium is equally essential. BiDil obtained market exclusivity but not a price premium as its formulation contained two active ingredients which are off-patent.

24. Lipitor shows us how an innovative pricing strategy can propel the product into the top position.

25. Johnson & Johnson's *Me without Migraine* case study teaches us that it is essential to seek to understand first and foremost in creating a social media campaign to improve awareness. It also highlights the importance of a patient-centric approach. We need to engage patients, help them understand the disease condition and manage it.

26. Involve and integrate the teams. Rally the troops. Like Ronald Cresswell did at Merck when he was a chief scientific officer at Warner-Lambert at the time of launching Lipitor. He integrated regulatory affairs and clinical research into the R&D organization with the intention of improving documentation packages submitted to the FDA. He also sought to involve marketing very early into the new product development process. As a result, both marketing and R&D had a clear sense of Lipitor's potential long before it received approval. In case of Viagra, the top management of Pfizer rallied the entire troops with unprecedented enthusiasm behind Viagra by clearly explaining the potential of Viagra and its significance not only to the company but to the whole patient community. Viagra became the most remembered product of the century.

27. Top management involvement and support are vital for success. Everyone agrees with this principle, but not many would practice it. Paul Girolami of GlaxoSmithKline was an exception. He led his troops from the front in the development and launching of Zantac. He was not only the chief executive of the company, but he conducted himself as the chief product manager of Zantac. Zantac created history by becoming the first-ever prescription drug to pass the coveted $1 billion mark and later the first to pass even the $4 billion mark.

Critical Success Factors

Any pharmaceutical marketer, who studies these cases assiduously and attentively would be able to identify the critical success factors for achieving excellence in launching new products, managing them effectively throughout their lifetime and build enduring therapeutic leadership in their chosen areas. Here is an indicative list of key success factors for achieving marketing excellence in pharmaceuticals and the companies that have excelled in putting them into practice:

Key Success Factors and Companies That Excelled At Them

Key Success Factors	Reference Brands and Companies
1. Early Start	Januvia, Janumet, Fosamax (Merck), Lipitor (Parke-Davis, which is Pfizer now)
2. Good to Great Science (Clinical Evidence)	Sovaldi (Gilead Life Sciences), Humira (AbbVie), Lipitor (Parke-Davis, which is Pfizer now), Gleevec (Novartis)
3. Disease Awareness	Viagra (Pfizer), Lipitor (Parke-Davis, which is Pfizer now), Fosamax, Januvia, Janumet (Merck), Zantac, Requip (GlaxoSmithKline), Prozac (Eli Lilly, Novartis (Ritalin), Shire (Adderall)
4. Celebrity Advertising Campaigns (DTCA)	Viagra (Pfizer), Lipitor (Merck), Januvia, Janumet (Merck),
5. Differentiation	Cialis (Eli Lilly, Prilosec, Zantac (GlaxoSmithKline)
6. Product Positioning	Cialis (Eli Lilly), Rocephin (Hoffman-la-Roche), Zantac (GlaxoSmithKline),
7. Education of Physicians, Patients, and other stakeholders	Viagra (Pfizer), Lipitor, Januvia, Janumet, Fosamax (Merck), Humira (AbbVie, Novartis (Ritalin),
8. Engaging and Extending Stakeholders	Fosamax (Merck), Januvia, Janumet (Merck), Novartis (Ritalin)
9. Disease Branding	Zantac (GlaxoSmithKline), Viagra (Pfizer), Requip (GlaxoSmithKline), Listerine (Warner-Lambert, which is Pfizer now), Detrol (Pharmacia), Xanax (Upjohn), Zoloft (Pfizer)
10. Life Cycle Management	Cipro (Bayer), Zantac (GlaxoSmithKline), Fosamax (Merck), Prilosec (AstraZeneca),
11. Improving Access	Humira (AbbVie), Gardasil (Merck), Lipitor (Pfizer), Gleevec (Novartis)

Table Contd...

Key Success Factors	Reference Brands and Companies
12. Creative Advertising Communication	Viagra, Cialis, Gardasil, Rocephin, Ritalin
13. Building and Developing a Franchise	Risperdal, Invega Sustenna (Eli Lilly), Keppra (UCB), Prilosec, Nexium (AstraZeneca), Insulin and Diabetic Care (Novo Nordisk)
14. Therapeutic Leadership	Eli Lilly's Diabetic Franchise, Xylocaine, Lidocaine (AstraZeneca), Novartis (ADHD), Shire (ADD),
15. Strategic Lobbying	Merck (Fosamax, Gardasil), BiDil (NitroMed), Gilead Life Sciences (Sovaldi)
16. Beyond-the-pill services	Januvia, Janumet, Fosamax (Merck),
17. Innovative Pricing	Lipitor (Parke-Davis, which is now Pfizer),
18. Blue Ocean Strategic Moves	Novopen (Novo Nordisk), Viagra (Pfizer), Requip (GlaxoSmithKline),
19. Media and Public Relations	Pfizer (Viagra), Merck (Fosamax, Gardasil, Januvia, Janumet),
20. Digital Marketing Initiatives	Merck (Januvia, Janumet, Gardasil, Fosamax),
21. Involve and integrate the teams (Regulatory, R&D and Marketing). And rally the troops behind the product.	Merck (Lipitor), Pfizer (Viagra)
22. Top management involvement and support	Zantac (GlaxoSmithKline)

In addition to these key success factors, the cases in the book also caution us against some of the practices that would take us on the road to failure. We need to avoid the following.

Practices to Avoid	Reference Brands and Cases
1. Excessive focus on Efficacy, Ignoring Safety	Baycol (Bayer), Exubera (Pfizer), Xigris (Eli Lilly), Zelnorm (Novartis)
2. Inadequate preparation before launch	Exubera (Pfizer), Baycol, (Bayer)
3. Off-label promotion	Neurontin (Parke-Davis, which is Pfizer now)
4. Use of MSLs for product promotion and selling	Neurontin (Parke-Davis, which is Pfizer now)
5. Predatory Pricing	Daraprim (Turning), Isupril (Valeant), Nitropress (Valeant), Vimovo (Horizon)

Secret Sauce for Achieving Marketing Excellence: Ten Active Ingredients

What is marketing excellence? Is there a formula for it? Or a secret sauce that can turn the conventional marketing activities into excellent marketing practices? A careful study of these hundred cases would also reveal ten active ingredients of a secret sauce for turning our marketing activities into excellent marketing practices. These secret ingredients are:

1. Start marketing planning early on in the development process. As Alexander Graham Bell, the inventor of the telephone says: before anything else, preparation is the key to success.

2. Identify the currently unmet needs and fit your product to fill them.

3. Build awareness of the disease condition among all the stakeholders and the general public. Use celebrities with the disorders who are on treatment with your product to accelerate the process of awareness.

4. Invest in educating all the stakeholders about diagnosing the condition and how your product can be a valuable tool in treating it.

5. Differentiate your product from competitive offerings and position it in the minds of the prescribing physicians, patients, and other stakeholders.

6. Think portfolio. It is imperative to follow a portfolio approach in product development as patent life is very limited.

7. Aim to achieve therapeutic leadership. Leverage customer and stakeholder relationships by continually developing new products in the therapeutic are of your choice. Maximize switching opportunities.

8. Manage the life cycle of the product effectively and proactively. Use all lifecycle management strategies to the best of your product advantage. Expand indications. Introduce new formulations and dosage forms. Field successive new drug candidates.

9. Follow an innovative and socially responsible pricing strategy.

10. Focus on efficacy as well as safety when you are developing and marketing a product. Excessive focus on efficacy and turning a blind eye to possible side effects have cost many a company dearly.

References

1. Giles D. Moss, *Pharmaceuticals - Where's the brand logic? Branding lessons and strategy,* Pharmaceutical Products Press, an imprint of The Hayworth Press, New York, 2007

2. Jie Jack Li, *Triumph of the heart: The story of statins,* Oxford University Press, 2009

3. Jie Jack Li, *Blockbuster drugs: The rise and decline of pharmaceutical industry,* Oxford University Press, 2014

4. Robert J. Thomas, *New product success stories: Lessons from leading innovators,* John Wiley & Sons Inc. New York, 1995

5. Keith Wailoo, *Pain: A political history,* Johns Hopkins University Press, Reprint edition, November 6, 2015

6. Rajiv Narang, *Devika Deviah, Orbit-shifting innovation: The dynamics of ideas that create history*, Random House India, 2013

7. Carl Elliott, *White coat, black hat: Adventures on the dark side of medicine,* Beacon Press, Boston, 2010

8. John Griffin, Editor, *The Textbook of pharmaceutical medicine,* 6th Edition, BMJ Books, Wiley - Blackwell, A John Wlley & Sons Publications Ltd., Chichester, West Sussex, UK, 2009

9. Greg Critser, *Generation Rx: How prescription drugs are altering American lives, minds, and bodies*, Houghton Mifflin Company, New York, 2015

10. Howard Brody, Hooked: *Ethics, the medical profession, and the pharmaceutical industry*, Rowman&Littlefield Publishers Inc. Maryland, USA, 2007

11. Jamie Reidy, *Hard sell: The evolution of a Viagra salesman,* Andrews McMeel Publishing, Kansas City, USA, 2005

12. W. Chan Kim, Renée Mauborgne, *Blue ocean strategy: How to use uncontested market space and make competition irrelevant*, Harvard Business School Publishing Corporation, Boston, 2015

13. Eileen Gambrill, *Propaganda in the helping professions,* Oxford University Press Inc. New York, 2012

14. Julie Froud, Sukhdev Johal, Adam Lever, and Karel Williams, *Financialization and strategy: Narrative and numbers,* Routledge, Taylor & Francis Group, New York, 2006

15. Edited by: Louise Hill Curth, *From physics to pharmacology: 500 Years of British drug retailing*, Ashgate Publishing, 2006

16. Enrico Gnaulati, PhD, *Saving Talk Therapy: How health insurers, Big Pharma, and slanted science are ruining good mental healthcare,* Beacon Press, Boston

17. Derek Lowe, Pfizer: *Four lessons from the Exubera Failure,* Seeking Alpha, October 22, 2007, www.seekingalpha.com

18. Avery Johnson, *Insulin Flop costs Pfizer $ 2.8-billion,* The Wall Street Journal, October 19, 2007, www.wsj.com

19. Gardiner Harris, Staff Reporter, *Prilosec's maker switches users to Nexium, thwarting generics,* The Wall Street Journal, June 06, 2002, www.wsj.com

20. Sarah Ellison, Staff Reporter, *Prilosec OTC blitz by P&G represents new drug foray*, The Wall Street Journal, September 12, 2003, www.wsj.com

21. Fritz Allhoff, *Daraprim and predatory pricing: Martin Shekril's 5000% hike,* Stanford Law School Blogs, Law and Biosciences Blog, October 05, 2015, https://law.stanford.edu/2015/10/05/daraprim-and-drug-pricing/

22. Andrew Pollack, *Big price increase for Tuberculosis drug is rescinded,* Business Day, The New York Times, September 21, 2015, www.nytimes.com

23. Sibyl Shalo, *The life cycle of Cipro,* Pharmaceutical Executive, August 01, 2004, www.pharmexec.com

24. Joshua Slatko, *Lucky and Good - Medicine of the Year: Januvia, 22nd Annual Report,* Med Ad News 200, MedAd News 30th Anniversary, Volume 31, Number 7, www.medadnews.com

25. Kao DP, *What can we learn from drug marketing efficiency?* BMJ, December 02, 2008

26. *Acomplia - Pharma's biggest flops,* Fierce Pharma, www.fiercepharma.com

27. Alex Berenson, *3 Doctors assail Lilly study of sepsis drug,* Business Day, The New York Times, October 19, 2006, www.nytimes.com/2006/10/19/business/19lilly.html

28. *Inhalable insulin,* Wikipedia, https://en.wikipedia.org/wiki/inhalable_insulin

29. Matthew Herper, Forbes Staff, *Medical flops of the decade,* Pharma & Healthcare, Forbes, June 17, 2010, www.forbes.com

30. Matthew Herper, Forbes Staff, *A buyout is Bristol's best hope,* Pharma & Healthcare, Forbes, March 20, 2002

31. Reinhard Angelman, Fellow in Healthcare Management, and Professor of Marketing, INSEAD, *The rise and fall of Baycol / Lipobay,* Journal of Medical Marketing, January 2007

32. Warren Allen, *The unexpected regulator: Regulation through settlement after Vioxx and Bextra,* Brooklyn Journal of corporate, financial & commercial law, Article 6, Volume 6/issue 2, 2012

33. Jeanne Whalen, *How Glaxo marketed a malady to sell a drug,* Healthcare, The Wall Street Journal, October 25, 2006

34. Siddhartha Mukherjee, *The science and history of treating depression*, The New York Times, April 19, 2012

35. Snigdha Prakash, Vikki Valentine, *Timeline: The rise and fall of Vioxx,* NPR, November 10, 2007

36. Stan Bernard, M.D. *Rethinking product lifecycle management, Pharmaceutical Executive,* February 01, 2013, www.pharmexec.com

37. Kristina Fiore, John Fauber, and Matt Wynn, *Drug firms helped create $US3 billion over active bladder market, MedPage Today and Milwaukee Journal Sentinel,* Journal Sentinel, October 15, 2016

38. Charlene Prounis, *10 steps to product positioning, Medical Marketing & Media,* February 01, 2007

39. Kathryn Greengrove, *GlaxoSmithKline, USA*, *Needs-based segmentation: Principles and Practice*, International Journal of Market Research, Vol 44, Quarter 4, 2002, https://pdfs.semanticscholar.org/dca1/3f93369c10a9fa1b25ea42182c8ec05b95be.pdf

40. Carl Elliott, Special to CNN, *How to brand a disease and sell a cure, October 11, 2011*, http://edition.cnn.com/2010/OPINION/10/11/elliott.branding.disease/index.html

41. David T. Wong, Kenneth W. Perry, and Frank P. Bymaster, *The Discovery of Fluoxetine Hydrochloride (Prozac)*, Reviews - Drug Discovery, Nature, September 2005, Volume 4, www.nature.com/reveiws/drugdisc

42. Anna Moore, *Social Care*, The Observer, Eternal Sunshine, Sunday 13 May, 2007, https://www.theguardian.com/society/2007/may/13/socialcare.medicineandhealth

43. Bali Sunset, *Prozac print campaign - Marketing campaign case studies*, October 15, 2008, http://marketing-case-studies.blogspot.com/2008/10/prozac-print-campaign.html

44. Stuart Elliott, *A new campaign by Leo Burnett will try to promote Prozac directly to consumers*, The New York Times, July 1, 1997, https://www.nytimes.com/1997/07/01/business/a-new-campaign-by-leo-burnett-will-try-to-promote-prozac-directly-to-consumers.html

45. Tara McKelvey, *How Prozac entered the lexicon, BBC News Magazine, April10, 2013*, https://www.bbc.com/news/magazine-22040733

46. William E. Sheeline, Reporter Associate Mark Colodny, *Glaxo's Goal: New Wonder Cures The US Patent of Zantac, the world's best selling drug is running out. At Britain's pharmaceutical powerhouse, the heat is on the American Boss,* Fortune Magazine, November 6, 1999, http://archive.fortune.com/magazines/fortune/fortune_archive/1989/11/06/72708/index.htm

47. Ernst R. Berndt, Linda T. Bui, David H. Lucking-Reiley, and Glen L. Urban, *The roles of marketing, product quality, and price competition in the growth and composition of US drug industry:* The Economics of Growth, University of Chicago Press, 1996, http://www.nber.org/chapters/c6070.pdf

48. Gerrie David, *Can marketing keep Glaxo in pole position?,* Marketing, Questia, October 18, 1990, https://www.questia.com/read/1G1-9275226/can-marketing-keep-glaxo-in-pole-position

49. Melody Petersen, *A bitter pill for Big Pharma,* Los Angeles Times, January 27, 2008, http://www.latimes.com/la-op-peterson27jan27-story.html

50. Jay Baglia, *The Viagra AdVenture: Masculinity, media, and the performance of sexual health*, Peter Lang Publishing Inc., July 2005, New York, USA

51. Jacque Wilson, *Viagra: The little blue pill that could*, CNN, March 27, 2013, https://edition.cnn.com/2013/03/27/health/viagra-anniversary-timeline/index.html

52. Robin McKie, *Ten years on: It's time to count the cost of the Viagra revolution,* February 24, 2008, The Guardian, https://www.theguardian.com/theobserver/2008/feb/24/controversiesinscience

53. Brittaney Kiefer, *Pfizer tackles erectile dysfunction taboo in a new campaign,* Campaign, April 18, 2018, https://www.campaignlive.co.uk/article/pfizer-tackles-erectile-dysfunction-taboo-new-campaign/1462450

54. Larry Dobrow, *7 ways Viagra changed how drugs are marketed, Medical Media & Marketing,* October 03, 2016, https://www.mmm-online.com/commercial/7-ways-viagra-changed-how-drugs-are-marketed/article/526011/

55. Beth Snyder Bulk, *Pfizer's latest Viagra TV ad pitches mobile texting for discounts,* Marketing: Fierce Pharma, January 19, 2017, https://www.fiercepharma.com/marketing/text-to-save-drugs-pfizer-s-latest-vaigra-ad-includes-text-promotion-for-discounts

56. Associated Press, *Pfizer to sell Viagra online, in first for Big Pharma,* CBS News, May 6, 2013, https://www.cbsnews.com/news/pfizer-to-sell-viagra-online-in-first-for-big-pharma-ap/

57. Megan Garber, *Jagged little (blue) pill: Released to the public 20 years ago, Viagra changed the way Americans have sex - and the way they talked about it,* Culture, The Atlantic, March 27, 2018, https://www.theatlantic.com/entertainment/archive/2018/03/20-years-of-viagra/556343/

58. Jack Neff, *Viagra takes more direct approach to get rise out of men,* Ad Age, September 30, 2014, http://adage.com/print/295206

59. Kurian M. Tharakan, *How Cialis outsmarted Viagra?...Or how to strategically outsmart a strong, entrenched competitor,* Strategy Peak, https://strategypeak.com/sex-romance-cialis-outsmarted-viagra/

60. Michael Arndt, *Is Viagra vulnerable? Eli Lilly's Cialis lasts for 36 hours - and a $100 million ad blitz will spread the word,* Bloomberg Business Week, October 27, 2003, https://www.bloomberg.com/news/articles/2003-10-26/is-viagra-vulnerable

61. Niraj Dawar, *When marketing is strategy*, Harvard Business Review, December 2013

62. Jim Edwards, *The name game: Why Pfizer's generic version of Viagra will be renamed Avigra,* Money watch, May 24, 2011, https://www.cbsnews.com/news/the-name-game-why-pfizers-generic-version-of-viagra-will-be-renamed-avigra/

63. Chris Wienke, *Male Sexuality, medicalization and the marketing Cialis and Levitra, Sexuality & Culture, Fall 2005,* Vol 9, No 4, pp 29-57

64. Beth Snyder Bulik, Updated: *My bathtub or yours? How a panned Cialis ad became promotional gold,* DTC Advertising: Fierce Pharma, May 27, 2015, https://www.fiercepharma.com/dtc-advertising/updated-my-bathtub-or-yours-how-a-panned-cialis-ad-became-promotional-gold

65. Jim Edwards, *Hard luck: Why did Viagra is about to lose its No 1 status to Cialis,* Money Watch: CBS News, February 9, 2011, https://www.cbsnews.com/news/hard-luck-why-viagra-is-about-to-lose-its-no1-status-to-cialis/

66. Robert Steyer, *Cialis dares to be different,* The Street, April 12, 2004, https://www.thestreet.com/story/10153065/1/cialis-dares-to-be-different.html

67. Michael Stephens, *PopMatters, Media: Erectile Dysfunction* TV, Alternet, August 15, 2004,https://www.alternet.org/story/19551/e%28rectile%29_d%28ysfunction%29_tv

68. John Russell, *For Lilly's Cialis, glory days are over, Indianapolis Business Journal,* February 20, 2016, https://www.ibj.com/articles/57284-for-cialis-glory-days-are-over

69. Michael A. Steinman, MD, Lisa A. Bero, PhD, Mary-Margaret Chren, MD, Seth Landefeld, MD, *Narrative Review: The promotion of Gabapentin: An analysis of Internal industry documents,* Annals of Internal Medicine, 15 August, 2006, http://annals.org/aim/article-abstract/727539

70. Michael A. Steinman, MD, C. Seth Landefeld, MD, *Perspective: The Neurontin legacy - Marketing through misinformation and manipulation,* The New England Journal of Medicine, January 8, 2009: 360:103-106, https://www.nejm.org/doi/pdf/10.1056/NEJMp0808659

71. Melody Petersen, *Business Day: Doctor explains why he blew the whistle,* The New York Times, March 12, 2003, https://www.nytimes.com/2003/03/12/business/doctor-explains-why-he-blew-the-whistle.html

72. Laura Clark, *How Halitosis became a medical condition with a 'cure',* Smart News - keeping you current, Smithsonian Magazine, January 29, 2015, https://www.smithsonianmag.com/smart-news/marketing-campaign-invented-halitosis-180954082/

73. Esther Inglis-Arkell, *The medical condition invented by Listerine, Science History*, ios9 - We Come From the Future, January 27, 2015, https://io9.gizmodo.com/the-medical-condition-invented-by-listerine-1682070561

74. Heather Ashton, *A view from the shoulders of giants: A review of David Healey's,* " The Psychopharmacologists III, Arnold, London, 2000, www.benzo.org.uk, https://benzo.org.uk/ashreview.htm

75. Jennifer Daw, Cover Story: *Is PMDD real? Researchers, physicians, psychologists fall on various sides of the debate over premenstrual dysphoric disorder,* American Psychological Association, October 2002, Vol 33, No 9, Print version: Page 58, http://www.apa.org/monitor/oct02/pmdd.aspx

76. Paula J. Caplan, PhD., *Premenstrual mental illness: The truth about Sarafem,* www.paulajcaplan.net/attachments/Nwhn_sarafem_ar.doc

77. James Davies, *Big Pharma's Placebo Problem,* Salon, August 3, 2013, https://www.salon.com/2013/08/03/big_pharmas_placebo_problem/

78. Brendan I. Koerner, *Disorders made to order: Pharmaceutical companies have come up with a new strategy to market their drugs: First go out and find a new mental illness, then push pills to cure it,* Mother Jones, July/August 2002 Issue, https://www.motherjones.com/politics/2002/07/disorders-made-order/

79. Matthew J. Friedman, MD, PhD., *A brief history of PTSD, PTSD:* National Center for PTSD, US Department of Veteran Affairs, https://www.ptsd.va.gov/professional/ptsd-overview/ptsd-overview.asp

80. Marcus Baram, *EX-drug sales rep tells all,* ABC News, March 13, 2008, https://abcnews.go.com/US/story?id= 4438095 &page=1

81. W. Chan Kim, *Rene Mauborgne, Blue ocean strategic moves,* https://www.blueoceanstrategy.com/bos-moves/viagra/

82. Jon Hess, Shannon Litalien, *Battle for the market's branded drug companies' secret weapons generic drug firms must know,* Journal of Generic Medicines, Vol 3, No 1, 20-29, October 2005

83. Shabana Hussain, Mankind Pharma: *Formulating strategy to enter the big league,* Forbes India, May 8, 2014, http://www.forbesindia.com/article/boardroom/mankind- pharma-formulating-strategy-to-enter-the-big-league/37704/0

84. Andrea Sobrio, Aleksandar Ruzicic, and Meike Wenzel, *Dive In: Gaining leadership in a therapeutic area: Gaining long-term leadership in a therapy area can be commercially invaluable,* PMLIve, 12 September, 2014, http://www.pmlive.com/pharma_news/dive_in_gaining_ leadership_in_a_ therapeutic_area_598542

85. Managed Care, *Senate Report slams drug makers' "Predatory" pricing model,* Senate Report, December 22, 2016, https://www.managedcaremag.com/news/senate-report-slams-drug-makers-predatory-pricing-model

86. Tom Norton, *How Gilead "Blew out the lights with Sovaldi,"* Pharmaceutical Executive, November 18, 2014, http://www.pharmexec.com/how-gilead-blew-out-lights-sovaldi

87. Lisa Murch, Sarah Rickwood, *Bill McClellan, Dr. Simone Seiter, Launch Excellence V: Surviving and thriving when launching in an increasingly specialized world,* White Paper, Quintiles IMS, https://www.iqvia.com/-/media/quintilesims/pdfs/launch-excellence-v.pdf

88. Alix Spiegel, *How a bone disease grew to fit the prescription,* National Public Radio Inc., https://www.npr.org/2009/12/21/121609815/how-a-bone-disease-grew-to-fit-the-prescription

89. Matthew Herper, The *Gardasil problem, Forbes, April 4, 2012,* https://www.forbes.com/forbes/2012/0423/feature-neal-fowler-pharmaceuticals-gardasilproblem.html#533cc4772d75

90. Pray, L (2008), Gleevec: *The breakthrough in cancer treatment, Nature Education, 1(11):37,* https://www.nature.com/scitable/topicpage/gleevec-the-breakthrough-in-cancer-treatment-565

91. Paul Holmes, *The global launch of Gleevec,* The Holmes Report, March 4, 2003, https://www.holmesreport.com/latest/article/the-global-launch-of-gleevec

92. David Hanlon, *10 Key activities in measuring and communicating Pharma product launch excellence,* Quirks Media, Article ID: 20150307, Published: March 2015, https://www.quirks.com/articles/10-key-activities-in-measuring-and-communicating-pharma-product-launch-excellence

93. Lydia Ramsey, *The strange history of the Epipen, the device developed by the military that turned into a billion-dollar business*, Business Insider India, August 28, 2016, https://www.businessinsider.in/The-strange-history-of-the-EpiPen-the-device-developed-by-the-military-that-turned-into-a-billion-dollar-business/articleshow/53892570.cms

94. Pauline Bartolone, *EpiPen's dominance driven by competitors' stumbles and tragic deaths,* NPR, September 7, 2016, https://www.npr.org/sections/health-shots/2016/09/07/492964464/epipen-s-dominance-driven-by-competitors-stumbles-and-tragic-deaths

95. Cynthia Koons, and Robert Langreth, *How marketing turned the EpiPen into a billion-dollar business,* BloombergSeptember 23, 2015, Bloomberg Business Week, https://www.bloomberg.com/news/articles/2015-09-23/how-marketing-turned-the-epipen-into-a-billion-dollar-business

96. Cara McDonough, *Medical necessity or marketing success?* Finding Dulcinea, October 9, 2008, http://www.findingdulcinea.com/news/health/September-October-08/Gardasil--Medical-Necessity-or-Marketing-Success-.html

97. Pharmaceutical Executive Editors, *Gardasil campaign taps public fear of cancer*, PharmExec.com, Issue 1, November 29, 2006

98. Laurie McGinley, *Do the new Merck HPV ads guilt-trip parents or tell hard truths? Both, To Your Health*, The Washington Post, August 11, 2016, https://www.washingtonpost.com/news/to-your-health/wp/2016/08/11/do-the-new-merck-hpv-ads- guilt-trip -parents-or-tell-hard-truths-both/?utm_ term=.2b496b 19ddec

99. S. Gottileib, MHS, PhD, *Vaccine promotion in the hands of a corporation: The missed opportunity of Merck's marketing of Gardasil,* Corporations and Health Watch, June 1, 2010, http:/ /www.corporationsandhealth.org/2010/06/01/vaccine-promotion-in-the-hands-of-a-corporation-the-missed-opportunity-of-mercks-marketing-of-gardasil/

100. Sheryl Attkisson, *Gardasil researcher speaks out,* CBS News, https://www.cbsnews.com/news/gardasil-researcher-speaks-out/

101. Sankar, Pamela and Kahn, Jonathan D, BiDil: *Race medicine or Race marketing,* Health Affairs, October 11, 2005, https://papers.ssrn.com/sol3/papers.cfm?abstract_id=825645

102. *Paragraph Four Explained*, Parry AshFord Publications, https:/ /www.paragraphfour.com/explained/why_challenge.html

103. Lucy Rana, India: *The Road ahead after patent grant*, mondaq.com, February 8, 2016, http://www.mondaq.com/india/x/464420/Patent/The+Road+Ahead+After+Patent+Grant

104. James O'Rourke, *Merck & Co Inc: Communication lessons from the withdrawal of Vioxx,* Journal of Business Strategy, July 2006

105. Reinhard Angelmar, *Marketing Case: The rise and fall of Baycol / Lipobay,* Journal of Medical Marketing (2007) 7, 77 - 88, http:/ /test-www.palgrave-journals.com/jmm/journal/v7/n1/full/5050068a.html

106. Dr. Neal Hansen, *Expert Insight: 10 Critical success factors for Pharma life cycle management,* cellforpharma.com, March 2017, https://www.celforpharma.com/insight/10-critical-success-factors-pharma-lifecycle-management

107. Sherry Baker, *David L. Martinson, The TARES Test: Five principles for ethical persuasion,* J647: The Theoretical Foundation of Communication Ethics, https://j647commethics.weebly.com/uploads/6/4/2/2/6422481/the_tares_test_-_five_principles_for_ethical _persuation_ _baker___ martinson_.pdf

108. John LaMattina, Pharma & Healthcare: *Even Pharma's good deeds are criticized, Forbes,* https://www.forbes.com/sites/johnlamattina/2013/05/06/even-pharmas-good-deeds-are-criticized/

109. Eric Dalton, *4 secrets of successful drug launches marketers must know*, PM 360, October 18, 2017, https://www.pm360online.com/4-secrets-of-successful-drug-launches-marketers-must-know/

110. Kathlyn Stone, *Biotech Industry - Sales and Marketing: A guide to the top generic drug companies,* The Balance, May 10, 2018, https://www.thebalance.com/top-generic-drug-companies-2663110

111. *Top 10 pharmaceutical markets worldwide 2016, IQVIA*, https://www.iqvia.com/-/media/iqvia/pdfs/canada-location-site/top-10-worldwide-sales-en-2016.pdf

112. Evaluate Pharma: *World Preview 2018 Outlook to 2024,* 11th Edition, http://info.evaluategroup.com/rs/607-YGS-364/images/WP2018.pdf

113. Allen Lefkowitz, Tim Opler, Vimal Vaderah, *Generic Pharmaceutical Industry Year Book,* Torreya Partners, GPhA Conference Edition 2016, February 2016, https://torreya.com/publications/generic-pharmaceutical-industry-yearbook-torreya-feb2016-gpha.pdf

114. Patricia M. Danzon, *Economics of the pharmaceutical industry,* NBER Reporter: Research Summary, Fall 2006, http://www.nber.org/reporter/fall06/danzon.html

115. S.S. Rana & Co, Working of patents statements in India, http://www.ssrana.in/Intellectual%20Property/Patents/Patents-Working-of-Patented-in-India.aspx

116. Tom Norton, *How Gilead "Blew out the lights" with Sovaldi,* Pharmaceutical Executive, November 18, 2014, http://www.pharmexec.com/how-gilead-blew-out-lights-sovaldi

117. John LaMattina, *Gilead's CEO admits to 'Failures' in setting price of $ 1000-A-Pill Breakthrough,* Editors Pick, Forbes, December 8, 2016, https://www.forbes.com/sites/johnlamattina/2016/12/08/gileads-ceo-apologetic-about-sovaldis-1000-per-pill-price-tag/#7872a901a97c

118. Truth Investor, *Stop panicking about Gilead's Hep-C competition*, Seeking Alpha, October 28, 2016, https://seekingalpha.com/article/4016497-stop-panicking-gileads-hep-c-competition

119. Emma Court, *Merck Hepatitis C exit could lift the space's two remaining drug makers*, Market Watch, October 1, 2017, https://www.marketwatch.com/story/merck-hepatitis-c-exit-could-lift-the-spaces-two-remaining-drugmakers-2017-09-29

120. Peter Bach and Mark Trusheim, *The US Government should buy Gilead for $156 billion to save money on Hepatitis C,* Forbes, January 12, 2017, https://www.forbes.com/sites/sciencebiz/2017/01/17/the-u-s-government-should-buy-gilead-for-156-billion-to-save-money-on-hepatitis-c/#4705236471a2

121. Allison Gatlin, *AbbVie's new Hepatitis C drug chipping away at Gilead's share,* Investor's Business Daily, September 15, 2017, https://www.investors.com/news/technology/abbvies-new-hepatitis-c-drug-chipping-away-at-gileads-share/

122. Allison Gatlin, How *AbbVie could hammer Gilead's Hepatitis C. Franchise, July 19, 2017,* https://www.investors.com/news/technology/how-abbvie-could-hammer-gileads-hepatitis-c-franchise/

123. Sy Mukherjee, *The FDA just approved the first drug that can treat all Hepatitis C strains in just 8 weeks,* Health–Drug Development, Fortune, August 3, 2017, http://fortune.com/2017/08/03/fda-hepatitis-c-mavyret/

124. Karen Andersen, *Despite Hepatitis C pressure, Gilead's portfolio supports strong cash flow and a wide moat*, Business Strategy and Outlook, May 2, 2018, www.analystreport.morningstarcom, May 2, 2018

125. Max Macaluso, *How Gleevec changed the game for Novartis,* The Motley Fool, December 18, 2013, https://www.fool.com/investing/general/2013/12/18/how-gleevec-changed-the-game-for-novartis.aspx

126. Steve Miller, *The Sovaldi Tax: Gilead can't justify the price it's asking for hepatitis C therapy,* Forbes, June 17, 2014, https://www.forbes.com/sites/theapothecary/2014/06/17/the-sovaldi-tax-gilead-cant-justify-the-price-its-asking-americans-to-pay/#22919bce5670

127. Megan Smith-May, *Celebrity drug endorsements: Are consumers protected?* American Journal of Law & Medicine, Sage Journals, September 6, 2007, http://journals.sagepub.com/doi/full/10.1177/0098858817707988

128. Piotr Wizosiski in Pharma Marketing, K. Message, *Gamification in Pharma marketing explained with examples,* December 25, 2013, http://www.k-message.com/gamification-in-pharma-marketing-explained-examples/

129. David Evans, *The Fair Price Coalition (FPC) applauds the Wyden-Grassley US Senate bipartisan Sovaldi investigation spotlighting - greed driven pricing strategy behind Gilead's $1,000 per pill Hepatitis C drug launch,* December 3, 2015, https://fairpricingcoalition.org/tag/sovaldi/

130. Bruce E. Levine, *What's it going to take to lock up drug company execs?* Alternet - Personal Health, January 15, 2009, https://www.alternet.org/story/119912/what%27s_it_going_to_take_to_lock_up_drug_company_execs/

131. History of Parke, Davis & Co, The Herb Museum, http://herbmuseum.ca/content/history-parke-davis-co

132. Eli Lilly & Company, International Directory of Company Histories, encyclopedia.com, September 15, 2018, https://www.encyclopedia.com/social-sciences-and-law/economics-business-and-labor/businesses-and-occupations/eli-lilly-company#3446600100

133. Suranjan Das, Strategic Thinking: *Blue Ocean strategic moves - Novo Nordisk,* October 1, 2011, http://suranjanmktg.blogspot.com/2011/10/blue-ocean-strategic-moves-novo-nordisk.html

134. Douglas Martin, T*he Nation: Thanks a bunch, Viagra; The pill that revived sex, or at least talking about it,* The New York Times, Archives 1998, https://www.nytimes.com/1998/05/03/weekinreview/nation-thanks-bunch-viagra-pill-that-revived-sex-least-talking-about-it.html

135. Y & R, *London launches Pfizer's Viagra Connect, Y & R, London, April 18, 2018,* https://london.yr.com/yr-london-launches-pfizers-viagra-connect/

136. ICMR India, *Glaxo SmithKline's marketing strategy for Requip*: A study in product lifecycle *management*, *IBS Center for Management Research, 2007,* http://www.icmrindia.org/casestudies/catalogue/Marketing/Glaxosmithkline %20Marketing%20Strategy-Requip-Product % 20 Lifecycle %20Management%20Case%20Studies.htm

137. Ruhi Kandhari, *Indian Pharma doesn't have a choice but to market digitally, The Ken,* November 1, 2017, https://the-ken.com/story/indian-pharma-market-digitally/

138. Ron Winslow, *Market Place - The Birth of a blockbuster: Lipitor's route out of the lab,* The Wall Street Journal, Updated January 24, 2000, https://www.wsj.com/articles/SB948677773420632448

139. Adam Gaffeney, *How ADHD was sold, The New Republic, September 23, 2016*, https://newrepublic.com/article/137066/adhd-sold

140. Bertrand Tappy, *Every molecule tells a story: Ritalin,* InVivomagazine.com, http://www.invivomagazine.com/en/corpore_sano/chronique/article/235/every-molecule-tells-a-story-ritalin

141. David Rotman, *Rewriting Life - Race and Medicine, MIT Technology Review, April 1, 2005,* https://www.technologyreview.com/s/403895/race-and-medicine/

142. *NitroMed Acquires BiDil NDA for CHF therapy,* www.thepharmaletter.com, September 22, 1999, https://www.thepharmaletter.com/article/nitromed-acquires-bidil-nda-for-chf-therapy

143. Britt M. Rusert, PhD and Charmaine D.M. Royal, *PhD, Grassroots marketing in global era: More lessons from BiDil, Journal of Law and Medical Ethics,* 2011 Spring: 39 (1): 79-90

144. *AbbVie's revenue from top product Humira from 2011 to 2017 (in million US dollars), Statista, The Statistical Portal, h*ttps://www.statista.com/statistics/318206/revenue-of-humira/

145. Cynthia Koons, *This shield of patents protects the world's best selling drug,* Bloomberg Business Week, September 7, 2017, https://www.bloomberg.com/news/articles/2017-09-07/this-shield-of-patents-protects-the-world-s-best-selling-drug

146. Simon King, *The best selling drugs since 1996 - why AbbVie's Humira is set to eclipse Pfizer's Lipitor, Pharma & Healthcare,* Forbes, July 16, 2013, https://www.forbes.com/sites/simonking/2013/07/15/the-best-selling-drugs-since-1996-why-abbvies-humira-is-set-to-eclipse-pfizers-lipitor/

147. Emery James Baker, MS, MBA, *PMP, Humira - A historical marketing perspective, SCRIBD, December 10, 2011,* https://www.scribd.com/document/80712983/Humira-a-Historical-Marketing-Perspective

148. Jeremy A. *Greene, M.D, PhD, "For me there is no substitute": Authenticity, uniqueness and the lessons of Lipitor*, AMA Journal of Ethics, October 2010, https://journalofethics.ama-assn.org/article/me-there-no-substitute-authenticity-uniqueness-and-lessons-lipitor/2010-10

149. Associated Press, *It took a brilliant marketing campaign to create the best-selling drug of all time,* Business Insider, December 28, 2011, https://www.businessinsider.com/lipitor-the-best-selling-drug-in-the-history-of-pharmaceuticals-2011-12?IR=T

150. Christopher Bowe, *Say farewell to Lipitor but don't forget its lessons,* Strategy: Harvard Business Review, November 18, 2011, https://hbr.org/2011/11/say-farewell-to-lipitor-but-do

151. Executive Summary: Targeting Cancer: *Innovation in the treatment of chronic myelogenous leukemia,* New England Healthcare Institute, March 2004, https://www.nehi.net/writable/publication_files/file/cml_report_exec_summary.pdf

152. Max Macaluso, *How Gleevec changed the game for Novartis: Novartis' first rule of innovation - forget the forecasts, focus on science,* The Motely Fool, December 18, 2013, https://www.fool.com/investing/general/2013/12/18/how-gleevec-changed-the-game-for-novartis.aspx

153. Justin Heifetz, *Pharma: Gleevec, Fierce Pharma,* https://www.fiercepharma.com/special-report/gleevec

154. *John Adams, Chinmoy Bhatt, and Brent Hooper, Shaping how your drug's target disease is perceived by medical professionals and the public can make a difference to the success of your launch,* Beyond the Storm: Establishing unmet needs, Mckinsey& Company,

155. Ned Pagliarulo, *Gilead forecasts steep slide in 2018 hepatitis C revenues,* BiopharmaDive, February 6, 2018, https://www.biopharmadive.com/news/gilead-hepatitis-c-revenues-slide-fourth-quarter-earnings/516494/

156. NIH - National Cancer Institute, *How Imatinib transformed leukemia treatment and cancer research, Updated April 11, 2018,* https://www.cancer.gov/research/progress/discovery/gleevec

157. Claudia Driefus, *Science: Research behind the drug Gleevec - A conversation with Dr. Druker,* The New York Times, November 2, 2009, https://www.nytimes.com/2009/11/03/science/03conv.html

158. Dr. Jason Fung, *Gleevec's false dawn,* Medium, November 1, 2017, https://medium.com/@drjasonfung/gleevecs-false-dawn-4315062d690d

159. *ADHD History*, www.adhd-brain.com

160. Vincent Innelli, M.D, *A history of medication timeline of ADHD, Very Well Mind, September 05, 2018,* https://www.verywellmind.com/adhd-history-of-adhd-2633127

161. Alan Schwarz, *The selling of Attention deficit disorder,* The New York Times, November 14, 2013, https://www.nytimes.com/2013/12/15/health/the-selling-of-attention-deficit-disorder.html?_r=0#videoModal

162. Peter Conrad, *Meredith R. Bergey*, The Impending globalization of ADHD: Notes on the expansion and growth of a medicalized disorder, Social Science & Medicine, Volume 122, December 122, Pages 31-43

163. Levi Sharpe, Kim Kardashian'sInstagram is only the latest victim of FDA campaign, Popular Science, August 12, 2015, https://www.popsci.com/fda-began-targeting-social-media-long-kim-kardashians-instagram

Index

Symbols

ABOUT THE AUTHOR

Subba Rao Chaganti

Has a masters in business administration and over fifty-two years of experience in pharmaceutical marketing covering the whole gamut and all facets of the industry from selling to sales management, product management to heading the total marketing activity. His experience includes domestic and international marketing, and also Indian and multinational sectors.

He also taught for a few years a course on Advertising and Brand Management at Gitam Institute of Foreign Trade (now part of Gitam University) at Visakhapatnam as an adjunct professor and also taught a class on Marketing at Jawaharlal Nehru Technological University (JNTU) School of Management, Hyderabad as a visiting faculty.

He lives in Hyderabad and can be reached at subbarao.chaganti@gmail.com

Here is a list of his publications:

Books Published:

1. Pharmaceutical marketing in India: Concepts, Cases, Strategy
2. Game Plans for Post-Gatt Era: Action Agenda of Indian Pharmaceutical Industry
3. Compete or Forfeit: Strategies for Sustainable Competitive Advantage in Pharma Product Patents Era
4. Pharmaceutical Marketing in India for Today and Tomorrow - 25th Anniversary Edition

www.ingramcontent.com/pod-product-compliance
Lightning Source LLC
Chambersburg PA
CBHW050658190326
41458CB00008B/2614